Faith, Hope, and Love:
The Space Between Therapy Sessions

Faith, Hope, and Love: The Space Between Therapy Sessions

A Holistic Approach for Treating Adolescents and Young Adults with Anxiety and Depression

DAVID J. HEAVNER

foreword by Andrew Ricci

RESOURCE *Publications* • Eugene, Oregon

FAITH, HOPE AND LOVE: THE SPACE BETWEEN THERAPY SESSIONS
A Holistic Approach for Treating Adolescents and Young Adults with Anxiety and Depression

Resource Publications
An Imprint of Wipf and Stock Publishers
199 W. 8th Ave., Suite 3
Eugene, OR 97401

www.wipfandstock.com

PAPERBACK ISBN: 979-8-3852-5563-4
HARDCOVER ISBN: 979-8-3852-5564-1
EBOOK ISBN: 979-8-3852-5565-8
VERSION NUMBER 02/25/26

For my son, Aven

Who braved the shadows of anxiety as a child
And rose with courage to lead with compassion as a man.
Your journey from panic to purpose is the living heartbeat of this work.
May your life continue to build not only strong foundations beneath your feet but also bridges of understanding for those still searching for theirs.

This isn't about becoming someone new.
It's about remembering who you've always been—loved.

—David J. Heavner

Contents

Lists of Illustrations and Tables

Lists of Illustrations and Tables

Foreword

In my pastoral work as a parish priest, one of the most powerful questions I can ask people in crisis is, "How does your faith help you?" This simple question becomes the starting point for a deeper discussion into the needs and concerns that are present. Do they need to know more about Jesus? Do they need to grow in faith, hope, or love? Do they know what they need to do but are struggling to find the strength to carry it out? Does the darkness of fear, uncertainty, doubt, or worry obscure the path that needs to be taken?

As I read David Heavner's book, I was struck with how he brings the power of our Christian faith to focus upon the crippling aspects of anxiety and depression that are widespread in our world today. The struggle is real, and for those in anguish it can be difficult to find tools that affirm and empower our faith in Jesus Christ. This text serves as a spiritual companion, offering practical insight and encouragement to place God at the center of our lives, using as its framework the Scriptural Way of the Cross given to the church by Pope John Paul II.

If you are new or just beginning your Christian faith, you will find in these pages a beautiful introduction to Jesus Christ through the timeless power of the Bible that comforts us in our need and challenges us to an ongoing conversion of heart. For those who have committed their lives to Christ, what follows is a powerful testament of the gospel message that meets us where we are and inspires us to change and grow as we live for the Lord.

Many of us know and love people who are struggling on the inside. They carry heavy burdens that are often overlooked or even ignored. In these situations, we find ourselves wondering how we can help and offer encouragement. I suggest that we read this book first for our own continuing conversion of heart, keeping in mind the very points that might help others. That way, when we share it with them, our own familiarity serves as a second companion that provides opportunities for discussion.

Our Christian faith calls us into community as we follow the Lord and live according to his commands. We need each other, and our faith inspires us to reach out to those in crisis. As we strive to help those suffering with anxiety and depression with the healing power of Jesus Christ, David Heavner gives us a tool to accompany those we love along the way.

Fr. Andrew Ricci
Cathedral of Christ the King, Superior, WI
Diocese of Superior
Host of *Catholic Inspiration* podcast

Preface

I AM PROUD TO say that I was born and raised in Pittsburgh, Pennsylvania. All my academic accomplishments, from my high school diploma to my graduate degrees, were earned at institutions within the Commonwealth of Pennsylvania. For the past thirty years, I've dedicated my career to serving students in the public education system of Western Pennsylvania. I've had the honor of being a social studies teacher, a school counselor at both the middle and high school levels, a varsity head football coach, and a licensed professional counselor.

Western Pennsylvania is a place rich with tradition, shaped by resilience, and grounded in a deep sense of identity. While every region has its own personality, I've learned that the struggles facing young people here are not all that different from those experienced across our country. Regardless of location, many adolescents and young adults today are facing overwhelming pressure, isolation, and uncertainty.

This preface is written especially for *you*, the young person who may be feeling anxious, depressed, disconnected, or simply lost. If you've opened this book, you're likely searching for answers, for relief, and for something deeper to hold onto. I want you to know this: *you are not alone* in how you feel, and there is a way forward.

In my years as a teacher, counselor, and coach, I've met countless students who carry emotional burdens that few can see. I've watched the rise of anxiety and depression among your generation, and I've seen how common it has become to rely on therapy, and too often on medication alone, to find relief. Therapy can be powerful and essential, but healing doesn't stop when the session ends. That's where this book comes in.

Faith, Hope, and Love: The Space Between Therapy Sessions; A Holistic Approach for Treating Adolescents and Young Adults with Anxiety and Depression is not just another self-help guide. It's a conversation—one rooted in faith, grounded in lived experience, and written with you in mind. This book will help you explore the source of your emotional pain, understand your mind and heart more deeply, and most importantly begin to build a spiritual foundation that can support lasting change.

At the center of this journey is Jesus Christ, not as a religious figure to be studied from a distance but as a personal Savior who longs to walk beside you. The exercises, reflections, and lessons within these pages are designed to help you experience a spiritual awakening, one that brings strength to your heart, clarity to your mind, and peace to your soul. Whether you are already familiar with Christian faith or approaching it for the first time, this book invites you to discover that the light of the world still shines for you and always has.

My hope is that this book becomes a companion on your path. When therapy ends and the silence returns, when the pressure builds, or when darkness creeps in, may the words in these pages point you toward the kind of healing that doesn't fade.

May your faith grow stronger. May your hope be renewed. And may you come to know, without a doubt, that you are loved.

You are not broken, you are becoming. And you are never alone.

Acknowledgments

First and foremost, I offer my deepest thanks to my Lord and Savior, Jesus Christ. It is through his grace, guidance, and unending mercy that I found the strength and courage to complete this project. The gifts of time, talent, and treasure he has so generously bestowed upon me have allowed me to carry out my calling and, in some small way, expand his kingdom.

To my beloved mother, Martina, and my late father, Daniel, thank you for your unwavering love and support. The value you placed on both faith and education has been the bedrock of my life. Your example continues to guide me each day.

To my brother, Gregory, your life has been my blueprint. Your dedication to education and your service as a teacher, counselor, administrator, and coach has shaped not only your students but also me. I am proud to walk in your footsteps.

To my son, Aven, you are the greatest blessing the LORD has ever given me. Your humility, compassion, and servant's heart are daily reminders of what truly matters. The highest compliment I can give is to say that you are a man of faith, character, and purpose. I thank God for the honor of being your father.

To my best friend and wife, Christina, your intelligence, loyalty, and unwavering love have brought light and peace to my life. You are living proof that God's timing is perfect. Your presence has made this journey joyful and meaningful in ways words cannot fully express.

To my spiritual brother, Dr. Walt Chambers, your words were a choir of angels during moments of doubt and discouragement. Your encouragement reminded me of my mission and the higher calling I serve. Thank you for being a voice of calm, purpose, and faith.

To my mentor in clinical mental health, Michele Majcher, your compassion and clinical wisdom introduced me to the transformative power of Christian counseling. You are a true angel of mercy, and your faith-driven care has saved countless lives. I will deeply miss our powerful and soul-nourishing conversations.

To my professors at Lock Haven University, Indiana University of Pennsylvania, and the University of Pittsburgh, thank you for fueling my passion and helping shape a career devoted to young minds and hearts.

To every colleague I have worked alongside in classrooms, counseling offices, or locker rooms, your dedication and purpose have directly influenced my own teaching, counseling, and coaching style. I am a better educator and person because of you.

To every student and player that I have had the privilege of knowing, you were my reason for showing up each day with a smile. It has been my greatest hope to play even the smallest role in helping you move closer to your dreams.

I extend my heartfelt gratitude to the ministries and individuals whose daily Scripture studies and spiritual insights have deepened my walk with Jesus Christ. Your words have guided my heart, shaped my days, and helped illuminate the path of healing and faith that this book seeks to share.

To Presentation Ministries, your daily Mass reflections, retreats, events, and publications continue to stir my soul and draw me closer to the living Word.

To Father Andrew Ricci of studyprayserve.com, your *Catholic Inspiration* podcast sets the tone for my mornings and lifts my spirit with wisdom and grace.

To My Catholic Life!, your Catholic Daily Reflections help me encounter Scripture with clarity and compassion, making the word of God ever more alive.

To Dr. Tony Evans, your powerful daily radio sermons on tonyevans.com inspire both reflection and redirection. You've helped me close each day with peace and begin the next with purpose.

To all of you, may the Lord bless your ministries as you continue to shepherd his flock.

Finally, to the entire team at Wipf and Stock Publishers, thank you for believing in my voice and helping bring this book to life. I am forever grateful that you took a chance on a middle-aged "Yinzer" from Pittsburgh and gave me the platform to share this story with the world.

Prologue

The Culture of Death

Be alert and of sober mind.
Your enemy the devil prowls around like a roaring lion
looking for someone to devour.
—1 Pet 5:8

On March 5, 1995, Pope John Paul II issued an encyclical titled *Evangelium Vitae*, translated as "The Gospel of Life."[1] Within this 188-page document, the pope coined the phrase "culture of death."[2] Saint John Paul II used theological and philosophical underpinnings to condemn the growing and widespread moral "crimes" that were occurring in the world. Topics like abortion, euthanasia, capital punishment, and artificial reproduction were seen by the pope as "choices once unanimously considered criminal and rejected by the common moral sense [that now] are gradually becoming socially acceptable."[3]

At the dawn of a new century, "the evil one" has been working twenty-four hours a day and seven days a week to expand the culture of death that Pope John Paul II uncovered. He has been recruiting his demons on this earth to attack Christians striving for the gates of heaven. Just look on your latest technological gadget to see this raging war! The list of topics that the pope shined the Lord's light on in 1995 still exists today. The more troubling news is that the list has grown! The World Economic Forum surveys

1. John Paul II, *Evangelium Vitae*, §1.
2. John Paul II, *Evangelium Vitae*, §12.
3. John Paul II, *Evangelium Vitae*, §4.

the younger generations every year about the biggest problems facing the world. The data collected is put through the modern methods of analysis and is reported and defined through a wide spectrum. For this book, I would like to share the top ten results from those who participated in this survey (Generation Y and Z—ages ten to forty).[4]

10. Lack of economic opportunity and unemployment
9. Safety / security / well-being
8. Lack of education
7. Food and water security
6. Government accountability and transparency / corruption
5. Religious conflicts
4. Poverty
3. Inequality (income, discrimination)
2. Large scale conflicts / wars
1. Climate change / destruction of nature

> *One day the angels came to present themselves before the Lord, and Satan also came with them. The Lord said to Satan, "Where have you come from?" Satan answered the Lord, "From roaming throughout the earth, going back and forth on it."*
> *—Job 1:6–7*

In America, a certain percentage of our youngest generations may agree with the descriptors from the World Economic Forum, however because we live in such a unique country that allows our adolescents and young adults to exercise their free will every second of their existence, there are a few more descriptors that they would add to the list of the biggest problems they are facing in "their" world today!

SINGLE-PARENT HOUSEHOLDS

According to the last US Census Bureau report, in 2017 about 19.97 million children (under the age of eighteen) in the United States lived with one parent. Approximately 16.77 million of them (84 percent) lived

4. Jackson and Loudenback, "10 Most Critical Problems."

with their mother![5] In the twenty-first century, family life in the United States is changing rapidly. Two-parent households are on the decline as divorce, remarriage, and cohabitation are on the rise. Today, four in ten births occur to women who are single or living with a nonmarital partner. Nonmarital cohabitation and divorce, along with the prevalence of remarriage and (nonmarital) recoupling, make for family structures that in many cases continue to evolve throughout a child's life. Today, a child's living arrangement changes with each adjustment in their relationship status of their parents. For example, one study found that over a three-year period, about three in ten (31 percent) children younger than six had experienced a major change in their family or household structure in the form of parental divorce, separation, marriage, cohabitation, or death.[6]

How do adolescents / young adults decode their parent(s) relationship issues while trying to survive in a disintegrating family structure?

ALCOHOL SATURATION

Have you watched or listened to some type of sporting event on television, radio, or some other streaming device? With collegiate and professional sports producing hundreds of billions of dollars a year, it is hard not to stumble across an amateur or professional event throughout the fall, winter, spring, or summer months! It is inevitable that you will either see or hear some type of alcohol sponsorship. Every alcohol brand is vying to be the "official" sponsor of a league, association, event, team, broadcast, program, or channel (television, radio, podcast, live streaming, etc.). Consumption and profit margins have proven that the prevalence and sophistication of sponsorship is a significant marketing tool. Although this may make business sense, it's destroying moral sense! Recent studies have tied beverage company sponsorships with health and societal consequences. Empirical evidence from consumer studies relating to alcohol sponsorship has repeatedly demonstrated that sponsorship has an impact on adolescent / young adult product recall, product related attitudes, and behavioral intentions.[7] But you don't need to read or analyze empirical studies to educate yourself on the invasion of alcohol in our nation. Go to

5. US Census Bureau, "Families and Living Arrangements."
6. Standberry, "Top 10 Issues."
7. US Preventive Services Task Force, "Unhealthy Alcohol Use."

an NCAA or NFL football game four hours prior to kickoff. Mingle with the crowd in the parking lots of musical concerts several hours before the performance begins. Visit a college campus over a weekend and observe the overcrowded bars or standing room only house parties. Listen and observe a high school hallway, classroom, or cafeteria to hear about the upcoming weekend events. No, you don't need a professor lecturing you or pushing his/her study about the direct negative correlation that alcohol has on the mental, physical, and emotional state of a young person. The five senses (sight, sound, smell, taste, and touch) that the LORD has given you is all that you need to understand the grip that alcohol has on our society!

However, if you enjoy lectures and reading empirical evidence (like I do), then listed below are the most recent statistics from the Centers for Disease Control and Prevention.[8]

Underage Drinking

Alcohol is the most used and abused drug among youth in the United States.

- Excessive drinking is responsible for more than 4,300 deaths among underage youth each year, and it cost the United States twenty-four billion dollars in economic costs in 2010.
- Although drinking by persons under the age of twenty-one is illegal, people aged twelve to twenty years drink 11 percent of all alcohol consumed in the United States. More than 90 percent of this alcohol is consumed in the form of binge drinks.
- On average, underage drinkers consume more drinks per drinking occasion than adult drinkers.
- In 2010, there were approximately 189,000 emergency rooms visits by persons under the age of twenty-one for injuries and other conditions linked to alcohol.

8. Centers for Disease Control and Prevention, "About Underage Drinking."

Drinking Levels Among Youth

The 2015 Youth Behavior survey[9] found that among high school students, during the past thirty days

- 33 percent drank some amount of alcohol.
- 18 percent binge drank.
- 8 percent drove after drinking alcohol.
- 20 percent rode with a driver who had been drinking alcohol.

The 2015 National Survey on Drug Use and Health reported that 20 percent of youth aged twelve to twenty years drink alcohol and 13 percent reported binge drinking in the past thirty days.[10] The 2015 Monitoring the Future survey reported that 10 percent of eighth graders and 35 percent of twelfth graders drank during the past thirty days, and 5 percent of eighth graders and 17 percent of twelfth graders binge drank during the past two weeks.[11]

How do adolescents / young adults shield themselves from the prevalent and sophisticated promotion of alcohol and the extreme peer pressure that comes with using and/or abusing it?

DRUG EPIDEMIC

Wars are waging around us each day. Whether we know it or not, enemies are advancing on many different fronts to capture our mind, body, heart, and soul. Our conscious and subconscious are constantly devising offensive and defensive battle plans to protect our well-being. One formidable enemy is drugs. There are numerous studies that prove humans have consumed mind-altering substances since the dawn of time. In fact, drug use is almost as old as food and drink. Here in the United States, our federal government "officially" recognized this enemy in June of 1971. President Nixon declared a "war of drugs" when he learned that 10 to 15 percent of servicemen in Vietnam were addicted to heroin.[12] The first weapon used by our country to try to defeat the drug invasion was strict judicial regulation for possession, use, and sale of illegal drugs. However,

9. Kann et al., "Youth Risk Behavior Surveillance."
10. Center for Behavioral Health Statistics and Quality, *Key Substance Use.*
11. Johnston et al., *Monitoring the Future.*
12. Nixon, "Program for Drug Abuse Prevention."

this did not stop or slow the enemy. In the 1980s, First Lady Nancy Reagan began the famous anti-drug campaign "Just Say No." It has been debated how effective this campaign was; however, everyone agrees that she helped shape the idea that adolescents should get educated on drugs and make their own informed decisions. During the 1990s and early 2000s, presidential administrations began to reexamine the primary and consistent weapon used since the 1970s: imprisonment of everyone connected to drug abuse—the users, the dealers, and those who bring drugs across state and international lines. Because this weapon was deemed ineffective against the enemy, a new and improved tactic was used to slow the invasion. The new battle strategy was to help those abusing drugs by mandating drug rehabilitation programs to help stop their addiction, instead of adjudication. Once again, this did not stop the enemy's advancement. As a matter of fact, the enemy has gotten larger and stronger, and it continues to conquer land and life throughout the United States.

I know that you didn't grow up in the 1980s, but you may have heard about or seen a famous campaign by the Partnership for a Drug Free America. A man asks if there is anyone out there who still doesn't understand the dangers of drug use. He holds up an egg and says, "This is your brain." Looking at a frying pan he says, "This is drugs." He then cracks open the egg, fries the contents, and says, "This is your brain on drugs." He then looks up at the camera and says, "Any questions?"[13]

Yes! Our youngest generations have many questions about the abundance of drugs that are available to them daily. The ever-advancing enemy has many ways to influence our youth and enter their bodies. Marijuana, cocaine, painkillers, stimulants, heroin, sedatives, tranquilizers, hallucinogens, and psychotherapeutics are the weapons of choice. Studies have been conducted by government agencies as well as private industries tracking the drug epidemic. Statistics tell us that someone in your family or someone you know is currently addicted to some type of drug. According to the National Institute on Drug Abuse, every day 115 people in the United States die after overdosing on opioids.[14] The fields of science and medicine have proven how substance abuse physically changes the brain. Most importantly, scientists and doctors know that brains of teenagers continue to develop until their mid-twenties. These

13. Partnership for a Drug-Free America, "Your Brain on Drugs."

14. National Institute on Drug Abuse, "Opioid Overdose Crisis."

experts have also found that anxiety and depression are consequences of substance abuse.

The enemy known as drugs has infiltrated the human conscious and subconscious since the beginning of human existence. This enemy is relentless in its pursuit to control all those who meet it. Studies, statistics, and personal relationships tell me who is currently winning the war. However, we still have time because this war will rage on until the end of time!

How do adolescents / young adults arm themselves with battle strategies and tactics to protect their most precious resources (mind, body, heart, and soul) against powerful drugs?

SOCIAL MEDIA

Today's youth have tailored their life around technology—a word that impacts their every waking moment. According to a recent Pew Research Center survey, smartphone ownership has become a nearly ubiquitous element of teen life. Ninety-five percent of teens now report they have a smartphone or access to one. These mobile connections are in turn fueling more persistent online activities. Forty-five percent of teens now say they are online on a near constant basis.[15] Generations Y and Z spend a large portion of their day using social media applications to interact with friends by posting statuses, pictures, music, videos, or playing games. Many have profiles on different platforms depending on their needs. Facebook, which once dominated the social media landscape, now finds itself down on the list of most popular online platforms among teens and young adults. YouTube, Snapchat, Instagram, and Twitter now rank higher than Facebook.[16]

What is attracting our youth to these online communities? To find the answer, all you must do is read Abraham Maslow's 1943 paper "A Theory of Human Motivation"! If that doesn't sound exciting, then at least analyze his universally recognized hierarchy of needs pyramid.[17] Right smack in the middle of his pyramid, you will find the answer: social needs. The social needs in Maslow's hierarchy include such things as love, acceptance, and belonging. At this level, the need for emotional

15. Anderson and Jiang, "Social Media and Technology."
16. Anderson and Jiang, "Teens' Social Media Habits."
17. Cherry, "Maslow's Hierarchy of Needs."

relationships drives human behavior. Some of the things that satisfy this need include friendships, romantic attachments, family, social groups, and community groups. According to Maslow, in order to avoid problems such as loneliness, depression, and anxiety, it is important for people to feel loved and accepted by other people.[18]

When used properly, social media applications can deliver some of the emotional relationships that are needed to satisfy the social needs portion of Maslow's hierarchy of needs. Unfortunately, social media applications have spawned some unattended (or attended) circumstances. When studying the latest *Diagnostic and Statistical Manual of Mental Disorders*, I did not find an entry or description for social media addiction. However, in section 3 ("Conditions for Further Study") Internet Gaming Disorder (IGD) is included and research is ongoing to determine if it warrants formal inclusion in a future edition.[19] When scientists catch up with social media, they may have to add a new type of addiction under this classified disorder.

Because of the influence that technology has on our daily lives, there have been some recent studies uncovering compulsive behaviors related to the use of social media applications. Scientists are now inventing scales to identify possible addictions to social media / smartphones. In the spring of 2017, the television newsmagazine *60 Minutes* reported on a story titled "Hooked on Your Phone?"[20] Within this story, they reported that Silicon Valley programmers are engineering smartphones and their social applications so that the users will check them constantly. This is why I wrote in the last paragraph that social media applications may have some attended circumstances. After all, social media apps are a delivery system for aids aimed directly at the user, and companies can tell a lot about who is using these social media apps.

Some of these new scientific studies are finding behaviors that are aligned with additional criteria: neglect of personal life, mental preoccupation, escapism, mood modifying experiences, tolerance, and concealing the addictive behavior. Additional studies have concluded that when a person enters the world of social media for more than two hours a day, their mental health begins to change. Feelings of sadness, anxiety, depression, jealousy, envy, dependence, isolation, and loneliness begin to

18. Maslow, "Theory of Human Motivation."

19. American Psychiatric Association, *Diagnostic and Statistical Manual*, 795–98.

20. Hacking, "Hooked on Your Phone?"

increase in the user's psyche.[21] In addition to mental health issues, millennials have to deal with hate speech, cyber bullying, inadequate sleep, identity theft, cyber stalking, rumors/slander, manipulation, underdeveloped interpersonal skills, and inadequate achievement at school or work.[22] I wonder what Abraham Maslow would think if he could witness how social media has negatively impacted the middle portion of his pyramid.

In today's technological world, how do adolescents / young adults satisfy their social needs without damaging their physical, mental, and spiritual essence?

VIOLENCE

The Bible is comprehensive in its teaching about the reality of Satan. His existence is taught from Genesis to Revelation. Seven Old Testament books teach his existence (Genesis, 1 Chronicles, Job, Psalms, Isaiah, Ezekiel, and Zechariah), and every New Testament writer refers to his reality and activity as a personal being. More importantly, Christ also affirmed the fact of Satan and his activity as a personal being. Satan, the deceiver, never likes to be revealed for who and what he is and how he operates. Satan has many faces, schemes, and approaches. Some are obvious: hate, violence, death, and destruction. Some aren't always obvious. They may appear very lovely, handsome, sophisticated, educated, polite, and apparently good. But it is all a dangerous sham designed to deceive and defeat your soul!

Because the "serpent" is secretive in his movement and direction, he is finding it easier to manipulate a generation whose attention span is no longer than a fleeting moment. If you open your eyes and ears, you can see and hear his work being done daily on the world stage. Just take a moment to watch your local news or read your local newspaper. Watch the numerous cable news shows or listen to the nationally syndicated radio shows. Watch and listen to what is being posted on your favorite social media application. If you do, it won't take you long to recognize the unrelenting work of the devil.

Satan loves to feast on the world's newest generation. Although some millennials are aware of the power of darkness, most are too young

21. Robinson and Smith, "Social Media."

22. *The Week* Staff, "Is Social Media Bad."

and inexperienced to deal with the sophistication of the devil's intelligence, emotions, and will. The greatest weapon that the "evil one" uses against millennials is the promotion of violence. For adolescents and young adults, violence is like a vaccine that the "prince of darkness" injects into their mind, body, and soul. These injections decrease sensitivity to violence and often lead to beliefs of apathy, rationalization, condonation, and affiliation. For millennials to build up immunity or tolerance for violence, the "father of lies" and his army of demons work in two phases. The first phase is the build-up phase. This involves dispensing injections with increasing amounts of violence daily. The length of this phase depends upon how often the injections are received and accepted in the human psyche. The delivery device used to disburse violence can come in many forms (environment, domestic/child abuse, insufficient parental supervision, peer pressure, drug use, traumatic events, etc.), but it can be constantly found in the favorite things our youngest generations like to invest their time in—video games, music, movies/television, and social media posts. This subtle strategy ensures that violence will invade a large portion of the waking hours of each adolescent and young adult.

The maintenance phase is the second phase that is used to reinforce tolerance for violence. This begins once the effective dose is reached. The effective maintenance dose depends on each millennial's sensitivity to violence and their response to the build-up phase. During the maintenance phase, exposure of violence helps develop customs, habits, and expectations for how adolescents and young adults will react to violence.

How are the "King of Darkness" and his minions doing? Pick any recent scholarly article that focused on youth violence and you will read about the increase in explosive temper tantrums, physical aggression, fighting, threats or attempts to hurt others (including thoughts of wanting to kill others), use of weapons, cruelty toward animals, fire setting, intentional destruction of property and vandalism, bullying, child sex trafficking, dating violence, child abuse, gun violence, suicide, and self-harm.[23] Because of these recorded statistics, it seems the youth of today are at the very least desensitized toward violence and at the very worst becoming perpetrators and/or victims of violence.

In a violent world, how do adolescents / young adults protect their moral compass while battling daily events that erode societal norms?

23. American Academy of Child and Adolescent Psychiatry, "Violent Behavior."

SCHOOL SHOOTINGS / GUN VIOLENCE

In 2018, the *Washington Post* ran a series of investigative articles centering on mass school shootings in the United States. These articles were in response to our nation's troubling conscience. Twenty-one weeks into 2018, there was already twenty-eight school shootings in which forty were killed and sixty-six were injured. That averaged out to be more than one shooting a week.[24] To expose the gun violence crisis in our America schools, the *Washington Post* ran a front page story in late May titled "2018 Has Been Deadlier for Schoolchildren than Deployed Service Members."[25] This revelation caught the attention of the majority in our nation. In subsequent articles, the *Post* spent a year determining how many children were exposed to gun violence during school hours since the Columbine High massacre in 1999. Their research tabulated more than 215,000 children at 217 schools witnessed gun violence. That meant that the number of children who have been shaken by gunfire in the places they go to learn exceeds the population of Spokane, Washington, or Birmingham, Alabama. They also found that at least 141 children, educators, and other people have been killed in assaults, and another 287 have been injured in schools because of guns.[26]

In March of 2018, *Newsweek* magazine claimed that the number of children killed by gunfire in the United States since the 2012 mass shooting at Sandy Hook Elementary School in Newtown, Connecticut, surpassed the total of American soldiers killed in overseas combat since 9/11, according to a Department of Defense report. The report accounted for total deaths in the five military operations since the war on terror began following the September 11, 2001, attacks. Over seventeen years of combat, the United States lost 6,950 soldiers. In the five years and three months since the December 14, 2012, massacre at Sandy Hook in Newtown, when a twenty-year-old killed twenty first graders and six adults with an AR-15-style rifle, about seven thousand children have died by gunfire. *Newsweek* arrived at that figure based on an American Academy of Pediatrics report, which said that about fourteen hundred children are killed by guns every year.[27]

---

24. Cox and Rich, "Scarred by School Shootings."
25. Bump, "2018 Has Been Deadlier."
26. Dvorak, "Kids Fear Being Killed."
27. Sit, "Killed by Guns."

Statistics can sometimes be confusing, intimidating, and hard to comprehend. However, the numbers reported above may give you pause to reflect upon the violent nation that we live in. The United States remains an outlier in the developed world when it comes to gun violence. That includes not just school shootings but shootings in general—of which America has far, far more of than any other developed nation in the world. The United States has nearly six times the gun homicide rate of Canada, more than seven times that of Sweden, and nearly sixteen times that of Germany, according to United Nations Data.[28] According to CNN, the United States makes up less than 5 percent of the world's population but holds 31 percent of global mass shooters.[29] Because of the prevalence of guns, we have become world experts in lethal violence. With lethal violence comes casualties. These casualties can be categorized as dead, wounded, or profoundly traumatized. Death is final, and being wounded by a bullet can be life altering. But the sound of gunfire, the smell of gunpowder, the sight of mayhem, and the taste of fear pierces the human core forever. Once thing is for certain: an altercation with a gun will end your life or change it forever.

Generations Y and Z were born and raised in a society where mass shootings are a reality. Their norm is to enter buildings that look like fortresses instead of schools. Digital cameras record every inch of the building twenty-four hours a day. Bulletproof windows have replaced glass windows. Classrooms are always locked. Armed resource officers patrol the halls and the surrounding campus. Schools conduct active-shooter drills in which kids as young as four hide in darkened closets and bathrooms from imaginary murderers. Threats inside or outside of the school send classrooms into lockdowns. Bomb threats are called into schools, causing mass evacuations into ball fields or parking lots. All these things can put children and adolescents into states of hypervigilance, which makes them perceive danger even where there is none, much like combat veterans with post-traumatic stress disorder.

How do adolescents / young adults enter school or college campuses and not worry about a violent confrontation involving a gun?

28. United Nations Office on Drugs and Crime, *Global Study on Homicide.*
29. Willingham and Ahmed, "Mass Shootings in America."

OBESITY / BODY SHAMING

According to the Centers for Disease Control and Prevention, the percentage of children and adolescents in the United States affected by obesity has more than tripled since the 1970s. Data from 2015 to 2016 shows that nearly one in five school age children and young people (six to nineteen years) has obesity.[30] Public health professionals agree that overweight and obesity have reached epidemic proportions in this country. They also say physical inactivity and poor diet are catching up to tobacco as a significant threat to health.

In many ways, obesity is a puzzling disease. How the body regulates weight and body fat is not well understood. On one hand, the cause appears to be simple in that if a person consumes more calories than he or she expends as energy, then he or she will gain weight. However, the risk factors that determine obesity can be a complex combination of genetics, socioeconomic factors, metabolic factors, and lifestyle choices, as well as other factors. Some endocrine disorders, diseases, and medications may also exert a powerful influence on an individual's weight.

Obesity has a far-ranging negative effect on health. Each year obesity-related conditions cost over one hundred billion dollars and cause premature deaths in the United States. The health effects associated with obesity include high blood pressure, diabetes, heart disease, joint problems, respiratory problems, cancer, and cardiovascular diseases. However, adolescents and young adults who suffer from obesity are more aware and concerned with the psychosocial effects it brings. In a culture where often the ideal of physical attractiveness is to be overly thin, people who are overweight or obese frequently suffer disadvantages. Adolescents and young adults who are obese often experience significant social pressure, stress, and difficulties accomplishing developmental tasks. They are often blamed for their condition and may be considered lazy or weak-willed. It is not uncommon for overweight or obese conditions to result in millennials having lower self-esteem or having fewer or no romantic relationships. Disapproval of overweight persons expressed by some individuals may progress to bias, discrimination, and even torment.

There is a relatively new concept being exercised in our culture today called body shaming. According to the *Oxford English Dictionary*, body shaming is the act or practice of humiliating a person based on their body type by making critical and/or mocking statements about

30. Hales et al., "Prevalence of Obesity," 1.

their body shape and size.[31] Why would our society turn this act into a sport? Unfortunately, we live in an image-focused society, and the most efficient tool being used to point out "deficiencies" are social media platforms. The internet has promoted public commentary on all matters all the time, especially bullying and shaming individuals for their weight and appearance. Body shaming statistics indicate that 94 percent of teenage girls have been body shamed. However, the practice isn't exclusive to the female gender. Teen boys and men are subjected to thoughtless opinions and hurtful comments made as well. Nearly 65 percent of teen boys reported having been body shamed.[32] No one is safe from this cruel practice. The Huffington Post has a link online in which they log body shaming articles to show their readers how rampant and devastating body shaming can be. Victims in these articles include actors, musicians, athletes, models, television personalities, and everyday citizens.[33]

How do adolescents / young adults deal with the stigma of obesity?

RELATIONSHIP DEVELOPMENT

As children turn into adolescents and adolescents turn into young adults, so do their physical and cognitive development. There are many changes that need to be navigated through this phase of life. One change that is usually embraced during these confusing times is in relationships with others. Family relationships are often reorganized due to a desire for increased autonomy. This autonomy leads to increased emotional distance between teens / young adults and their parents. Their attention often shifts to a more intense focus on social interactions and friendships expanding from same-sex friends to same-sex groups of friends to heterosexual groups of friends.

This expansion leads to a new understanding of self. Concepts of independence, identity, and self-esteem are explored at a deeper level for the very first time in their life. They begin to realize that they can work out their own problems independently. They experience new responsibilities and reflect on their own independent thoughts and actions. They

31. *Oxford English Dictionary*, s.v. "body shaming," https://www.oed.com/dictionary/body-shaming_n?tl=true.

32. Vargas, "Body-Shaming.

33. HuffPost, "Body Shame."

begin to strategize about their future life (post-secondary education, occupation, marriage, children, etc.). They begin to develop a sense of personal identity and a secure sense of self. They create their own unique personality. Finally, they begin to look within and learn to love themselves. All these seeds are cultivated through relationships which in time will help them blossom.

Sexual maturity marks the need to reorganize friendships once again. This transition is influenced by sexual interest and by social and cultural influences and expectations. Social and cultural expectations and behaviors in sexual relationships are learned from observations and practice. During adolescence, developmental tasks include struggles to gain control over sexual and aggressive urges and discovering potential or actual love relationships. Sexual behaviors during adolescence may include impulsive behavior, a wide range of experimental interactions of mutual exploring, and eventually intercourse. Biological differences, and differences in the socialization of males and females, set the stage for males and females to have different expectations of sexual and love relationships that may influence sexual experiences and may also have consequences for later sexual behavior and partnerships. Ultimately, achievement of a mutually satisfying sexual partnership within a loving relationship is the end goal.

How do adolescents / young adults ensure themselves that they will meet their physical and cognitive benchmarks to fully lead a productive life?

ACUTE FINANCIAL STRESS

CBS News recently published an article pointing out that millennials finally outnumber baby boomers among the American population, according to the latest population estimates.[34] Millennials, defined by those born between 1981 and 1997, now number 75.4 million, which pushes them past the 74.9 million baby boomers that currently live in the United States. Until this point, baby boomers, defined by those born between 1946 and 1964, have constituted the United States' largest living generation and have carried enormous economic, political, and cultural clout as a result. Now this title belongs to the millennials. However, with this throne comes a heavy crown.

34. Gunaratna, "U.S. Population Milestone."

Millennials have a lot on their minds. They are entering or exiting a post-secondary school. They are also balancing education/training with full-time/part-time work while calculating future endeavors (career, marriage, family). As their minds process these daily dilemmas, one topic short-circuits their mental drive—financial stress. According to most studies, personal finances are often the number one source of stress for this newest largest living generation. Usually, these stressors come with a lack of coping skills such as life experiences and financial knowledge. Even though millennials made all the "right" decisions on the road to success, they often wind up stalling or hitting dead ends financially. According to a LendingTree survey, the top three money stressors for millennials are too much debt, inability to afford rent and other necessities, and difficulty managing a budget.[35]

For millennials, too much debt is their number one source of financial stress. They are most stressed about credit card debt and student loan debt. It can be incredibly discouraging to a young adult when they allocate monthly income toward their debt and barely cover interest, let alone making a dent in the principal. Since credit cards have higher interest rates compared to other forms of debt, it's no wonder millennials are stressed out trying to pay back what they owe. Student loan debt can be frustrating for different reasons. Millennials with student debt are mostly stressed out about the length of time it will take to pay it off, as well as how high their student loan balances are.

According to Nielsen, millennials prefer cities to suburbs and subways to driveways.[36] This makes sense since career opportunities and higher-paying jobs are abundant in metropolitan areas rather than small towns. However, populated areas equate to higher costs of living, which in turn diminish discretionary income. This leads to a conflict of fulfilling physiological and safety needs (which leads us right back to Abraham Maslow's hierarchy of needs pyramid).

Finally, because the millennial generation was accompanied by helicopter parents, many were never told *no* and therefore always got what they wanted. This unlimited generosity never allowed budgetary lessons and strategies to be introduced or prescribed. Now as young adults, necessity dictates that they need to create and follow a budget. Something that is easier said than done!

35. Kirkham, "No. 1 Source of Money Stress."

36. Nielsen, "Millennials Prefer Cities."

How do millennials balance their financial stress with their daily pursuit of happiness?

EXISTENTIAL AND INTERPERSONAL STRESS

Adolescents and young adults suffer from high rates of apocalyptic anxiety and existential doom. According to a study by the American Psychological Association, they have the highest perceived amount of stress of any living generation.[37] They feel so anxious and depressed about their present and future, it is hard for them to sustain two consecutive productive days. They tie their entire value and worth on the demands they put upon society. If they get what they want, they perceive themselves as worthy. If they are denied access to their requests, they feel worthless. This is the roller coaster ride of emotion they grapple with during their waking and sleepless hours each day.

Their culture has taught them to constantly compare their lives to others. This approach leads them to lose life's daily battles before they roll out of bed each morning. These perpetuating losses have forced them to create an exoskeleton of happiness—a distorted public image that hides their sadness, confusion, loneliness, disappointment, and desperation. They find themselves emotionally sentenced to solitary confinement with no eligibility for parole. Compounding these interpersonal feelings are external events that leave this generation with a doomsday outlook toward the future. Whether it is the melting ice caps, rising seas levels, holes in our ozone, climate change, trash in our oceans, wildfires, deforestation, animal extinction, starvation, threat of war, disenfranchisement, racism, discrimination, sexual harassment, economic inequality, infectious diseases, etc., Generations Y and Z take up the guilt of past generations and are left to rectify enormous environmental and societal sins.

How do adolescents / young adults function productively with the amount of internal and external pressures they impose upon themselves?

37. Gander, "Most Stressed Out Group."

When Jesus landed and saw a large crowd, he had compassion on them, because they were like sheep without a shepherd. So he began teaching them many things.

—*Mark 6:34*

Why are adolescents and young adults suffering from high amounts of anxiety and depression today? In the last two sections, I listed for you twenty possible reasons from a world and US perspective. Of course, these twenty items do not comprise the complete list of reasons why anxiety and depression have increased in our adolescents and young adults; however, it does provide you with some clear triggers that bring on these two mental health issues. From the American perspective, I presented the following descriptors: single-parent households; alcohol saturation; drug epidemic; social media; violence; school shootings / gun violence; obesity / body shaming; relationship development; acute financial stress; and existential and interpersonal stress.

At the end of each subset, I posed a question for you to reflect upon. Below is the reprinted list of those questions. Take some time to generate as many solutions as you can to solve these problems.

- How do adolescents / young adults decode their parent(s) relationship issues while trying to survive in a disintegrating family structure?
- How do adolescents / young adults shield themselves from the prevalent and sophisticated promotion of alcohol and the extreme peer pressure that comes with using and/or abusing it?
- How do adolescents / young adults arm themselves with battle strategies and tactics to protect their most precious resources (mind, body, heart, and soul) against powerful drugs?
- In today's technological world, how do adolescents / young adults satisfy their social needs without damaging their physical, mental, and spiritual essence?
- In a violent world, how do adolescents / young adults protect their moral compass while battling daily events that erode societal norms?
- How do adolescents / young adults enter school or college campuses and not worry about a violent confrontation involving a gun?

- How do adolescents / young adults deal with the stigma of obesity?
- How do adolescents / young adults ensure themselves that they will meet their physical and cognitive benchmarks to fully lead a productive life?
- How do millennials balance their financial stress with their daily pursuit of happiness?
- How do adolescents / young adults function productively with the amount of internal and external pressures they impose upon themselves?

How did you do? Did you come up with multiple solutions for each problem? I'm guessing it was a struggle! The emotions you experienced trying to solve these difficult problems is the exact same feeling that adolescents and young adults carry with them daily.

When you buy a puzzle at a store, you expect all the pieces to be in the box. You expect each piece to fit into another piece to complete the picture. If pieces are missing or do not properly fit together, then the picture will never be complete. What happens when some of the pieces in your life are missing? What happens if events in your life don't fit together the way they should? What happens if you never have an opportunity to live the life that you want to live? Just like the puzzle, your life will never be complete.

When pieces of your life's puzzle are missing or incomplete, your mind tries to substitute other things to complete the picture. When your mind realizes that its efforts are futile, anxiety and depression fill the empty spaces. However, your mind, body, and soul sometimes need to be reminded that there are additional puzzle pieces that are within you that can make your life complete. With the help of faith, hope, and love, your life's dreams will come true!

WHO THIS BOOK IS WRITTEN FOR

First and foremost, this book is written for all those who are suffering from anxiety and depression. Even though the client focus of this book is on adolescents and young adults, the information provided in the ensuing pages will help the young and old. Mental health issues can be debilitating and sometimes life threatening if never diagnosed or treated. It can and will affect every aspect of your life. However, if you educate yourself about these diseases and seek proper medical attention and therapeutic techniques, you can control and even eradicate these mental obstacles and live an extraordinary life.

The second group that can gain growth by reading this book is the family and friends of those who suffer from anxiety and depression. Mental health issues are something that most people don't like to talk about. It makes people uncomfortable to hear about it, and as a result people who are suffering from the effects of mental issues don't get to do the one thing that can ease some of their burden—talk. It is easier to tell someone that you have cancer than a mental health issue. When you tell someone you have cancer, they react with sympathy. When you say you have a mental issue, they don't know how to react, or they try to change the subject. It's exacerbating to be diagnosed with a mental health issue such as a panic or depressive disorder. It's also difficult when a loved one is experiencing one of these diseases. When a person is living with a mental health issue, the whole family may be affected. Most mental issues often have genetic, biological, psychological, and environmental components. They are not the result of bad parenting, and they probably couldn't have been prevented by anything that you, as a friend or family member, might have done differently. It's not abnormal to feel ashamed, or hurt, or embarrassed by a family member or friend whose behaviors can be difficult to understand and deal with. Sometimes you may feel anger at the circumstances and even at the person who has been diagnosed. Such feelings of shame and anger may also go together with feelings of guilt and grief. The information contained in this book will help educate the patient and his/her circle of support to understand each disease from a genetic, biological, psychological, and environmental approach, as well as expand upon holistic approaches that promote faith, hope, and love!

The third group that can find this book beneficial is the clinicians that help their clients travel the road to recovery so that they can experience all the colorful landscapes that life can provide. I hope this book adds to the pallet of techniques that psychiatrists, psychologists, and licensed professional counselors use to help their patients who are suffering from anxiety and depression. The holistic techniques and exercises presented within this text may be new paradigms that these professionals can use to naturally unlock the mysteries of mental health issues.

The fourth group that can add this book to its office library is made up of the counselors, social workers, home school visitors, nurses, administrators, and teachers/professors who work in middle/high school settings as well as post-secondary schools. These professionals are usually on the first line of defense when it comes to observing abnormal academic/social behaviors in a structured public setting. They are also usually the first to initiate contact with family members and friends to discuss their observations, as well as dispense critical information about process and procedures within the mental health field.

Finally, this book was written for those bachelor's, master's, and doctoral degree students who are in training to become psychiatrists, psychologists, licensed professional counselors, school counselors, social workers, home school visitors, nurses, administrators, and teachers. The mental health and educational fields need intelligent, passionate, and compassionate professionals who understand the importance of their profession when it comes to easing mental, physical, emotional, and spiritual pain that is caused be anxiety and depression. I am hoping that this book will provide you with new insight into combating mental health issues that are eviscerating life experiences from our adolescents and young adults.

HOW TO READ THIS BOOK

Of course, the first thing that I would like you to do is read this book from cover to cover. After you familiarize yourself with the information provided in the units and chapters, I would like you to begin to use it as a guidebook—in other words, a daily manual in which you can specifically turn to a unit, chapter, quote, technique, or exercise that will help your mind, body, and spirit ease your pain or take another step on the road to recovery. The book is constructed so you can quickly go to a page or section to help you deal with what life has dealt you on that day. Maybe you need education or motivation or inspiration or time for reflection. Holistic tools are provided in this book so you can hook them onto your tool belt and use them when an uncomfortable situation arises. However, you must familiarize yourself with each tool and understand how and when to use it. Like all tools, the more you use it the more effective and efficient your life becomes.

THE HEART OF THIS BOOK

Near the end of each chapter there will be a section titled the "Road to Resurrection." Here you will walk behind Jesus Christ on the road to Calvary. You will learn the pain and anguish he went through to wash away your sins, conquer evil, and give you everlasting life. First you will reflect upon each Station of the Cross, which is a fifteen-step Catholic devotion that commemorates Jesus Christ's last days on earth as the Son of Man. The fifteen stations focus on specific events of his crucifixion, resurrection, and ascension into heaven. Finally, you will take up your own cross and follow Jesus Christ on your journey. Reflective exercises and questions will be posed to you for you to wash away your anxiety or depression and live a fruitful life. I encourage you to experience this journey once a week. Each time you revisit one of the fifteen stations, you will receive grace and growth and expand upon your experiences and responses to the reflective exercises and questions. By participating in this activity, you will uncover that Jesus Christ has already been through what you are experiencing. He has conquered evil and death! He will go before you and protect you always, if you follow him.

A COMPANION TO THIS BOOK

This first words printed on the first page of this book were Scripture taken from the Bible. For you to fully experience the essence of this book, you will need to have a Bible at an arm's length from you as you read. Do you own a Bible? If so, do you know where it is at this very moment? Do you know how to locate specific Scripture in the Bible? If you answered yes to these three questions, then you are in the starting blocks ready to go! If you answered no, don't panic. There are various ways you can access a Bible. You can purchase one or use your favorite digital delivery device to read it for free! There are hundreds of different translations of the Bible in more than two thousand languages. For this book, I used the New International Version (NIV). Choosing a version is a personal preference. Don't get intimidated when you research a Scripture passage and see a list of versions for the same Scripture passage. Choose a version that you are comfortable with when it comes to reading and comprehending.

The most important question that I should ask is, when was the last time you read the Bible? Hopefully your answer is *today*! However, if it has been a while, there is no need to fret. In each chapter of this book,

I provide you with Scripture or ask you to read a particular Scripture passage on your own. These activities will allow you to become familiar with the greatest book ever written. So, before you go any further, stop reading and go find *your* Bible. I promise you that this action will be a life-changing event! If you need assistance in obtaining one, contact me and I will send one to you! Reading this book without using your Bible is like driving across the country without checking your car's oil, tire pressure, or gas gauge. This book will get you moving forward, but the Bible will provide you with the confidence and the peace of mind that you will reach your destination.

In youth we learn; in age we understand.
—Marie von Ebner-Eschenbach[38]

PROLOGUE SUMMARY

Only faith in Christ gives rise to a culture
contrary to egotism and death.
—Pope John Paul II[39]

Who is the greatest magician of all time? Is it Henry Houdini, David Copperfield, David Blaine, or maybe the Penn and Teller duo? There is no doubt that these magicians were/are masters of their craft, but the greatest street magician of all time is Satan. I'm positive that you have met the GOAT (greatest of all time) on many occasions and watched him perform his magic right in front of your eyes. I bet he mesmerized you with his personality, performance skills, persistence, realism, connection, and brand. At first, you may have never heard of him or seen his dynamic show, but it was only a matter of time before he found you and invited you to experience him personally. Wasn't it amazing? It was like his tricks were specifically designed for you. You were so impressed and entertained that you wanted more. No one has ever understood your

38. Ebner-Eschenbach, *Aphorisms*, 11.
39. "Pope Gets Rousing Farewell," *Hereford Brand*, Jan. 26, 1999.

wants more than him. You felt so alive while being in his presence that you consciously or subconsciously yearned for his next visit.

Let me see if I can describe some the tricks that he performed for you. Was his first performance all about deception? Did he perform the trick entitled "Empty Promises"? You know, the one where he tells you the lie that you will be happier and more fulfilled if you sin or deny aspects of the truth. His skills are so sharp that he hid the fact that great and accumulated suffering eventually comes from almost all sinful activity. What about the trick entitled "Excuses"? This is the one where he seeks to confuse you and conceal the fundamental truth about your actions. He teaches you how to deflect blame. You learn to become a victim by constantly asking others, "What about this?" or "What about that?"

When he visited you for the second time, did he show you the power of division? Did he ask you about your hopes and dreams and then twist them until you gave up on them? Did he trick you to give him permission to scatter internal strife within you? Did he fracture the connection between your mind and soul? Did he flood your heart with anger, past hurts, resentments, fears, misunderstandings, greed, pride, and arrogance? Did he persuade you to abandon your family, friends, church, and community in search of the elusive goal of finding better and more perfect people and situations? If so, then you experienced the mentalism portion of his act. His only goal was to divide you internally and externally.

For his third performance, did he come to you, or did you go to him? Either way, you may have noticed that things began to "heat up" (pardon my pun) between you two. His third visit is more about recruitment than entertainment. He begins to teach rather than perform. He goal is to recruit you to become his understudy. He shows you that his hand is quicker than your eye as he diverts you away from your primary goal (which is God) and task (which is to work toward the kingdom of heaven). Thus, the devil does all that he can to fracture your relationship with God. He will trick you into thinking that you are too busy to pray, go to church, or seek other forms of spiritual nourishment. He will point out to you that your flesh is more powerful than your spirit and that the world has more to offer than heaven. He will cloud your vision and thoughts until you believe that you are your own god and can accomplish anything you want on your own.

How do I know all the devil's tricks? Like everyone else in the world, he visits me at least once a day. His motto is "The show must go on!"

He is always trying to find new ways to increase his audience size. He uses the latest and greatest strategies (cell phones, social media, etc.) to advertise his soul-altering performances. If Satan has performed for you, don't panic. His traveling show comes to everyone's hometown. He even visited Jesus Christ every day on his way to Jerusalem (Luke 14:1–13). The next time Satan comes to visit you, with a whole new set of tricks, tell him that Jesus Christ is your Lord and Savior, and watch him disappear in thin air.

OPENING PRAYER

God of power and mercy, in love you sent your Son so that we might be cleansed of sin and live with you forever. Bless us as we read and reflect upon his suffering and death so that we may learn from his example the way we should go.

We ask this through that same Christ, our Lord. Amen.

FIRST STATION: JESUS IN THE GARDEN OF GETHSEMANE

> Watch and pray so that you will not fall into temptation. The spirit is willing, but the flesh is weak. (Matt 26:41)

We adore you, O Christ, and we bless you.

Because by your holy cross you have redeemed the world.

> Then Jesus went with his disciples to a place called Gethsemane, and he said to them, "Sit here while I go over there and pray." He took Peter and the two sons of Zebedee along with him, and he began to be sorrowful and troubled. Then he said to them, "My soul is overwhelmed with sorrow to the point of death. Stay here and keep watch with me."

> Going a little farther, he fell with his face to the ground and prayed, "My Father, if it is possible, may this cup be taken from me. Yet not as I will, but as you will."
>
> Then he returned to his disciples and found them sleeping. "Couldn't you men keep watch with me for one hour?" he asked Peter. "Watch and pray so that you will not fall into temptation. The spirit is willing, but the flesh is weak." (Matt 26:36–41)

Lord, grant us your strength and wisdom that we may seek to follow your will in all things. Lord Jesus, help us walk in your steps.

FIRST STATION: REFLECTIVE EXERCISES AND QUESTIONS

Like our Lord, your afflictions may cause you to feel sorrow and stress. Follow Jesus' lead and find your "Gethsemane" so that you can focus on your mind, body, and soul! In the prologue of this book, I listed twenty possible reasons why adolescents and young adults may be suffering with anxiety or depression. Below, I re-listed these reasons for you. Take several minutes to review and reflect upon these reasons. Once you have given each reason its due consideration, list the top ten reasons (in ascending order) of why you believe you have anxiety and/or depression. If you have additional reasons that are not listed in the twenty that were presented in the prologue, please add them to your top ten list. Once you have listed the ten reasons, I would like you to go back and write out specific facts on why you placed each reason into a specific rank. This exercise will help you determine the main stressors and/or triggers that bring about your mental health issues.

Top Ten Reasons Why You Believe You Suffer from Anxiety and/or Depression			
Lack of Economic Opportunity and Unemployment	Safety/Security/ Well-Being	Lack of Education	Food and Water Security
Government Accountability Transparency / Corruption	Religious Conflicts	Poverty	Inequality (Income, Discrimination)
Large Scale Conflicts / Wars	Climate Change Destruction of Nature	Single-Parent Households	Alcohol Saturation

Drug Epidemic	Social Media	Violence	School Shootings Gun Violence
Obesity / Body Shaming	Relationship Development	Financial Stress	Existential and Interpersonal Stress

Rank	*Reason(s)*
#1	
#2	
#3	
#4	
#5	
#6	
#7	
#8	
#9	
#10	

Review your rankings. Are your stressors and/or triggers clearer now than they were before? Review your reasons. Do you understand the circumstances that cause these stressors and/or triggers? The first step on the "Road to Resurrection" is to know where you are and how you got there. The stress and strain of life comes upon us all. If you can find your current coordinates in life, you no longer need to look back but cast your eyes forward to see that you are following in the LORD's footsteps. He will break the shackles that bind you. He will heal all your afflictions. He will provide for your every need!

See, I am doing a new thing!
Now it springs up; do you not perceive it?
I am making a way in the wilderness
and streams in the wasteland.
—Isa 43:19

THE ROAD  RESURRECTION

SECOND STATION: JESUS, BETRAYED BY JUDAS, IS ARRESTED

> While he was still speaking a crowd came up, and the man who was called Judas, one of the Twelve, was leading them. He approached Jesus to kiss him, but Jesus asked him, "Judas, are you betraying the Son of Man with a kiss?" (Luke 22:47–49)

We adore you, O Christ, and we bless you.

Because by your holy cross you have redeemed the world.

> Just as [Jesus] was speaking, Judas, one of the Twelve, appeared. With him was a crowd armed with swords and clubs, sent from the chief priests, the teachers of the law, and the elders.
>
> Now the betrayer had arranged a signal with them: "The one I kiss is the man; arrest him and lead him away under guard." Going at once to Jesus, Judas said, "Rabbi!" and kissed him. The men seized Jesus and arrested him. (Mark 14:43–46)

Lord, grant us the courage of our convictions that our lives may faithfully reflect the good news you bring.

Lord Jesus, help us walk in your steps.

SECOND STATION: REFLECTIVE EXERCISES AND QUESTIONS

Judas, one of Jesus' twelve disciples, lost his way. His afflictions weren't physical or mental but spiritual. He suffered from a crippled spirit. He was consumed with greed, envy, and pride. These sins eroded his life's mission. Have you lost your way? Do you allow your afflictions to distract or change your life's mission? Do you know your life's mission?

To be who you want to be and go where you want to go, you must travel the Road to Resurrection. Sometimes this road is straight, and sometimes it curves. Sometimes you can travel on it for free, and sometimes you will have to pay a toll. Expect to be detoured more than once while traveling this road due to construction and unforeseen obstacles. These detours will force you to take exits that you never thought existed. However, this road is full of signs and signals, so you won't lose your way. It provides rest areas and gas stations to help fill up your soul! And even though you may have to travel farther than others on this road, you have a guarantee through your Heavenly Father that you will reach your destination—which is everlasting life!

The following exercise will help you find or revitalize your sense of mission. Take the appropriate amount of time to answer the following three questions. The more thought and reflection you put into each of these questions, the easier it will be to find the on-ramp to the Road to Resurrection.

Finding Your Sense of Mission
Who are you?
Why are you here?
What are you supposed to be doing?

Did it take you more time than you thought it would to answer these questions? These are questions that require you to scan your mind, body, and soul. The answers to these questions will bring you closer to your true essence as a human being. Keep in mind, the answers that you provided today will not be the same answers you will provide yourself a month, a year, or ten years from now. As you travel down the Road to Resurrection, your sense of self will change. When your sense of self changes, so does your sense of mission. I encourage you to repeat this exercise when you feel that you have lost your way. Your answers will bring you closer to faith, hope, and love, which in turn will jettison you further down the Road to Resurrection. If Judas asked himself these three questions, he would have not sold our Lord for thirty silver pieces!

> *"You know the way to the place where I am going." Thomas said to him, "Lord, we don't know where you are going, so how can we know the way?" Jesus answered, "I am the way and the truth and the life. No one comes to the Father except through me."*
> *—John 14:4–6*

Part 1

The Afflictions

Then Pilate took Jesus and had him flogged
—John 19:1

They stripped him and put a scarlet robe on him, and then twisted together a crown of thorns and set it on his head. They put a staff in his right hand. Then they knelt in front of him and mocked him. "Hail, king of the Jews!" they said. They spit on him, and took the staff and struck him on the head again and again. After they had mocked him, they took off the robe and put his own clothes on him. Then they led him away to crucify him.
—Matt 27:28–31

When they came to the place called the Skull,
they crucified him there, along with the criminals—
one on his right, the other on his left.
—Luke 23:33

Instead, one of the soldiers pierced Jesus' side with a spear,
bringing a sudden flow of blood and water.
—John 19:34

Chapter 1

Anxiety

He withdrew about a stone's throw beyond them, knelt down and prayed, "Father, if you are willing, take this cup from me; yet not my will, but yours be done." An angel from heaven appeared to him and strengthened him. And being in anguish, he prayed more earnestly, and his sweat was like drops of blood falling to the ground.
—Luke 22:41–44

It is earlier September on a late Sunday afternoon and Paul has hardly touched his full plate of meatloaf, mashed potatoes, and corn. It is not because he ate a big lunch; as a matter of fact, he hasn't eaten anything all day. When his family asks him to take a few bites from his plate, he tells them that he can't because he has a headache and his stomach hurts. Paul's parents are familiar with these symptoms because their son suffers from them every day. Paul excuses himself from the table and goes to his room to do whatever he can stop thinking about Monday morning. As the clock turns, so does his mind. He creates thousands of negative scenarios about the hours before and during school. He mentally watches each of them play out like we binge-watch our favorite shows on Netflix. There is no stopping his mind. He is on a mental treadmill going twenty miles per hour with no end in sight. Does this description sound familiar? It is just a small glimpse into what an adolescent or young adult goes through daily with anxiety.

In the above scenario, Paul's mind is defining his present and near-future experiences. Where Paul's mind goes, his body follows! While his mind acts like a runaway train, Paul's body begins to react.

Immediately, his hypothalamus, a tiny control tower in his brain, sends stress hormones to his central nervous system. Suddenly, his adrenal glands release adrenaline. These stress hormones are the same ones that trigger his body's "fight or flight" response. Paul's heart races, his breath quickens, and his muscles are ready for action. His body is in "emergency mode" and is preparing him to react quickly. However, he is not actually in immediate danger. His mind is triggering realistic simulations that are possible but not likely. Because of this, his central nervous system keeps releasing stress hormones that interrupt his normal bodily functions. Normally, when a perceived fear is gone, the hypothalamus tells all systems to go back to normal, but with an individual who suffers from anxiety, the hypothalamus fires many times a day—every day.

Paul's mind is also affecting his respiratory and cardiovascular systems. The adrenaline released into his body makes him breathe faster to quickly distribute oxygen-rich blood to his body. The adrenaline causes his blood vessels to constrict and divert more oxygen to his muscles so he'll have more strength to act. This raises his blood pressure, which makes his heart work too hard for too long. Over time, if Paul doesn't seek help in controlling his anxiety, he will increase his chances of having a heart attack or stroke.

Paul's digestive system is also responding to his mental distress. Why didn't Paul eat his dinner? One reason may be that Paul is suffering from heartburn or acid reflux due to increased stomach acid. Or maybe Paul has a stomach ulcer. Or Paul has a negative response on how food moves through his body. In past experiences, when he finished eating while under the influence of anxiety, he may have experienced diarrhea, constipation, nausea, vomiting, or a stomachache. All of these are biological reactions that disseminate from the digestive system due to increased levels of anxiety.

After Paul excused himself from the dinner table and went into his room, he probably felt his entire muscular system tense up. This is a normal reaction when your body is in "fight or flight" mode. It becomes your armor to protect your internal organs from injury. But Paul isn't in a dangerous situation—he is in his bedroom! Paul's tight muscles will probably cause him headaches, back and shoulder pain, and body aches. This can lead to unhealthy decisions like lack of exercise and/or self-medication due to muscular pain.

I bet that Paul is embarrassed to tell anyone that he has lost his sexual desire. He is probably frustrated and sad because he doesn't know the reasons why. Stress will take a toll on the entire human body, which includes sexuality and the reproductive system. Long-term anxiety usually causes a man's testosterone levels to begin to drop. This can interfere with sperm production and cause erectile dysfunction or impotence. It also may increase the risk of infection for male reproductive organs like the prostate and testes. For women, stress can affect the menstrual cycle. It can lead to irregular, heavier, or more painful periods.

Finally, I'm sure Paul has a difficult time attending school or other social activities because he is chronically tired and/or sick. One reason may be that the constant release of stress hormones into his body weakens his immune system and reduces his body's response to foreign invaders. People that suffer with anxiety are more susceptible to viral illnesses like the flu and the common cold, as well as other infections. Stress can also increase the time it takes Paul to recover from an illness or injury.[1]

Scripture tells us the body is one and has many members, and all the members of the body, though many, are one body; so it is with Christ (1 Cor 12:12). This statement is certainly true, but the body part that has a direct impact on the rest is the brain. A mental health issue like anxiety puts strain on the brain, which in turn impacts the entire body. However, faith, hope, and love are the antidotes that Paul can use to control his stress and allow his body to function normally, regardless of the situation he finds himself in.

Anxiety is a thin stream of fear trickling through the mind. If encouraged, it cuts a channel into which all other thoughts are drained.

—Attributed to Arthur Somers Roche

1. Cherney, "Effects of Anxiety."

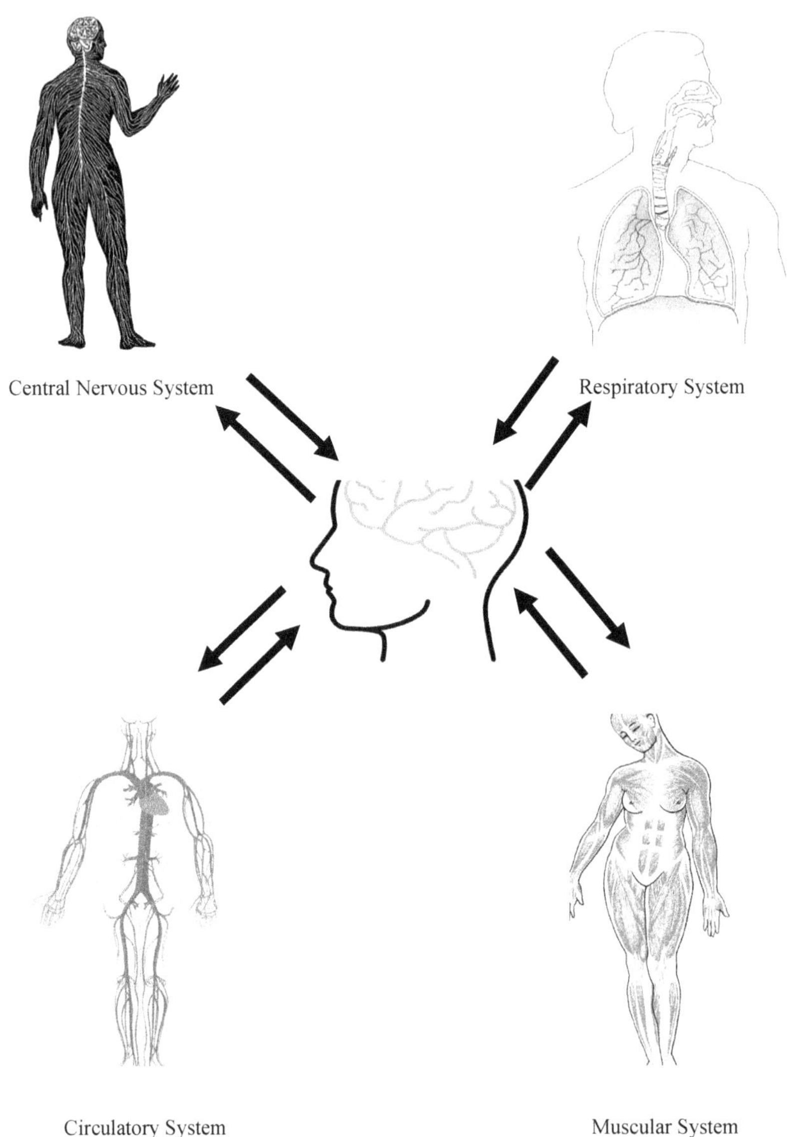
Central Nervous System
Respiratory System
Circulatory System
Muscular System

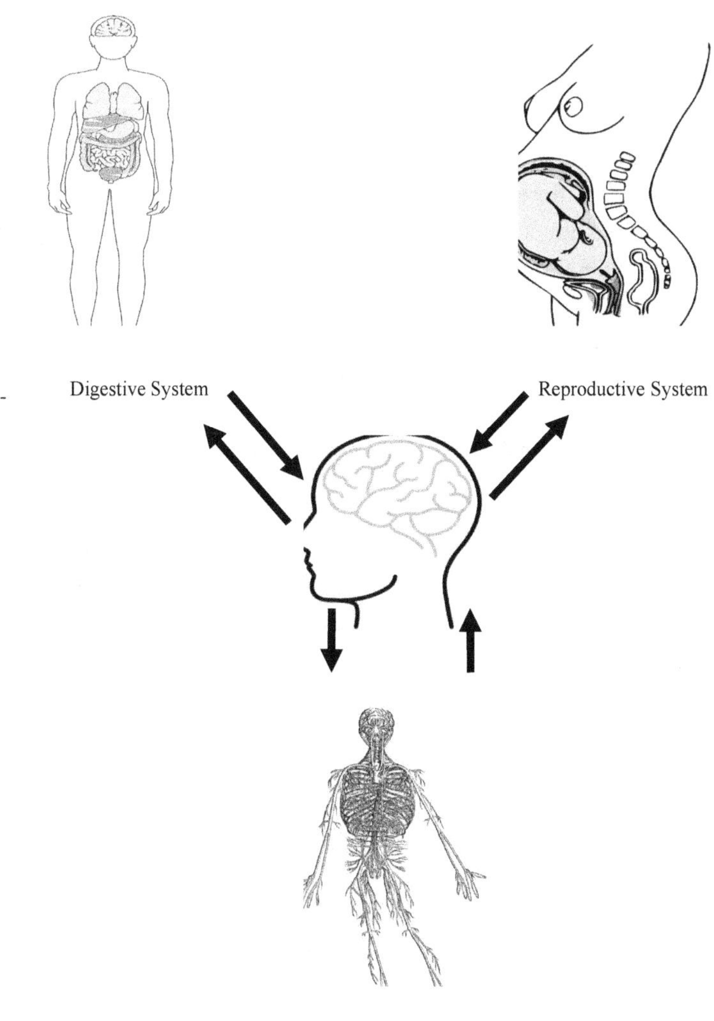

Anxiety's like a rocking chair.
It gives you something to do, but it doesn't get you very far.
—*Jodi Picoult*[2]

2. Picoult, *Sing You Home*, 322.

Nervousness, fear, apprehension, and worrying affect how you feel and behave. It is natural for all of us to experience these feelings sometimes throughout our life. Mild anxiety alerts our body that we are entering an atypical event. These feelings surface when we must speak in public, go on a blind date, take a test that we didn't study for, have an interview, etc. Furthermore, transitional moments in our life are usually accompanied by these feelings—for example, the first day of elementary school, junior high school, high school; moving away from your home for college, military, or work; deciding to marry, buy a house, or have children. These shining life moments are shared by the shadows of anxiety. However, as you read above, having anxiety on a minute-by-minute, hour-by-hour, and day-by-day basis is unhealthy for your body, mind, and soul.

According to the Anxiety and Depression Association of America,

- anxiety disorders are the most common mental illness in the United States, affecting forty million adults in the United States age eighteen and older, or 18.1 percent of the population every year;
- anxiety disorders are highly treatable, yet only 36.9 percent of those suffering receive treatment;
- people with an anxiety disorder are three to five times more likely to go to the doctor and six times more likely to be hospitalized for psychiatric disorders than those who do not suffer from anxiety disorders.[3]

The American Psychological Association (APA) defines anxiety as "an emotion characterized by feelings of tension, worried thoughts and physical changes like increased blood pressure." The APA also describes a person with an anxiety disorder as "having recurring intrusive thoughts or concerns."[4] The APA goes out of its way to delineate the difference between normal feelings of anxiety and an anxiety disorder that requires medical attention. However, those who suffer with anxiety do not need the APA's definition to diagnose their problem. Their daily life provides them evidence that they suffer with some type of mental disorder.

Anxiety disorders can be classified into six main types. Below we have presented a section for each.

3. Anxiety and Depression Association of America, "Anxiety Disorders."
4. American Psychological Association, "Anxiety."

GENERALIZED ANXIETY DISORDER (GAD)

Generalized anxiety disorder (or GAD) is characterized by excessive, exaggerated anxiety and worry about everyday life events with no obvious reasons for worry. People with symptoms of generalized anxiety disorder tend to always expect disaster and can't stop worrying about health, money, family, work, or school. In people with GAD, the worry is often unrealistic or out of proportion for the situation. Daily life becomes a constant state of worry, fear, and dread. Eventually, the anxiety so dominates the person's thinking that it interferes with daily functioning, including work, school, social activities, and relationships.

Symptoms of GAD may include the following:

- excessive, ongoing worry and tension
- an unrealistic view of problems
- restlessness or a feeling of being "edgy"
- irritability
- muscle tension
- headaches
- sweating
- difficulty concentrating
- nausea
- the need to go to the bathroom frequently
- tiredness
- trouble falling or staying asleep
- trembling
- being easily startled[5]

PANIC DISORDER

People with panic disorder have sudden and repeated attacks of fear that last for several minutes or longer. These are called panic attacks. Panic

5. Anxiety and Depression Association of America, "Generalized Anxiety Disorder."

attacks are characterized by a fear of disaster or of losing control even when there is no real danger. A person may also have a strong physical reaction during a panic attack. It may feel like having a heart attack. Panic attacks can occur at any time, and many people with panic disorder worry about and dread the possibility of having another attack. If this kind of random event has happened to you at least twice, and you constantly worry and change your routine to keep from having one, you might have panic disorder.

A person with a panic disorder may become discouraged and feel ashamed because he or she cannot carry out normal routines like going to school or work, going to the grocery store, or driving. Panic disorder often begins in the late teens or early adulthood. But not everyone who experiences panic attacks will develop panic disorder.

Symptoms of panic disorder include a sudden strong feeling of fear. You'll have four or more of these signs:

- pounding or fast heartbeat
- sweating
- trembling or shaking
- shortness of breath or a feeling of being smothered
- a choking feeling
- chest pain
- nausea or stomach pain
- feeling dizzy or faint
- chills or hot flashes
- numbness or tingling in the body
- feeling unreal or detached
- a fear of losing control or going crazy
- a fear of dying[6]

6. Anxiety and Depression Association of America, *Panic Disorder*.

SOCIAL ANXIETY DISORDER

Have you ever had extreme anxiety when talking to strangers, speaking in public, dating, making eye contact, entering rooms, using public restrooms, going to parties, eating in front of other people, going to school or work, or starting conversations? If so, you may be suffering from social anxiety disorder. Social anxiety disorder (or social phobia) is an intense fear of being judged, negatively evaluated, or rejected in a social or performance situation. People with social anxiety disorder may worry about acting or appearing visibly anxious (e.g., blushing, stumbling over words) or being viewed as stupid, awkward, or boring. As a result, they often avoid social or performance situations, and when a situation cannot be avoided, they experience significant anxiety and distress.

This state of mind can create havoc on the lives of those who suffer from it. For example, individuals may decline a job opportunity that requires frequent interaction with new people, or avoid going out to eat with friends due to a fear that their hands will shake when eating or drinking. Symptoms may be so extreme that they disrupt daily life and can interfere significantly with daily routines, occupational performance, or social life, making it difficult to complete school, interview and get a job, and have friendships and romantic relationships.

Symptoms of social anxiety disorder may include the following:

- a rapid heart rate
- nausea
- sweating
- full-blown panic attacks when confronting a feared situation[7]

Although people who suffer from social anxiety disorder recognize that their fear is excessive and unreasonable, they often feel powerless against their anxiety.

Worrying is like walking around with an umbrella
waiting for it to rain.
—Attributed to Wiz Khalifa

7. Anxiety and Depression Association of America, *Social Anxiety Disorder.*

SPECIFIC PHOBIAS

Have you ever flown on a plane? How was your experience? Did you ever fly again? Have you ever ridden on an elevator? What did it feel like when the doors closed? Do you now take the stairs to get to your destination? Have you ever gone to a musical concert? Was it fun when the sound waves blew back your hair and you and the masses bumped into one another while you were singing and dancing to your favorite song? Or do you like to listen to your favorite musical group in your car or bedroom with the volume on low? The answer to the above questions may help you understand if you are suffering from a specific phobia.

A specific phobia (or simple phobia) is a lasting and unreasonable fear caused by the presence or thought of a specific object or situation that usually poses little or no actual danger. Exposure to the object or situation brings about an immediate reaction, causing the person to endure intense anxiety or to avoid the object or situation entirely. The distress associated with the phobia and/or the need to avoid the object or situation can significantly interfere with the person's ability to function. Those that suffer with a specific phobia recognize that the fear is excessive or unreasonable yet are unable to overcome it.

Different types of phobias may include the following:

Animal: includes the fear of dogs, snakes, insects, mice, etc.

Situational: involves a fear of specific situations, such as flying, riding in a car, driving, going over bridges or underneath tunnels, or being in a closed-in place (elevator)

Natural Environment: fear of storms, heights, water, etc.

Blood Injection / Injury: fear of being injured, of blood, or of invasive medical procedures

Other: fear of falling, loud sounds, costumed characters (clowns), etc.

Symptoms of specific phobias may include

- excessive or irrational fear of a specific object or situation, avoiding the object or situation, or enduring it with great distress;
- physical symptoms may include a pounding heart, nausea, diarrhea, sweating, trembling or shaking, numbness or tingling, problems

with breathing (shortness of breath), feeling dizzy or lightheaded, and feeling like you are choking;

- anticipatory anxiety, which involves becoming nervous ahead of time about being in certain situations or encountering the object of your phobia.[8]

OBSESSIVE COMPULSIVE DISORDER (OCD)

Do you bite your nails? Do you always have negative thoughts? If so, you have formed bad habits and need to walk on the sunny side of the street. You do not have OCD! However, if you think that your family members might get hurt if they don't put their clothing on in the exact same order every morning or if you wash your hands exactly seven times after touching something that might be dirty, you may be suffering from a form of OCD. People with OCD experience obsessions and compulsions. Obsessions are intrusive and unwanted thoughts, images, or urges that cause distress or anxiety. Compulsions are behaviors that the person feels compelled to perform to ease their distress or anxiety or suppress the thoughts. Some of these behaviors are visible actions, while others are mental behaviors. Common obsessions include concerns about contamination, cleanliness, aggressive impulses, or the need for symmetry. Common compulsions include checking, washing/cleaning, and arranging. There isn't always a logical connection between obsessions and compulsions. Often people with OCD experience a variety of obsessions and compulsions.

Many people with OCD recognize that their obsessions and compulsions are not rational. Nevertheless, they still feel a strong need to perform the repetitive behavior or mental compulsions. They may spend several hours every day focusing on their obsessions, performing seemingly senseless rituals. If left untreated, OCD can be chronic and can interfere with a person's normal routine, schoolwork, job, family, or social activities. Unlike adults, children and teens with OCD may not recognize that their obsessions and compulsions are excessive.

Obsessive thoughts can include

- fear of germs or getting dirty;

8. Anxiety and Depression Association of America, *Specific Phobias*.

- worries about getting hurt or others being hurt;
- need for things to be placed in an exact order;
- belief that certain numbers or colors are "good" or "bad";
- constant awareness of blinking, breathing, or other body sensations;
- unfounded suspicion that a partner is unfaithful.

Compulsive habits can include

- washing hands many times in a row;
- doing tasks in a specific order every time, or a certain "good" number of times;
- repetitive checking on a locked door, light switch, and other things;
- need to count things, like steps or bottles;
- putting items in an exact order, like cans with labels facing front;
- fear of touching doorknobs, using public toilets, or shaking hands.[9]

POSTTRAUMATIC STRESS DISORDER (PTSD)

In the first sentence in the book *The Road Less Traveled*, M. Scott Peck writes, "Life is difficult!"[10] No one who ever lived on this earth can dispute this fact. Life is a journey of peaks and valleys. One day your experiences will allow you to bump your head on the clouds; the very next day it may feel like you are walking alone in Death Valley (282 feet below sea level). Each person's journey is unique but similar when it comes to life-changing events. Unfortunately, negative life events can change the trajectory of your life. People who have experienced or witnessed a natural disaster, serious accident, terrorist incident, sudden death of a loved one, war, violent personal assault such as rape, or other life-threatening events have natural reactions such as shock, anger, nervousness, fear, and even guilt. These reactions are common and go away over time. For a person with PTSD, however, these feelings continue and even increase, becoming so strong that they keep the person from living a normal life.

9. Anxiety and Depression Association of America, "Obsessive Compulsive Disorder."

10. Peck, *Road Less Traveled*, 10.

People with PTSD have symptoms for longer than one month and cannot function as well as before the event occurred.

The disorder is characterized by four main types of symptoms:

Reliving: People with PTSD repeatedly relive the ordeal through thoughts and memories of the trauma. These may include flashbacks, hallucinations, and nightmares. They also may feel great distress when certain things remind them of the trauma, such as the anniversary date of the event.

Avoiding: The person may avoid people, places, thoughts, or situations that may remind him or her of the trauma. This can lead to feelings of detachment and isolation from family and friends, as well as a loss of interest in activities that the person once enjoyed.

Increased Arousal: These include excessive emotions; problems relating to others, including feeling or showing affection; difficulty falling or staying asleep; irritability; outbursts of anger; difficulty concentrating; and being "jumpy," or easily startled. The person may also suffer physical symptoms, such as increased blood pressure and heart rate, rapid breathing, muscle tension, nausea, and diarrhea.

Negative Cognitions and Mood: This refers to thoughts and feelings related to blame, estrangement, and memories of the traumatic event.[11]

The twelve-step program remains a commonly recommended and used treatment modality for various types of addiction. The basic premise of the twelve-step model is that people can help one another achieve and maintain abstinence from substances or behaviors to which they are addicted. The model gives people a framework from which to surrender their addiction, process their experience, and move forward into new patterns. The third step on the Road to Resurrection is to take a personal inventory of your thoughts, emotions, and behaviors. This data may help uncover whether you have an anxiety disorder. If you think that you may suffer from anxiety, make an appointment with your doctor so that they can collect medical documentation on your condition and recommend a psychiatrist, psychologist, or licensed professional counselor if needed.

11. Anxiety and Depression Association of America, *Posttraumatic Stress Disorder*.

THIRD STATION: JESUS CONDEMNED BY THE SANHEDRIN

> And he said, "The Son of Man must suffer many things and be rejected by the elders, the chief priests and the teachers of the law, and he must be killed and on the third day be raised to life." (Luke 9:22)

We adore you, O Christ, and we bless you.

Because by your holy cross you have redeemed the world.

> At daybreak the council of the elders of the people, both the chief priests and the teachers of the law, met together, and Jesus was led before them. "If you are the Messiah," they said, "tell us."
>
> Jesus answered, "If I tell you, you will not believe me, and if I asked you, you would not answer. But from now on, the Son of Man will be seated at the right hand of the mighty God."
>
> They all asked, "Are you then the Son of God?"
>
> He replied, "You say that I am."
>
> Then they said, "Why do we need any more testimony? We have heard it from his own lips." (Luke 22:66–71)

Lord, grant us your sense of righteousness that we may never cease to work to bring about the justice of the kingdom that you promised.

THIRD STATION: REFLECTIVE EXERCISES AND QUESTIONS

The night before the last day of Jesus' earthly life, he had an opportunity to express his personal inventory of thoughts, emotions, and behaviors to the elders, chief priests, scribes, and the Sanhedrin. This moment of clarity prepared him for his final mission of mercy and forgiveness (the road leading to Calvary). For you to find your moment of clarity on whether you suffer from a form of anxiety, I have provided you with screening tools for the specific anxiety diagnoses that were explained in this chapter. The goal in participating in these screening tools is for the results of these tests to be shared with your doctor to inform further conversations about diagnosis and treatment.

A screening can be an important first step in getting needed care for mental health concerns and can be an easy way for you or someone you care about to get a better understanding of concerning experiences or feelings. The screenings are not a substitute for professional assessment and care. If you have further questions or serious concerns, contact your health care provider or a mental health professional.

Generalized Anxiety Disorder (GAD) Screening Tool

This is a screening measure to help you determine whether you might have a generalized anxiety disorder (GAD) that needs professional attention. This screening tool is not designed to make a diagnosis of GAD but to be shared with your primary care physician or mental health professional to inform further conversations about diagnosis and treatment.[12]

Are you troubled by the following?		
Yes	*No*	*Question*
		Do you experience excessive worry?
		Is your worry excessive in intensity, frequency, or amount of distress it causes?
		Do you find it difficult to control the worry (or stop worrying) once it starts?
		Do you worry excessively or uncontrollably about *minor things* such as being late for an appointment, minor repairs, homework, etc.?
		During the *last six months*, have you been bothered by excessive worries more days than not?
Please list below the most frequent topics about which you worry excessively or uncontrollably.		

12. Questionnaire reproduced from Newman et al., "Generalized Anxiety Disorder Questionnaire-IV" with permission.

During the past six months, have you often been bothered by any of the following symptoms? Check one square next to each symptom that you have had more days than not.									
	Not at all		A little		Moderately		Quite a bit		Extremely
Restless or feeling keyed up or on edge	0	1	2	3	4	5	6	7	8
Irritability	0	1	2	3	4	5	6	7	8
Difficulty falling/staying asleep or restless/unsatisfying sleep	0	1	2	3	4	5	6	7	8
Being easily fatigued	0	1	2	3	4	5	6	7	8
Difficulty concentrating or mind going blank	0	1	2	3	4	5	6	7	8
Muscle tension	0	1	2	3	4	5	6	7	8

How much do worry and physical symptoms interfere with your life, work, social activities, family, etc.?								
0	1	2	3	4	5	6	7	8
None		Mild		Moderate		Severe		Very Severe
How much are you bothered by worry and physical symptoms (how much distress does it cause you)?								
0	1	2	3	4	5	6	7	8
None		Mild		Moderate		Severe		Very Severe

The remaining tools in this Third Station are designed to help you reflect on additional experiences you may have had with anxiety. These screening instruments are supported by the American Psychiatric Association and often used by clinicians. However, for this exercise, please think of it as a personal check-in rather than a scientific test. Take a few minutes to read each question carefully and think about how you've been feeling over the past 7 days. You can ignore the last column, the bottom rows, and the numbering system - they aren't needed for your reflection. Focus instead on your experiences and emotions. If your responses suggest that you may be struggling with specific anxiety symptoms, consider sharing your results with your primary care doctor or a mental health professional. They can help you explore next steps and provide the support you need.

Severity Measure for Panic Disorder—Adult[13]

Instructions: The following questions ask about thoughts, feelings, and behaviors about panic attacks. A panic attack is an episode of intense fear that sometimes comes out of the blue (for no apparent reason). The symptoms of a panic attack include: a racing heart, shortness of breath, dizziness, sweating, and fear of losing control or dying. **Please respond to each item by marking (✓ or X) one box per row.**

							Clinician Use
	During the PAST SEVEN DAYS, I have . . .	*Never*	*Occasionally*	*Half of the time*	*Most of the time*	*All of the time*	*Item score*
1	felt moments of sudden terror, fear or fright, sometimes out of the blue (i.e., a panic attack)	0	1	2	3	4	
2	felt anxious, worried, or nervous about having more panic attacks	0	1	2	3	4	

13. Assessment reproduced from American Psychiatric Association, "Panic Disorder"; used with permission.

3	had thoughts of losing control, dying, going crazy, or other bad things happening because of panic attacks	0	1	2	3	4	
4	felt a racing heart, sweaty, trouble breathing, faint, or shaky	0	1	2	3	4	
5	felt tense muscles, felt on edge or restless, or had trouble relaxing or trouble sleeping	0	1	2	3	4	
6	avoided, or did not approach or enter, situations in which panic attacks might occur	0	1	2	3	4	
7	left situation early, or participated only minimally, because of panic attacks	0	1	2	3	4	
8	spent a lot of time preparing for, or procrastinating about (putting off), situations in which panic attacks might occur	0	1	2	3	4	
9	distracted myself to avoid thinking about panic attacks	0	1	2	3	4	

10	needed help to cope with panic attacks (e.g., alcohol or other medication, superstitious objects, other people	0	1	2	3	4	
Total/Partial Raw Score:							
Prorated Total Raw Score (if one to two items left unanswered)							
Average Total Score:							

Severity Measure for Social Anxiety Disorder (Social Phobia)—Adult[14]

Instructions: The following questions ask about thoughts, feelings, and behaviors that you may have had about *social situations.* Usual social situations include: public speaking, speaking in meetings, attending social events or parties, introducing yourself to others, having conversations, giving and receiving compliments, making requests of others, and eating and writing in public. **Please respond to each item by marking (✓ or X) one box per row.**

							Clinician Use
	During the PAST SEVEN DAYS, I have . . .	*Never*	*Occasionally*	*Half of the time*	*Most of the time*	*All of the time*	*Item score*
1	felt moments of sudden terror, fear, or fright in social situations	0	1	2	3	4	

14. Assessment reproduced from American Psychiatric Association, "Social Anxiety Disorder"; used with permission.

2	felt anxious, worried, or nervous about social situations	0	1	2	3	4	
3	had thoughts of being rejected, humiliated, embarrassed, ridiculed, or offending others	0	1	2	3	4	
4	felt a racing heart, sweaty, trouble breathing, faint, or shaky in social situations	0	1	2	3	4	
5	felt tense muscles, felt on edge or restless, or had trouble relaxing in social situations	0	1	2	3	4	
6	avoided, or did not approach or enter, social situations	0	1	2	3	4	
7	left social situations early or participated only minimally (e.g., said little, avoided eye contact)	0	1	2	3	4	
8	spent a lot of time preparing what to say or how to act in social situations	0	1	2	3	4	
9	distracted myself to avoid thinking about social situations	0	1	2	3	4	
10	needed help to cope with social situations (e.g., alcohol or medications, superstitious objects)	0	1	2	3	4	

Total/Partial Raw Score:	
Prorated Total Raw Score (if one to two items left unanswered)	
Average Total Score:	

Severity Measure for Specific Phobia—Adult[15]

Instructions: The following questions ask about thoughts, feelings, and behaviors that you may have had in a variety of situations. Please check (✓) the item below that makes you most anxious. Choose only one item and make your ratings based on the situations included in that item.

Driving, flying, tunnels, bridges, or enclosed spaces	Animals or insects	Heights, storms, or water	Blood, needles, or injections	Choking or vomiting

Please respond to each item by marking (✓ or X) one box per row.							*Clinician Use*
	During the PAST SEVEN DAYS, I have . . .	*Never*	*Occasionally*	*Half of the time*	*Most of the time*	*All of the time*	*Item score*
1	felt moments of sudden terror, fear, or fright in these situations	0	1	2	3	4	
2	felt anxious, worried, or nervous about these situations	0	1	2	3	4	

15. Assessment reproduced from American Psychiatric Association, "Specific Phobia"; used with permission.

3	had thoughts of being injured, overcome with fear, or other bad things happening in these situations	0	1	2	3	4	
4	felt a racing heart, sweaty, trouble breathing, faint, or shaky in these situations	0	1	2	3	4	
5	felt tense muscles, felt on edge or restless, or had trouble relaxing in these situations	0	1	2	3	4	
6	avoided, or did not approach or enter, these situations	0	1	2	3	4	
7	moved away from these situations or left them early	0	1	2	3	4	
8	spent a lot of time preparing for, or procrastinating about (i.e., putting off), these situations	0	1	2	3	4	
9	distracted myself to avoid thinking about these situations	0	1	2	3	4	
10	needed help to cope with these situations (e.g., alcohol or medications, superstitious objects, other people)	0	1	2	3	4	
Total/Partial Raw Score:							
Prorated Total Raw Score (if one to two items left unanswered)							
Average Total Score:							

Repetitive Thoughts and Behaviors—Adult: Adapted from the Florida Obsessive-Compulsive Inventory (FOCI) Severity Scale (Part B)[16]

Instructions: The questions below ask about things that might have bothered you. For each question, circle the number that best describes how much (or how often) you been bothered by each problem during the **past TWO (2) WEEKS**

How much (or how often) have you been bothered by the following problems							*Clinician Use*
	During the past TWO (2) WEEKS, I have . . .	*None* Not at all	*Slight* Rare, less than a day or two	*Mild* Several days	*Moderate* More than half the days	*Severe* Nearly everyday	*Item score*
1	unpleasant thoughts, urges, or images that repeatedly enter your mind?	0	1	2	3	4	
2	feeling driven to perform certain behaviors or mental acts over and over again?	0	1	2	3	4	

Instructions: If you answered the above questions at a mild or greater level of severity, please continue with this inventory. The questions below ask about these feelings in more detail and especially how often you have been bothered by a list of symptoms **<u>during the past 7 days.</u> Please respond to each item by marking (✓ or X) one box per row.**

16. Assessment reproduced from American Psychiatric Association, "Repetitive Thoughts and Behaviors"; used with permission.

During the PAST SEVEN (7) DAYS . . .							*Clinician Use*
1	On average, how much *time* is occupied by these thoughts or behaviors each day?	*None* 0	*Mild* (less than an hour a day 1	*Moderate* (1 to 3 hours a day) 2	*Severe* (3 to 8 hours a day) 3	*Extreme* (more than 8 hours a day) 4	*Item score*
2	How much *distress* do these thoughts or behaviors cause you?	*None* 0	*Mild* (slightly disturbing) 1	*Moderate* (disturbing but still manageable) 2	*Severe* (very disturbing) 3	*Extreme* (overwhelming distress) 4	
3	How hard is it for you to *control* these thoughts or behaviors?	*None* (complete control) 0	*Much Control* (usually able to control thoughts or behaviors) 1	*Moderate Control* (sometimes able to control thoughts or behaviors) 2	*Little Control* (infrequently able to control thoughts or behaviors) 3	*No Control* (unable to control thoughts or behaviors) 4	
4	How much do these thoughts or behaviors cause you to *avoid* doing anything, going anyplace, or being with anyone?	*No avoidance* 0	*Mild* (occasional avoidance) 1	*Moderate* (regularly avoid doing these things) 2	*Severe* (frequent and extensive avoidance) 3	*Extreme* (nearly complete avoidance; house bound) 4	
5	How much do these thoughts or behaviors *interfere* with school, work, or your social or family life?	*None* 0	*Mild* (slight interference) 1	*Moderate* (definite interference with functioning, but still manageable) 2	*Severe* (substantial interference) 3	*Extreme* (near total interference; incapacitated) 4	

Total/Partial Raw Score:	
Prorated Total Raw Score (if 1-2 items left unanswered)	
Average Total Score:	

Severity of Posttraumatic Stress Symptoms—Adult[17]

Please list the traumatic event that you experienced:
Date of the traumatic event:
Instructions: People sometimes have problems after extremely stressful events or experiences. How much have you been bothered during the PAST SEVEN (7) DAYS by each of the following problems that occurred or became worse after an extremely stressful event/experience? **Please respond to each item by marking (✓ or X) one box per row.**

							Clinician Use
		Not at all	*A little bit*	*Moderately*	*Quite a bit*	*Extremely*	*Item score*
1	Having "flash-backs," that is, you suddenly acted or felt as if a stressful experience from the past was hap-pening all over again (for example, you reexperienced parts of a stressful experience by see-ing, hearing, smell-ing, or physically feeling parts of the experience)?	0	1	2	3	4	

17. Assessment reproduced from American Psychiatric Association, "Posttraumatic Stress Symptoms"; used with permission.

2	Feeling very emotionally upset when something reminded you of a stressful experience?	0	1	2	3	4	
3	Trying to avoid thoughts, feelings, or physical sensations that reminded you of a stressful experience?	0	1	2	3	4	
4	Thinking that a stressful event happened because you or someone else (who didn't directly harm you) did something wrong or didn't do everything possible to prevent it, or because of something about you?	0	1	2	3	4	
5	Having a very negative emotional state (for example, you were experiencing lots of fear, anger, guilt, shame, or horror) after a stressful experience?	0	1	2	3	4	
6	Losing interest in activities you used to enjoy before having a stressful experience?	0	1	2	3	4	
7	Being "super alert," on guard, or constantly on the lookout for danger?	0	1	2	3	4	

8	Feeling jumpy or easily startled when you hear an unexpected noise?	0	1	2	3	4	
9	Being extremely irritable or angry to the point where you yelled at other people, got into fights, or destroyed things?	0	1	2	3	4	
Total/Partial Raw Score:							
Prorated Total Raw Score (if one to two items left unanswered)							
Average Total Score:							

When Jesus stood in front of the elders, chief priests, scribes, and the Sanhedrin, he knew this was going to be the last day of his earthly life. He responded to their questions with a clear mind, heart, and soul. He knew what brought him to this moment. He knew that he was the Son of Man. Finally, he knew his earthly mission was coming to an end. I am hoping you took some time to fill out one of these screening tools. By reflecting upon your thoughts and responses, you too brought clarity toward the anxiety that you are suffering with. Like Jesus, you have a better understanding of the events that led you to this moment. Like Jesus, you have a better understanding of who you are and how this anxiety is impeding your daily life. Finally, like Jesus, you realize that you are on a mission to end the misery that is preventing you to lead a productive and happy life.

> *Now as they went on their way, he entered a certain village, where a woman named Martha welcomed him into her home. She had a sister named Mary, who sat at the Lord's feet and listened to what he was saying. But Martha was distracted by her many tasks; so, she came to him and asked, "Lord, do you not care that my sister has left me to do all the work by myself? Tell her then to help me." But the Lord answered her, "Martha, Martha, you are anxious and troubled by many things; there is need of only one thing. Mary has chosen the better part, which will not be taken away from her."*
>
> —*Luke 10:38–42*

Chapter 2
Depression

The righteous cry out, and the Lord hears them;
he delivers them from all their troubles.
The Lord is close to the brokenhearted
and saves those who are crushed in spirit.
—Ps 34:17–18

It was a cold February morning, and Amy's mother was frantically trying to help her get out of bed, get dressed, eat breakfast, and make it to a 9:00 a.m. parent/student meeting at her high school. It will be a minor miracle if they arrive on time for the meeting. The meeting had been initiated by the school counseling department after a "needs assessment" had been completed on Amy. Mom contacted the counseling secretary to inform her that they will be thirty minutes late due to Amy's "inactivity." Mom had a very difficult time getting Amy out of bed. She literally had to open the blinds, take the blankets and sheets off the bed, and forcibly push and pull her off the mattress. Once out of bed, Mom had to help Amy brush her teeth and wash her face in the bathroom. After that uncooperative battle, Mom had to literally dress Amy in an outfit that she had once adored. Taking her by the hand, Mom walked Amy downstairs and begged her to eat the breakfast that she had prepared an hour earlier. Because it was getting close to 9:00 a.m., Mom relented and told Amy that since she did not eat breakfast she would have to have a big lunch instead! It took fifteen minutes of negotiating to get Amy into the car. Mom and Amy finally arrived at the high school at 9:40 a.m. Amy's father (who seemed visibly upset) had been waiting in the main office for forty minutes for them to arrive.

Upon entering the counseling conference room, Amy and her soon-to-be divorced parents were greeted by the principal, assistant principal, school counselor, school psychologist, licensed clinical social worker, home school visitor, and the school nurse. As the school professionals introduced themselves around the large conference room, Amy crossed her arms and laid her head on the table. The school counselor took the lead by informing Amy and her parents why the meeting had been convened. The school counselor handed Amy (whose head was still down on the table) and her parents a copy of the "needs assessment" that had been completed by the school district. The detailed packet was a record-based timeline of Amy's academic and extracurricular career since ninth grade. Amy was now a junior.

The school psychologist began explaining the information detailed in the first section of the needs assessment. Before entering high school, Amy had been tested and accepted into the GATE (Gifted and Talented Education) program in middle school. Amy had a rewarding experience while attending middle school. She excelled academically by taking a challenging schedule and scoring "distinguished" on all her state assessments. She also took a leadership role in many of the extracurricular activities that the middle school offered. Amy's positive attitude and aptitude continued as she entered high school. During her freshman and sophomore years, she expanded her imprint by being elected student government president, as well as playing an active role in the fall and spring musicals. Unfortunately, Amy had disconnected from these activities since the beginning of the current school year.

It was now the assistant principal's turn as he reviewed the second section of the needs assessment, which focused on Amy's current high school transcript. Amy's first two years of high school represented a student who participated in a rigorous academic schedule with high honor roll results. Entering her junior year, she was ranked fifth out of four hundred students in her class. She had also been recognized by the College Board for receiving a National Merit Scholar nomination. These nominations were sent to students who scored in the top 1 percent on the PSAT. However, Amy's junior schedule included no honors or AP courses, nor had she registered to take the SAT or ACT. Her first semester grades reflected an apathetic, lost student who was failing all her core classes and was now behind on graduation credits.

The principal and home school visitor then reviewed the third section of the needs assessment, which detailed Amy's school attendance and behavioral record. Amy had perfect attendance during her middle school years as well as her first two years of high school. But the current school year had shown a 180-degree turn. Amy had already missed forty days of school and had been late an additional thirty times. Because these absences and tardies were unexcused, Amy and her parents had to appear before the local magistrate to explain why she was being truant from school. When in school, Amy was either indifferent or disruptive. The principal emphasized that prior to this school year, Amy did not have one behavioral infraction on her record. In fact, she had been recognized by the school board for the random acts of kindness she displayed within the school and community. However, within the current one hundred days of school, Amy had been in the office for various discipline matters (disrespect, class cuts, fighting, etc.), which had resulted in detentions and suspensions.

The fourth section of the needs assessment was a copy of the current logbook that the school nurse maintained . The school nurse reviewed with Amy and her parents the days and times that Amy had visited her. The nurse calculated that Amy had visited her almost every day that she attended school. Some of the medical complaints that Amy reported to the nurse included headaches, stomachaches, lower back pain, fatigue, difficulty concentrating, restlessness, decreased appetite and weight loss, and memory loss. Since Amy already missed a significant amount of school, the nurse comforted her until she was ready to re-engage in the classroom. More importantly, the nurse communicated with Amy's mom each time her daughter visited and provided her with local and county services to help Amy address these medical issues.

The last group of school professionals that spoke about the information contained in the needs assessment were the school counselor and the licensed clinical social worker. They reviewed with Amy and her parents the numerous individual and group counseling sessions that Amy had participated in. It was recorded that Amy had reported to her school counselor just as many times as she had reported to the school nurse while attending school. Amy had talked about many issues with the counselor and social worker. Some of the issues were repeated feelings and others were streams of consciousness that bubbled up from deep within her. Some of the areas that were uncovered and discussed included excessive guilt, sadness, anxiety, feelings of hopelessness, social isolation, and difficulty making daily decisions. The school counselor and social worker did their best to reassure Amy that her feelings were normal and natural and that most people contemplate these issues at some point in their lives. However, they also contacted Mom to alert her to the number of times Amy had sought counseling and emotional comfort while attending school.

After the school personnel completed their presentation, they provided Amy and her parents the opportunity to expand upon some of the issues that had been reported. It should not have surprised anyone that Amy had nothing to say. Throughout the entire presentation she either had her head down on the table or was looking at the floor while slouched in her seat. Amy's parents were distraught, even though all the information that had been reported was not "breaking news." Amy's mom began to tell those in the room how her marriage to her soon-to-be ex-husband had started to disintegrate in the spring of Amy's sophomore year. She also shared that Amy was an only child, and that the marital split had taken an emotional toll on her. She continued to report that Amy's behavior outside of school had also changed. She expressed concern about Amy sneaking out of the house late in the evening and "disappearing." She also reported finding marijuana and prescription pills in her room. Amy's mom began to visibly break down when she told those present that her daughter had unintentionally found herself in the "quicksand" of life and was sinking rapidly. She could hardly contain herself as she explained that she did not know what to do or who can help "rescue" her daughter!

Does this story sound familiar to you? Does it pierce your soul? Are you Amy? Are you Amy's mother? Are you one of the school professionals that participated in this meeting? This storyline happens in America many times over each day. According to a 2017 Mental Health America study, 11 percent of youth (ages twelve to seventeen) reported suffering from at least one major depressive episode during a calendar year. In this study, Mental Health America defined major depression as a marked significant and pervasive feeling of sadness that is associated with suicidal thoughts and/or an impairment of a young person's ability to concentrate or engage in normal activities.[1] If this percentage is correct, which I believe that it is, then 2.6 million of our American youth are suffering from depression. This number does not consider the members

1. Mental Health America, "Mental Health in America 2017."

of the millennial generation (ages twenty-two to thirty-seven). If you add this generation, it would not surprise me if the number grew to over ten million young adults suffering with some kind of depressive disorder.

Depression, suffering, and anger are all part of being human.
—Janet Fitch[2]

Do you recall the discussion I had with you earlier about post-traumatic stress disorder? I opened our dialogue with the first sentence from the book *The Road Less Traveled*, in which M. Scott Peck writes, "Life is difficult!"[3] I'm sure whomever is reading this book will agree with Mr. Peck's statement. God never promised us an easy journey in life, just a safe arrival! Because of this, you may experience more valleys than peaks in your life. Valleys may come in the form of losing a loved one, relationship break-ups, divorce, rejection from post-secondary/workforce opportunities, and unfulfilled dreams. With these disappointments come feelings of sadness, loneliness, anger, and frustration. These are normal reactions to unfortunate circumstances. Experiencing these feelings does not mean that you are depressed. It means that you are human!

Depression, however, is a serious mental health problem that causes a persistent feeling of sadness and loss of interest in activities. It affects how you think, feel, and behave, and it can cause emotional, functional, and physical problems. The key words in the above definition are *persistent feelings*. Short-term negative feelings generated from natural life events is not depression, it's your body's natural way of dealing with life! However, if you feel like Amy felt for an extended period (more than two weeks), then you may be suffering from some kind of depressive disorder.

If I asked you to list adjectives to describe yourself, what words would you use? Would your list include vibrant, personable, motivated, productive, and confident? Or would your list be sad, lonely, scared, nervous, and anxious? Is your mental self-portrait large and colorful or small and dark? Are your todays and tomorrows full of hope and possibilities, or are you in so much pain that you want today to be your last day on earth? These questions will help you determine if you are suffering from depression.

2. Curran-Hackett, "WD Interview."

3. Peck, *Road Less Traveled*, 10.

Depression

Depression is being colorblind and constantly told how colorful the world is.

—Atticus[4]

What really causes depression? Here's the thing, depression isn't a one-size-fits-all condition, and scientists haven't yet cracked the code on what exactly causes it. Some people seem more likely to experience depressive episodes, while others appear more resilient. But why is that? Let's explore the main pieces, keeping in mind that each plays a role in the bigger puzzle but that the final picture is still incomplete.[5]

COULD IT BE IN YOUR GENES?

Have you ever wondered if feeling low runs in your family? Well, there's a chance it might. Researchers believe depression might be inherited—meaning, if someone in your family struggles with it, you could be more likely to face it too. However, scientists haven't yet pinpointed the exact genes responsible for the propensity toward depression. If future research can find these genes, they may be able to edit or switch them off altogether.

IS IT ALL IN THE BRAIN?

Another possibility lies deep inside the brain itself. People with depression often show changes in brain function, especially in how their neurotransmitters behave. These chemical messengers (like serotonin, dopamine, and norepinephrine) are linked to feelings of joy, motivation, and pleasure. But if these chemicals are out of balance, could that explain depression? Possibly. Yet scientists still don't fully understand why the balance tips or how it triggers such intense emotional shifts.

4. Atticus (@atticuspoetry), "Depression," X, Nov. 20, 2021. https://x.com/atticuspoetry/status/1462150759194279936.

5. The following sections draw from Gabbey, "Causes of Depression."

WHAT ABOUT HORMONES?

Your hormones (chemical messengers) might be the reason for the heaviness that you feel from within. Major hormonal changes, such as those during puberty, pregnancy, menopause, or due to thyroid issues, can stir up emotional chaos. Could a hormonal shift be the quiet storm behind a depressive episode? It's certainly a possibility.

SHOULD YOU BLAME THE SEASON?

Have you ever felt gloomy in the dead of winter, when the sunlight is scarce and the days feel endless? You are not alone. Some people experience what's called Seasonal Affective Disorder (yes, the acronym is SAD), where shorter days and less daylight trigger feelings of sadness, fatigue, or disinterest. The good news? These symptoms often melt away when spring returns, but why our brains react this way remains something of a mystery.

OR IS IT LIFE JUST BEING LIFE?

Sometimes, depression isn't about chemistry or genes, it's about life's circumstances knocking the wind out of you. Big changes, personal loss, trauma, or ongoing stress can shake the emotional foundation of anyone. In these cases, depression may be the mind's response to overwhelming experiences. But what makes some people more vulnerable than others in the same situation? That's yet another question researchers are still exploring.

Depression is complex, an emotional puzzle with many interlocking pieces. Some of the causes might be biological, others situational, and some still unknown. But understanding the possibilities is the first step toward compassion for yourself and others. And who knows? Maybe God will bless you with the time, talents, and treasures to be a scientist who helps solve the mystery of depression!

Causes of Depression

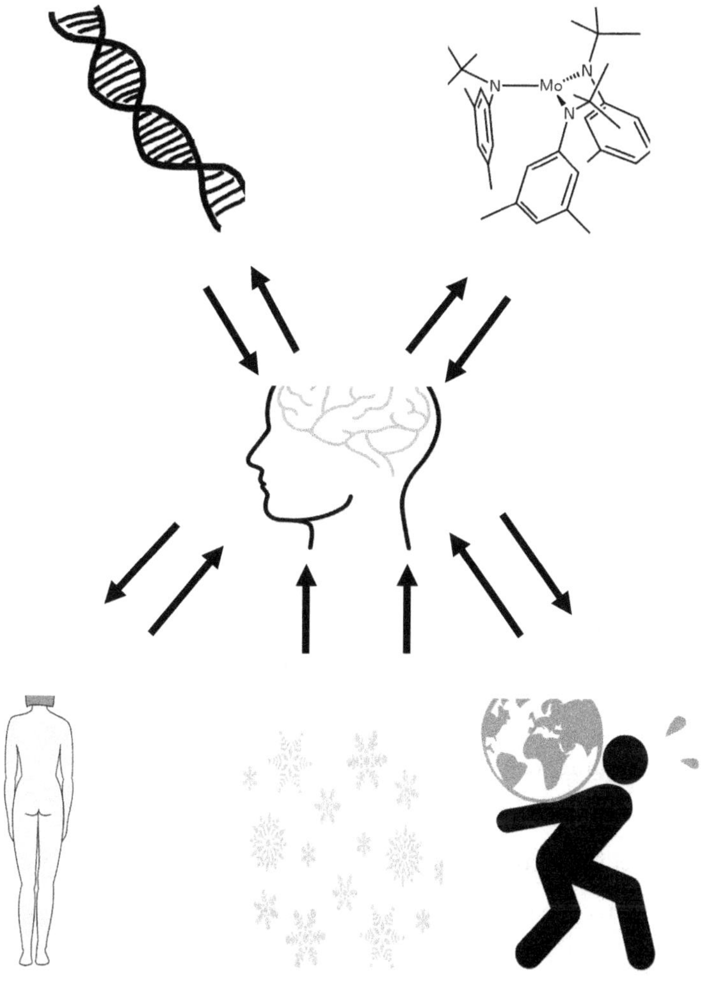

Every thought is a battle. Every breath is a war,
and I think I'm not winning anymore.

—Anonymous

Family members and friends often tell a loved one who is experiencing depression to "walk on the sunny side of the street," "be a glass half full kind of person," "pull yourself up by your bootstraps," and "quit feeling sorry for yourself." However, these catchy phrases are not going to help someone who is depressed. Depression is not a sign of weakness or a character flaw. More times than not, a person suffering from depression will need some kind of treatment plan to get better.

Depression signs and symptoms include a change from a person's previous attitude and behavior that can cause significant distress and problems at school or home, in social activities or other areas of life. Depression symptoms can vary in severity, but changes in emotions and behavior may include the examples below.[6]

EMOTIONAL CHANGES

- Persistent sadness that may include crying without an obvious reason
- Feeling emotionally drained or without purpose
- Easily irritated or frequently in a bad mood
- Intense frustration or anger, even in minor situations
- Losing interest in hobbies or everyday routines
- Feeling distant from or in conflict with friends and family
- Struggling with poor self-worth
- Overwhelmed by guilt or feelings of failure
- Dwelling on past mistakes or harsh self-judgment
- Overreacting to rejection or setbacks, and needing constant reassurance
- Difficulty focusing, remembering details, or making decisions
- A constant sense that things won't get better
- Recurring thoughts about death or suicide

BEHAVIORAL CHANGES

- Feeling drained or fatigued most of the time
- Trouble sleeping or sleeping excessively

6. Lists of the symptoms draw from Mayo Clinic Staff, "Teen Depression."

- Eating habits change—either eating much less or much more than usual
- Turning to alcohol, nicotine, or drugs to cope
- Showing signs of restlessness or agitation (e.g., fidgeting, pacing)
- Moving or speaking more slowly than usual
- Frequent physical complaints like headaches or stomachaches, often leading to repeated visits to the nurse
- Withdrawing socially or avoiding interactions
- Falling behind in schoolwork or missing class often
- Paying less attention to personal hygiene or appearance
- Angry reactions, impulsive behavior, or risk-taking
- Intentional self-injury (e.g., cutting or burning)
- Creating or acting on a plan to end one's life

The following are characteristics that may increase the risk of developing or triggering depression.

RISK FACTORS

- Struggles with self-image due to issues like bullying, academic challenges, or being overweight
- Experiencing or witnessing trauma, such as abuse or violence
- Living with other mental health concerns, such as anxiety, eating disorders, or bipolar disorder
- Managing conditions like ADHD or learning difficulties
- Coping with chronic illnesses such as asthma, diabetes, or cancer
- Living with a physical disability
- Having personality traits like excessive self-criticism, dependency, or pessimism
- Substance use, including alcohol or tobacco
- Identifying as LGBTQ+ in an environment that lacks acceptance or support

FAMILY HISTORY / FAMILY ISSUES

- A close relative has experienced depression, bipolar disorder, or struggled with alcohol misuse
- A family member has died by suicide
- Living in a high-conflict or unstable family situation
- Recently facing major life stressors, like parental separation, deployment, or a death in the family

There are different types of depressive disorders, and while there are many similarities among them, each depressive disorder has its own unique set of symptoms.[7]

MAJOR DEPRESSIVE DISORDER

The most diagnosed form of depression is major depressive disorder. Major depression is characterized by at least five of the diagnostic symptoms, of which at least one of the symptoms is either an overwhelming feeling of sadness or a loss of interest and pleasure in most usual activities. The other symptoms that are associated with major depression include decrease or increase in appetite, insomnia or hypersomnia, psycho motor agitation or retardation, constant fatigue, feelings of worthlessness or excessive and inappropriate guilt, recurrent thoughts of death and suicidal ideation with or without specific plans for committing suicide, and cognitive difficulties, such as diminished ability to think, concentrate, and make decisions. The symptoms persist for two weeks or longer and represent a significant change from previous functioning. Social, occupational, educational, or other important functioning is also impacted. For instance, the person may start missing work or school or stop going to classes or their usual social activities.[8]

7. For more information, see American Psychiatric Association, "What Is Depression?"

8. American Psychiatric Association, *Diagnostic and Statistical Manual*, §§303.02, 303.03.

PERSISTENT DEPRESSIVE DISORDER (DYSTHYMIA)

Another type of depression is called persistent depressive disorder (dysthymia). The essential feature of this mood disorder is a low, dark, or sad mood that is persistently present for most of the day and on most days for at least two years (children and adolescents may experience predominantly irritability and the mood persists for at least one year). For the individual to receive the diagnosis of persistent depressive disorder, they should also have two of the diagnostic symptoms which include poor appetite or overeating, insomnia or hypersomnia, low energy or fatigue, low self-esteem, poor concentration, difficulty making decisions, or feelings of hopelessness. During this period, any symptom-free intervals last no longer than two months. The symptoms are not as severe as with major depression. Major depression may precede persistent depressive disorder, and major depressive episodes may also occur during persistent depressive disorder.[9]

PREMENSTRUAL DYSPHORIC DISORDER

Premenstrual Dysphoric Disorder (PMDD) is a serious and often debilitating condition that represents a more intense form of premenstrual syndrome (PMS). While both PMDD and PMS involve physical and emotional symptoms tied to the menstrual cycle, the psychological effects associated with PMDD are significantly more severe. These emotional disturbances can interfere with daily life, affecting social relationships, academic or work performance, and overall well-being.

Typically, symptoms of both PMS and PMDD emerge approximately seven to ten days before menstruation begins and may continue into the early days of the menstrual period. Common physical symptoms include fatigue, breast tenderness, bloating, and changes in sleep and eating patterns.

What sets PMDD apart is the intensity of its emotional and behavioral symptoms. Individuals with PMDD may experience overwhelming feelings of sadness and hopelessness, heightened anxiety or tension, frequent and intense mood swings, increased irritability, and episodes

9. American Academy of Family Physicians, "Persistent Depressive Disorder."

of anger. These symptoms can disrupt a person's ability to function normally and may require clinical attention and treatment.[10]

DEPRESSIVE DISORDER

Sometimes, symptoms of depression can be caused by an underlying medical condition. When this happens, it is known as Depressive Disorder Due to Another Medical Condition. In these cases, treating the medical issue may help relieve the depressive symptoms.

Certain health problems, especially those related to the endocrine (hormone) and reproductive systems, are more likely to be linked with depression. For instance, hypothyroidism—a condition where the body doesn't produce enough thyroid hormones—can lead to symptoms like tiredness, weight gain, irritability, memory problems, and a persistently low mood. In many cases, once the thyroid hormone levels are brought back to normal with treatment, the depression also improves.

Another example is Cushing syndrome, which happens when the body produces too much of the hormone cortisol. This hormone imbalance can also lead to depressive symptoms. Other serious medical conditions have also been connected to depression including HIV/AIDS, diabetes, strokes, and Parkinson's disease. In these cases, the physical effects of the illness, as well as the emotional stress of managing a chronic condition, can both contribute to the development of depression.[11]

ADJUSTMENT DISORDER WITH DEPRESSED MOOD

Adjustment Disorder with Depressed Mood happens when a person develops symptoms of depression within about three months after experiencing a stressful life event. This event, called a stressor, can be something negative, like a breakup, family conflict, or moving away from home, but it can also be something positive that still brings a lot of change, such as starting a new job, getting married, or having a baby.

What makes this condition stand out is that the person's emotional reaction is stronger or lasts longer than what would normally be expected in that situation. The sadness, worry, or lack of motivation can interfere with school, work, relationships, or daily life.

10. Yonkers and Casper, "Clinical Manifestations and Diagnosis."
11. World Health Organization, "Depressive Disorder."

The good news is that Adjustment Disorder with Depressed Mood usually improves within six months, either when the person adapts to the change or when the stressor is no longer present. Treatment often focuses on short-term support, like counseling, healthy coping strategies, or simply having someone to talk to, which can help the person recover and adjust more smoothly.[12]

SEASONAL AFFECTIVE DISORDER (SAD)

The final type of depression is related to changes in the length of days or seasonality. This type of depression is called Seasonal Affective Disorder (SAD). People with SAD experience many of the same symptoms as Major Depressive Disorder, such as low mood, loss of interest in activities, fatigue, and changes in sleep or appetite, but these symptoms occur in a pattern connected to the seasons.[13]

She says she's fine but she's going insane.
She says she feels good but she's in a lot of pain.
She says it's nothing but it's really a lot.
She says she's okay but she's really not.

—*Anonymous*

It wasn't a coincidence that I opened this chapter sharing Amy's story with you. Study after study has confirmed that women more than men, girls more than boys, suffer from depression. What are the factors that make this statement true? And why are girls at such a higher risk? These matters are still under investigation, but mental health professionals are beginning to uncover clues about why there is such a disparity when it comes to gender and depression.

Depression occurs in both genders, but by teenage years, girls are much more at risk than boys. Before puberty, the prevalence of depression is about the same in boys and girls (3 to 5 percent). But by mid-adolescence, girls are more than twice as likely to be diagnosed with depression as boys (14 to 20 percent).[14] What constitutes this change? By

12. Cleveland Clinic, "Adjustment Disorders."
13. National Institute of Mental Health, "Seasonal Affective Disorder."
14. Steingard, "Mood Disorders."

looking at brain scans, the medical field has deduced that there are differences in the way girls and boys process stimuli. Girls mature, in terms of their emotional recognition, faster than boys, and that sensitivity could make them more vulnerable to depression. Girls also may be wired to tune in earlier to emotional stimuli because of their innate ability to nurture. Another medical reason for the gender disparity is that females produce less serotonin than males. Serotonin is the positive, "don't worry, be happy" neurotransmitter in the brain. Finally, other studies have found that female risk factors concerning depression are heightened in a variety of categories, including genetic, biological, emotional, cognitive, behavioral, and social-interpersonal compared to their male counterparts.[15]

These professional studies and their outcomes are important to all who are involved in helping adolescents and young adults lead productive lives. It is obvious that every person's social and emotional well-being matters. However, it is particularly important for us to pay careful attention to those girls and young women in our lives so we can detect early signals and symptoms of depression. Whether its girls or boys, young women or young men, we can't wait and expect things to get better without helping them!

FOURTH STATION: JESUS IS DENIED BY PETER

> "Simon, Simon, Satan has asked to sift all of you as wheat. But I have prayed for you, Simon, that your faith may not fail. And when you have turned back, strengthen your brothers."
>
> But he replied, "Lord, I am ready to go with you to prison and to death."
>
> Jesus answered, "I tell you, Peter, before the rooster crows today, you will deny three times that you know me." (Luke 22:31–34)

We adore you, O Christ, and we bless you.

Because by your holy cross you have redeemed the world.

15. McGrath, "Teen Depression."

> Now Peter was sitting out in the courtyard, and a servant girl came to him. "You also were with Jesus of Galilee," she said.
>
> But he denied it before them all. "I don't know what you're talking about," he said.
>
> Then he went out to the gateway, where another servant girl saw him and said to the people there, "This fellow was with Jesus of Nazareth."
>
> He denied it again, with an oath: "I don't know the man!"
>
> After a little while, those standing there went up to Peter and said, "Surely you are one of them; your accent gives you away."
>
> Then he began to call down curses, and he swore to them, "I don't know the man!"
>
> Immediately a rooster crowed. Then Peter remembered the word Jesus had spoken: "Before the rooster crows, you will disown me three times." And he went outside and wept bitterly. (Matt 26:69–75)

Lord, grant us the gift of honesty that we may not fear to speak the truth even when difficult.

FOURTH STATION: REFLECTIVE EXERCISES AND QUESTIONS

As the Earth spun on its axis for the final time in Jesus' earthly life, he had an opportunity to spend his last hours before his persecution with his friends (disciples). Jesus was preparing himself as well as his disciples on what was to occur when the "Light" penetrated darkness. Because Jesus was like us in all things except sin, he shares in your thoughts and emotions. He has experienced what you have experienced, are experiencing, and will experience in your life.

- He has experienced pain (crucifixion = physical and emotional).
- He knows what isolation feels like (his disciples deserted him when he was arrested).
- He has been moved to tears (when his friend Lazarus died).
- He was tempted by Satan (after forty days of prayer and fasting).
- He was unfairly labeled and persecuted for spreading the "good news" (by the Sanhedrin).

- He was slandered for his beliefs and actions (teachers of the law accused him of being possessed by Satan. Even his family wanted to take charge of him because they said, "He was out of his mind!").

Your feelings, perceptions, and experiences are not unfamiliar to the Lord. The Son of Man struggled in his life like you sometimes struggle in your life. Have you ever been misunderstood? Jesus Christ has! Has your heart ever been broken? Jesus Christ's heart has! Have one of your best friends ever betrayed you? Jesus Christ's best friends did! If you find yourself suffering from a bout of depression, take comfort in knowing that you are not alone. Jesus Christ has already traveled the road that you are on. Through his earthly mission of mercy and salvation, he has proven to you that you shall overcome the current darkness that you find yourself in and move into the "Light" of faith, hope, and love!

For you to more fully understand the pain that you are experiencing, I have provided you with a screening tool to help you determine whether you might have depression that needs professional attention. This screening tool is not designed to make a diagnosis of depression but to be shared with your primary care physician or mental health professional to inform further conversations about diagnosis and treatment. This screening can be an important first step in getting needed care for mental health concerns and can be an easy way for you or someone you care about to get a better understanding of concerning experiences or feelings. This screening is not a substitute for professional assessment and care. If you have further questions or serious concerns, contact your health care provider or a mental health professional.

DEPRESSION SCREENING TOOL[16]

Over the last two weeks, how often have you been bothered by any of the following problems? Check one square next to each problem that you have had.				
Problems	Not at all	Several days	More than half the days	Nearly every day
Little interest or pleasure in doing things				

16. Kroenke et al., "PHQ-9," 606.

Feeling down, depressed, or hopeless				
Trouble falling/staying asleep or sleeping too much				
Feeling tired or having little energy				
Poor appetite or overeating				
Feeling bad about yourself or that you are a failure or have let yourself or your family down				
Trouble concentrating on things such as reading or watching television				
Moving or speaking so slowly that other people have noticed. Or being so fidgety or restless that you have been moving around a lot more than usual				
Thoughts that you would be better off dead or of hurting yourself in some way				

If you checked any of the problems above, how difficult have they made it for you to do your work, take care of things at home, or get along with other people?			
Not Difficult	Somewhat Difficult	Very Difficult	Extremely Difficult

The three holiest days of the Catholic Church (the Sacred Triduum) begin with the Thursday evening celebration Mass of the LORD's Last Supper. It is followed by Good Friday, in which we solemnly celebrate our LORD's passion and death, and concludes with the Easter Vigil celebration when our Lord and Savior conquers evil and death by resurrecting from the grave. It is during Holy Thursday where the fourth station takes place. Many important things are said and done (literally and symbolically) during our LORD's Last Supper on earth. One of the many things that occurs is that Jesus predicts to Peter that he will deny him three times before the rooster crows the next morning. How important was this conversation between Jesus and Peter? All four Gospels chronicle this event!

Even though Peter was only one of twelve missionaries that Jesus sought out, he was given special insight from the Father about his Son. Jesus had never explicitly taught Peter and the other disciples the fullness of his identity. However, when he asked his disciples who they thought he was, Peter answered, "You are the Messiah, the Son of the living God" (Matt 16:16). Upon hearing the gift that the Father gave Peter, Jesus declared that he would build his church on Peter and give him the keys to the kingdom of heaven. Peter went on to be the first to proclaim the gospel on the day of Pentecost and was the first to take the gospel to the gentiles.

You may be asking yourself, "What does this have to do with me?" Well, you are Peter! I am Peter! We are all Peter! What lessons can we learn from Peter's life that we can apply to our life?

- *Jesus overcomes fear.* Whether stepping out of a boat onto a tossing sea or stepping across the threshold of a gentile home for the first time, Peter found courage in following Christ.
- *Jesus forgives unfaithfulness.* After he had boasted of his fidelity, Peter fervently denied the LORD three times. It seemed that Peter had burned his bridges, but Jesus lovingly rebuilt them and restored Peter to service. Peter was a former failure, but with Jesus, failure is not the end.
- *Jesus patiently teaches.* Repeatedly, Peter needed correction, and the LORD gave it with patience, firmness, and love. The Master Teacher looks for students willing to learn.
- *Jesus sees you as he intends you to be.* The very first time they met, Jesus called Simon "Peter." The rough and reckless fisherman was, in Jesus' eyes, a firm and faithful rock.
- *Jesus uses unlikely heroes.* Peter was a fisherman from Galilee, but Jesus called him to be a fisher of men. Being with Jesus makes all the difference.

I have told you these things, so that in me you may have peace. In this world you will have trouble. But take heart! I have overcome the world.

—John 16:33

Part 1 Summary

As for everyone who comes to me and hears my words and puts them into practice, I will show you what they are like. They are like a man building a house, who dug down deep and laid the foundation on rock. When a flood came, the torrent struck that house but could not shake it, because it was well built. But the one who hears my words and does not put them into practice is like a man who built a house on the ground without a foundation. The moment the torrent struck that house, it collapsed and its destruction was complete.

—Luke 6:47–49

IN A FEW PAGES, you will move from part 1 ("The Afflictions") to part 2 ("The Cornerstone"). The pages associated with part 1 set the footers for this book. For those of you unfamiliar with construction, footers are the foundation of any construction site. Their purpose is to support the structure and prevent settling. Footings are especially important in areas with troublesome soils. This is a perfect metaphor when reflecting upon the information that was presented in the prologue and in chapters 1 and 2. Your life will always be a construction site. You will be constantly building, rebuilding, and/or reorganizing depending on your life's experiences. Before learning how to construct holistic approaches to help you relieve the stress and strain caused by your mental health struggles, you need to assess the "soil conditions" which your life is built upon. Part 1 helped you interpret your "soil assessment"!

What did your soil assessment tell you?

- Did you uncover one or more of the biggest problems that you are facing in your world today?
- Are you willing to follow Jesus on the road to Calvary to experience his and your resurrection?
- Did you find your sense of mission?
- Did you learn about the six main types of anxiety disorders?
- Did you participate in the screening measures to help you determine whether you might have one of the anxiety disorders? What was the outcome?
- Did you learn about the six main types of depression disorders?
- Did you participate in the screening measure to help you determine whether you might have one of the depression disorders? What was the outcome?
- Did the stories of Paul and Amy resonate with you? Could you exchange your name with theirs?

The answers to the above questions can help you determine the current "soil of your life." These answers, in turn, will help you decide the placement of your life's "footings" as well as how deep and wide your life's footings need to be. The dimensions and placement of your life's footings will depend upon where you were—or are—and want to be. Unsettling soil (negative life events) can crack the foundation of a structure (your life), which can cause undue stress and pressure on the structure (your life) and may cause it to collapse (live an unproductive life). Therefore, placement of your life's footings is crucial in providing the proper support when life's unexpected events occur. Solid soil (based on faith, hope, and love) along with well-placed concrete footers (mind, body, spirit) will ultimately lead you to a productive life!

There are a couple of loose ends that I must tie together before we enter part 2. The first, that was not mentioned in part 1, is that research tells us that anxiety and depression disorders are different, but people with depression often experience symptoms like those of an anxiety disorder. But each disorder has its own causes and its own emotional and behavioral symptoms. Many people who develop depression have a history of an anxiety disorder earlier in their life. However, there is no evidence one disorder causes the other, but there is clear evidence that many people suffer from both disorders.

Finally, it is worth emphasizing again that recent studies have shown that girls and young adult women are two times more likely to experience major depression than boys and young adult men.[1] They are also up to three times more apt to suffer from anxiety disorders or to attempt suicide than their gender counterpart.[2] As reported in the last chapter, the reasons for these gender differences are not clear but hormonal changes, biological factors, inherited traits, personal life circumstances, and culture have something to do with the gender discrepancies when it comes to diagnosing anxiety and depression.

We are ready to move into part 2 ("The Cornerstone"). The three chapters within this unit will begin to build holistic approaches to help you break the chains of anxiety and depression so that you can move into the "Light" and produce "good fruit." Jesus told his disciples (you) that a healthy tree cannot bear bad fruit (Matt 7:18)! Through your primary care physician and/or mental health professional, along with the holistic approaches detailed in the rest of this book, you will receive the "fruit of the Spirit," which Gal 5:22–23 defines as love, joy, peace, patience, kindness, goodness, faithfulness, gentleness, and self-control.

> *I am the true vine, and my Father is the gardener. He cuts off every branch in me that bears no fruit, while every branch that does bear fruit he prunes so that it will be even more fruitful. You are already clean because of the word I have spoken to you. Remain in me, as I also remain in you. No branch can bear fruit by itself; it must remain in the vine. Neither can you bear fruit unless you remain in me.*
>
> *I am the vine; you are the branches. If you remain in me and I in you, you will bear much fruit; apart from me you can do nothing. If you do not remain in me, you are like a branch that is thrown away and withers; such branches are picked up, thrown into the fire, and burned. If you remain in me and my words remain in you, ask whatever you wish, and it will be done for you. This is to my Father's glory, that you bear much fruit, showing yourselves to be my disciples. (John 15:1–8)*

1. Kuehner, "Depression More Common."
2. Bommersbach et al., "More Likely to Attempt Suicide."

Part 2

The Cornerstone

For God so loved the world that he gave his one and only Son, that whoever believes in him shall not perish but have eternal life. For God did not send his Son into the world to condemn the world, but to save the world through him.
—John 3:16–17

But he was pierced for our transgressions,
he was crushed for our iniquities;
the punishment that brought us peace was on him,
and by his wounds we are healed.
—Isa 53:5

Part 2 | The Cornerstone

For even the Son of Man did not come to be served, but to serve, and to give his life as a ransom for many.
—Mark 10:45

Haven't you read this passage of Scripture:
"The stone the builders rejected
has become the cornerstone."
—Mark 12:10

Chapter 3
Faith

So I say to you: Ask and it will be given to you; seek and you will find; knock and the door will be opened to you. For everyone who asks receives; the one who seeks finds; and to the one who knocks, the door will be opened.
—Luke 11:9–10

Mitch Albom is an internationally renowned author, screenwriter, playwright, nationally syndicated columnist, broadcaster, and musician. He is the author of six consecutive number one *New York Times* bestsellers. His book *Tuesdays with Morrie* is the bestselling memoir of all time.[1] It has sold over seventeen million copies in more than fifty editions around the world! *Tuesdays with Morrie* is the final lesson between a college professor, Morrie, and one of his long-lost students, Mitch Albom. After seeing his professor in an interview on the show *Nightline*, the author is reminded of a promise he made sixteen years ago to keep in touch with him. Now stricken with ALS, Morrie does not have much time left, and Mitch recognizes this fact. He travels from Michigan to Massachusetts to meet with him. This meeting goes well and affects Mitch and Morrie so much that they meet for the next fourteen consecutive Tuesdays, up until Morrie passes away. During each of these meetings, they discuss a different topic about life. These topics make up the content of the book and include death, love, culture, marriage, regret, and the world we live in, among many others.

1. Albom, *Tuesdays with Morrie.*

One Tuesday, Morrie reflected upon one of the many lessons that he taught his students. In class, Morrie had said that he had an exercise for his class to try. They were to stand, facing away from their classmates, and fall backward, relying on another student to catch them. Most of the students were uncomfortable with this and could not let go for more than a few inches before stopping themselves. Most laughed in embarrassment. Finally, one student, a thin, quiet, dark-haired girl, crossed her arms over her chest, closed her eyes, leaned back, and did not flinch! For a moment, the whole class thought she was going to crash onto the floor. At the last instant, her assigned partner grabbed her head and shoulders and yanked her up harshly. Several students gasped. Some clapped. Morrie smiled and said to the young lady, "You see you closed your eyes. That was the difference. Sometimes you cannot believe what you see. You must believe what you feel. And if you are ever going to have other people trust you, you must feel that you can trust them too—even when you're in the dark. Even when you're falling."[2]

These words by Morrie Schwartz are words to live by, especially for those who struggle with anxiety and depression. The important life lesson that Morrie was teaching his students that day centered on trust, which can be translated into faith. *Merriam-Webster* defines faith as a complete trust or confidence in someone or something.[3] Trust and/or faith is something that we all need in our lives to be productive. Some people attain this intangible characteristic early in their life, while others learn it later. Some people possess it, lose it, and repossess it, while others maintain it once they find it. Where, when, how, or why you find faith doesn't really matter. The most important thing about faith is that you possess it now!

To experience all the good things life has to offer, you will need faith. Faith is the bridge between mental "illness" and mental "wellness." Many scholars believe faith is personal and mysterious and individualistic and inexpressible and indefinable. However, people like Morrie believe that faith is linked to the concepts of trust and loyalty. Personal and spiritual faith are often intertwined, although not always codependent. Whether you are suffering from anxiety, depression, or any other obstacle that life puts in your way, you will need to tap into your personal and spiritual faith to find and fulfill your destiny.

2. Albom, *Tuesdays with Morrie*, 61.

3. *Merriam-Webster*, s.v. "faith," https://www.merriam-webster.com/dictionary/faith.

The remaining pages of this book will provide you holistic ways to live in earthly paradise before reuniting with the Father. The tools that you will obtain will only work if you have a fountain of faith from within. The first step in moving toward mental wellness is to find a mental health professional who specializes in your struggle. A mental health professional who specializes in adolescent and young adult anxiety and/or depression is an important base block to fit onto your personal "footers." Their past client experiences and successes will further add to your "fountain of faith." How do you choose a qualified mental health professional to help you on your journey toward mental wellness? The answer to this question will take time, energy, and diligence on your part. The following activity will provide some prompts that can help get you started on finding the right mental health professional for you.

STEP 1: KNOW WHAT YOU'RE LOOKING FOR

Before you start searching, take a moment to reflect on your preferences. Grab a notebook or journal and jot down your answers to these prompts:

- Do I want my therapist to have a certain type of training or background? (For example: psychiatrist, psychologist, counselor, social worker, nurse specialist, etc.)
- Does it matter to me if they can prescribe medication?
- Would I feel more comfortable with someone who has experience working with young people who struggle with anxiety and/or depression?
- What kind of person do I open up to most easily? (Think about gender, age, religion, language, or cultural background.)
- How much time can I realistically commit to therapy right now?
- What's my insurance situation? (Does it cover therapy? Do I have to pick from a specific list of providers? Do I need a referral from a doctor? Am I okay with paying some costs out of pocket if needed?)

STEP 2: QUESTIONS TO ASK DURING A CONSULTATION

When you meet a therapist for the first time, it's totally okay (and important!) to ask questions. Here are some you might write down and bring with you:

- How long have you been practicing, and what's your professional background?
- What licenses, certifications, or professional groups are you a part of?
- What are your fees, and how do payments work (insurance, up front, or later)?
- If I miss a session, do I still have to pay for it?
- Have you worked with people who are dealing with challenges like mine? How recently?
- What kind of clients do you work with best?
- What do you see as your strengths and your limits as a therapist?
- How would you describe your style of therapy (more structured/directive or more open/guiding)?
- Do you offer individual sessions only, or also group or family sessions?
- What's your perspective on using medication as part of treatment?
- What are your office hours, and how long is each session?
- How often do you usually recommend sessions at the beginning?
- What happens if I need help outside of normal hours? (Are you or someone else available in emergencies? How do you handle between-session contact?)
- Have you been in therapy yourself? How recently?
- Do you consult with other professionals for feedback or support in your practice?

STEP 3: REFLECTION AFTER YOUR FIRST SESSION

Once your first meeting is over, take some quiet time to check in with yourself. Answer these reflection questions honestly:

- Did I feel at ease with this therapist quickly, or did it take a while?
- Did I feel pressured to rush through my questions, or was there enough space to talk?
- Did the therapist seem to understand me, or did I have to keep explaining myself?
- Did our conversation flow naturally, or did it feel awkward?
- Were the therapist's answers clear, or were they hard to understand (too much jargon or vague statements)?
- Do I feel like I could share my personal struggles or deepest worries with this person?

Remember: therapy is about you. Finding the right fit is worth the effort, and it's okay to meet more than one therapist before deciding.[4]

Throughout your journey on the Road to Resurrection, you will have many passengers that will help you navigate the topography of recovery. Each will play a specific role to help you become a champion in life. Your passengers will be meaningful people, places, and things that you can depend on when the road becomes steep and narrow. The one person that will travel with you the longest will be your therapist. He or she will have a deep interest in you as an individual and will see and relate to you in ways that are sensitively tailored to your specific needs. The first thing that you will work on, regardless of your mental health condition, will be establishing a solid therapist/client relationship based on trust and understanding (faith). In the mental health profession, there is no one proven method of therapy, no one-size-fits-all approach to treatment. You are a unique person, with unique needs. Your therapist will guide you, and sometimes be guided by you, to move you toward your goal: mental wellness. Over the years, research has confirmed that the therapeutic relationship itself is essential to the success a client experiences. Some studies have even called it the most important common factor to successful outcomes. Change in a client's experiences and/or

4. Bloudoff-Indelicato, "14 Questions You Should Ask."

behaviors often have a direct correlation to the kind of relationship they have with their therapist. Simply put, you're much better off seeing a graduate student you connect with than a thirty-year veteran and author with whom you don't feel understood.

Do you have

- faith in yourself?
- faith in the process (your journey)?
- faith in your passengers?

If so, your growth and healing will be expedited!

Morrie Schwartz's lesson retold in *Tuesdays with Morrie* reminds me of the letter that Paul wrote to his Christian brothers and sisters in Corinth when he learned that their church had recently been struggling due to divisions and quarrels. Paul told these troubled Christians that they (you) need to walk by faith and not by sight (2 Cor 5:7).

Morrie smiled and said to the young lady, "You see you closed your eyes. That was the difference. Sometimes you cannot believe what you see. You must believe what you feel. And if you are ever going to have other people trust you, you must feel that you can trust them too—even when you're in the dark. Even when you're falling."[5]

Have you found your "bridge of faith" between mental "illness" and mental "wellness"? Are you ready to take your first step onto this bridge? Our Lord Jesus Christ said to his disciples (you) that the spirit is willing, but the flesh is weak (Matt 26:41). How full is your well of faith? Can you fill your mind, heart, and soul up with faith when Satan visits you with all his empty promises (John 4:4–26)?

> *Again, Jesus said, "What shall we say the kingdom of God is like, or what parable shall we use to describe it? It is like a mustard seed, which is the smallest of all seeds on earth. Yet when planted, it grows and becomes the largest of all garden plants, with such big branches that the birds can perch in its shade."*
>
> —*Mark 4:30–32*

5. Albom, *Tuesdays with Morrie*, 61.

Faith

> *Jesus replied, "Because you have so little faith. Truly I tell you, if you have faith as small as a mustard seed, you can say to this mountain, 'Move from here to there,' and it will move. Nothing will be impossible for you."*
>
> *—Matt 17:20*

In the first part of this chapter, we discussed the importance of your personal faith as it relates to your journey toward living a new life with mental wellness. The rest of this chapter will be devoted to your spiritual faith! Your spiritual faith comes from the LORD and his mighty powers. "Put on the full armor of God, so that you can take your stand against the devil's schemes. . . . In addition to all this, take up the shield of faith, with which you can extinguish all the flaming arrows of the evil one" (Eph 6:11, 16).

Faith is the substance of your life! The secret about faith is that it requires assistance. For you to fill your eternal well, you will need to lean on the word of God (Scripture) and those people in your life that exercise their faith through word and action. Faith is something that is not gained but given. According to Rom 12:3, God has distributed faith to each of us. You see, God gets everyone started off the same way. He doesn't give one person more faith than he gives another. He gives everyone the same measure of faith. What you do with that faith will determine whether it grows strong or weak, becomes developed or underdeveloped. God is a true believer in free will. He will always give you freedom to make your own decisions. However, when you exercise this gift from God, you must realize that you are still responsible for the choices that you make. You can choose to sow whatever you want, but you cannot choose what you will reap! Deciding what you want to do with the faith that the LORD has given you reminds me of a parable that Jesus taught his disciples:

> *A man going on a journey, called his servants and entrusted his wealth to them. To one he gave five bags of gold, to another two bags, and to another one bag, each according to his ability. Then he went on his journey. The man who had received five bags of gold went at once and put his money to work and gained five bags more. So also, the one with two bags of gold gained two more. But the man who had received one bag went off, dug a hole in the ground, and hid his master's money.*
>
> *After a long time, the master of those servants returned and settled accounts with them. The man who had received five bags of gold brought the other five. "Master," he said, "you entrusted*

> *me with five bags of gold. See, I have gained five more." His master replied, "Well done, good and faithful servant! You have been faithful with a few things; I will put you in charge of many things. Come and share your master's happiness!" The man with two bags of gold also came. "Master," he said, "you entrusted me with two bags of gold; see, I have gained two more." His master replied, "Well done, good and faithful servant! You have been faithful with a few things; I will put you in charge of many things. Come and share your master's happiness!"*
>
> *Then the man who had received one bag of gold came. "Master," he said, "I knew that you are a hard man, harvesting where you have not sown and gathering where you have not scattered seed. So, I was afraid and went out and hid your gold in the ground. See, here is what belongs to you." His master replied, "You wicked, lazy servant! So, you knew that I harvest where I have not sown and gather where I have not scattered seed? Well then, you should have put my money on deposit with the bankers, so that when I returned I would have received it back with interest. So, take the bag of gold from him and give it to the one who has ten bags. For whoever has will be given more, and they will have an abundance. Whoever does not have, even what they have will be taken from them."* (Matt 25:14–29)

Who do you relate to in this parable? Are you the servants who doubled their master's money (faith) from five bags to ten and two bags to four? Or are you the servant that left his master's money (faith) hidden and dormant in the ground, only to return it without interest? It is up to you what you do with the measure of faith God has given you. Your measure of faith can be increased. But you are the one who increases it, not God.

You may ask yourself, "How can I double the measure of faith that God has given me?" You are not the only person to ask or request this. Jesus Christ's own disciples said to him, "Lord, increase our faith" (Luke 17:5)! There are boundless ways the LORD will provide for you to increase your faith exponentially. Before I provide you with three simple ways to help build and increase your reliance on God, I want to share with you a belief and understanding that you must possess to open the "faucet of faith."

> *Be strong and courageous. Do not be afraid or terrified because of them, for the Lord your God goes with you; he will never leave you nor forsake you.*
>
> *—Deut 31:6*

Faith in the Lord begins with knowing that the Holy Trinity loves you with all its power and might. It is a pure and spotless love that guarantees that you are never alone. Regardless of your circumstance, your Savior walks in front of you! Your experiences were his experiences. Jesus constantly tells you, "Be not afraid," "I go before you always," "Come and follow me, and I will give you rest" (Deut 31:8, Matt 4:19, 11:28). He knows where your life is now, and he knows what shall become of your life in the future. Today he is calling you to follow him in a more loving and personal way: Are you listening? He knows where you are going and is waiting to receive you with open arms; be not afraid! If you begin with this belief, then the mustard seed of faith that is already planted into your soul will blossom into a large tree that will support your future endeavors.

The following are three simple ways you can fill your fountain of faith.

READ THE BIBLE

> Faith comes from hearing the message, and the message is heard through the word about Christ. (Rom 10:17)

Make it a goal to open the greatest book ever written (or for those belonging to Generation Y and Z, open your phones, tablets, laptops, etc.). Here you will be introduced to God's will. You will see and hear his word, his wisdom, his goodness, his intentions, his judgments, his heart, and most importantly his love for you.

> Jesus answered, "It is written: Man shall not live on bread alone, but on every word that comes from the mouth of God." (Matt 4:4)

Your faith is contained within your spirit. Your spiritual food comes from the New Testament. Digesting food and water are essential to your physical life. Digesting Scripture is essential to your spiritual life. You can feed your spirit on God's word, and thereby feed your faith, because God's word is faith food. In Rom 10:8, Paul called the message he preached the word of faith. He called the word of God the word of faith, because the word will cause faith to come into your heart. God's word will build assurance, confidence, and faith in your spirit.

> Your word is a lamp for my feet,
> a light on my path.

(Ps 119:105)

Begin reading the Bible today! Make an appointment with your Creator each day to hear his voice. His light (word) will show you "the way." It will prevent you from stumbling over obstacles or wandering off into paths which will lead you into danger. His light will guide you right into his arms, where he can love and protect you for all of eternity.

LIVE THE BIBLE

> Do not merely listen to the word and so deceive yourselves. Do what it says. (Jas 1:22)

As I mentioned above, food and water are essential for your physical life. The substances that you put into your body daily maintain your life but do not sustain your life. What do I mean by that? Well, you can eat and drink everyday but be out of physical shape. Without exercise, your muscular and cardiovascular systems will not work at optimum levels. The key to physical health is proper diet and exercise. One without the other can lead to a weakened state. This is also true about your spiritual life. You can read, research, and recite Scripture just like a religious scholar, but if you do not live the word, your spirit (faith) will not operate at its capacity.

Always preach the gospel, and when necessary, use words.
—Saint Francis of Assisi[6]

The New Testament is a living, breathing document. It is more important to live it than read it. The Gospels are history; they are a declaration of something that happened. And since the Gospels are the saving work of Jesus Christ, it is something that you can announce, but more importantly it is "the Way" to live. The teachings and actions of our Lord need to be anchored to your soul through your life experiences. The ultimate worshiping of God is to literally follow in the footsteps of Jesus Christ. Each teaching you abide by and each action you follow are two steps closer to reuniting with our Lord. Your fountain of faith will overflow with confidence and joy by imitating your Lord and Savior.

6. This sentiment highlights the importance of living a life that reflects Christian values. While commonly attributed to Saint Francis of Assisi, the true origin is unknown.

Faith

TRUST THE BIBLE

> That day when evening came, he said to his disciples, "Let us go over to the other side." Leaving the crowd behind, they took him along, just as he was, in the boat. There were also other boats with him. A furious squall came up, and the waves broke over the boat, so that it was nearly swamped. Jesus was in the stern, sleeping on a cushion. The disciples woke him and said to him, "Teacher, don't you care if we drown?"
>
> He got up, rebuked the wind, and said to the waves, "Quiet! Be still!" Then the wind died down and it was completely calm.
>
> He said to his disciples, "Why are you so afraid? Do you still have no faith?" (Mark 4:35–40)

Few of life's battles are ever won overnight, so it is safe to assume that you are going to confront suffering. You will experience pain, loss, abandonment, rejection, burden, heartache, fatigue, anger, and betrayal. Why will you experience these things in your life? Because Jesus Christ experienced these things in his life!

> For we do not have a high priest who is unable to sympathize with our weaknesses, but we have one who in every respect has been tested as we are, yet without sin. (Heb 4:15)

Welcome to being a Christian. The trademark of being a disciple of Christ is that you will not be immune to trials and tribulations. God loves his children, and he works all things together for good, which means your sufferings must have a divine purpose. The Lord wants you to grow more into the image of Jesus Christ. Everything in your life (the sun as well as the rain) is designed to enable you to reach this goal.

> Consider it pure joy, my brothers and sisters, whenever you face trials of many kinds, because you know that the testing of your faith produces perseverance. Let perseverance finish its work so that you may be mature and complete, not lacking anything. (Jas 1:2–4)

You will be periodically placed into a boat and sent out into a raging storm. Furious squalls will loosen your boat's rudder, which in turn will toss and turn you mercilessly until you lose all sense of direction. Waves will break over your boat until you almost capsize! How will you respond? Will you let Satan drain your fountain of faith and manipulate you into believing that God has left you or God doesn't care about you?

Or will you lower a bucket into your soul, fill it up with faith, and tell yourself, "God is good. He is for me. He has a plan"?

> What, then, shall we say in response to these things? If God is for us, who can be against us? (Rom 8:31)

Your attitude and actions are pivotal when your faith is being tested. Will you become terrified and panic like those disciples in Jesus' boat? Or will you be joyous and thankful for the opportunity to gain endurance, like Saint James? Whether God is awake or in the stern sleeping on a cushion, he is always with you! He will provide you with situations and circumstances that will cause your faith to grow.

> Remember what I told you: "A servant is not greater than his master." If they persecuted me, they will persecute you also. If they obeyed my teaching, they will obey yours also. (John 15:20)

Faith (whether personal or spiritual) grows through new challenges. Whether these challenges emerge from the social, emotional, physical, or spiritual realm, you will need internal fortitude to change your circumstance. Trusting in yourself, family, friends, mental health professionals, and God will ensure passage through the bumpy roads of life.

> When Jesus had entered Capernaum, a centurion came to him, asking for help. "Lord," he said, "my servant lies at home paralyzed, suffering terribly."
>
> Jesus said to him, "Shall I come and heal him?"
>
> The centurion replied, "Lord, I do not deserve to have you come under my roof. But just say the word, and my servant will be healed. For I myself am a man under authority, with soldiers under me. I tell this one, 'Go,' and he goes; and that one, 'Come,' and he comes. I say to my servant, 'Do this,' and he does it."
>
> When Jesus heard this, he was amazed and said to those following him, "Truly I tell you, I have not found anyone in Israel with such great faith." Then Jesus said to the centurion, "Go! Let it be done just as you believed it would." And his servant was healed at that moment. (Matt 8:5–10, 13)

THE ROAD  RESURRECTION

FIFTH STATION: JESUS IS JUDGED BY PILATE

> *Jesus said, "My kingdom is not of this world. If it were, my servants would fight to prevent my arrest by the Jewish leaders. But now my kingdom is from another place."*
>
> *"You are a king, then!" said Pilate.*
>
> *Jesus answered, "You say that I am a king. In fact, the reason I was born and came into the world is to testify to the truth. Everyone on the side of truth listens to me."*
>
> *"What is truth?" retorted Pilate. (John* 18:36–38*)*

We adore you, O Christ, and we bless you.

Because by your holy cross you have redeemed the world.

> Very early in the morning, the chief priests, with the elders, the teachers of the law and the whole Sanhedrin, made their plans. So they bound Jesus, led him away and handed him over to Pilate.
>
> "Are you the king of the Jews?" asked Pilate.
>
> "You have said so," Jesus replied.
>
> The chief priests accused him of many things. So again Pilate asked him, "Aren't you going to answer? See how many things they are accusing you of."
>
> But Jesus still made no reply, and Pilate was amazed. . . .
>
> Wanting to satisfy the crowd, Pilate released Barabbas to them. He had Jesus flogged, and handed him over to be crucified. (Mark 15:1–5, 15)

Lord, grant us discernment that we may see as you see, not as the world sees.

FIFTH STATION: REFLECTIVE EXERCISES AND QUESTIONS

If you read each Gospel from Matthew, Mark, Luke, and John when they describe the arrest, interrogation, and judgment of our Lord, you will be struck by the limited number of words that Jesus spoke to his accusers. He did not answer every question posed to him, nor did he elaborate on his short responses. Most everyone would agree that if someone was unfairly accused of crimes that he/she did not commit, they would vigorously argue their innocence and demand their freedom. Jesus Christ, however, acted in the exact opposite way.

> He was oppressed and afflicted,
> yet he did not open his mouth;
> he was led like a lamb to the slaughter,
> and as a sheep before its shearers is silent,
> so he did not open his mouth.
> (Isa 53:7)

Jesus had faith in his Father and accepted his destiny to fulfill the Scriptures. Jesus is your Father, and he wants you to have faith in him to fulfill the plan that he has for you. In Jer 1:5 the Lord says, "Before I formed you in the womb, I knew you!" In Luke 12:7, Jesus tells you that his relationship with you is so intimate that he knows how many hairs you have on your head. During your many life struggles, have faith in your Father and ask him to provide you with strength, courage, and trust that the "Light" that you carry from within will lead you to mental wellness.

The following questions will help you measure your personal and spiritual faith. Find a quiet, comfortable place to ponder and answer the following questions. You may need time for reflection to provide yourself direction to generate answers. Digging into your mind, heart, and soul takes time, energy, and commitment. Maybe you can answer all these questions in one sitting. Maybe you want to answer one question per day. There are no rules for this exercise except to be open and honest with yourself. The answers that you generate will provide you with your current location on "Faith Mountain." This is your starting point. It will be up to you to equip yourself with the proper climbing gear and start taking your personal journey to the peak one step at a time. It will take time and effort to get yourself into personal and spiritual shape, but the more you climb "Faith Mountain," the better you will feel about yourself, life, and God. Slow and steady will be your accent until you reach your goal, the peak. There you will experience your destination—a personal, loving relationship with your Lord and Savior Jesus Christ.

A Test of Faith

1. On a scale of one to ten, how strong is your faith and why did you give yourself that rating?
2. What would you have to do to grow your faith?
3. What new direction do you need to take in your life?
4. What fear would a stronger faith help you to conquer?
5. If you grew your faith, who would benefit from it?
6. How often do you read God's word?
7. Do you deliberately try to follow what God's word says?
8. Do your closest friends have a strong faith?
9. What books do you need to start reading to grow your faith?
10. What pain are you going through right now that you need to trust God with?

Submit yourselves, then, to God. Resist the devil, and he will flee from you. Come near to God and he will come near to you.
—Jas 4:7–8

And the God of all grace, who called you to his eternal glory in Christ, after you have suffered a little while, will himself restore you and make you strong, firm, and steadfast.
—1 Pet 5:10

Jesus answered him, "Truly I tell you, today you will be with me in paradise."
—Luke 23:43

Chapter 4
Hope

"For I know the plans I have for you," declares the Lord, "plans to prosper you and not to harm you, plans to give you hope and a future."
—Jer 29:11

Once upon a time a daughter complained to her father that her life was miserable and that she didn't know how she was going to make it. She was tired of fighting and struggling all the time. It seemed just as one problem was solved, another one soon followed. Her father, a chef, took her to the kitchen. He filled three pots with water and placed each on a high fire. Once the three pots began to boil, he placed potatoes in one pot, eggs in the second pot, and ground coffee beans in the third. He then let them sit and boil, without saying a word to his daughter.

The daughter moaned and impatiently waited, wondering what he was doing. After twenty minutes he turned off the burners. He took the potatoes out of the pot and placed them in a bowl. He pulled the boiled eggs out and placed them in a bowl. He then ladled the coffee out and placed it in a cup. Turning to her he asked, "Daughter, what do you see?" "Potatoes, eggs, and coffee," she hastily replied. "Look closer," he said, "and touch the potatoes." She did and noted that they were soft. He then asked her to take an egg and break it. After pulling off the shell, she observed the hard-boiled egg. Finally, he asked her to sip the coffee. Its rich aroma brought a smile to her face. "Father, what does this mean?" she asked.

He then explained that the potatoes, the eggs, and coffee beans had each faced the same adversity—the boiling water. However, each one reacted differently. The potato went in strong, hard, and unrelenting, but in boiling water, it became soft and weak. The egg was fragile, with the thin outer shell protecting its liquid interior, until it was put in the boiling water. Then the inside of the egg became hard. However, the ground coffee beans were unique. After they were exposed to the boiling water, they changed the water and created something new.

"Which are you?" he asked his daughter. "When adversity knocks on your door, how do you respond? Are you a potato, an egg, or a coffee bean?"[1] The moral of this short story is that in life, things happen around you, things happen to you, but the only thing that truly matters is what happens within you. Which one are you?

Hope is a key ingredient to mental wellness. Hope is defined in the dictionary as a feeling of expectation and desire for a certain thing to happen.[2] For a simple one-syllable word, hope carries a tremendous amount of stress, strain, and pain for you throughout your life. It is a lever that lifts unwanted circumstances off your heart, mind, and soul. Hope, like faith, only grows through daily physical, mental, and spiritual exercise. Your hope is directly correlated to your future. The stronger your hope, the brighter your future.

Hope is always projected into the future; however, its power is created in the present. Hope is fueled with positive thoughts, words, and actions. It grows and blossoms with experiences that are coupled with support. Hope disinfects the darkness of your physical and emotional challenges with a bright spiritual light! Hope breaks the chains and ropes that bind you from living a productive life.

Have you ever heard the story of the Elephant Rope? As a man was passing the elephants, he suddenly stopped, confused by the fact that these huge creatures were being held by only a small rope tied to their front leg—no chains, no cages. It was obvious that the elephants could, at any time, break away from their bonds, but for some reason, they did not. He saw a trainer nearby and asked why these animals just stood there and made no attempt to get away. "Well," the trainer said, "when they were very young and much smaller, we used the same size rope to tie them, and at that age, it was enough to hold them. As they grew up, they were

1. Story based on the lessons from Gordon and West, *Coffee Bean*, 35.

2. *Merriam-Webster*, s.v. "hope," https://www.merriam-webster.com/dictionary/hope.

conditioned to believe they could not break away. They believe the rope can still hold them, so they never try to break free." The man was amazed. These animals could at any time break free from their bonds, but because they believed they couldn't, they were stuck right where they were.[3]

The elephants tried to exercise their hope when they were young but were not successful, so they accepted their circumstance and misery. Don't be like the elephants and stand in one place. The world is too big not to explore and experience all that it offers. Your life is too important to waste minutes, hours, days, months, and years standing stagnant and unproductive. Let your hope move your feet down the Road to Resurrection.

But those who hope in the Lord
will renew their strength.
They will soar on wings like eagles;
they will run and not grow weary;
they will walk and not be faint.
—Isa 40:31

THE ROLE OF HOPE IN THERAPY

Do you know what a placebo is? Have you ever read, heard, or witnessed the power of the placebo effect? In the medical field, the power of the placebo effect is a psychological phenomenon; however, for me it is hard evidence that the power of hope works!

A placebo is anything that seems to be a "real" medical treatment—but isn't. It could be a pill, a shot, or some other type of "fake" treatment. What all placebos have in common is that they do not contain an active substance meant to affect health. Sometimes a person can have a response to a placebo. The response can be positive or negative. For instance, the person's symptoms may improve, or the person may have what appears to be side effects from the treatment. These responses are known as the "placebo effect."

There are some conditions in which a placebo can produce results even when people know they are taking a placebo. Studies have shown that placebos can influence conditions such as anxiety and depression. The reason for this is that the placebo has an impact on the relationship between the mind and body. One of the most common theories is that

3. Marcus, *Elephant and the Rope.*

the placebo effect is due to a person's hope. If a person expects a pill to have an effect, it's possible that the body's own chemistry produces effects similar to what the medication might have caused. Experts also say that there is a relationship between how strongly a person hopes to have results and whether results occur. The stronger the feeling, the more likely it is that a person will experience positive effects.

Because of these medical studies, psychiatrists, psychologists, and other mental health care professionals now strongly agree that a client's hope is key for successful therapy. Therapists are taking a detour from traditional therapies, which often focused on what was wrong, and are now navigating their clients toward their strengths or teaching them how to recognize and develop their interpersonal strengths. This approach (hope therapy) is producing significant change in measures of self-esteem, life meaning, and anxiety/depression symptoms.

Hopeful people have goals, the inspiration to go after those goals, and the skills to make them happen. If you feel you know how to get what you want out of life, and you have that desire to make that happen, then you have hope. Do you have the following components of hope?

- *Goals*: Do you have long-term and short-term meaningful goals?
- *Pathway*: Do you have a plan or pathway to get there and the ability to seek alternative routes, if needed?
- *Agency*: Do you have willpower (habits of thought) that will push you to reach your long-term and short-term goals?

THE TRAIT HOPE SCALE

To help you measure your hope, I have provided you the Trait Hope Scale that was developed by C. R. Snyder. This hope scale measures Snyder's cognitive model of hope which defines hope as "a positive motivational state that is based on an interactively derived sense of successful (a) agency (goal-directed energy), and (b) pathways (planning to meet goals)."[4] The hope scale contains twelve items: four items that measure pathways thinking, four items that measure agency thinking, and four items that are fillers.

4. Snyder et al., "Hope and Health," 285.

Please respond to each item using an eight-point scale ranging from "Definitely False" to "Definitely True." This will only take a few minutes to complete, but the composite scores will help you understand the level of hope that you have from within.[5]

The Trait Hope Scale							
Directions: Read each item carefully. Using the scale shown below, please select the number that best describes you and put that number in the blank provided.							
1 Definitely False	2 Mostly False	3 Somewhat False	4 Slightly False	5 Slightly True	6 Somewhat True	7 Mostly True	8 Definitely True

Score	*Statement*
	1. I can think of many ways to get out of a jam.
	2. I energetically pursue my goals.
	3. I feel tired most of the time.
	4. There are lots of ways around any problem.
	5. I am easily downed in an argument.
	6. I can think of many ways to get the things in life that are important to me.
	7. I worry about my health.
	8. Even when others get discouraged, I know I can find a way to solve the problem.
	9. My past experiences have prepared me well for my future.
	10. I've been successful in life.
	11. I usually find myself worrying about something.
	12. I meet the goals that I set for myself.

Add the responses from the following questions		
The Pathway Subscale Score	The Agency Subscale Score	The Hope Scale Score
Question 1	Question 2	Question 1
Question 4	Question 9	Question 2
Question 6	Question 10	Question 4

5. Trait Hope Scale reprinted from Snyder et al., "Will and the Ways," with permission.

Question 8	Question 12	Question 6
		Question 8
		Question 9
		Question 10
		Question 12
Total Points:	Total Points:	Total Points:

THE PATHWAY SUBSCALE SCORE

Scores on this subscale can range from four to thirty-two. A higher score indicates higher levels of pathway thinking. Pathway thinking is the ability to develop a pathway to reach a goal. This skill is essential when you pursue complex, challenging goals, since often the path you imagine might not be the correct one. The most effective response in case you hit an obstacle is to say, "I know there is another way, I just do not know what it is yet." In this way you allow your mind to explore and look for alternative solutions. Your attention will be focused on the future and not on the problem, and this will let you progress and spot new opportunities. Pathway thinking also increases motivation; the more you can rapidly find alternative solutions, the more motivated you become, which in turn increases your ability to find new pathways.

What was your score?

Do you agree with the result?

THE AGENCY SUBSCALE SCORE

Scores on this subscale can range from four to thirty-two. A higher score indicates higher levels of agency thinking. Agency thinking is essential for you to feel in control of your life: to believe in your capacity to influence your own thoughts and behavior and have faith in your ability to handle a wide range of tasks or situations. Having a sense of agency influences your stability as a separate person; it is your capacity to be psychologically stable, yet resilient or flexible, in the face of conflict or change.

What was your score?

Do you agree with the result?

TOTAL HOPE SCORE

Scores on this measurement can range from eight to sixty-four. The higher the score, the higher levels of hope that you have. Scores of forty to forty-eight are hopeful; forty-nine to fifty-six, moderately hopeful; and fifty-seven or higher are identified as high hope.

What was your score?

Do you agree with the result?

But blessed is the one who trusts in the Lord,
whose confidence is in him.
They will be like a tree planted by the water
that sends out its roots by the stream.
It does not fear when heat comes;
its leaves are always green.
It has no worries in a year of drought
and never fails to bear fruit.
—Jer 17:7–8

Science is the concerted human effort to understand the history of the natural world and how the natural world works, with observable physical evidence as the basis of that understanding. When scientists turn their expertise to the human mind, heart, and soul, their understanding becomes less concrete. C. R. Snyder used his talents to create a measuring tool meant to reach deep into the essence of your being. The science world does give him credit because his Trait Hope Scale is valid and reliable according to scientific standards. Many of you may have even agreed with where you scored on his subscales and total hope measurement.

However, all the scales and mathematical equations in the world cannot calculate or solve what occurs in the spiritual world. How can science measure what the Lord means to you? What the Lord gives you? How the Lord protects you? What lessons he teaches you? Science can't and doesn't even try. If you reread the definition of science that I provided above, it clearly states it is the concerted human effort to understand the history of the *natural world* and how the *natural world* works. Scientists have been blessed by God to leave his work alone.

Do you recall the short story that introduced this chapter? The experiment that the father demonstrated for his troubled daughter. How the potatoes, the eggs, and coffee beans had each faced the same adversity—the boiling water. And how each one reacted differently. The potato became soft and weak. The egg became solid and hard. But the ground coffee beans changed the water and created something new. Jesus Christ, our Lord and Savior, is the ground coffee beans in the experiment.

> He who was seated on the throne said, "I am making everything new!" Then he said, "Write this down, for these words are trustworthy and true." (Rev 21:5)

The first miracle that Jesus ever did was to change water into something new!

> On the third day a wedding took place at Cana in Galilee. Jesus' mother was there, and Jesus and his disciples had also been invited to the wedding. When the wine was gone, Jesus' mother said to him, "They have no more wine."
>
> "Woman, why do you involve me?" Jesus replied. "My hour has not yet come."
>
> His mother said to the servants, "Do whatever he tells you."
>
> Nearby stood six stone water jars, the kind used by the Jews for ceremonial washing, each holding from twenty to thirty gallons.
>
> Jesus said to the servants, "Fill the jars with water"; so, they filled them to the brim.
>
> Then he told them, "Now draw some out and take it to the master of the banquet."
>
> They did so, and the master of the banquet tasted the water that had been turned into wine. He did not realize where it had come from, though the servants who had drawn the water knew. Then he called the bridegroom aside and said, "Everyone brings out the choice wine first and then the cheaper wine after the guests have had too much to drink; but you have saved the best till now."
>
> What Jesus did here in Cana of Galilee was the first of the signs through which he revealed his glory; and his disciples believed in him. (John 2:1–11)

Jesus Christ is hope. His words are the definition of hope. His actions are examples of hope. Throughout the New Testament, in every interaction that our Lord had with someone (either friend or foe, believer or nonbeliever), he left them with the hope of everlasting life. Jesus Christ can provide you with goals, pathways, and agency. As a matter of fact, his hope can be your hope. His goals can be your goals. His pathway can be your pathway. His thinking can be your thinking. He is full of hope, love, and compassion, and he is waiting for you to come to him so he can fill you with his grace.

God's mission is to help you restore your relationship with him. He has proven to you, through his words and deeds, that he loves you and wants the very best for you. Because the Lord created you, he knows you perfectly. He knows how to break through your resistance to his will. He knows how to penetrate your heart and transform you. He knows how to love you. In his infinite wisdom, he has decided to make you his productive disciple by providing you with astounding miracles of conversion, repentance, deliverance, and healing. You can experience him and all that he promises today if you fill your life with faith, hope, and trust in him. The following Scripture will help you understand the priceless gifts that the Lord will provide you if you let him into your mind, body, and soul.

> Immediately Jesus made the disciples get into the boat and go on ahead of him to the other side, while he dismissed the crowd. After he had dismissed them, he went up on a mountainside by himself to pray. Later that night, he was there alone, and the boat was already a considerable distance from land, buffeted by the waves because the wind was against it.
>
> Shortly before dawn Jesus went out to them, walking on the lake. When the disciples saw him walking on the lake, they were terrified. "It's a ghost," they said, and cried out in fear.
>
> But Jesus immediately said to them: "Take courage! It is I. Don't be afraid."
>
> "Lord, if it's you," Peter replied, "tell me to come to you on the water."
>
> "Come," he said.
>
> Then Peter got down out of the boat, walked on the water, and came toward Jesus. But when he saw the wind, he was afraid and, beginning to sink, cried out, "Lord, save me!"
>
> Immediately Jesus reached out his hand and caught him. "You of little faith," he said, "why did you doubt?"
>
> And when they climbed into the boat, the wind died down. Then those who were in the boat worshiped him, saying, "Truly you are the Son of God."

> When they had crossed over, they landed at Gennesaret. And when the men of that place recognized Jesus, they sent word to all the surrounding country. People brought all their sick to him and begged him to let the sick just touch the edge of his cloak, and all who touched it were healed. (Matt 14:22–35)

I would like to fill this space on why I chose to share this Scripture with you in the chapter devoted to hope. At the beginning of this passage, it states that Jesus dispatched his disciples to get into a boat and go to the other side while he dismissed the crowd of people that surrounded him. Like all Scripture, every word or phrase is packed with meaning that can help you in the present situation that you find yourself in. Jesus' heart is so full of love that he is willing to send his disciples from their present tasks to help rekindle the relationship he longs to have with you. Though you may not realize it, you meet his disciples numerous times throughout each day. To recognize the LORD's disciples, you must open your eyes, ears, heart, and soul to the LORD. Once your spiritual senses are opened, you will be given internal and external motivation to find Jesus. The LORD's disciples could be your parents, siblings, extended family, friends, teachers, therapist, or someone that God will put into your life today. They were sent to you on a mission of mercy from God. They will provide you a map that you will need in order to come back to the "Good Shepherd."

The final statement in the introduction of this passage explains how Jesus stayed with the crowd after dispatching his disciples. There is always a crowd around the LORD. The reason for this is that Jesus declared, "I am the bread of life. Whoever comes to me will never go hungry, and whoever believes in me will never be thirsty" (John 6:35). No matter how large the crowd, Jesus always stays with his followers to teach and serve them, until they are reunited with him in their resurrection. Jesus was scanning the crowd looking for you. When he realized that you were not there, he sent his angels to find you. This should prove to you how much he loves you and needs you!

Before reuniting with his disciples and you, Jesus provided himself an opportunity to fill his soul with hope through prayer. The passage states, "He went up on a mountainside by himself to pray." Faith, hope, and love are created through prayer. Each day of Jesus' ministry, he made it a point to spend some alone time with his Father to strengthen his resolve so that he could fulfill his earthly mission. *Prayer* is the name of the road that you will walk on to reunite with the LORD. Prayer is necessary.

Is your life busier than Jesus' life was? If he found time to pray each day, I'm sure you can generate an empty space in your daily calendar to pray. When you do pray, model yourself after our Lord and Savior and find a quiet place. Make it a personal goal to unplug from the world before you speak to the One who made the world. Don't assume that your prayer life will be easy. Persistence ought to be the hallmark of your prayers. You will need to plead with God faithfully, fervently, and passionately. When you pray to the LORD, do it with adoration (deep love and respect). When you pray to the LORD, confess your sins because you need forgiveness daily. When you pray to the LORD, provide him with thanksgiving for all that you have. Finally, when you pray to the LORD, ask him to provide because he knows what you need. This is a template for you to pray with a purpose. Speak to the Father like Jesus spoke to the Father.

After this introduction, Matthew details the body of this Scripture passage. He lets the reader, you, know that it has been a considerable amount of time since Jesus sent disciples to find you. I am assuming that they left sometime in the afternoon, and it is now just before dawn. I am also assuming that his disciples have found you and that you are now in the boat. The boat represents your life in Christ, since he sent the boat to find you. The lake represents life itself. Matthew tells you that you are a considerable distance from land (Jesus) and therefore are experiencing the afflictions that life provides through Satan. It is the darkest part of the night (of your life). You are at the mercy of the traps that Satan has set for you. The wind and the rain are moving you further away from the LORD while you take on the waters of life that soon will drown you. When your hope is all but lost, the "Light of the World" defies all human logic and walks on water to save you. Jesus immediately tells you, "Take courage! It is I. Don't be afraid." In your disbelief that it is him, you challenge him and ask him to allow you to close the distance between the both of you by walking over the devil's traps. When Jesus tells you to come, your heart, mind, and soul are not fully freed from the claws of the evil one, and you begin to sink into hell. As you sink further down into the netherworld, you cry out, "LORD, save me!" Immediately Jesus reaches out his hand and pulls you toward him and says to you, "You of little faith, why did you doubt?" And when you climb into the LORD's arms, you realize that the wind has died down, and the devil has been defeated once again.

The conclusion of this passage is just as important as the introduction and main body. You are now with Jesus. You firmly believe that he is truly the Son of God. You lay your head in his bosom and feel the radiance of his light penetrate your body. You have now rekindled your relationship with him. You are filled with faith, hope, and love and are ready to lead a productive Christian life. You have earned your "angel wings" and now work for the Lord.

When you arrive at the next chapter in your life, your spiritual senses will allow you to witness a new crowd of people that have been afflicted by the devil. Even though Satan has tried to cripple their spirit, the Lord will dispatch you in his boat to find them and bring them to him so that he can heal them and pull them into his arms.

Hope is one of the building blocks in life. It is something that you need to build and reinforce throughout the events of your life. In this chapter, I have shown you a way that science can measure the amount of hope that you have and strategies that mental health professionals have created for you to increase your hope. I have also discussed with you the importance of hope through the Lord's eyes. Through Scripture, you have read how Jesus Christ creates and sustains hope in your mind, body, and soul. It is also important to know that science and God can work in harmony to help increase your hope. Hope is a living and ever-changing substance. It can increase or decrease. A surplus of it can make you productive. A shortage of it can make you unproductive. Hope is something that you can control. It is a mindset, a belief, a lifestyle that you can use and share daily. For those of you who are struggling with anxiety and/or depression, begin to explore the concept of hope and measure how much you have. Use science and the word of God to help you understand how hope can bring an immediate positive change to the current mental health condition that you find yourself in today.

Let your hopes, not your hurts, shape your future.

—Robert H. Schuller[6]

6. Schuller, *Tough Times Never Last*, 107.

SIXTH STATION: JESUS IS SCOURGED AND CROWNED WITH THORNS

> I offered my back to those who beat me,
> my cheeks to those who pulled out my beard;
> I did not hide my face
> from mocking and spitting.
> (Isa 50:6)

We adore you, O Christ, and we bless you.

Because by your holy cross you have redeemed the world.

> Then Pilate took Jesus and had him flogged. The soldiers twisted together a crown of thorns and put it on his head. They clothed him in a purple robe and went up to him again and again, saying, "Hail, king of the Jews!" And they slapped him in the face. (John 19:1–3)

Lord, grant us patience in times of suffering that we may offer our lives as a sacrifice of praise.

SIXTH STATION: REFLECTIVE EXERCISES AND QUESTIONS

Jesus' death sentence was all-encompassing. It included an unjust trial, a forced execution, and a public display of humiliation that included physical abuse (spitting, punching, kicking, and whipping) as well as emotional abuse (chanting, cheering, daring, and false worshiping). This was all before he had to carry his own cross to which he would be nailed. How and why would Jesus go through this? Throughout the Gospels, Jesus would predict his passion, death, and resurrection to his disciples. They either chose not to understand it or were too afraid to ask more about it. Either way, Jesus' closest friends never fully understood who he was and why he came. It was only after Jesus ascended into heaven and sent the Holy Spirit down to his disciples (Pentecost) that they truly understood his earthly mission.

Do you feel misunderstood by your friends because of your mental health diagnosis?

Do you feel like you are being unfairly persecuted due to your anxiety and/or depression?

Have you been unfairly sentenced to thoughts, feelings, and actions that others don't understand or experience?

Has your anxiety and/or depression ever humiliated you in public?

Have you ever received verbal, physical, and/or emotional abuse because someone does not understand your mental health affliction?

Has someone ever symbolically crowned you with the thorns of your diagnosis and only recognized you as someone who is mentally unstable?

Do you feel like you are carrying a heavy cross daily due to your mental health condition?

If you answered yes to each of these questions, fear not. As a matter of fact, rejoice! Rejoice in the fact that you have or are experiencing what Jesus Christ experienced while living on earth. He knows firsthand your pains and struggles. He knows firsthand the power of temptation from Satan. Remember the prediction that Jesus told to his disciples—passion, death, and resurrection. There cannot be a resurrection without pain and struggle. He has already conquered what you are presently going through. He has defeated the demons that are inside of you or around you. He has conquered death! He wants his story to be your story. He has tailor-made a life strategy for you to rise out of your darkness. He has shined the light of hope down upon you so that you can see the path to resurrection. Use your faith, hope, and love to follow his footsteps.

The following questions will help you recognize the hope you have from within. Like in previous chapters, find a quiet, comfortable place to ponder and answer the following questions. You may need time for reflection to provide yourself direction to generate answers. Digging into your mind, heart, and soul takes time, energy, and commitment. Maybe you can answer all these questions in one sitting. Maybe you want to answer one question per day. There are no rules for this exercise except to be open and honest with yourself. The answers that you generate will help you define hope in your terms. They will allow you to put a "face" on hope so that you can recognize it and retrieve it when you need it the most. If you take your time and thoroughly search your mind, heart, and soul, you may uncover the face of God!

The Face of Hope

1. What does hope look like in your life?
2. If you could photograph it, what might you see?
3. How could you "instill" it or invoke it or strengthen it in your life? What might undermine it?
4. How could you protect it from those factors that might seek to undermine it?
5. What does it feel like for you to hope?

   Daring?

   Foolish?

   Reckless?

   Painful?

   Strong?

   (and how does that impact how you see yourself in the world?)

6. Could hope form a solid foundation for you, or does it feel too shapeless for that?

> *Therefore, since we have been justified through faith, we have peace with God through our Lord Jesus Christ, through whom we have gained access by faith into this grace in which we now stand. And we boast in the hope of the glory of God. Not only so, but we also glory in our sufferings, because we know that suffering produces perseverance; perseverance, character; and character, hope. And hope does not put us to shame, because God's love has been poured out into our hearts through the Holy Spirit, who has been given to us.*
>
> *—Rom 5:1–5*

Chapter 5

Love

A new command I give you: Love one another. As I have loved you, so you must love one another. By this everyone will know that you are my disciples, if you love one another.

—John 13:34–35

My name is Brian Riley, and I am a senior at Walnut Heights High School. I was fortunate enough to be elected to student council to represent our senior class. Throughout the school year, one of the missions of student council is to organize fundraisers to offset the cost of school dances. One of the most popular and profitable fundraisers occurs during the month of February. From the first to the thirteenth, the student body has an opportunity to purchase and send carnations (with a personal message) to a person / people of their choice. These carnations are delivered to the recipients in homeroom on Valentine's Day (February 14). The student body can choose from several colors to send to someone. . A pink carnation represents gratitude. It symbolizes that a person's character, attitude, and friendship has made a difference in someone's life. A light red carnation represents admiration. It symbolizes that a person's words and actions are held in deep respect and appreciation and that the person that sent it to the recipient is attracted to them. The final choice of carnation color is dark red, which represents affection and love. Receiving a dark red carnation means that someone in the school loves and values the recipient. A dark red carnation is a powerful reminder that the recipient has shown attraction, respect, acceptance, selflessness, loyalty, forgiveness, companionship, and communication toward someone they love. A pink carnation costs three dollars, a light red carnation costs four dollars, and a dark red carnation costs five dollars.

After the holiday break, the students in my school count down the days until the carnation sale begins. Because money didn't grow on trees, I had to be very particular about who I planned to send carnations to. During the month of January, I spent time in the hallways, classrooms, and cafeteria observing girls to create my carnation list. My top ten ranking kept changing because I was constantly inventing and reinventing my criteria. By the time February arrived, I was even more confused than when I started ranking in January. . Who was ranked where and why? What did the carnation colors mean again? How many carnations should I send out? What should I write down in my personal message? These and a thousand other questions ran through my mind throughout each school day leading up to Valentine's Day. My friends weren't struggling as much as I was during the carnation sale. My friend Mike sent out a dozen light red carnations to a dozen girls, trying to secure a date for the prom. My friend Chad sent a red carnation to his ex-girlfriend, trying to re-spark their relationship that flamed out over the holiday break. Finally, my friend Donny sent three pink carnations to a group of friends that helped him through a difficult time earlier in the school year. Mike, Chad, and Donny asked me daily about my top ten ranking list and who I was going to send carnations to and what color they were going to be. My daily response to them was the same: "I don't know!"

It was now February 13, the last day to purchase carnations, and I had not yet decided on who to send carnations to. Knowing that lunch was the last opportunity to purchase carnations, I mentally checked out of my morning classes and focused all my energy on my top ten list. Even though I missed out on all the content of the morning lessons, I was able to accomplish my goal and decided who to send a carnation to. As I entered the cafeteria, I immediately went to the student council booth and filled out a form to purchase one dark red carnation and wrote a personal message to the recipient. I paid my five dollars and went to my table to eat lunch. As I sat down, Mike, Chad, and Donny asked me about who I purchased a dark red carnation for, and I told them that they would have to wait until tomorrow to find out. I was relieved, yet anxious, about the next day—Valentine's Day.

The morning of February 14 arrived, and I got into homeroom earlier than usual. I spotted on Mr. Cutler's desk a massive bouquet of carnations of different colors. After going through the normal routine of taking attendance and saying the Pledge of Allegiance, Mr. Cutler organized the flowers and shuffled through the thick stack of cards. The room filled with anticipation as he was ready to announce the names and deliver the carnations with the cards. Mike received six light red carnations, which meant he now could choose who he wanted to go to the prom with. Chad received one dark red carnation from his ex-girlfriend, which meant he could remove the prefix *ex-* from ex-girlfriend. Donny received three pink carnations from his group of friends that he valued. The carnations and cards were running out, but I wasn't worried. I still had hope that I would be receiving at least one. There was one flower and card left when Mr. Cutler announced my name. "Brian Riley, here is a dark red carnation for you!" My three friends let out a yell and clapped. When I went back to my seat, I looked down at the card and confirmed exactly what I expected. It wasn't from any of the girls that appeared on my top ten list over the past month. The message on the card simply read, "Happy Valentine's Day. Love, Brian Riley." When my friends asked who sent it, I told them it was from someone that I love with my whole mind, heart, and soul. They wanted a name, but I did not give them one. They didn't need to know!

Do you love yourself?

Do you tell yourself "I love you"?

Do you treat yourself the way you want others to treat you?

Most of the shadows of this life are caused
by standing in one's own sunshine.
—Attributed to Ralph Waldo Emerson

LOVE YOURSELF

Do you know what it means to love yourself unconditionally?

Do you know how to totally accept and embrace yourself fully?

Like most people, you will probably struggle with the concept of love in your life. You want it! You will search for it! And if you are lucky, you will find it. The biggest problem with love is when you find it, there is no guarantee that it will be everlasting. Throughout your life, love will wax and wane. It will increase and decrease in size, strength, and intensity like the phases of the moon. Internal and external circumstances will have a direct impact on the amount of love that will permeate your body at any given time. However, once you experience love, you will realize that it is the greatest commodity that the universe can offer. It is more precious and priceless than any tangible item you will discover in your life. Love is light. Light uncovers hope. Hope brings joy. Joy fuels confidence. Confidence creates accomplishment. Accomplishment strengthens mental wellness. Mental wellness guarantees a productive life.

> Why do you look at the speck of sawdust in your brother's eye and pay no attention to the plank in your own eye? How can you say to your brother, "Let me take the speck out of your eye," when all the time there is a plank in your own eye? You hypocrite, first take the plank out of your own eye, and then you will see clearly to remove the speck from your brother's eye. (Matt 7:3–5)

The Scripture above was taken from the Sermon on the Mount. The Sermon is the longest continuous discourse of Jesus found in the New Testament. The lessons sent from the mount emphasize Jesus' moral teachings. In this passage, Jesus attacks the hypocrites who attack others for their small flaws while ignoring their own massive ones. He's focusing on those who judge others but do not evaluate themselves. Jesus specifically uses the human eye as a symbol to make his point because the eye is the window to the soul. So why would I include this Scripture verse in the section entitled "Love Yourself"? Well, you can take this lesson and apply it to yourself when it comes to self-love. When you insert the words *heart* and *love* into this passage, your "eyes" will be opened to the importance of loving yourself first and foremost:

> Why do you constantly evaluate the hearts of others and pay no attention to your own? How can you tell others "I love you" when you don't love yourself? You hypocrite, first look within your own heart and love yourself for who you are, and then you will fully understand the meaning of love and will be able to love others as you love yourself.

You're always with yourself, so you might as well enjoy the company.
—Attributed to Diane Von Furstenberg

What is self-love? Is it materialistic (e.g., showering yourself with gifts)? Is it motivational (e.g., immersing yourself into novels, poems, and movies that speak to your heart)? Is it social (e.g., receiving attention from family, friends, and romantic partners)? The answer to these questions is *no*! Self-love is not a state of feeling good. Self-love is a state of appreciation for yourself that grows from actions that support your physical, psychological, and spiritual growth. Self-love is dynamic; it grows by actions. When you act in ways that expand your self-love, you begin to accept your weaknesses as well as your strengths. You have less need to explain away your shortcomings. You have compassion for yourself as you struggle to find personal meaning. Finally, you are more centered on your life's purpose and expect to be fulfilled through your own efforts.

The million-dollar question is, how do you arrive at this state of mind? What actions do you need to execute for your self-love to grow and sustain itself during your lifetime? The following are some stimulants that you can try to get self-love flowing to your mind, body, and soul.

ALLOW YOURSELF TO BE YOUR BEST FRIEND

Do you have a best friend? If so, do you always know what he or she is thinking, feeling, and wanting? Of course you don't. It is unreasonable and impossible to know what another person's thoughts are every second of every day. However, there is one person that you know better than anyone else. You always know their wants and needs. That person is you! Since you know all these things about yourself, who then can better support your physical, psychological, and spiritual growth than you? The key to becoming your own best friend is that you need to search your mind, heart, and soul daily to gauge what support is needed for you to be productive.

How much do you agree with each of the following statements?

I trust my intuition.

I am honest with myself.

I can depend on myself regardless of what occurs in my life.

I am loyal to my thoughts, emotions, values, and goals.

I care about my social, emotional, physiological, and spiritual well-being.

I can trust myself.

I experience and express empathy for myself.

I can be nonjudgmental toward myself.

I listen to my inner voice.

I support myself in good times.

I am support myself in bad times.

I am self-confident.

I can see the humor in life.

I know what makes me happy.

If you find that you strongly agreed with many of these statements, then you have a positive relationship with yourself. You can discern your daily psychological and emotional state and provide your mind, heart, and soul with the nourishment it needs to be productive. If you find that you disagree with many of the statements, you may be struggling to develop a meaningful, lasting relationship with yourself. You are probably wrestling with your daily psychological and emotional state because you have yet to find pieces of your mind, heart, and soul that will make you complete. Finding these pieces begins with loving yourself!

When you learn to Accept instead of Expect, you will have few disappointments.

—Anonymous

ACCEPT WHO YOU ARE AND WHERE YOU ARE

Love will flow into your mind, heart, and soul if you accept your current condition. You are unique. There is no one else in the world exactly like you. You were brought onto this earth to share your talents and gifts with others. But before you can share you must prepare. How do you prepare? You must ignite your eternal "Light." Regardless of your current condition, the love that you generate for yourself will cast out the darkness of your affliction and reveal the gifts that God blessed you with. If it only takes a spark to start a forest fire, then it only takes a spark to set your mind, heart, and soul ablaze. Sometimes when you find yourself in the cold, dark, damp days of your life, it is hard to generate an internal spark. However, these three survival mindsets are guaranteed to start a fire:

- Love yourself
- Approve yourself
- Accept yourself

I have come to bring fire on the earth, and how I wish it were already kindled!
—Luke 12:49

Life is full of transitions. It is like a river—ever flowing. There is no such thing as being stagnant. You are on the white water rafting journey of a lifetime. The raft that you are in is specifically made for you. The course that you will traverse will only be run by you. Where you are today is not where you will be tomorrow. Instead of holding onto the side of the raft with white knuckles, grab your oar and dip it into the water. Enjoy where the currents of life take you. Whether you find yourself in deep waters or shallow waters, rough waters or calm waters, going straight or bending, you must remind yourself that these experiences are molding you into the person that you are meant to be, and that you are only experiencing these life lessons today to fully appreciate tomorrow.

The point of life (and white water rafting) is the journey. That's where the fun is! You are not meant to rush through life. Life's about savoring every moment of each day. It's about how and why you learn lessons along the way. It's about the hardships and the challenges that you will face and how you work through them. It's about the joy and happiness that you will experience. It's about learning the importance of self-love. Therefore, don't waste a day or an opportunity. Embrace all your experiences, good and bad, and learn from them because where you are today you won't be tomorrow.

Part 2 | The Cornerstone

I am not what I ought to be,
Not what I want to be,
Not what I am going to be,
But thankful that I am not what I used to be.

—*John Wooden*[1]

Life is not a problem to be solved, but a reality to be experienced.

—*Jacobus Johannes Leeuw*[2]

CLEAR YOUR SYSTEM'S CACHE

If you haven't been organizing and discarding files as you go, it's likely your hard drive is stuffed with downloads and unwanted files. You probably have been experiencing the dreaded spinning circle on your screen. This symbolizes slow performance! Deep cleaning your computer of unwanted files and streamlining your folder system daily can not only free up storage space but improve your computer's performance.

This piece of advice is not only useful for your laptop but for your mind. Your mind is the most powerful computer in the world. Because it is a computer, it receives and stores billions of bits of information a day. However, you are the programmer of your mind. You can install software programs that search and analyze your hard drive for files that are no longer of any use and therefore can be moved to the trash bin.

Only a lucky few can install software that filters real time information and decides whether it's worthy of filing or deleting. Most of us take in the billions of bits of information daily and internalize it. Without ever organizing and/or discarding these files, we begin to function at a sub-optimal level due to over-storage. Unwanted downloads and files begin to drain our energy, emotions, body functions, and thought processes. It brings about a physical and psychological crisis that makes us unproductive (a human spinning circle).

1. Impelman, "7-Point Creed."
2. Leeuw, *Conquest of Illusion*, 89.

To protect yourself from mental over -storage, you need to install a mental wellness cleaner. This will optimize your mind, body, and soul so that they can function at their ultimate speed and performance. Below are the install directions to start using this software.

- Schedule thirty minutes of alone time prior to going to bed.
- Read Scripture, say prayers, and have a conversation with God.
- Run the following mental wellness cleaning program:

List each significant event that occurred in your life today.

Was this event external or internal?

How did this event impact your mind, body, and spirit?

Did you perceive this event as a positive experience or negative experience?

Why was this event a positive experience or negative experience?

Regardless of whether it was positive or negative, did it teach you something about yourself?

Regardless of whether it was positive or negative, did it teach you a life lesson that you can use in the future?

Do you want to mentally download this event into a file?

If yes, what is the name of the file that you are placing it in?

If no, are you willing to place this event into your trash bin and click *erase*?

- Accept and appreciate all that happened to you today.
- Mentally mark the distance that you traveled on your day's journey.
- Close your eyes and get your much-needed rest for tomorrow's journey.

Respect Others.
Help Others.
Love Others.
These are the keys that unlock your soul.
—Anthony Douglas Williams[3]

LOVE OTHERS

Within the book *Chicken Soup for the Soul*, Eric Butterworth tells of a college sociology class that was sent into the Baltimore slums to take case histories of two hundred young boys.[4] The students were required to write an evaluation of each boy's projected future, and in virtually every case, they wrote, "He hasn't got a chance." Some twenty-five years later, another professor came across the earlier study and decided to do a follow-up study. Except for twenty boys who had died or moved, the study revealed that 176 of the remaining 180 boys had gone on to surprising success, with many becoming lawyers, doctors, and leading businessmen. When the men were asked what contributed to their successes, they all pointed to one teacher who had influenced them. The teacher was still alive, so the professor went to visit her to ask how she had influenced boys seemingly destined for poverty and crime to become such success stories. "It's really very simple," she responded. "I loved those boys."[5]

The most powerful object in our solar system is the sun. Without it, life would not exist. The most powerful emotion on earth is love. Without it, life would not be worth living. The sun and love have many other things in common. For example, the sun warms our planet. It heats the surface, oceans, and atmosphere. Love warms your daily existence. It heats your mind, heart, and soul. The energy generated from the sun drives our climate and weather. The energy generated from love drives your psychological and emotional outlook. The sun's gravitational pull holds our planet in orbit. Love's gravitational pull holds you in a state of joy. Sunlight is essential for vegetation to grow. Humans and animals need plants for food and oxygen. Love is essential for your mind, heart,

3. Williams, *Inside the Divine Pattern*.
4. Butterworth, "Love."
5. Butterworth, "Love," 4.

and soul to grow. Having a strong mind, heart, and soul will lead you to a productive life. Without heat from the sun, the Earth would freeze. There would be no winds, ocean currents, or clouds to transport water. Without the heat from love, your life would be cold and lonely. You would wander aimlessly without hope and faith. As you can see, the sun and love provide you with life as you know it. Without either of them you would not exist.

How powerful is love? So powerful that 176 boys from the Baltimore inner city became lawyers, doctors, and leading businessmen all due to the love of a particular teacher! How powerful is love? So powerful that it can be the antidote for all afflictions (including anxiety and depression).

Have you ever heard someone use the idiom "silver bullet"? This term refers to something that provides an immediate and extremely effective solution to a given problem or difficulty, especially one that is normally very complex or hard to resolve. The phrase is almost always used within a statement that such a solution does not exist. All mental health professionals believe that there is not one type of therapeutic approach or delivery system that can heal one or every mental health affliction. Because of the complexities of a therapeutic relationship, it would be unethical for mental health professionals or associations to create a diagram of all the diagnoses found in the *Diagnostic and Statistical Manual of Mental Disorders* and connect them to a particular therapeutic approach (psychodynamic, behavior, cognitive, humanistic, or integrative). Unfortunately, it just doesn't work like that. There is no silver bullet! However, it is my belief, regardless of the therapeutic approach you are participating in or plan to participate in, that loving others can expedite the recovery time when suffering from anxiety and/or depression. As detailed in the beginning of this section, love has been proven to be a powerful antidote.

My command is this: Love each other as I have loved you.
—John 15:12

FOLLOW "THE WAY"

Saint Bernadette Soubirous once said, "Every human being is precious in God's eyes."[6] The LORD has made you in his own image. He has blessed

6. McEachern, *Holy Life*, 123.

your life with everything that you had, have, and will have. Sometimes, his blessings come in the form of opportunities. He will place you in certain situations so that you can use your unique talents to do his work. Sometimes these life situations are pleasing and pleasant, and sometimes they are stressful and burdensome. When seizing upon these opportunities, the Holy Spirit will wash over you and cleanse your mind, body, and soul. You will feel the healing power of the Lord when he provides you with peace and tranquility on your most challenging days.

To receive this great gift from the Lord, you will need to follow "the way." The way will lead you to Jesus Christ. By entering the narrow gate (Matt 7:13–14), your life's mission will overlap Christ's life mission. Upon your first step through the narrow gate, you will realize that "the Way" is paved in love and service to God and others. As you struggle with your current mental affliction(s), whether you know it or not, your family and friends are interceding on your behalf. They are investing their time and energy to ensure a compassionate, cooperating environment to ease some of the pain and anguish that you are experiencing with anxiety and/or depression. Because you are preoccupied with your condition, you may sometimes lash out at them and not comprehend and/or appreciate the love and support that they are providing you. By traveling "the way," the Lord will strip away the self-centered attitude that comes with mental affliction and free you to experience the power of love.

Love on "the Way" is not a feeling or emotion, instead it is a concentrated action to live for someone else. It is a complete separation from one's own egotism. The person that experiences true love on "the Way" is not interested in reciprocation but simply in the good of the other, and therefore is willing to wait out any resistance. This is why Saint Paul uses the adjective *patient* to first describe love in 1 Cor 13:4. True love has no resentment for it wants success for another. True love never ends. True love is the way, the truth, and the life! So, you may be asking yourself, how can I receive and experience this true love? The answer is that you must strive for the divine life each day. The life of Christ must be repeated in your daily life. Does this sound impossible? Matthew 19:26 tells us that "Jesus looked at his disciples and said, 'With man this is impossible, but with God all things are possible.'"

BE KIND TO OTHERS

Because you suffer from anxiety and/or depression, you may often find it difficult to experience happiness. By traveling "the way," you will discover that happiness is attainable by being kind to others. The heavenly gift of true love is embedded in your soul. The only thing that you need is your will to uncover this skill! This starts by giving expression to your impression. When you use your heart to connect with another, a heavenly seed will be produced in both you and the recipient. Your kindness to others will be the water that helps both seeds blossom into God's "fruit." The secret to kindness is that it tenderizes the human heart. A simple kind word on your part will cheer another's heart. Your kindness will not diminish when you give it away—it will grow! Your kindness to others will be a concrete expression of true divine love. I hope that you realize that life and death are in the power of your tongue. When you speak to others, provide them with expressions of faith, hope, and love. Use your words to build instead of demolish, strengthen instead of weaken, and inspire instead of discourage. Out of the abundance of your heart, you are speaking. How full is your heart and what is coming out of it?

I would like to take time to further explain the power of divine true love by providing you a passage from the gospel that Saint Paul wrote to the Romans. Who better than Paul to help me further explain to you how the power of divine love can offer you and others salvation?

> Love must be sincere. Hate what is evil; cling to what is good. Be devoted to one another in love. Honor one another above yourselves. Never be lacking in zeal, but keep your spiritual fervor, serving the Lord. Be joyful in hope, patient in affliction, faithful in prayer. Share with the Lord's people who are in need. Practice hospitality.
>
> Bless those who persecute you; bless and do not curse. Rejoice with those who rejoice; mourn with those who mourn. Live in harmony with one another. Do not be proud but be willing to associate with people of low position. Do not be conceited.
>
> Do not repay anyone evil for evil. Be careful to do what is right in the eyes of everyone. If it is possible, as far as it depends on you, live at peace with everyone. Do not take revenge, my dear friends, but leave room for God's wrath, for it is written: "It is mine to avenge; I will repay," says the Lord. On the contrary:
>
> "If your enemy is hungry, feed him; if he is thirsty, give him something to drink. In doing this, you will heap burning coals

> on his head." Do not be overcome by evil but overcome evil with good. (Rom 12:9–21)

You have just read a Scripture passage that provides you with a road map for "the way." It details for you what divine love is and how you can harness and spread this love to promote healing and harmony within yourself and others. Before Saint Paul instructs you on divine love, he describes it to you as being sincere. To me, this means that divine love comes from the innermost core of your soul—the deepest and purest place in your being. The place of clarity and truth. Your "spirit" and not your "flesh." Are you familiar with this "white light" (John 8:12) within you? Have you taken time in your life to find this portal? If you answered no to these two questions, then you must take inventory from within to mentally and spiritually prepare yourself for this expedition into your soul. You will need to frequently visit and explore your "white light" (John 9:5) from within to walk through the "narrow gate" (Matt 7:13–14) onto "the way" (John 14:6).

After Saint Paul describes to you what divine love is, he instructs you on what divine love looks like by providing you daily living examples:

- Be devoted to one another in love.
- Honor one another above yourselves.
- Serve the LORD.
- Be joyful in hope, patient in affliction, and faithful in prayer.
- Share with the LORD's people who are in need.
- Practice hospitality.
- Bless those who persecute you.
- Rejoice with those who rejoice.
- Mourn with those who mourn.
- Live in harmony with one another.
- Do not be proud. Do not be conceited.
- Be willing to associate with people of low position.
- Do not repay anyone evil for evil.
- Do what is right in the eyes of everyone.
- Live at peace with everyone.

- Do not take revenge.
- If your enemy is hungry, feed him; if he is thirsty, give him something to drink.
- Overcome evil with good.

I wish I could comment on each one of these Christlike actions, but if I did, this book would be too big to fit on your bookshelf and/or too heavy for you to carry around everywhere you go. Better yet, I think it would be a great idea for you to stop reading and take the appropriate amount of time to review and reflect upon this Scripture from Saint Paul and the list that I generated above. Make each Christlike action in the list into a closed question (yes or no) by inserting "Am I" or "Do I" at the beginning. Once you answer each question, go back and change the format to an open-ended question by asking, "Why did I answer yes or no?" for each action in the list. This exercise will get you moving toward your inner soul in preparation for traveling on "the way."

Let no debt remain outstanding, except the continuing debt to love one another, for whoever loves others has fulfilled the law.
—Rom 13:8

GIVE TO AND SERVE OTHERS

There are many roads along "the way." The Lord tells us that all of them are narrow and winding. In this chapter, you have learned that all these roads are created through divine love. In the last section we discussed roads along "the Way" named after kindness. In this section we will discuss other roads named after service. When the Lord blesses you with his divine love, he relies on Isaac Newton's third law of motion, which states that "for every action there is an equal and opposite reaction."[7] In other words, *action* equals the Lord providing you with his divinity. *Reaction* equals you experiencing his love, compassion, forgiveness, and healing and passing on these gifts to others through kindness and service! This is a perfect analogy because God's action produces an equal and opposite reaction in you. His divine love fills you and frees you from the shackles of your flesh, which in turn allows the "white light" of your soul to radiate throughout your body to help you with your healing process. Also, his

7. Newton, *Mathematical Principles*, 3.

divine love will reduce the impulses of your id and kick start your super ego to share the LORD's love through action (devotion and service). This, my friend, is an example of religion and science working together—a bond between the Spirit and physics!

> *But when you give a banquet, invite the poor, the crippled, the lame, the blind, and you will be blessed. Although they cannot repay you, you will be repaid at the resurrection of the righteous.*
> —*Luke 14:13–14*

Any act of genuine love you do for another will echo into eternity. Let me repeat that: any act of genuine love you do for another will echo into eternity! Divine love changes perspectives, circumstances, and most importantly lives. With divine love in your heart and labor on your mind, you will experience heaven on earth for yourself and all those you encounter. Through your words and actions, momentous miracles will occur for you and others daily (John 14:12–14). You may be saying to yourself at this moment, "How can I help others when I cannot help myself?" Unfortunately, your human condition enslaves you to your flesh. It causes you to understand through seeing and not believing (John 20:24–29). It forces you to seek for yourself instead of others. It demands insurances before any type of movement. The Spirit, however, is rooted in faith, hope, and love. It is independent and free from doubt and constraint. It is beyond human thought and reproach (Isa 55:8–9).

Once you surrender to divine love, it will drive you to respond to those around you that are in genuine need of your love. Once the radiant light of God shines through your eyes, it will be easy to identify those in need of your love. Perhaps one of them may be in your immediate family. One may be a friend. One may live in your neighborhood. One may attend your school, or one may be a random person that God has placed into your life. Through God's grace, he will lead you to them. Once you identify them, what should you do? Allow God to guide your thoughts and actions. Maybe God's task for you is to listen, console, consult, support, facilitate, appreciate, donate, volunteer, teach, etc. Don't allow your flesh to infiltrate your "Light" and cast shadows onto your service to others. React to the gift of divine love and leave the results to God!

I would be remiss if I did not share the following two Gospel passages with you concerning service. These will be powerful reminders to you that kindness and service toward others is the fundamental character of Jesus Christ and his followers. Hopefully they will have a profound effect upon you when it comes to the power of divine love. The first selection is taken from Luke 10:25–37. This passage is titled the parable of the good Samaritan.

> *On one occasion an expert in the law stood up to test Jesus. "Teacher," he asked, "what must I do to inherit eternal life?" "What is written in the Law?" he replied. "How do you read it?" He answered, "'Love the Lord your God with all your heart and with all your soul and with all your strength and with all your mind'; and 'Love your neighbor as yourself.'" "You have answered correctly," Jesus replied. "Do this and you will live." But he wanted to justify himself, so he asked Jesus, "And who is my neighbor?"*
>
> *In reply Jesus said: "A man was going down from Jerusalem to Jericho, when he was attacked by robbers. They stripped him of his clothes, beat him, and went away, leaving him half dead. A priest happened to be going down the same road, and when he saw the man, he passed by on the other side. So too, a Levite, when he came to the place and saw him, passed by on the other side. But a Samaritan, as he traveled, came where the man was; and when he saw him, he took pity on him. He went to him and bandaged his wounds, pouring on oil and wine. Then he put the man on his own donkey, brought him to an inn, and took care of him. The next day he took out two denarii and gave them to the innkeeper. 'Look after him,' he said, 'and when I return, I will reimburse you for any extra expense you may have.'*
>
> *"Which of these three do you think was a neighbor to the man who fell into the hands of robbers?" The expert in the law replied, "The one who had mercy on him." Jesus told him, "Go and do likewise."*

What must you do to inherit eternal life?

What is written in the Bible about inheriting eternal life?

More importantly, how do you interpret it?

How is it possible to be able to correctly recite the greatest commandments in the Bible and still not have them "installed" in your life?

What is your definition of "neighbor"?

Have you ever been a robber in your life—robbing a person or a group of people of their dignity, pride, justice, mercy, or faithfulness?

Have you ever experienced a "neighbor" in need and removed yourself from their situation by "passing them on the other side of the road"?

Have you ever tried to justify a less-than-Christian attitude or action? Why do you constantly try to justify your actions? What motivates justifying yourself?

What does the parable of the good Samaritan teach you about love? About mercy? About selfishness?

How many times has the LORD shown mercy to you in your life?

If the LORD has shown mercy to you, then why haven't you shown mercy to others?

How are you to emulate the good Samaritan by "doing likewise"?

What is God speaking to you from this passage?

The second Gospel passage I would like to share with you is taken from John 13:1–15. This passage is titled "Jesus Washes His Disciples Feet" in the NIV.

> It was just before the Passover Festival. Jesus knew that the hour had come for him to leave this world and go to the Father. Having loved his own who were in the world, he loved them to the end.
>
> The evening meal was in progress, and the devil had already prompted Judas, the son of Simon Iscariot, to betray Jesus. Jesus knew that the Father had put all things under his power, and that he had come from God and was returning to God; so, he got up from the meal, took off his outer clothing, and wrapped a towel around his waist. After that, he poured water into a basin and began to wash his disciples' feet, drying them with the towel that was wrapped around him.
>
> He came to Simon Peter, who said to him, "Lord, are you going to wash my feet?"
>
> Jesus replied, "You do not realize now what I am doing, but later you will understand."
>
> "No," said Peter, "you shall never wash my feet."
>
> Jesus answered, "Unless I wash you, you have no part with me."
>
> "Then, Lord," Simon Peter replied, "not just my feet but my hands and my head as well!"

> Jesus answered, "Those who have had a bath need only to wash their feet; their whole body is clean. And you are clean, though not every one of you." For he knew who was going to betray him, and that was why he said not everyone was clean.
>
> When he had finished washing their feet, he put on his clothes and returned to his place. "Do you understand what I have done for you?" he asked them. "You call me 'Teacher' and 'Lord,' and rightly so, for that is what I am. Now that I, your Lord, and Teacher, have washed your feet, you also should wash one another's feet. I have set you an example that you should do as I have done for you."

Jesus loved his own "to the end," without limits. Where do you place limits on your love of others?

How would you feel if you saw Jesus rise from the table and approach you, kneel before you, and prepare to wash your feet?

Would you allow him to wash your feet, just as they are?

Would you be moved, perhaps to tears, by what he does?

Do you have the courage to accept his humble service and unconditional love?

What are you called to do in your life circumstances?

How can you bear witness to a servant God in your life today?

Jesus washes Judas's feet. Knowing that Judas is shortly going to betray him, Jesus still washes his feet. After reading this, is there anyone whom you can justifiably not love or serve?

Will your acts of service be for the good of the world and for the glory of God?

Through this Gospel passage, Jesus explains that he himself lives out a life of loving and humble service and that he wants you to copy what he has done for you. Ask him to show you, day by day, whose needs he wants you to meet. He promises to be with you until the end of time (Matt 28:20), especially when you love and serve others. By receiving his divine love and acting upon it, you will find meaning in this life and the afterlife!

This is my command: Love each other.
—John 15:17

LOVE THE LORD

One day, if it is God's plan, you will meet someone very special, fall in love, and partake in the sacrament of marriage. This unity, blessed in heaven, will take the both of you and make you *one* in the eyes of the LORD. You and your spouse will probably discuss and prepare to reproduce children to further solidify God's plan of "producing fruit" for his kingdom. God willing, he will bless you with multiple children and fill your household and life with cherished memories. You and your spouse will sacrifice everything that you have to provide each of your children with every opportunity life has to offer them. You will protect them, teach them, and serve them so that all their dreams will come true. In return, you will see the fruits of your labor. Your family vine will increase with each year that passes. You will experience a loving and supportive marriage. Your children will grow to be God-fearing, productive citizens and one day provide you and your spouse with the greatest gift that life can offer—being grandparents! If God provided you with this life, would you agree to it?

Let me provide another scenario for you to contemplate. What if God gave you the opportunity to be all-powerful, wise, successful, and richer than any other in the universe? Would there be any reason for you to want to get married? Let's say the only reason that you wanted to get married is to have a son in order to pass everything that you have accomplished in your life on to him. However, let's say that your child would experience heartache and pain each day of his life. That he would be perceived as an "outcast." That he would be ridiculed and mocked for his beliefs and way of life. That he would have his reputation smeared and must escape continuous death threats. That he would be disowned by his family and betrayed by his friends. That he would be accused of false crimes and be put on trial for his life. That he would be found guilty by a bloodthirsty mob. That he would be humiliated, spat upon, scourged, and nailed to a tree. That he would be abandoned by all in his hour of need and die a violent death at the young age of thirty-three. Would you be willing to have this child, or would you be satisfied with your powerful, wise, successful, rich life?

> For God so loved the world that he gave his one and only Son, that whoever believes in him shall not perish but have eternal life. (John 3:16)

Your flesh yearns for good over bad, reward over punishment, victory over defeat, joy over pain, sun over rain, harmony over stress, and life over death! Your flesh moves you along the path of least resistance. It manipulates your moral compass to always point to "me first." Because of this human condition, you are self-serving and always want what is best for *you*. When viewing life events (past, present, future) through this lens, it is easy for you to pick the first scenario presented above because you want to live a fairy-tale life. Or in the second scenario, you would choose to be an individual (without a spouse and child who would suffer) that is powerful, wise, successful, and rich. Do you want a life of isolation, disappointment, strife, failure, regret, and unfulfilled dreams? Of course you don't!

The biggest difference between you and God is that you live by the creed "me first" while he lives by the creed "you first." God believes that "we > me." He is the definition of unconditional love. How great is his love for you? Greater than the highest mountain, deeper than the deepest ocean, and wider than the widest sea. He loves you so much that he "made himself nothing by taking the very nature of a servant, being made in human likeness. And being found in appearance as a man, he humbled himself by becoming obedient to death—even death on a cross!" (Phil 2:7–8). If you haven't guessed by now, the individual in the second scenario is God, and the child is the Son of God, Jesus Christ. God, the Creator of the universe, the Alpha and the Omega, the Almighty, sacrificed his only Son so that you can live a life void of sin and full of faith, hope, and love. This is the quintessential act of divine love. The LORD loves you unconditionally, and there is nothing that you can do about it!

Love is the adhesive bond that holds a relationship together. To appreciate the good times and persevere in the bad times, unconditional love is needed in equal doses from each participant. Whether you know it or not, your Heavenly Father has a paternal relationship with you. He proves his unconditional love for you every moment of your life. Each day he speaks to you and tells you, "Never will I leave you; never will I forsake you" (Heb 13:5). The question is, are you providing him with an equal dose of unconditional love?

WHAT IS YOUR RELATIONSHIP WITH THE LORD?

1. I do not know the LORD.
2. I know about the LORD, but I don't follow him.
3. I follow the LORD but need to know how to mature in it.
4. I want to follow the LORD, and I am pursuing him.
5. I am willing to make sacrifices to help others follow the LORD.

What number do you find yourself on?

What number would you like to be on?

What number do you think the LORD wants you to be on?

When placing yourself on this scale, you essentially are measuring the amount of unconditional love that you have for the LORD. Please keep in mind, this tool is a beginning point and not an ending point. You have every moment, minute, hour, day, week, month, and year to grow in your love for the LORD. Regardless of where you placed yourself on this scale, the LORD reminds you to "be strong and courageous. Do not be afraid or terrified, for the LORD your God goes with you; he will never leave you nor forsake you" (Deut 31:6). I am hoping that your goal and the LORD's goal are one and the same—that is, for you to live and act on the fifth point in this scale.

To help you grow in your unconditional love for the LORD, I would like to prove to you how much God loves you and what he has done for you (and will continue to do for you) in your life. Below is a reflection tool that I like to call a "Gratitude List." It is my hope that you will complete this exercise at least twice a year. It will provide you an opportunity to look through the lens of the "spirit" instead of the lens of the flesh. This exercise will take some time and reflection but will provide you with the perspective of the LORD's love and dedication that he has for you. There are two columns listed below. The first asks you to list all the problems that you are experiencing in your present condition. The second column asks you to list all the things that you are grateful for (that the LORD has provided you) in your life. Take as much time as you need to make an exhaustive list for each column.

Gratitude List

Problems that I am currently experiencing	*Things that I am grateful for*

Which list is longer?

The second column should *always* be longer than the first column!

Your gratitude should *always* outweigh your sufferings!

The "spirit" will *always* overcome the "flesh"!

Maybe in your current state of mind, your first column is longer than your second column. Don't panic! The LORD tells you, "For I know the plans I have for you, plans to prosper you and not to harm you, plans to give you hope and a future" (Jer 29:11). If your first column is longer than your second column, take a moment and ask yourself why. Could it be that when you participated in the "What Is Your Relationship with the LORD?" scale, you placed yourself within the first or second description? If so, the LORD understands. You see, he was in the garden of Eden when the serpent tempted and tricked Eve to eat the apple from the tree of knowledge. He was in the garden of Eden when Adam and Eve's eyes were opened and they realized they were naked and therefore hid from him. You and Jesus have a lot in common. You both are familiar with anxiety, depression, and temptation. You both have experience living in the flesh. Jesus Christ has walked the road that you are currently traveling. He understands the human condition that you are struggling with. He was introduced to it, suffered from it, but more importantly overcame it. He promises you that you will do the same if only you will love him unconditionally.

How do you go about loving the LORD unconditionally? How do you uncover the treasure (Matt 13:44) that he has for you? I will attempt to answer these questions in the final portion of this chapter!

> One of the teachers of the law came and heard them debating. Noticing that Jesus had given them a good answer, he asked him, "Of all the commandments, which is the most important?"
>
> "The most important one," answered Jesus, "is this: 'Hear, O Israel: The Lord our God, the Lord is one. Love the Lord your God with all your heart and with all your soul and with all your mind and with all your strength.'" (Mark 12:28–30)

LOVE THE LORD YOUR GOD WITH ALL YOUR HEART

Your relationship with the LORD will change when your heart changes. The straightest path to the LORD is through your heart. Loving the LORD unconditionally begins with spiritual surrender. Spiritual surrender means completely trusting in the LORD. This occurs by completely turning your life over to him—conforming your entire existence toward his love. Though this may seem impossible, it is not complicated to do. You simply must dedicate yourself to these four words: thy will be done. These words should sound familiar to you, for they come from the Lord's Prayer (Matt 6:9–13). Hopefully you say these words daily when you give God yours prayers and thanksgiving. Are these just words that you say as part of the Lord's Prayer, or do you know the meaning behind them?

"Thy will be done" is the third of the seven petitions in the Lord's Prayer (the first three address God, the second four are prayers related to your needs and concerns). The third request is that God's will occurs. By stating this, you are aligning your will with God's will, you are submitting yourself to him and asking that his way triumphs. Praying these words and believing in them are the first two steps toward unconditional love for the LORD. When you allow the Spirit of the LORD to enter your heart, he will bring to you the knowledge and understanding of the kingdom of heaven. This divine knowledge and understanding will help you find and unlock the treasures that the LORD has secured for you in your life. Allow me to remind you one more time, the flesh is in direct opposition to "thy will be done." Satan and the fallen world that you live in would much rather have you live by "*my* will be done." However, with your heart full of the LORD's grace, you will not be tempted or tricked by the serpent to disobey the LORD, thus giving you the keys to unlock the gates of heaven.

> You will seek me and find me when you seek me with all your heart. (Jer 29:13)

LOVE THE LORD YOUR GOD WITH ALL YOUR SOUL

Have you ever contemplated how you were created? Have you ever thought about why you were created? Let's tackle the less complicated of the two questions by first looking at how you were created. The answer to the first question can be found in Gen 2:7: "Then the LORD God formed a man from the dust of the ground and breathed into his nostrils the breath of life, and the man became a living being." Yes, the LORD God formed you and breathed life into you. We are all formed through the image of God (Gen 1:27). Have you ever seen God? Look at yourself in the mirror, and you will see him. Look at your family and friends; you will see him. Look at a stranger; you will see him. How have you been treating God? Let me try to make this question a little easier to answer. How have you been treating yourself? How have you been treating your family and friends? How have you been treating strangers that you meet daily? The answers that you provided for the three questions above are one and the same to the first question I asked you: How have you been treating God?

> Then the righteous will answer him, "Lord, when did we see you hungry and feed you, or thirsty and give you something to drink? When did we see you a stranger and invite you in, or needing clothes and clothe you? When did we see you sick or in prison and go to visit you?"
>
> The King will reply, "Truly I tell you, whatever you did for one of the least of these brothers and sisters of mine, you did for me." (Matt 25:37–40)

Whether you know if or not, the LORD has been with you even before you were conceived in your mother's womb (Jer 1:5). Therefore, a logical question to ask after hearing this revelation is, "Well where is he?" In our human condition (the flesh) we breathe through our lungs to sustain our life on earth. However, Gen 2:7 tells you that the first breath to enter your earthly vessel was created by the LORD. This means that the LORD's breath is still within you. You have an opportunity to be refreshed by his breath by visiting your soul. The LORD uses your soul (not your lungs) to help sustain your spiritual life. His breath shapes and reshapes you each time you visit your soul. It provides you with a joy that you will not be able to contain. You will need to share his breath with others because it provides eternal life with a guarantee to be raised up on your last earthly day into his kingdom.

The second question, why were you created, is a bit more complicated to explain. This question is more perplexing because only you and God know the answer. See, God has a plan for us all. Unfortunately, he does not unveil it to us when we enter kindergarten. As a matter of fact, it may seem like his plan for you is always under construction and ever-changing. However, the Lord is omnipotent and never makes mistakes and therefore doesn't need to update his plan for you! Journeying inward into your soul will help you take inventory on the past and present steps of God's plan for you. Events that you experienced in the past may make sense to you in the present. The pain and suffering you are experiencing in the present with your anxiety and/or depression may be necessary for you to cross the bridges of tomorrow. Basking in the radiant "Light" of your soul will prevent you from getting frustrated and worried about where you are today. Yesterday brought you to today, and today will get you to tomorrow. The secret to God's plan is for you to live it one day at a time—to be fully engaged and productive in the opportunities that the Lord has blessed you with in the last twenty-four hours. Finally, please realize that the Lord's plan for you will be fully revealed when he shows you the place that he has made for you in his Father's house (John 14:2–3).

Truly my soul finds rest in God;
my salvation comes from him.
(Ps 62:1)

LOVE THE LORD YOUR GOD WITH ALL YOUR MIND

The brain is the most complex object in the known universe. With its one hundred billion neutrons, it can solve mankind's mysteries as well as cause affliction from mental illness. When you ask the leading neuroscientists and psychiatrists about the human brain, they will tell you that they know enough about the brain to realize that there is a whole lot that they still do not know about the brain. However, you don't need to study the brain to understand your mind! Do you know the difference between a neuron and an astrocyte? If you do, give yourself a gold star and put it on your brain—by that, I mean your forehead! Most of us don't and we probably never will. However, I bet you can tell me why you would choose ice cream over broccoli, or why your favorite song makes you sing and dance in front of the mirror in your bedroom (or, like me, in the shower)! You can provide me with these answers because you understand your mind.

Unfortunately, when it comes to your mind, you *think* you know, but you don't know! For example, why does your mind force your body to go into a panic attack? Why does your mind tell you to cut yourself? Why does your mind always think of the worst-case scenario? Why does your mind make you feel sad and lonely for no good reason? If you and I knew these answers, then there would be no need for me to write this book and no need for you to read this book. However, there is no guarantee that you will find meaning in everything that you ponder or experience in your life, especially when it comes to your brain and/or mind.

There is only one spirit that puts meaning behind everything found in the universe. That spirit is our Lord (the Father, Son, and Holy Spirit). Jesus Christ fully comprehends your brain and mind because he created it! He knows the capability of the untapped power within you. He has generated this power and has given it especially to you. This power will transform your life if only you have the spiritual will to search for it.

Why does Jesus Christ have an interest in your mind? Because he yearns for you to be single-minded toward him. Single-mindedness in the Lord means to live as he lived, think as he thought, embrace your destiny as he embraced his, and share in his mercy. Can you do this on your own? No, you cannot! But, with the grace from God, he will allow you to tap into the power that he gifted to you, which will enable you to give and receive divine love. Being single-minded toward the Lord will restore you, heal you, and make you whole.

When you request the Light of the World to enter your mind, the darkness will disappear. The cold emptiness that you feel will dissipate into the warmth of the Lord's divine love. This occurs because there are no limits to God's mercy. No matter how deep you are in life's pits, you have not traveled deeper than Jesus Christ has! No matter where your anxiety and/or depression has led you, Jesus Christ has already been there! No matter how much pain and suffering you are currently in, Jesus Christ has suffered more! No matter how confused or frightened you are, Jesus Christ has experienced even more anguish—to the point where he even sweat his own blood (Luke 22:44). Jesus Christ will meet you at whatever depth life has put you in. He will call you by your name, extend his hand, and pull you up into his kingdom.

The contrast between the Light of the World (Jesus Christ) and the "cold, dark, empty world" (Satan) reminds me of the great literature classic *Inferno* by Dante Alighieri. Have you read it? Wait a minute, weren't you required to read it in high school? (Did you read it or watch the movie?) Anyway, Dante's *Inferno* details Dante's journey through the nine circles of hell (Limbo, Lust, Gluttony, Greed, Anger, Heresy, Violence, Fraud, Treachery). The voyage begins during Easter week in the year 1300. The descent through hell started on Good Friday. After meeting the Roman poet Virgil, Dante begins his descent through a baleful world of doleful shades, horrifying tortures, and unending lamentation.

When they reach the ninth circle of hell, it is divided into four rings, according to the seriousness of the sin. All the residents of this circle are frozen in an icy lake. Those who committed more severe sins are deeper within the ice. Each of the four rings is named after an individual who personifies the sin. The deepest ring (the fourth) is named Judecca after Judas Iscariot, the apostle who betrayed Jesus with a kiss. When Virgil and Dante proceed to the lowest depth of hell, they see those who betrayed their benefactors, spending eternity in complete icy submersion.

In the middle of the icy lake is a huge three-headed giant (Lucifer). He is plunged waist-deep into the ice. His body pierces the center of the earth, where he fell when God hurled him down from heaven. Each of Lucifer's mouths chews one of history's three greatest sinners: Judas, the betrayer of Christ, and Cassius and Brutus, the betrayers of Julius Caesar. Virgil leads Dante on a climb down Lucifer's massive form, holding on to his frozen tufts of hair. Eventually, they both reach the river of forgetfulness and travel from there out of hell and back onto earth. They emerge from hell on Easter morning, just before sunrise.

To me what is so interesting about Virgil and Dante's adventure into hell is that the deepest part of hell is made of ice and not flames, like we were all taught. You may ask, "Why ice?" The reason for the ice is the absence of "Light." The deepest part of hell is the furthest you can be from the Light of the World, and therefore it is exactly what Virgil and Dante experienced: frozen darkness! When Virgil and Dante climb down Lucifer's massive form to reach the river of forgetfulness, Satan does not even notice them because he is living in the epitome of the flesh: self-absorption.[8]

God's divine love is like the sun that shines on the good and the bad. He has enough for everyone. The question is, how will you respond

8. Alighieri, *Inferno of Dante*, 25.

to God's divine love? Will you freely accept it and allow it to enter your mind to free you from the chains of sin? Or will you resist it and believe that your flesh is stronger and smarter than your spirit to navigate between heaven and hell?

God's divine love is eternal! God's divine love is absolute! God's divine love is free!

What will you do with God's divine love?

We take captive every thought to make it obedient to Christ.
(2 Cor 10:5)

LOVE THE LORD YOUR GOD WITH ALL YOUR STRENGTH

The LORD loves you unconditionally! He wants you to know that he is your loyal friend and that you can always count on him. However, a loving relationship is reciprocal. It is based on mutual love, trust, and respect. The LORD wants you to be a part of his loving family. The LORD is ready to call you his son or daughter. For this to occur, he wants and needs your constant and continuous allegiance!

Do you believe that God the Almighty, the Creator of heaven and earth, needs loving, loyal friends? Of course, he does! He is like you in every way except sin. Because of this, he (like you) yearns for meaningful companionship. Do your mental afflictions sometimes make you anxious, nervous, sad, lonely, frustrated, depressed, angry, annoyed, discouraged, and apathetic? I bet they do! Jesus' mental and spiritual afflictions also made him anxious, nervous, sad, lonely, frustrated, depressed, angry, annoyed, discouraged, and apathetic. The best way that I can explain this to you is to paraphrase Luke 9:51–58 when Jesus experienced Samaritan opposition. This Scripture passage explains that as the time approached for Jesus to accomplish his earthly mission, he resolutely set out for Jerusalem where he would be crucified. He sent messengers on ahead who went into a Samaritan village to get things ready for him to stay and rest because of the long journey that he was embarking on. But when Jesus arrived, the people of the town did not welcome him. So, he and his disciples had to venture on to another village. As they were walking along the road to the next town that would accept him, a man said to him, "I will follow you wherever you go." Jesus replied, "Foxes have dens and birds have nests, but the Son of Man has no place to lay his head" (Matt 8:19–20).

Jesus desperately needed love, support, friendship, and companionship as he marched to his earthly death. But as Luke reports to us, he could not find a loyal friend when he needed one the most. He was rejected and dismissed. He was abandoned by all and had to experience his pain and suffering in isolation. Does this Scripture passage resonate with you? Have your mental afflictions placed you into a situation similar to what Jesus was in as he entered the Samaritan town? Has your anxiety and/or depression caused you to be rejected and dismissed? Are you experiencing pain and suffering in isolation? Jesus Christ wants you to know that you are not alone. He is your loyal friend. He will never reject you or dismiss you. He will never abandon you. In your darkest moments, he will provide you with light in the form of love, support, friendship, and companionship.

The Lord is with me; I will not be afraid.
What can mere mortals do to me?
The Lord is with me; he is my helper.
I look in triumph on my enemies.
It is better to take refuge in the Lord
than to trust in humans.
—Ps 118:6–8

How strong is your love for the Lord?

Do you consider yourself a loyal friend of his?

Does he call you "my son" or "my daughter"?

Do you follow his commandments and observe them?

Do you exist at the service of the Lord?

Or . . .

Is the Lord in your life at your convenience (when you need him)?

Loving relationships are fluid because they are constantly growing. They need energy and attention to blossom. The Lord will provide the light for your loving relationship to grow with him. You just need to be willing to find his breath in your soul. As mentioned earlier in the chapter, finding this is easier said than done. For example, let's take a closer look at the first five questions I asked you above. If you are being truthful with yourself, I'm sure you struggled answering them. As a matter of fact, I am willing to say that these questions made you feel uneasy. The reason for the uneasiness is that these questions drove right through your flesh and pierced your soul. They forced your mind to listen to your spirit. Once this occurred, you were caught in the middle of a game of tug-of-war between your flesh and spirit. As always, the spirit defeated the flesh, and you were left with a sense of guilt and regret because you knew the correct answers but have not yet acted upon them. But again, don't beat yourself up too much because the LORD understands the human condition—because he lived it!

I'm sure the last question was a bit easier to answer since it can be answered by the flesh and not the spirit. We all believe in God and call upon him when we need him. This play is taken out of the human playbook and is called being egotistical! However, we need to be very careful when calling this play because Jesus tells us in Matt 7:21, "Not everyone who says to me, 'Lord, Lord,' will enter the kingdom of heaven, but only the one who does the will of my Father who is in heaven."

This brings me to the completion of the Scripture passage that I started a few paragraphs ago about the Samaritan opposition to Jesus in Luke 9. After the people of the town rejected and dismissed Jesus, he was back on the road trying to find a place to stay and rest. According to Luke 9:59–62, "Jesus said to a man on the road, 'Follow me.' But he replied, 'Lord, first let me go and bury my father.' Jesus said to him, 'Let the dead bury their own dead, but you go and proclaim the kingdom of God.' Still another said, 'I will follow you, Lord; but first let me go back and say goodbye to my family.' Jesus replied, 'No one who puts a hand to the plow and looks back is fit for service in the kingdom of God.'"

This Gospel passage fits perfectly with the question that I asked you earlier: Is the LORD in your life at your convenience (when you need him)? From verse 58 to 62 Jesus tells his disciples, "Follow me." Then he waits for each of them to respond. The first man responds to Jesus by telling him, "First let me go bury my father." The man's answer was not pleasing to the LORD. Why? Because this man wanted to be a convenient follower. Convenient followers are not followers at all because they will only accompany Jesus when it is convenient for their schedules. Jesus challenged him to set his priorities in place.

Another disciple also answered Jesus' call to follow him. He said, "I will follow You, Lord; but first permit me to say good-bye to those at home." Jesus did not accept his response either. It appears (from Jesus' response to him) that he was also suffering from being a convenient disciple. Notice how he also said, "But first let me . . ." he was making bargains with the LORD. He understood what Jesus told him but wanted to tell the LORD what he wanted to do first. The problem is that this man was really looking for an excuse not to follow. He wanted to keep his options open and not be tied down with sacrifice and commitment. He undoubtedly liked Jesus, but he liked his freedom too. He is the distracted disciple who gets excited and devoted for a while, and then you do not see him for a while. He is off involved in some other matter.

How do you personally respond to Jesus' command, "Follow me"?

Do you tend to make bargains with the LORD?

Are you a convenient disciple or a loving devoted disciple? Do you *tell* the LORD, "I have this to do today, but tomorrow I can help you." Or do you *obey* the LORD by saying, "Thy will be done"? Loving relationships are reciprocal. They are based on mutual love, trust, and respect. They take absolute commitment. Jesus wants and needs you to be his loving, devoted disciple. He wants you to stay focused. He wants you to be committed. He wants your priorities in the right order. He wants you to sign a lifetime contract with him. The terms of the contract are simple: the more you give, the more you will receive. Jesus is on the same road that you are on. He is telling you, "Follow me!" He is waiting for your response.

As the Father has loved me, so have I loved you.
Now remain in my love.
—John 15:9

SEVENTH STATION: JESUS BEARS THE CROSS

> Then Jesus said to his disciples, "Whoever wants to be my disciple must deny themselves and take up their cross and follow me. For whoever wants to save their life will lose it, but whoever loses their life for me will find it." (Matt 16:24–25)

We adore you, O Christ, and we bless you.

Because by your holy cross you have redeemed the world.

> As soon as the chief priests and their officials saw him, they shouted, "Crucify! Crucify!"
>
> But Pilate answered, "You take him and crucify him. As for me, I find no basis for a charge against him." . . .
>
> But they shouted, "Take him away! Take him away! Crucify him!"
>
> "Shall I crucify your king?" Pilate asked.
>
> "We have no king but Caesar," the chief priests answered. Finally Pilate handed him over to them to be crucified. So the soldiers took charge of Jesus. Carrying his own cross, he went out to the place of the Skull (which in Aramaic is called Golgotha). (John 19:6, 15–17)

Lord, grant us strength of purpose that we may faithfully bear our crosses each day.

SEVENTH STATION: REFLECTIVE EXERCISES AND QUESTIONS

I wish I could tell you that I am smart enough and clever enough to have constructed this book to insert the seventh station after the chapter on love. However, I cannot take credit for this because I believe the Holy

Spirit is working through me so that the LORD can have a conversation with you! At this point in the book, I am hoping that the LORD's voice is growing in clarity and volume for you. Chapter 5 focused on loving yourself, loving others, and loving the LORD. Hopefully this information delivered insight to you about what it means to be a loving, devoted disciple of Jesus Christ. There can be no greater or clearer teaching anywhere in the Bible that crystallizes the meaning of discipleship than that in Matt 16:24–25. This introductory Scripture passage to the seventh station depicts how the LORD lived and how his disciples must live. It reinforces the divine love that Jesus has for you and what you must do to return your love back to him.

When Jesus took up his cross, he was carrying more than wood. Unknown to the many spectators that day, Jesus was carrying the sins of mankind. He willingly faced the punishment those sins deserved by literally and figuratively carrying them on his back. After reading Matt 16:24–25, it becomes very evident what "Follow me" really means. Jesus' statement in this Scripture passage isn't a casual invitation but a demanding expectation that requires you to surrender every fiber of your being to the Father, just like he did. Those who accept his invitation, he said, would have to bear their own cross. Thus, you don't "piggyback" off his cross, but you learn from him how to bear your own personal challenges as you follow in his steps.

How will you respond to this invitation while currently facing many challenges in your life?

For every question that you may have about your life, the answer can be found in the Bible. There is no exception to this rule! Because of this, the LORD, through Scripture, can help you with the last question I asked you above. In Luke 14:28 the LORD states, "Suppose one of you wants to build a tower. Won't you first sit down and estimate the cost to see if you have enough money to complete it?" How can this Scripture verse help you to respond to the LORD's invitation in Matt 16:24–25? Well, the LORD wants you to sit down and consider what it will cost you to become a loving, devoted disciple (a tower for the LORD). He wants you to figure out what old habits (foundations) need to be dug up and discarded. He wants you to discover his ways and make them the new foundation of your life. Finally, he wants you to realize that being a loving, devoted disciple means laying stones of mercy and kindness for God, yourself, and others daily. As I remind you (like, all the time!) be aware and consider what oppositions the fallen world, the flesh, and Satan has in store for you while you transition into becoming a tower for the LORD.

The following exercise will help you "estimate the costs" while preparing to accept the LORD's invitation to deny yourself, take up your cross, and follow him. There are three columns within this reflective exercise. The first asks you to list the old habits (foundations) you are willing to dig up and discard for the LORD. The second column asks you to list the ways of the LORD that you are willing to adopt to create a new foundation for your life. The final column asks you how the fallen world, the flesh, and Satan will try to stop you from successfully transitioning into a loving, devoted disciple of Jesus Christ. As I always tell you when completing these activities, take as much time as you need to exhaust all your thoughts into each one of these columns. The more detailed each column is, the closer you are to accepting the invitation the LORD has sent you.

Estimate the Costs		
Old Habits Willing to Discard	New Foundations in My Life	Opposition to Discipleship

EIGHTH STATION: JESUS IS HELPED BY SIMON THE CYRENIAN TO CARRY THE CROSS

> Carry each other's burdens, and in this way you will fulfill the law of Christ. (Gal 6:2)

We adore you, O Christ, and we bless you.

Because by your holy cross you have redeemed the world.

> A certain man from Cyrene, Simon, the father of Alexander and Rufus, was passing by on his way in from the country, and they forced him to carry the cross. (Mark 15:21)

Lord, grant us willing spirits that we may be your instruments on earth.

EIGHTH STATION: REFLECTIVE EXERCISES AND QUESTIONS

The Gospel of Mark does not provide us with much detail about this event. As a matter of fact, Saint Mark only uses one verse to report it. But we may conclude that Jesus had fallen under the weight. He seemed unable to bear the cross any further. Perhaps he had fainted from the loss of blood and from the long fasting. He sank on the pavement and could bear the wood no longer. Something like this must have occurred, or the centurion would not have halted the convoy and ordered that the cross be transferred to someone else. This was not done out of compassion but out of necessity. Jesus could not bear it any further; therefore, in order that the place of execution might be quickly reached, someone else had to be assigned to carry the cross. No Roman would carry the cross. To do so would dishonor him. The soldiers needed to assign this job to someone else. Enter Simon the Cyrenian! Who was this man? Most biblical scholars believe he was an African from Libya. Why was he in Jerusalem on that day? No one will ever know; however, some speculate that he was a pagan who had turned up quite unwittingly in Jerusalem to discover that the city was packed with hundreds of thousands of men and women to attend a feast called the Passover. While enjoying the festivities, he came across a grim procession of three condemned men going to their deaths.

Have you ever been a bystander, like Simon, and witnessed an event that put a person or people into a precarious situation?

How did you react while viewing this event?

If this was the case, then Simon was a man on vacation in Jerusalem, a sightseer, a bystander, not wanting to get involved, not wanting to be pressurized about religion and Jesus. "Back off! This is a private debate.

I don't want to get involved; I want to enjoy myself," he might have been thinking, and then suddenly a Roman legionnaire comes right up to him and says, "Pick up that cross and come along with us." That's the command, and Simon has no time to debate the issue. Before he knows it, everybody in Jerusalem is looking at him, following this beaten-up, unsteady man surrounded by four soldiers. Simon is ashamed, embarrassed, and resentful. He is annoyed with the soldier for seizing him and angry with the prisoner for not shouldering his own burden. "I was in the wrong place at the wrong time," he might have imagined himself saying to his friends later as he described to them the events of that day. However, Simon would soon realize that things were not as they first appeared.

Have you ever experienced an incident where you felt that you were in the wrong place at the wrong time?

What kind of emotions did you feel throughout this incident?

What a day it was for Simon. If he had been on his way in from the country an hour later, he would have missed it all. If he had walked a little faster or a little slower or taken another gate into the city, he'd have seen nothing. If he'd pressed back into a doorway, the Roman legionnaire wouldn't have spotted him. But none of that happened. It was in God's providence that he was there at that place and at that time. Simon was known, loved, and chosen by God before the foundation of the world. God focused the soldier's eyes on Simon, not because he was in the wrong place at the wrong time but because God's grace was placed upon him. God was determined to save Simon by bringing him and Jesus together.

How do you know that you are currently in the right place and the right time?

Jesus was pleased that Simon came to his aid because he needed his help to fulfill his earthly destiny. He also wanted Simon's help to remind you that you must also enter a fellowship of his sufferings, take up your personal cross when he requires you, endure provocations, be patient under affliction, love those that hate you, abstain from the temptations of the flesh, and seek to bring comfort to others. These are the lessons to glean from the eighth station.

Do you feel the weight of the personal crosses that you are currently carrying on your back?

Would you like a "Simon" to come along and take some of the burden off you?

Close your eyes for a moment and picture the scene from the eighth station: Jesus on one side of the cross and Simon on the other. This signifies that no one ever needs to carry a whole cross alone (not even Jesus Christ). The Father will place a person or people in your life to carry one end of the pain and suffering you feel due to your anxiety and/or depression. He will ask you to carry the other end to help you come closer to him. Finally, he will come and take hold of the middle of the cross. Once you accept his will and enter his light, your spirit will free you from your flesh, and you will be able to deliver up to him the crosses that you carry. He will bless you, heal you, and remove the weight from you.

The following exercise will help you find the "Simons" in your life. Just like in the last reflective exercise, this one will also provide you with three columns for you to complete. The first column asks you to list all the "wooden beams" that you are currently carrying on your back. This may include thoughts, emotions, mental and/or physical pain, events, people, etc. This list should detail all the trials and tribulations that you experience daily. The second column asks you to list all the people (whether you met them or not) who you feel can help you relieve some of the weight from the wooden beams that you carry. The final column asks you to specifically list how each person in the second column can help you relieve some of the stress and strain you experience daily. I know that you are tired of me reminding you, but please take as much time as you need to complete each column. The more detailed each column is, the closer you are to seeking out the "Simons" that appear on the side of the road that you are traveling on.

Who Are the "Simons" in My Life?		
My "Wooden Beams"	The "Simons" in My Life	Ways "Simons" Can Help Me

Your current thoughts may be like Simon's that fateful day when he entered Jerusalem—"I'm just in the wrong place at the wrong time." You may feel that you don't need a "Simon." That you have it all figured out. That you are strong enough to carry your current burdens on your back. That you just need time and space to figure everything out. There is no shame in asking for help. If God Almighty needed help, so do you. Pray for strength and courage that you will be able to visit each of the "Simons" you listed above and share with them the information that you detailed in each column. Especially the second and third columns, where you entered their name and the things they can do for you to relieve some of the weight from the wooden beams you currently carry. God's plan for you is always the right plan. You are at exactly the right place and the right time to cross paths with him and the "Simons" he has placed in your life. Be willing to carry your one-third of the wooden beam, and trust that he and the "Simons" in your life will be there to carry the other two-thirds for you!

Jesus replied, "Anyone who loves me will obey my teaching. My Father will love them, and we will come to them and make our home with them."

—John 14:23

Part 2 Summary

Consequently, you are no longer foreigners and strangers, but fellow citizens with God's people and also members of his household, built on the foundation of the apostles and prophets, with Christ Jesus himself as the chief cornerstone. In him the whole building is joined together and rises to become a holy temple in the Lord. And in him you too are being built together to become a dwelling in which God lives by his Spirit.

—Eph 2:19–22

Do you remember when I summarized the prologue and part 1 of this book? I used metaphors concerning construction materials and techniques to review all that we discussed. Do you remember assessing the "soil conditions" of your life or deciding where to place your life's "footings"? Well, I would like to continue using these construction metaphors to summarize part 2. This makes total sense to me since you are in the process of rebuilding your life!

Part 2 of this book was aptly entitled "The Cornerstone." The cornerstone, in an architectural sense, is the first stone set in the construction of a masonry foundation. This stone is usually the largest, the most solid, and the most carefully constructed of any other stone in the structure. All other stones are set in reference to this stone, thus determining the position of the entire structure. After completing part 2, you can clearly see that it is my belief that Jesus Christ is the cornerstone of your recovery from anxiety and/or depression!

Through all your attacks, bouts, trials, tribulations, and failures, you will need to rely on your cornerstone (Jesus Christ) to unconditionally love you, support you, bind and heal your wounds, raise you up, and motivate you to fight the good fight and cross the finish line (2 Tim 4:7). Chapters 3, 4, and 5 stressed to you that the Lord wants to be the center of your life above anything else and everyone else (Matt 10:37–38). By accepting him as your cornerstone, the position of the magnificent structure known as "your life" will always point to physical, mental, and emotional productivity.

When someone observes you or interacts with you, they should see, hear, and feel your cornerstone. Your words and actions should narrate a daily story about your total love and devotion to the Lord. Your faith, hope, and love should permeate the darkest circumstances, and your attitude should reflect the kingdom of God. These are the lessons that have been embedded into part 2 of this book.

According to Saint Paul (1 Cor 13:13), these things will last forever:

FAITH

- Do you have faith in the Lord?
- Do you have faith in yourself?
- Do you have faith in others?

HOPE

- Do you anticipate a future event with a confident expectation of its fulfillment?
- Do you have hope in today, tomorrow, next week, next month, and next year?
- Where does your hope come from? How do you fuel it?

LOVE

- Do you have unconditional love for the Lord?
- Do you have unconditional love for yourself?
- Do you have unconditional love for others?

The answers to these questions along with the material covered in chapters 3, 4, and 5 will provide the additional stones needed around the cornerstone to build a spiritual structure dedicated to the LORD and mental wellness!

Before we enter part 3 of this book, I would like to reserve this space to present my disclaimer when it comes to treating adolescents and young adults that suffer from anxiety and/or depression. The last part of the long title of this book is *A Holistic Approach for Treating Adolescents and Young Adults with Anxiety and Depression*. The main reason for writing this book is provide you and your loved ones with a spiritual and natural path to mental wellness. However, let me be clear: I am not opposed to medication for anxiety and depression. In my life's work as a school counselor and a licensed professional counselor, I have met students and clients that have shown improvement and/or been given relief from symptoms created by their anxiety and/or depression using medication. But unfortunately, I've also seen students and clients complicate their mental health issues by taking prescribed medications. Medications can be very effective when targeted properly after a thorough workup, but they can also be a disaster when not used appropriately.

While I am not opposed to medication for anxiety and depression, I am deeply opposed to the indiscriminate use of these medications and the way many physicians and other health care professionals prescribe them, without a comprehensive workup and without clearly telling patients about the potential side effects, poor long-term outcome studies, and alternative treatment options. It is my belief that the rampant use of these medications is hurting your generation (Y and Z).

We are ready to enter the final unit of this book, part 3 ("The Way, the Truth, the Life"). The final four chapters ("Conversion," "Mission," "Resurrection," and "Ascension") will detail holistic approaches that you can practice each day to experience "the Way" without the chains of anxiety and/or depression weighing you down and limiting your productivity. The theme that has been established in the prologue, part 1, and part 2 will continue in part 3. That theme can be best defined in Heb 13:8: "Jesus Christ is the same yesterday and today and forever." This means if you are committed to the spirit and not the flesh, the LORD will honor his promises that he made to you when he created you (Prov 1:33).

> *Do not be anxious about anything, but in every situation, by prayer and petition, with thanksgiving, present your requests to*

God. And the peace of God, which transcends all understanding, will guard your hearts and your minds in Christ Jesus.

Finally, brothers and sisters, whatever is true, whatever is noble, whatever is right, whatever is pure, whatever is lovely, whatever is admirable—if anything is excellent or praiseworthy—think about such things. (Phil *4:6–8)*

Part 3

The Way, the Truth, the Life

]

My feet have closely followed his steps;
I have kept to his way without turning aside.
—*Job 23:11*

Then you will know the truth, and the truth will set you free.
—*John 8:32*

Jesus said to her, "I am the resurrection and the life. The one who believes in me will live, even though they die; and whoever lives by believing in me will never die. Do you believe this?"
—*John 11:25–26*

Part 3 | The Way, the Truth, the Life

Jesus answered, "I am the way and the truth and the life.
No one comes to the Father except through me."
—John 14:6

Chapter 6

Conversion

Those who live according to the flesh have their minds set on what the flesh desires; but those who live in accordance with the Spirit have their minds set on what the Spirit desires. The mind governed by the flesh is death, but the mind governed by the Spirit is life and peace.

—Rom 8:5–6

Long ago, when the world was very new, there was a certain lobster who was determined that the Creator had made a mistake. So, he set up an appointment to discuss the matter.

"With all due respect," said the lobster, "I wish to complain about the way you designed my shell. You see, just as I got used to one outer casing then I must shed it for another. Very inconvenient and rather a waste of time."

To which the Creator replied, "I see. But do you realize that it is the giving up of one shell that allows you to grow into another?" "But I like myself just the way I am," the lobster said. "Your mind's made up?" the Creator asked. "Indeed!" the lobster stated firmly. "Very well," smiled the Creator. "From now on, your shell will not change, and you may go about your business just as you do right now." "That's very kind of you," said the lobster, and left.

At first, the lobster was very content wearing the same old shell. But as time passed, he found that his once light and comfortable shell was becoming quite heavy and tight. After a while, in fact, the shell became so cumbersome that the lobster couldn't feel anything at all outside himself. As a result, he was constantly bumping into others. Finally, it got to the point where he could hardly even breathe. So, with great effort, he went back to see the Creator.

"With all due respect," the lobster sighed, "contrary to what you promised, my shell has not remained the same; it keeps shrinking!" "Not at all," smiled the Creator, "your shell may have gotten a little thicker with age, but it has remained the same size. What happened is that you changed—inside, within your shell."

The Creator continued, "You see, everything changes continuously. No one remains the same. That's the way I've made things." "That's very sensible," said the lobster. "If you like," offered the Creator, "I'll tell you something more." "Please do," encouraged the lobster.

"When you let go of your shell and choose to grow," said the Creator, "you build new strength within yourself. And in that strength, you'll find new capacity to love yourself—to love those around you—to love life itself. This is my plan for each one."[1]

The secret of change is to focus all of your energy, not on fighting the old, but building on the new.

—Attributed to Socrates

Do you relate to the lobster? Are you content with your life? Do you feel that there is no need for change? Or, do you realize that change is necessary for you to conquer your current affliction(s)? Is there a voice from within preaching to you that change is inevitable and necessary? If so, then why are you still living in your current "shell"? The lobster and you (and I) have something in common—we are creatures of habit. This means regardless of our current circumstance, we usually resist change due to its uncertainty.

Take some time to examine your current "shell." Is it becoming heavy and tight? Is it becoming so cumbersome that it's not allowing you to freely move and experience life? Is your current shell hindering you to the point that it is the only thing that occupies your mind? Does your shell dominate and control your emotions and bodily functions? If so, you (like the lobster) must realize that this old shell (infected with anxiety and/or depression) must be shed for a new shell (created by faith, hope, and love)!

1. Martin, "Modern Parable About Change"; reproduced here with permission.

This chapter will uncover a "new" world and a "new" life that is waiting for you (Matt 9:16). To experience this new world and life, you will need to be ready, willing, and able to experience a personal *conversion*. The content in this chapter is designed to open your senses (eyes) to the possibility of total mental wellness. It will lead you to a realization that there is a mansion that has been built just for you (John 14:2–3) inside a gated community made of pearls on a street that has been paved with pure gold (Rev 21:21). There will be no need for the sun in this new dwelling place because there is a "Light" that always shines (Rev 22:4–5) that will provide you with daily nourishment and healing (Rev 22:2). It sounds like a great place! Would you like to know the address? Before you type it into Google Maps, you will need to shed your current shell and experience change.

Amazing grace, how sweet the sound
that saved a wretch like me!
I once was lost, but now am found,
was blind, but now I see.

—John Newton[2]

A MAN NAMED SAUL

> But Saul began to destroy the church. Going from house to house, he dragged off both men and women and put them in prison. (Acts 8:3)

I would like to introduce you to a man named Saul. He was likely born between the years of 5 BC and AD 5. He was raised in the city Tarsus (which now is in the country of Turkey). Saul came from a family of artisans. He was a Roman citizen and a Jew who lived in the Roman Empire. While he was still young, he was sent to Jerusalem to receive his education. He was given a balanced education and was exposed to classical literature, philosophy, and ethics. Because of his zeal for the Roman Empire and his membership among the Jewish Pharisees, he became a natural enemy for the upstart religion known as Christianity.

2. Newton, "Amazing Grace," stanza 1.

His thuggish behavior helped create a reputation defined by intolerance, intimidation, and violence. He personally led a program to eradicate Christians from Jerusalem. Saul first appears in the biblical record as a witness to the stoning of Stephen, the first martyr to the cause of Christ—even "consenting" to his death (Acts 7:58, 9:1). However, his frenzied ambition to exterminate Christianity from the face of the earth was to radically change.

THE ROAD TO DAMASCUS

> Meanwhile, Saul was still breathing out murderous threats against the Lord's disciples. He went to the high priest and asked him for letters to the synagogues in Damascus, so that if he found any there who belonged to the Way, whether men or women, he might take them as prisoners to Jerusalem. (Acts 9:1–2)

According to Luke's historical record (Acts 9:18), Saul, armed with arrest warrants for those of the Christian "Way," departed from Jerusalem in route to ancient Damascus, some one hundred and forty miles to the north. As he drew near that city, a light brighter than the noonday sun suddenly engulfed him. A voice inquired, "Saul, Saul, why do you continue to persecute me?" Saul responded, "Who are you?" The voice was identified as Jesus of Nazareth! The stunned persecutor was instructed to enter Damascus where he would be informed as to what he "must do." Blinded because of this miraculous vision in which Christ appeared to him (Acts 9:17, 1 Cor 15:8), Saul was led into the city. For three agonizing days he fasted and prayed. Finally, Ananias, a messenger selected by God, arrived. He restored Saul's sight and commanded him to "arise, and be baptized, and wash away your sins, calling on his name" (Acts 22:16). After certain days passed, the former persecutor began to proclaim among his fellow Jews that Jesus "is the Son of God" (see Acts 9:19–22).

THE CONVERSION OF THE APOSTLE PAUL

> *As he neared Damascus on his journey, suddenly a light from heaven flashed around him. He fell to the ground and heard a voice say to him, "Saul, Saul, why do you persecute me?"*
>
> *"Who are you, Lord?" Saul asked.*

> *"I am Jesus, whom you are persecuting," he replied. "Now get up and go into the city, and you will be told what you must do." (Acts 9:3–6)*

The furthest thing on Saul's mind as he traveled the dusty road from Jerusalem to Damascus was change. He was a young, strong, arrogant man with a plan. His fanatical energy and passion against Christians fueled his reputation as being armed and dangerous. He relished the warrior role by riding a white horse and wearing the accessories of a conqueror (armor, cape, helmet, and sword—take a few minutes to view art renditions of this event). He immersed himself into the three enemies that corrupt the spirit: the world, the flesh, the devil. However, while on his bloody mission of savagery against the church of Christ, the LORD offered Saul a new plan that would shed his "shell."

Saul ran into the Light of the World and was blinded by it. He was knocked off his horse by the grace of God. When he met and communicated with the crucified and risen Jesus Christ, his life was reconfigured at that very moment. Everything that he learned and experienced in life now had to be reassessed and rethought in the "Light" that blinded him. His eyes were instead opened to the heavens, the Spirit, and the Creator. His once-crippled spirit became strong and ever flowing. This new shell changed every aspect of his life. He literally became a changed man. He discarded the name Saul and took on the name Paul. Paul's conversion enabled Christianity to become what it is today. Hopefully you have your companion book (the Bible) next to you as you are reading this. Open it up to the New Testament. Thirteen of the twenty-seven books in the New Testament were written by Paul. Not bad for a bloodthirsty warrior who wanted to eradicate Christianity off the face of the earth!

THE CONVERSION OF (ENTER YOUR NAME)

"Return to me," declares the Lord Almighty, "and I will return to you," says the Lord Almighty.
—Zech 1:3

Do you find yourself traveling on a long dusty road like Saul? Do you know where you are? Do you know where you are going? Do you know the reasons for this journey? Do you know your destination and when you will reach it? These are thought-provoking questions that sometimes go unanswered. You and Saul may be on the same road but for different reasons. This road is marked with pain, affliction, heartache, regret, selfishness, delusion, disbelief, and arrogance. Please don't think that you and Saul are the only ones who have experienced this road. The entire human race, from the beginning of time until the end, will walk this road. Does this fact surprise you? Well, it shouldn't! We live in a broken world that promotes sin, hatred, violence, corruption, and self-absorption. Satan never wastes an opportunity to offer you his works and empty promises. He is the master deceiver who sets traps for you daily. His only goal is to separate you from God by distorting your appearance (Saul dressed like a warrior), thoughts (Saul wanted to eradicate Christianity), and behaviors (Saul tortured and murdered the followers of Jesus Christ).

Ask yourself these three basic questions:

1. Who or what is calling you?
2. What are you being called out from?
3. What are you being called into?

Your answers to these questions will give you a pretty good idea about how you view the world you currently live in. There are only two ways to look at the world: your way or God's "Way." Which lens are you currently looking through? Who are you serving? What are you serving? Is your daily creed "*My* will be done" or is it "*Your* will be done"? When you speak to God do you tell him, "Do what I want you to do!" or do you ask him, "What would you like me to do?" There is a constant battle from within between your flesh and your spirit. When your flesh overtakes your spirit, you control your life. When your spirit dominates your flesh, God controls your life. Which Uber driver have you chosen? Is it your flesh, or is it your spirit?

YOUR WAY

Do not let sin reign in your mortal body so that you obey evil desires.
—Rom 6:12

When God created you, he did not intend for you to die; he made you like himself—immortal. It was the devil's jealousy that brought pain and death into the world (Gen 3). Satan was a murderer from the beginning and does not stand for truth because there is no truth in him. When he lies, he speaks according to his own nature, for he is a liar and the "father of lies" (John 8:44). He will always offer you the "forbidden fruit" and tempt you to consume it so that he can put a chasm between you and the LORD. The evil one preys on your "flesh." He knows that your flesh is weak and can be manipulated (Matt 26:40–41). He will fill you up with false pride, arrogance, and power so you can pretend to be God-like. He will inflate your ego to crush your spirit. These are just a few of the tactics that he will use to ensure your flesh becomes your master (Matt 6:24). He is a tenacious recruiter. He wants you and needs you to be a member of his army of nonbelievers. He will say and do anything for you to turn your back on your spirit and sell your soul.

The greatest gift that God has given you is free will. He allows you to think and act freely. He loves you too much to force you to do anything. However, with this gift comes consequences. The daily decisions that you make have a direct impact on your life (present and future). Life is not easy! This broken world has placed you under various pressures and stressors that can become suffocating. During these strenuous times, your flesh entices you to

- live for yourself;
- define your own reality;
- define your own truth;
- create your own meaning in life.

These thoughts and actions are taken directly from Satan's playbook. They lead into a future of sin, bitterness, resentment, unforgiveness, self-hatred, and compulsions that will victimize you. They create feelings of indifference when it comes to having a relationship with God. Has your flesh influenced your free will? Is your heart, mind, and soul void of God? If you are having trouble answering these two questions, take some time to reflect upon the following exercise. Your reflections and answers to the following questions will further clarify your view of the world. Furthermore, it will allow you to measure the intensity between your flesh and your spirit.

1. Are you indifferent to God?
2. Do you ignore God's calling?

3. Are you bored with God?
4. Are you working to please yourself and not God?
5. Are you being commissioned by God to do his work but consciously opt out of it?
6. Do you see the truth about God or are you comfortable being spiritually blind?
7. Do you live in God's reality, or do you live in your reality?
8. Are you what God wants you to be, or do you define who you want to be?
9. Do you have a "darkened" mind?

How quickly were you able to answer these questions? Did you answer yes for the first five questions? Do you consider yourself spiritually blind? Do you define yourself and your reality? Is the Light of the World flickering in your heart, mind, and soul? Don't panic if your flesh is currently overwhelming your spirit. Even Jesus' closest companions (his disciples) struggled with their flesh (Matt 16:23).

Have you ever wondered:

- Why can't I be more at peace?
- Why do I allow my mind to control my attitude and feelings?
- Why am I anxious about the present and future?

The friction that you feel from within is caused by God's love for you! He refuses to lose even one sheep from his flock (Luke 15). He has promised you, "I am with you always" (Matt 28:20), "I go before you. I will never leave you. I will never desert you" (Deut 31:6). The fulfillment of these promises comes directly from the unconditional love that he has for you! He has forgiven you (Luke 23:34) and wants to relieve the pain that you feel from your flesh. Once again, I would like to remind you that he has experienced the emotional and physical pain that you are currently experiencing. The trials and tribulations in your life are the same trials and tribulations that were in his life. He is true God and true man and therefore can personally relate to your current struggles.

Did Satan tempt Jesus Christ? Every day! Did Satan wage war against Christ's spirit? Absolutely! To prove to you that the spirit is stronger than the flesh and that love will always conquer evil, I would like to present the following Scripture to you. This passage will provide you with additional insight on the battle that rages on between heaven and hell. It is taken from Luke 4:1–14 and is titled "Jesus Is Tested in the Wilderness" in the NIV.

> Jesus, full of the Holy Spirit, left the Jordan and was led by the Spirit into the wilderness, where for forty days he was tempted by the devil. He ate nothing during those days, and at the end of them he was hungry.
>
> The devil said to him, "If you are the Son of God, tell this stone to become bread."
>
> Jesus answered, "It is written: 'Man shall not live on bread alone.'"
>
> The devil led him up to a high place and showed him in an instant all the kingdoms of the world. And he said to him, "I will give you all their authority and splendor; it has been given to me, and I can give it to anyone I want to. If you worship me, it will all be yours."
>
> Jesus answered, "It is written: 'Worship the Lord your God and serve him only.'"
>
> The devil led him to Jerusalem and had him stand on the highest point of the temple. "If you are the Son of God," he said, "throw yourself down from here. For it is written:
>
> 'He will command his angels concerning you
> to guard you carefully;
> they will lift you up in their hands
> so that you will not strike your foot against a stone.'"
>
> Jesus answered, "It is said: 'Do not put the Lord your God to the test.'"
>
> When the devil had finished all this tempting, he left him until the next opportunity came.

So, what's this passage all about? It's about unconditional love! It's about God loving you so much that he was willing to endure every form of hardship and human suffering that enters your life. It's about God being able to look you square in the face and say, "Yes, I do understand what you're going through . . . I really do." God himself was willing to experience your weaknesses and pain so that he would be able to meet you there, console you amid whatever you are going through, and gently lift you out of it to the new life (new shell) he has in store for you.

In the introduction of this passage, Luke tells you that the Spirit "led" Jesus out into the desert. This is his way of telling you that Jesus' experience in the desert was the plan and will of God. God was willing to suffer for a purpose, suffer with an intention. And the intention was to experience and embrace all that you experience and must embrace. The LORD knows that temptation is real. He knows that it comes from your weakness but also from Satan. He knows that temptation can be a heavy burden and cause emotional, psychological, and spiritual pain. Jesus never gave in to the temptations in the desert, nor did he give in to temptations at any other time in his life. But he endured them and suffered them.

This tells you that he can be your strength and inspiration during whatever you are tempted with each day. When you feel the loneliness and isolation that your anxiety and/or depression brings, know that Jesus Christ freely allowed himself to experience this as well. For this reason, it is Jesus himself who can meet you in this desert within. He is there, waiting for you, looking for you, calling to you. He is there during anything and everything you may be going through. And it is he, the one who defeated this desert temptation, who will gently guide you out. He went to the desert to meet you and to bring you back to him. So, whether your "desert" is anxiety, depression, or any other mental, physical, emotional, or spiritual affliction, Jesus wants to meet you and bring you out. He has experienced and conquered his "forty days" in the desert and wants to help you conquer your days in life's desert!

There are only two ways to look at the world. You were tricked into believing (by Satan) that "your way" is the only way. That your flesh gives you the power and ability to conquer the world on your own. That you alone have the solutions to the problems that accompany your life. These lies have placed you on the desert road leading to Damascus. These lies have created distance between you and God. These lies have crippled your spirit. These lies have forced you to answer the three basic questions that I asked you earlier in these ways:

The World of Dsytopia	
Who or what is calling you?	*Satan / Sin*
What are you being called out from?	*A relationship with the Lord*
What are you being called into?	*Abandonment, pain, and suffering*

However, you have an opportunity to change your perspective to cure your "spiritual blindness." Look down the desert road that you are on. What do you see? Is there a crossroad coming up? Who is on the left side of the road? Is it Satan? Is he waving you toward him? Who is on the right side of the road? Is it the LORD? Is he waving you toward him? It is now time to decide. Will you turn left and travel "your way"? Or will you turn right and travel "the Way"?

GOD'S WAY

For the spirit God gave us does not make us timid, but gives us power, love and self-discipline.
—2 Tim 1:7

Regardless of where you have been or where you currently are, the LORD wants a relationship with you! He is willing to come to you and draw you into a more meaningful life. Jesus Christ wants to be your center of gravity. He wants to occupy your time and energy. He wants to fill you up with his love and blessings and give you a sense of happiness and satisfaction. He has given you an invitation to join him. Will you accept the invitation, or will you send it back "with regrets"?

Since the day you were born, you have been experiencing relationships with others in your life. Relationships come in different forms, levels, and intensity. Some relationships are short-lived, while others last a lifetime. The length of a relationship depends on the strength of the bond that you form with another person. In the world of science, bond strength is measured by the energy required to separate two bonded atoms. We can apply this scientific measurement to the laws of human behavior: the stronger a relationship bond is, the greater the energy it takes to break it. This seems to make sense! If this is the case, then the next two questions to ask are, "What does a bond consist of?" and "How is it strengthened?" Relationship bonds can be created many ways for many different reasons, but they always seem to have the same building blocks within each of them. These ingredients include respect, honesty, trust, and communication. The more that these ingredients are explored and used, the stronger the relationship becomes.

Having a strong everlasting relationship with the LORD is no different than having a strong lifelong relationship with a family member, friend, spouse, coworker, etc. It begins, continues, and ends with respect, honesty, trust, and communication.

Respect God

Therefore, let us be thankful, and worship God acceptably with reverence and awe.
—Heb 12:28

God is the Almighty (1 Chr 29:11)! The King of kings and the LORD of lords (Rev 19:16)! The Creator of heaven and earth (Ps 24:1)! He is the Alpha and the Omega (Rev 1:8)! He is your Father, and you are his child (1 John 3:1)! He is deserving of the highest level of reverence. Reverence is honor and respect that is deeply felt and outwardly demonstrated.

The best way to honor and respect the LORD is to humble yourself when going to him. Humility is the "mother of all virtue" because it opens you up to God's grace. It is the first step in the pursuit of God. It allows you to express your love for him by curing your selfishness and teaching you that you are not self-sufficient and all-powerful. Humility allows you to be honest with yourself about who and what you really are so that you can become what God made you to be. This helps clarify your thinking so that you can more fully entrust yourself to God and his holy will.

The best way I can express the importance of humility is to provide you with a Scripture passage from Luke 22:24–27, which takes place during the LORD's Last Supper.

> A dispute also arose among them as to which of them was considered to be greatest. Jesus said to them, "The kings of the Gentiles lord it over them; and those who exercise authority over them call themselves Benefactors. But you are not to be like that. Instead, the greatest among you should be like the youngest, and the one who rules like the one who serves. For who is greater, the one who is at the table or the one who serves? Is it not the one who is at the table? But I am among you as one who serves."

Humility and selflessness are to be the hallmarks of Christians. Yet the first students of Jesus Christ (his disciples) are debating which one of them is the greatest the night before Jesus is to go to the cross. This wasn't the first time that the twelve had gotten into this debate. They had argued about the same matter while they walked at some distance from Jesus, thinking that he couldn't hear what they were discussing (Mark 9:3–37). But he knew what they were discussing and used the occasion to teach them about childlike humility. On another occasion, the mother of James and John had come to Jesus to ask that her sons could sit on his right and left in the kingdom. The other disciples were indignant (Mark 10:35–45). What right had these two brothers to claim the top spots in the kingdom? Jesus taught them that the greatest should become the servant, and the one who wished to be first should be the slave of all, adding, "For even the Son of Man did not come to be served, but to serve, and to give his life a ransom for many" (Mark 10:45).

Despite these repeated lessons, here they were again, right on the eve of the LORD's death, arguing over which of them was the greatest! The LORD, in his infinite patience, reminds them (and you) once again that humility insists that you become a servant. God has blessed you not because you are great but because he loves you and wants you to serve him by sharing your compassion and talents with others. If your relationship with the LORD is firm, then your reverence for him will come in the form of obedience, suffering, service, and forgiveness.

Be Honest with God

Blessed are the pure in heart, for they will see God.
—Matt 5:8

Your Almighty Father wants to have an intimate relationship with you! For this intimate relationship to flourish, each of you must speak the truth to one another. On the last day of his earthly mission, Jesus said something truly amazing in Scriptures about himself and why he came to earth while speaking to Pontius Pilate during his trial. He told Pilate, "For this is why I was born, for this is the reason that I came into the world to bear witness to the truth. Everyone who is in the truth hears my voice" (John 18:37). Throughout the New Testament, Jesus Christ and his followers proclaim the truth. The truth is a road map that will lead you directly to the LORD. Within the truth lies the promise of an everlasting relationship with God!

The absence of truth brings dishonesty, hypocrisy, delusion, mistrust, and betrayal. In other words, it provides the energy that is needed to separate your relationship bond with the LORD. It is interesting to me the response that Pontius Pilate gave Christ after listening to his statement about his mission on earth. Pilate retorted, "What is truth?" (John 18:38). His response is tragic. It is phrased as a question, but it is really an admission of complete cynicism. He does not ask, "What is the truth?"

Such a question would indicate that Pilate believes in truth but does not know what the truth is. The question "What is truth?" is a completely different matter. It is as though Pilate had said, "Truth? You don't mean to tell me that you believe there is such a thing as truth, do you? Truth is whatever you want it to be." I am sure Pilate had heard many who claimed to know the truth and who were willing to reveal it to him. But here, it is as though Pilate has finally come to the point of giving up so far as ever knowing anything to be absolutely true. Therefore, Pilate would never accept Jesus' teachings because he could not "hear his voice."

What about you? Have you had an opportunity, like Pontius Pilate (John 18:33), to have a private conversation with Jesus Christ? If so, what did you say? What did you ask? How did he respond? What did he say? What did he ask? How did you respond? Like any father, Jesus loves to talk to his children. He wants to know everything that is on your mind, heart, and soul. He wants you to open up to him and tell him the good, bad, and the ugly. He wants a stream of truth to constantly flow between you and him. There is no freedom without the truth. There is no healing without truth. There is no peace without truth. There is no relationship with the Lord without truth!

Is there an area in your life where truth is missing?

Are you hiding from the truth?

Is your mind, heart, and soul darkened by dishonesty, hypocrisy, delusion, mistrust, betrayal?

Are you being shackled and chained by Satan?

Is his bondage keeping you from your freedom? From your Creator?

The absence of truth breaks relationships in heaven and on the earth. It fractures the bonds that you have with yourself, God, and your family/friends. Make the decision today to break free from the darkness and enter the light (the truth). The Lord is calling you to live in the truth. As you draw closer to him, he will plant seeds within you that will blossom into peace and well-being. Jesus said, "I am the way and the truth and the life" (John 14:6). If you want the source of truth, you must go to Jesus and be honest with him.

Trust God

Trust in the Lord with all your heart, and do not lean on your own understanding.
—Prov 3:5

Trusting others can transform your life! It can strip the pain and strain that life splatters upon you and provide you with a fresh new appearance (a new shell). Trust can add confidence, a sense of purpose, loyalty, truthfulness, reliability, accountability, and authenticity to your overall well-being. Trust is the most important bonding element that holds relationships together. Its presence allows you to live and work productively, feel safe in unfamiliar situations, and overcome vulnerabilities to experience new opportunities. Trust will make you feel eager to be part of a relationship. When trust is intact, you will be willing to share your dedication, talent, energy, and honesty so that the relationship flourishes. Therefore, trust is an element that nourishes growth internally and externally.

Trust is an intangible substance that is hard to define, but you will know when it's lost. When it dissipates, you will naturally withdraw your energy and level of engagement. You will go on an internal strike. You will share less and not follow through on commitments. Over time you will become indifferent, and the relationship will end. However, trust is a slippery substance because it is based upon an ongoing exchange between people and therefore is not static. Trust can be earned. It can be lost. And it can be regained.

Trust is something that two people need to build together early in a relationship. You can't demand or prove trust; trusting someone is a choice that you make! Since trust is so important in relationship building, you should find a way to monitor it, build upon it, and heal it when it becomes frayed. Take a few minutes to think about a relationship that you currently have in your life. What is the level of trust in that relationship? To help you measure that trust, I have provided a few test questions for you to answer.

1. Are both parties true to their word and fulfill their commitments toward one another?

2. Do both parties share their thoughts, feelings, and considerations about the relationship, or does one party hold important information from the other party?
3. Are both parties capable of doing what they promised?
4. Are both parties sincere, authentic, and congruent in their words and actions?
5. Are both parties' needs and desires equally met?
6. Do both parties acknowledge their mistakes and offer a timely apology?

Were you able to answer yes to all six questions? If so, your relationship bond is indestructible. Did you answer yes to half of the questions? If so, the cohesion in your relationship bond is faltering. Did you answer yes to less than three questions? If so, your relationship will soon end. I hope that you noticed that within these six questions, action-related activities were investigated. This means that trust is a verb. It depends upon mutual or reciprocal actions or obligations. You, as well as the other party, have equal responsibility in maintaining and sustaining trust.

I would like to revisit the questions that I asked you above. However, before answering these questions for a second time, I would like you to take a few minutes to think about the relationship that you currently have with God. What is the level of trust in your relationship with him? Again, to help you measure that trust, I would like you to answer the following questions.

1. Are you true to your word and fulfill your commitments to God?
2. Do you share your thoughts, feelings, and considerations about the relationship you have with God, or do you hold important information from him?
3. Do you fulfill the promises that you made to God?
4. Are you sincere, authentic, and congruent in your words and actions to God?
5. Do you meet God's needs and desires?
6. Do you acknowledge your mistakes to God and offer him a timely apology?

Were you able to answer yes to all six questions? If so, your relationship bond with God is indestructible. Did you answer yes to half of the questions? If so, the cohesion in your relationship bond with God is weak. Did you answer yes to less than three questions? If so, your relationship with God needs rebuilt. You may be asking yourself why each question focused on you and not God when we already established that trust depends upon mutual or reciprocal actions or obligations. Well, God has already established his everlasting love and trust with you when he became a human being in the person of Jesus Christ to take on your sins, be killed, and then be raised to life again, proving his victory over sin and death. God desperately wants a relationship with you. He has done his part to establish trust with you. He is now waiting for you to reciprocate. How will you respond?

Communicate with God

May these words of my mouth and this meditation of my heart
be pleasing in your sight,
Lord, my Rock and my Redeemer.
—Ps 19:14

All relationships depend upon communication. It's the lifeblood of any successful partnership. Communication, at its core, is about connecting through verbal and nonverbal means. Your behaviors are just as important as your words. However, your willingness to listen may be the key to opening the hearts, minds, and souls of those you would like to initiate and sustain relationships with. Just like trust, communication needs to flow two ways. If there is an interruption or shutdown in the communication process, the relationship may become endangered. Therefore, healthy communication is essential for relationship productivity.

Healthy communication in a relationship begins with giving the other person your full attention. Prioritizing time for those you are in a relationship with promotes respect, relevance, affection, and concern. It naturally provides genuine connections on a physical, emotional, and intellectual level. Therefore, when interacting with a loved one or friend, put down your phone, clear your mind, be present in the moment, and focus on the other person.

A second component to healthy communication is active listening. Does your mind wonder or daydream when someone is talking to you?

Are you always thinking about what to say next when you are engaged in a conversation? Do you judge others when they are speaking? Do you listen with a specific goal or outcome in mind? If you answered yes to these questions, then you are guilty of being a passive listener. Passive listeners never really hear what other people are saying because they are too consumed with their experiences, responses, and perceptions. Passive listeners are surface-level listeners that rarely connect to the essence of the conversation or explore the thoughts and feelings of the person who is delivering the message. Because of this, passive listeners have a difficult time establishing and sustaining relationships. On the other hand, active listeners engage in authentic relationships by using their empathy to drive their communication. Active listeners connect their verbal and nonverbal messages, resist the temptation to engage in their own thoughts, practice non-judgment, are comfortable with silence, check for understanding, and ask appropriate questions. Active listening not only deepens the connections that you make with others, but it also allows you to become more self-aware, which leads to better psychological health.

A third item that ensures healthy communication is being open and honest. If you are open and honest in the way you communicate, there is a good chance that the person with whom you are communicating will feel like reciprocating, which leads to meaningful dialogue. Being open and honest gives the impression of authenticity and integrity, which are the essential foundations for true collaboration. Open and honest communication leads to a mutual understanding and respect for a difference in views, interests, and needs. Simply put, being open and honest flushes out any impediments that may clog the flow of communication and provides you with a green light to be truthful to yourself and with others.

Take a moment and think about the relationships that you are currently committed to. How would you describe your communication channels with those people? Are they open, half opened, or closed? In other words, how strong or weak is the flow of communication? To help you analyze this, I have provided you the following questions to answer.

1. When called upon, do I give my relationship partner my undivided attention?
2. When called upon, does my relationship partner give me their undivided attention?
3. Do I consider myself an active listener or a passive listener? Why?

4. Do I consider my relationship partner an active listener or a passive listener? Why?
5. Am I open and honest with my relationship partner?
6. Is my relationship partner open and honest with me?

Because relationships are active and not static, the answers to the above questions can change quite frequently. Many circumstances can manipulate the valve which controls the flow of communication. Some of these circumstances may include the participant's mental and/or emotional outlook, attitude and behaviors, symptoms associated with anxiety and depression, or coping strategies that are used to deal with mental health afflictions. However, in general terms, healthy communication will occur when commitment, empathy, and honesty are valued in a relationship.

How would you describe your communication channel with God? When was the last time you spoke to him? Was it today? Was it last night? Was it last week? Was it last month? Was it last year? Have you ever spoken to him? Whatever your answer, he wants you to double, triple, quadruple the amount of time you speak to him (Matt 26:40). His love for you is infinite and everlasting. He has and will always forgive your transgressions. However, to fully experience the power of God, you must have ongoing conversations with him. He will always give you his undivided attention. He will always be an active listener, and he will always be open and honest with you.

You can speak to God anywhere, anytime. You can do it formally (in a church setting) or informally (in your own personal space). There is no right way or wrong way to approach God. The most important thing is for you to try to find him. Once you find Jesus Christ in your life, it will be easy to converse with him. He is a great conversationalist! The following are some tips to help you spark a conversation with the Lord.

- Set aside time to talk with the Lord without interruption from other people or distractions (phones, computers, or television).
- Think about what you want to say.
- Make your message clear so that the Lord hears it accurately and understands what you mean.
- Speak to him about what is happening in your life and how it is affecting you.

- Speak about what you want, need, and feel—use "I" statements such as "I need," "I want," and "I feel."
- Accept responsibility for your own feelings.
- Listen to the Lord! Put aside your own thoughts for the time being and try to understand his intentions, feelings, needs, and wants (receive the Holy Spirit).
- Share positive feelings with the Lord, such as what you appreciate and admire about him and how important he is to you.
- Be humble and show reverence.
- Admit to him that you are a sinner, and ask him to strengthen your faith, hope, and love.

Healthy communication provides a relationship with the nutrients that it needs to grow. Without it, the rest of the ingredients that define a relationship (respect, honesty, trust) weaken, wither, and die. Open your mind, heart, and soul to others to connect intellectually, emotionally, and spiritually with them. Seek and find Jesus Christ so that you can experience the peace and healing that only he can offer. Today is the day to speak to the Lord. He is waiting patiently to hear from you!

Choose God

Having a relationship with Jesus Christ is a life-changing event. You will be born again (John 3:1–21) into a new life of faith, hope, and love. Your senses will be open to the heavenly kingdom. You will strive to carry out the Lord's word and mission. You will realize that your flesh is only a vessel that carries you to the afterlife where you will be reunited with your Creator (1 Cor 6:19). All relationships are hard. They require commitment, patience, understanding, and forgiveness. These characteristics, as well as many others, will be demanded by the Lord for your relationship to grow with him. However, your small investment will reap the ultimate reward when you are able to spend the rest of eternity with your Heavenly Father (Luke 6:38).

For the third time in this section, I would like you to reflect upon the following three questions. Because of the old saying "the third time's a charm," I am hoping that you can internalize and understand each question and commit to the answers that I have provided for you.

Who or what is calling you?	*The Savior of the world*
What are you being called out from?	*Sin and death*
What are you being called into?	*An everlasting relationship with the Lord*

If you truly understand each question and freely respond in the manner presented above, then God's grace will be poured onto you (like the baptismal water that was poured over Saul's eyes that cured his blindness). With his grace comes faith: believing, receiving, and accepting Jesus' perspective. You no longer have to be confused, frustrated, stressed, or unhappy. Peace, happiness, and fulfillment are obtainable when you accept Jesus Christ as your Savior. Receive the abundant life (John 10:10) by accepting Jesus as Lord of your life.

THE BLIND WILL SEE

The Lord gives sight to the blind.
—Ps 146:8

When was the last time you had your vision checked? Was it in the nurse's office at school or in an optometrist's office? Regardless of the setting, I'm sure you went through a similar process. The nurse or eye doctor used an eye chart to measure how well you see at a specific distance (twenty feet). The examiner asked you to read the smallest line of letters that you could recognize. The smaller the text, the better you scored. The goal of this test was to measure your visual acuity and help you get to twenty-twenty vision (by prescribing glasses/contacts if needed). Most eye care professionals recommend that you have a comprehensive eye exam every two years. The reason for this recommendation is to help you protect one of the most vital organs in your body.

Of the five senses that you have been blessed with, your sight may be the most important to you. The eye is a wonderfully made, complex, sophisticated, and unique organ. Thousands of times a day, your eyes move and focus on images near and far, identifying images for interpretation. The eye transmits thousands of bits of information at any one time to the brain to interpret and decode. In essence, your eyes are your connection to the world and beyond. Because of this, Jesus Christ recommends that you get your eyes checked by him daily! Like the nurse or optometrist, the LORD wants to test and measure you. However, he is not measuring your visual acuity but your spiritual acuity. He will not ask you to read a chart but will ask you to defend your thoughts, words, and actions. His goal is to intensify the relationship that you have with him. Faith, hope, and love may be prescribed as needed.

Are you willing to go to the LORD daily and get your eyes checked? If so, you will help him fulfill his fundamental mission, "to seek and to save the lost" (Luke 19:10). During his earthly mission of divine mercy, he intentionally sought out those who lived in darkness—sin (John 11:10). Jesus did not passively wait for the lost to come to him, but he actively found them. He was proactive instead of reactive (Isa 42:16). As it was on the first day of creation (Gen 1:3), the LORD continues to proclaim, "Let there be light"! The only difference between night and day is "the Light." Jesus tells you, "I am the light of the world. Whoever follows me will never walk in darkness but will have the light of life" (John 8:12).

The natural parallels that occur in this book are heaven sent. For example, even though there are many complex parts to the eye, the actual mechanism of sight is a well-designed simple process. Light is projected through the cornea, the pupil, and then the lens. The lens muscles focus the light rays on the back of the retina. There the rods and cones turn the light into electrical impulses that are carried by the optic nerve to the brain. The brain interprets these messages into what you perceive as sight. Without light you have no sight. Without the Light of the World (John 9:5) you have no life! Are you ready for your consultation with Jesus Christ? What will he see when he looks into your eyes? Will he see "a formless void and darkness" (Gen 1:2), or will he see his reflection (Gen 1:27)?

The New Testament contains around seventy-five references to the healing work of Jesus. According to the Gospel accounts, Jesus performed thirty-four miracles during his time on earth. However, John 21:25 tells you that "Jesus did many other things as well. If every one of them were written down, I suppose that even the whole world would not have room for the books that would be written." When the LORD encountered the afflicted, he did not meet them in a clinic or hospital but rather in their homes or community centers. He didn't collect an oral history of their alignments or provide them with a physical examination. He already knew what their physical, mental, and/or spiritual alignments were (John 2:25). Furthermore, Jesus did not employ any medicines (drugs or herbs) but simply used such means as spitting, praying, touching, and laying on of hands. Jesus often put his hands on people to heal and bless, convey empathy, and/or channel God's help. Jesus seeks the afflicted. He is looking for you! He wants to put his nailed, scarred hands around you and take away your pain. He is offering you a rebirth, a new life, a new shell (2 Cor 5:17)! Are you willing to meet him?

As Jesus deliberately made his way toward Jerusalem (Luke 9:51) to fulfill God's plan (to die on the cross as atonement for the sin of those who put their faith in him, and to rise again from the dead in victory over sin and death), he continued to gather and heal his "lost sheep" (Luke 15). On his journey, he had several interactions with the blind. Why did Jesus seek out the blind? Matthew 6:22–23 may provide you with some insight. "The eye is the lamp of the body. If your eyes are healthy, your whole body will be full of light. But if your eyes are unhealthy, your whole body will be full of darkness." Jesus frequently made a comparison between those who were physically blind and those that were spiritually blind. He often used "blindness" to point out hypocrisy, as well as the state of being spiritually lost. This did not mean that the blind themselves were spiritually lost but that they were unable to see, as someone who is spiritually lost is unable to see the truth. Jesus frequently used the blind to demonstrate that he came to heal blindness—both of the eyes and of the heart.

I would like to share with you the four accounts in the Gospels when Jesus interacted with the blind. While reading these Scriptures, place yourself into the scene as the blind character. Take note of what you experience. What do you hear? What do you say? What do you feel? Ultimately, what do you see? I have provided you with key questions after each account to help further facilitate your understanding of these Gospel passages. I suggest that you take your time reading each account. You may want to read each passage several times before reflecting upon the key questions. I would also suggest that you write/type your responses to each question on paper or your favorite electronic device. Writing out your answers will provide you with an opportunity to exhaust all your thoughts and experiences while role playing as the blind character. If you properly commit to this exercise, you will expend tremendous mental energy, which in turn will ignite your spiritual flame. The goal for these role-playing scenarios is to introduce you to the love and compassion that the Lord specifically has for you. Take your time! The longer you spend on each passage, the stronger your spiritual flame will burn!

Jesus Heals the Blind

> *As Jesus went on from there, two blind men followed him, calling out, "Have mercy on us, Son of David!"*
>
> *When he had gone indoors, the blind men came to him, and he asked them, "Do you believe that I am able to do this?"*
>
> *"Yes, Lord," they replied.*
>
> *Then he touched their eyes and said, "According to your faith let it be done to you"; and their sight was restored. Jesus warned them sternly, "See that no one knows about this." But they went out and spread the news about him all over that region.* (Matt 9:27–31)

Why did you follow Jesus?

What gave you the confidence to petition him, "Have mercy on us, Son of David"?

Did you understand the question that he asked you?

How confident were you in your response to him?

How did his fingers feel on your eyes?

Why did he grant your request?

What was the first thing that you saw?

Why did you disobey his command and evangelize his name all over the region?

In what ways did this encounter with Jesus Christ change your life?

Blind Bartimaeus Receives His Sight

> *Then they came to Jericho. As Jesus and his disciples, together with a large crowd, were leaving the city, a blind man, Bartimaeus, was sitting by the roadside begging. When he heard that it was Jesus of Nazareth, he began to shout, "Jesus, Son of David, have mercy on me!"*
>
> *Many rebuked him and told him to be quiet, but he shouted all the more, "Son of David, have mercy on me!"*
>
> *Jesus stopped and said, "Call him."*

So, they called to the blind man, "Cheer up! On your feet! He's calling you." Throwing his cloak aside, he jumped to his feet and came to Jesus.

"What do you want me to do for you?" Jesus asked him.

The blind man said, "Rabbi, I want to see."

"Go," said Jesus, "your faith has healed you." Immediately he received his sight and followed Jesus along the road. (Mark 10:46–52)

- Why did Jesus come to your hometown (Jericho)?
- Why did you shout out, "Jesus, Son of David, have mercy on me"?
- Why did the community members rebuke you and tell you to be quiet?
- Why did you ignore their demands?
- How did you react when you received word that Jesus "called you"?
- What were your expectations when you stood in front of Jesus?
- Were you surprised that Jesus initiated the conversation with a question? If so, why?
- Were you prepared to answer Jesus' question?
- Why didn't Jesus have to touch you to heal your affliction?
- Where did Jesus want you to "go" after he restored your sight?
- What did you see "along the road" while following Jesus?

Jesus Heals a Blind Man at Bethsaida

They came to Bethsaida, and some people brought a blind man and begged Jesus to touch him. He took the blind man by the hand and led him outside the village. When he had spit on the man's eyes and put his hands on him, Jesus asked, "Do you see anything?"

He looked up and said, "I see people; they look like trees walking around."

Once more Jesus put his hands on the man's eyes. Then his eyes were opened, his sight was restored, and he saw everything clearly. Jesus sent him home, saying, "Don't even go into the village." (Mark 8:22–26)

Why did Jesus come to your hometown (Bethsaida)?

Who brought you to Jesus?

Where did Jesus take you? Why? How did he take you there?

How did Jesus go about healing your affliction?

Why did Jesus question you?

How did Jesus react to your response?

When your sight was restored, what did you see?

Where did Jesus want you to go and not to go? Why?

Jesus Heals a Man Born Blind

> *As he went along, he saw a man blind from birth. His disciples asked him, "Rabbi, who sinned, this man or his parents, that he was born blind?"*
>
> *"Neither this man nor his parents sinned," said Jesus, "but this happened so that the works of God might be displayed in him." . . .*
>
> *After saying this, he spit on the ground, made some mud with the saliva, and put it on the man's eyes. "Go," he told him, "wash in the Pool of Siloam" (this word means "Sent"). So, the man went and washed and came home seeing. (John 9:1–3, 6–7)*

How did Jesus meet you?

Why were Jesus' disciples so interested in you?

How did Jesus respond to the questions that his disciples had about you?

How did Jesus go about healing your affliction?

Where did Jesus command you to "go"?

Why is the translation of Siloam ("sent") so important to you?

What happened when you obeyed Jesus?

After receiving your sight, where did you "go"? What did you see?

How did you do? Do you feel that you added fuel to your spiritual flame by participating in this exercise? Did you feel the LORD's presence? Maybe you could not answer all the questions. That's OK. This shouldn't be the one and only time that you partake in this exercise. Once you allow the LORD to open your eyes, he will gradually allow you to see a new reality that is available to you. His "Light" will allow you to focus more clearly on the truth. Through revelation comes understanding. With understanding comes clarity. Clarity uncovers the truth, and the truth brings about the miracle of healing. Each time you receive revelation, understanding, clarity, truth, and healing, you should revisit this exercise. You will find that the LORD will provide you with a deeper understanding of each passage, which in turn will reinforce the growth you are achieving in your relationship with Jesus Christ.

Before we move into the first holistic strategy to help minimize the effects that anxiety and/or depression has on your daily life, I would like to share a statistic with you that I recently read. In the United States, someone goes blind every twenty minutes.[3] What a sad statistic that is. I would imagine that many of us would agree that being blind is not an enjoyable experience. Constantly living in the dark must be both frustrating and dangerous. This statistic made me wonder about how many people become spiritually blind during their lifetime. Is it one a day? One every hour? One every minute? One every second?

What is spiritual blindness? It is the lack of spiritual insight. In other words, it's the inability to understand, interpret, and apply the spiritual principals of God into one's life. A spiritually blind person cannot discern truth from lies, holiness from evil, or future heavenly riches from temporary earthly riches. They cannot "see" past this earthly life. They are blocked from mentally, soulfully, and willfully sacrificing the temporary things of this earth for much greater eternal things in heaven. It's not easy to recognize a spiritually blind person because they know biblical facts, speak the Christian lingo, and can reason through life's decisions with biblical logic. However, they do these things only on a superficial level. They allow themselves to be deceived about their own salvation. Their selfishness (flesh) does not allow their eyes to witness the truth. Thus, they are unable/unwilling to experience an authentic relationship with the God.

3. Centers for Disease Control and Prevention, "Vision Loss."

There will be times when you want to cling to the ways of the world and the pressure of your peers. You will be tempted in pride to assert that you know better than God and to do it "your way." There will be times when you are afraid—afraid of losing acclaim, acceptance, wealth, prestige, and even what you mistake for love—and you will be tempted to reject the Light of the World. The message of the world is loud and persistent, and if you let it, the message can be persuasive. You will be tempted to deny the obvious and to accept the lies of the evil one. However, a dose of faith, hope, and love will cure any and every alignment that you may encounter.

Are you part of the statistic that calculates those who are spiritually blind, or have you been healed by Jesus Christ and have spiritual faith? Seek the LORD with all your heart, cry out to him, "Jesus, Son of David, have mercy on me!" and he will come to you. Today is your day to see the Light. Today is your day to be healed physically, emotionally, and spiritually. Today is your day of salvation (2 Cor 6:1–2).

HOLISTIC APPROACH #1: BIBLIOTHERAPY

> Be strong and do not give up, for your work will be rewarded. (2 Chr 15:7)

When anxiety and/or depression invades your mind, body, and spirit, what kind of emotions do you exhibit? Are you sad and hopeless? Do you lack motivation? Do you feel restless? Are you always tired? Do you feel worthless or very guilty? Is it hard for you to focus? Does one thought dominate your mind? Do you generate future scenarios and simulate their outcomes? Are you worried about things you can and can't control? Do you get easily confused? Do you feel helpless? Do you get easily agitated? Do you become hostile to others? Do you become stubborn? Do you become impatient? Do you become pessimistic? Does your demeanor and attitude change? Do you consider harming yourself or taking your own life?

Symptoms of anxiety and/or depression have a way of putting you on a deserted island in the middle of the Pacific Ocean. They make you feel lost, lonely, and desperate (Ps 22:11). The deeper you retreat within yourself, the further away you are from those who can love, support, and heal you. However, you are not the only person that has experienced the "darkness" of these mental afflictions. There are people in the world, at this very minute, who are struggling with the same symptoms that you are experiencing. These people feel (and have felt) the same pain and strain that you are being consumed with. They are at the same mile marker as you on the road to recovery. As you walk toward mental wellness, you need to keep in mind that there are people behind you, next to you, and ahead of you. Because of this fact, I would like to introduce you to the first holistic approach that will help support you on your journey toward mental wellness. It is called *bibliotherapy*.

When dealing with personal issues, such as anxiety and/or depression, it can be difficult to make sense of what is happening in your mind, body, and spirit, especially if you don't have any other experience to compare it to. Bibliotherapy aims to bridge this gap by using literature to help improve your life by providing information, support, and guidance in the form of reading activities via books and stories. The idea of healing through books is not new; it can be traced as far back as the first libraries in ancient Greece. Although the term *bibliotherapy* may be unfamiliar, you have engaged in this therapy for most of your life and may not even know it. Think about it: when you open a book, you enter a world that is defined by the characters who are portrayed in it. You become invested and intimate with these characters. Their words and actions control your emotions, thoughts, attitude, and outlook. They allow you to reflect and gain insight into your own life. Many times, these reflections lead to enrichment and healing.

Using stories via fiction and nonfiction books, poetry, plays, short stories, and self-help materials, you can gain a deeper understanding of the concerns that are hindering you from leading a productive life. Bibliotherapy helps you develop strategies to address these issues. It also helps promote problem solving, understanding, self-awareness, empathy, insight, conversation, and self-growth. Another compelling reason for using bibliotherapy is that it can help you see how other people, such as characters in a book, address and deal with similar issues. When you identify with a fictional or non-fictional character, especially on an emotional level, you're able to see that there are others who are also navigating and coping with personal struggles. This understanding will help achieve universality, which basically means you are not the only person dealing with mental health symptoms and that anxiety and/or depression are mental afflictions that impact millions of people around the world. These facts are therapeutic in a sense that other people have gone through (or are going through) your exact mental afflictions and can share testimony that can help and heal you.

Bibliotherapy is an adjunct to other treatments rather than a treatment in itself. It can be used before, during, and after the therapeutic process. Its versatility and adaptability make it an excellent supplement to self-improvement of all kinds. This approach may be incorporated in one or more of the following ways.

Self-Help Books

If you walk into a bookstore and ask one of the workers to take you to the most popular section in the store, he or she will walk you to the psychology section. Here you will find rows and rows of self-help books. This genre is so popular that the *New York Times* gives self-help publications their own category in its bestseller list, distinguishable from fiction, nonfiction, and children's books. These facts should not surprise you. We all want to maximize our experiences each day. We yearn to be successful, popular, happy, and productive. Self-help books provide you with strategies to get where you want to go in life. Popular themes include accountability, career, commitment, communication, confidence, creativity, diet, fitness, health, goals, leadership, parenting, passion, purpose, relationships, retirement, self-control, self-esteem, strategic thinking, stress management, time management, vision—whew, I could list one hundred more, but I'm tired of typing! I think I proved my point of why self-help books are so popular today.

Out of all those categories I listed, I left out the two themes that are getting the most attention today. Those topics would be anxiety and depression. Do you like self-help books? I think that you do because you are reading one right now! I created this book to introduce you to the causes of anxiety and depression, their symptoms, and holistic coping mechanisms you can use to help recover from these temporary setbacks. In my humble professional opinion, I believe you are already on the road to recovery and may not even know it. You are currently reading my book (I interrupt this sentence for self-promotion) and your companion book, the Holy Bible, which is the greatest self-help book ever written! The goal of these two books is to prepare you for the therapeutic process, help you during the therapeutic process, and sustain you after the therapeutic process has ended. This is the power of bibliotherapy!

Prescribed Books

A good book has potential to be life-changing. The right read can unearth an inner passion, inspire you to take healthy risks, and shine a new light to guide your journey of self-expansion. Because of this, many therapists include elements of bibliotherapy in their treatment plans for their clients. If this book (and the Bible) has had an impact on you, then I would suggest that you find a mental health professional that is qualified and has experience with bibliotherapy. How will you know if a potential therapist has experience in bibliotherapy? In chapter 3, we discussed important questions you should ask a potential therapist at your consultation. Add the following questions to this list:

1. Are you familiar with bibliotherapy?
2. Are you qualified to use bibliotherapy?
3. Have you used bibliotherapy with prior clients?
4. If so, what were the outcomes of the use this therapeutic technique?
5. Do you plan on using bibliotherapy as part of my treatment plan?

The answers to these questions will allow you to evaluate the expertise and experience of your potential therapist when it comes to bibliotherapy, as well as allow you to take a proactive approach in your treatment plan. Mental health professionals who use bibliotherapy as part of your treatment plan can choose reading materials that target your specific mental health needs. By using resources like the Bibliotherapy Education Project, your therapist can find appropriate books for you that have been evaluated and approved by professionals in the field of psychology. In other words, these books have earned the stamp of approval as a possible tool to help you heal from your affliction.

As mentioned earlier in this book, the success rate of therapy depends upon the client (you). If you take ownership in your sessions by communicating, participating, and trusting, then you will expedite the healing process. The therapeutic framework is dependent upon the following correlation: the more you work, the more you heal! Because of this fact, you have an opportunity to work in conjunction with your therapist in picking out the book(s) that you think will appeal to you. This proactive approach is easier than you think. You see, you have access to the same list as your therapist. Most major libraries in the United States carry a set of books provided by the Bibliotherapy Education Project.

More importantly, these book titles can be accessed online. Here is the part of the book where I give a shout-out to my hometown, Pittsburgh, Pennsylvania! The Carnegie Library of Pittsburgh is one such library that can share this book list with you. Please visit their website, or better yet come and visit one of the most livable cities in America—the Steel City, the City of Bridges, the City of Champions, Sixburgh (winner of six Super Bowl titles)!

Alternative Modes of Expression

You don't have to wait until you enter therapy to start the healing process. You also don't have to wait for a mental health professional to guide you on the road to recovery. As a matter of fact, you can ignite the fuel for change by empowering yourself. Words have power and influence. Whether they are read or spoken, they can change your attitude, actions, reactions, outlook, and productivity. They can change the present and the future. Words can literally change your life! If you are willing to accept and understand this, then you have an opportunity to harness the power behind words and allow them to become the "wind beneath your wings." Have you ever heard of Bette Midler? I didn't think so.

Positive words create a positive mindset, which in turn creates positive experiences. Negative words activate your defense mechanisms, which in turn deny access to opportunities. Therefore, you should purposefully flood yourself with positive words to maximize opportunities throughout your life. In this technological age, you have been given tremendous freedom to craft and control the messages that you send and receive each day. Let me go out on a limb and say the most important possession that you currently own is your phone. It is on you or near you twenty-four hours a day! This revolutionary invention has become your personal wormhole for sending and receiving information. Therefore, it has a daily impact on your mental, physical, and spiritual condition. The words and sounds transmitted from your phone can intensify or diminish the symptoms generated from anxiety and/or depression. What affect has your phone had on your mental wellness? To help you answer this question, I humbly ask you to participate in the following experiment—remember, the more you work, the more you heal!

Screen Time Summary

Pick up your phone and check your screen time.

How long did you use your phone today?

How many minutes did you spend on *entertainment*?

What entertainment applications were you on?

How many minutes did you spend on *social networking*?

What social networking applications were you on?

How many minutes did you spend on *productivity*?

What productivity applications were you on?

How many minutes did you spend on *creativity*?

What creativity applications were you on?

How many minutes did you spend on *reading and reference*?

What reading and reference applications were you on?

Screen Time Effectiveness

Are you surprised about the amount of time and energy you invested into your phone today?

Has this investment helped or hindered your current mental, physical, and spiritual state?

Were your phone interactions mostly positive or negative?

Did your phone interactions inspire you or discourage you?

What category did you invest the most time in and why?

We have just created a baseline for our experiment. Every experiment needs a baseline because it establishes a standard against future results. I now would like you to track your phone usage from the time you get up tomorrow until you go to bed. This time, however, I would like you to use your phone as a tool to help diminish the symptoms generated from your anxiety and/or depression. I would like you to use it to inspire you. I would like you to use it so that it helps you create a positive mindset. Finally, I would like you to use it to flood your internal and external perspectives with positive messages and information. Do you need a strategy or some ideas to make this happen? Let me try to help you. Maybe you will only listen to music tomorrow that is upbeat and lyrically encouraging. How about listening to a podcast that will boost your mood? You can always use your creative talents and produce an artifact that will make you or someone else feel energized about the past, present, or future. You can read, listen, or watch novels, short stories, poetry, plays, and biographies that galvanize the meaning of life and/or how you can make the world a better place. Make a promise to yourself that you will only interact with positive, selfless, kind, and independent thinking people on social media or via talk/text. These are just a few things that you can do with your phone tomorrow that will help initiate change and begin to bring some relief to the mental, physical, and spiritual struggles that you are currently dealing with.

The day after tomorrow, I would like you to revisit the questions above concerning your "Screen Time Summary" and "Screen Time Effectiveness." Compare your answers from today and tomorrow. I hope that you will see a difference (whether slight or significant). Focus on the area of change and reflect upon why change occurred. Ask yourself if your new phone strategy was the reason for the change. If so, use your phone as a weapon against the suffering and pain that anxiety and/or depression brings. Own your phone instead of your phone owning you! Don't allow it to manipulate your emotions and thought patterns by stealing your light and leaving you darkness.

Bibliotherapy is a holistic technique that you can begin using today. The words that you digest daily have a direct impact on your psychological system. Positive words can act like antidotes to counteract the poisonous effects that anxiety and/or depression bring to your body. The right words can relieve the pain that you are currently feeling and prevent them from returning. Proper communication is vital to the therapeutic process. Many times, listening is just as important as speaking. Bibliotherapy allows you the opportunity to listen to others that have experienced your pain, confusion, frustration, helplessness, and hopelessness. It allows you to connect with someone who has experienced what you are experiencing. It also increases your faith, hope, and love by allowing you to walk in their shoes and preview the road to recovery that is ahead for you. Bibliotherapy works if you commit to it. As mentioned earlier in this section, it is a technique that you can use before, during, and after your therapy ends. If you incorporate it into your lifestyle, it will help fuel your light from within and provide you the skill and the will to be productive each day.

CHAPTER 6 SUMMARY

Open my eyes that I may see
wonderful things in your law.
—Ps 119:18

This chapter was strategically placed at this point of the book to introduce you to "the Way," "the Truth," and "the Life." Its content focused on the importance of opening your eyes and seeing what your "new" life has to offer you. Whether it was the lobster and his shell or Saul being visited by the Lord on a desert road, the lesson to be learned from this chapter is that conversion is the first step in the process of healing and living for and in the "Light." Before your conversion can take place, decisions need to be made. The first is how do you plan to live your life—your way or God's way? This will determine the direction of your life's journey. If you respect the Lord, are honest with the Lord, trust the Lord, communicate with the Lord, and choose the Lord, he will bless you with his grace and mercy and wash away the sin and pain that has blinded you. He will open your eyes so you can find the gifts he has created for you in his heavenly kingdom. Through Scripture, Jesus has proven to you that he can heal any type of affliction. He has healed others, and now he wants to heal you. Open your eyes to Jesus so he can lay his healing hands upon you so that you can find your way back to him. He will help you shed your "flesh" and enter your "spirit" so that you can take advantage of all of the unopened gifts he has given you.

Because the eye is the window to your soul (Prov 30:17), Jesus wants to bless you with spiritual twenty-twenty vision. He wants your eyes to work in high definition so that you can profit from bibliotherapy. He wants your refocused eyes to absorb images and information that will reduce the symptoms caused by anxiety and/or depression. He wants his other disciples to bless you with their revelations about how they overcame their challenges with mental afflictions. He wants other brothers and sisters in Christ to walk with you on the road to recovery. All of this is possible with one encounter with God (Mark 8:25).

> No one lights a lamp and puts it in a place where it will be hidden, or under a bowl. Instead, they put it on its stand, so that those who come in may see the light. Your eye is the lamp of your body. When your eyes are healthy, your whole body also is full of light. But when they are unhealthy, your body also is full of darkness. See to it, then, that the light within you is not darkness. Therefore, if your whole body is full of light, and no part of it dark, it will be just as full of light as when a lamp shines its light on you. (Luke 11:33–36)

NINTH STATION: JESUS MEETS THE WOMEN OF JERUSALEM

> Blessed are those who mourn, for they will be comforted. (Matt 5:4)

We adore you, O Christ, and we bless you.

Because by your holy cross you have redeemed the world.

> A large number of people followed him, including women who mourned and wailed for him. Jesus turned and said to them, "Daughters of Jerusalem, do not weep for me; weep for yourselves and for your children. For the time will come when you will say, 'Blessed are the childless women, the wombs that never bore and the breasts that never nursed!' Then 'they will say to the mountains, "Fall on us!" and to the hills, "Cover us!"' For if people do these things when the tree is green, what will happen when it is dry?" (Luke 23:27–31)

Lord, grant us gentle spirits that we may comfort those who mourn.

NINTH STATION: REFLECTIVE EXERCISES AND QUESTIONS

What a difference a week makes! Six days earlier, Jesus was making his triumphal entrance into Jerusalem on the back of a donkey (Matt 21:1–9). On his way in, a large celebrating crowd laid palms and garments in front of him, singing the words of a psalm, "Blessed is he who comes in the name of the LORD. We bless you from the house of the LORD" (Ps 118:25–26). He was hailed as their king. Now, Jesus is being forced out of Jerusalem under the weight of his cross. The crowds no longer have an interest in him. He is all alone. He is no longer being treated as a king but as a condemned criminal about to face crucifixion. There are only a few women witnessing his march uphill to Calvary. They are wailing in mourning and beating their breast in anguish at his plight. We don't know who these women are whom Luke references. Perhaps they are some of the women who brought him children to be healed or ate of the bread he shared when he fed the multitudes or witnessed him curing friends and relatives. The Gospels leave it up to us to fill in these blanks. What we can guess with confidence, however, is that whoever they were, they were not expecting Jesus to speak to them.

Jesus had not uttered a word since he was in the presence of Pontius Pilate. Through the mocking, the scourging, and the spitting, Jesus was silent. However, as he approached his final earthly destination, he continued to teach his flock. Before Jesus converses with the "daughters of Jerusalem," he *turned to them*. This means that he was in front of them—a physical description packed with symbolism. Once again, using Scripture, I would like to stress to you that you are not alone in your grief, pain, and confusion. Jesus Christ understands the human condition because he experienced it firsthand. Regardless of your current psychological condition, the LORD wants you to look ahead with the new eyes he gave you through your conversion. Do you see the footprints? These have been left by Jesus so that you can follow him. He wants you to carry your afflictions and symptoms on your back and bring them to him just as he carried the sins of all mankind on his back to his Father. Even though the road that you are on is long, winding, and uphill, the LORD has left you a path that ends in victory (mental wellness). You just need the courage to follow Jesus like the "daughters of Jerusalem" did.

To this you were called, because Christ suffered for you, leaving you an example, that you should follow in his steps.

—*1 Pet 2:21*

Every word that Jesus spoke had meaning. They were meant to teach and prepare his followers to enter his Father's heavenly kingdom. The themes of his teachings were simple but complex (Matt 11:5). The interactions that Jesus had with others changed their lives (physically, mentally, emotionally, and spiritually). The words that Jesus spoke to the "daughters of Jerusalem" were profound. They emphasized the past, appraised the present, and predicted the future. Jesus was more concerned for what lay ahead for them (you) than what lay ahead for him. Jesus was about to give his life in dreadful agony on a cross, yet, on "his way," Jesus modeled a level of care for others—loving his neighbor—far beyond anything most of us know or do. The LORD has provided you with a blueprint you must strive to follow. Because of your flesh, he knows it is a difficult standard to attain and sustain, but he encourages you to "take up your cross daily and follow [him]" (Matt 16:24–26). Through the LORD's grace (2 Cor 12:9) and mercy (Heb 4:16), he will never give you anything beyond what you cannot bear and will always provide you a way out so that you can endure it (1 Cor 10:13). Like the daughters of Jerusalem, he has turned to you and has spoken to you. How will you respond? Will you follow Jesus? Will you model Jesus?

> *Do nothing out of selfish ambition or vain conceit. Rather, in humility value others above yourselves, not looking to your own interests but each of you to the interests of the others. In your relationships with one another, have the same mindset as Christ Jesus: Who, being in very nature God, did not consider equality with God something to be used to his own advantage; rather, he made himself nothing by taking the very nature of a servant, being made in human likeness. And being found in appearance as a man, he humbled himself by becoming obedient to death—even death on a cross!*
>
> —*Phil 2:3–8*

While traveling the uphill journey to Calvary with Jesus, the daughters of Jerusalem were earning their salvation. Being "saved" by God is a lifetime journey that is measured daily. Salvation is not given but earned. Simply put, salvation rests on your union with Jesus Christ. You either have a relationship with the LORD or you don't. Regardless of where you are in your personal relationship with God, repentance and belief are the two actions that can gain and sustain salvation.

Repentance means that you are changing your mind about God and about yourself. You are laying down your own foolish efforts to save yourself. You are turning away from self-sufficiency. At the same time, you are turning toward Christ. You trust that he alone is the one who can save you. You are entrusting yourself to him. Where are you on the road to salvation? To help you locate your position behind Jesus Christ, I have generated the following questions for you to answer:

1. What function does God have in your life?
2. What kind of control does God have on your heart?
3. What kind of control does God have on your mind?
4. What kind of control does God have on your will?
5. Where are you in your personal knowledge of Jesus?
6. How much new revelation of Jesus have you received in the last year?
7. Are you letting the Holy Spirit lead you more deeply into the mystery of the person of Jesus?
8. Do you love Jesus more deeply than ever?
9. Is Jesus your life and your love?

The answers that you provided to each question above help measure how much salvation you have currently earned. With these answers in mind, circle the phrase the best describes your relationship with Jesus Christ.

How Much Salvation Have You Earned?	
I have been saved!	Rom 8:24
I am being saved!	1 Cor 1:18
I hope to be saved!	Rom 5:9

Which phrase did you circle? Why did you circle that specific phrase? What will you need to do in your daily life to move to the phrase above the one that you circled? Your goal should be to confidently recognize and evangelize that Jesus Christ is your Lord and Savior (Acts 4:12) daily.

We sinned for no reason but an incomprehensible lack of love, and He saved us for no reason but an incomprehensible excess of love.

Part 3 | The Way, the Truth, the Life

—*Peter Kreeft*[4]

TENTH STATION: JESUS IS CRUCIFIED

> It was nine in the morning when they crucified him. The written notice of the charge against him read: The King of the Jews. (Mark 15:25–26)

We adore you, O Christ, and we bless you.

Because by your holy cross you have redeemed the world.

> When they came to the place called the Skull, they crucified him there, along with the criminals—one on his right, the other on his left. Jesus said, "Father, forgive them, for they do not know what they are doing." And they divided up his clothes by casting lots. (Luke 23:33–34)

Lord, grant us merciful hearts that we may bring your reconciliation and forgiveness to all.

TENTH STATION: REFLECTIVE EXERCISES AND QUESTIONS

Jesus reached the end of the road. He scaled Calvary. He entered the place called Golgotha (which means the place of the skull). However, this did not mean that his ridicule and torture came to an end. The Roman soldiers, Pharisees, and even the criminals that were crucified alongside him mocked Jesus for the next three hours while he hung on the cross. The Gospel of Mark reports "they offered him wine mixed with vinegar,

4. Kreeft, *Jesus-Shock*, 7.

but he did not take it. Dividing up his clothes, they cast lots to see what each would get" (Mark 15:23–24).

> Those who passed by hurled insults at him, shaking their heads and saying, "So! You who are going to destroy the temple and build it in three days, come down from the cross and save yourself!" In the same way the chief priests and the teachers of the law mocked him among themselves. "He saved others," they said, "but he can't save himself! Let this Messiah, this king of Israel, come down now from the cross so that we may see and believe." Those crucified with him also heaped insults on him. (Mark 15:29–32)

How did Jesus respond to these slurs and insults? He offered the first of seven phrases that he would share while hanging on the cross: "Father, forgive them, they know not what they do" (Luke 23:34). To fully appreciate Jesus' response, try inserting yourself into his position—an innocent person nailed to a cross several feet off the ground. Take his point of view and reflect on his perspective. Who did he see? He saw the soldiers who mocked, scourged, and tortured him. He saw Caiaphas and the high priests of the Sanhedrin who sentenced him. He saw two criminals (one on his right and one on his left) who were sentenced on the same day as him. At the foot of his cross, he saw his mother and aunt (mother's sister), as well as Mary of Clopas and Mary Magdalene. He saw only one (John) of his twelve closest friends. The rest deserted him (like we sometimes do). How do you think these visuals made him feel? How would they make you feel?

The Lord wants you to think as he thinks and feel as he feels. If this is the case, then you need to see as he sees. As Jesus looked down from his cross, he didn't see his enemies; he saw his brothers and sisters. The soldiers, Pontius Pilate, the chief priests and scribes, the Pharisees and Sadducees, family members and friends, you and I were all created by the Heavenly Father. Therefore, we are all related (through our Father, God Almighty). Because of this, Jesus took this opportunity to break his silence and say a prayer on your behalf. It is remarkable that Jesus isn't praying for himself! How terrified and overwhelmed would you be in this situation? Your (and my) prayer would probably be, "Father, help me!" instead of "Father, forgive them!" But Jesus' life was based upon unconditional love. He was concerned for the people who were responsible for crucifying him and was asking God to forgive them. Instead of thinking of himself and his own needs, he was thinking of those whose souls were in much greater peril than his own. At the height of his physical suffering, his love prevailed, and he asked his Father to forgive!

Right up to his final hours on earth, Jesus preached forgiveness. Forgiveness transcends all human understanding because it comes from the spirit and not the flesh. The by-product of forgiveness is resurrection. Hate turns into love, hurt turns into relief, anger turns into joy, and blame turns into peace. Today is the day for you to forgive. Start with forgiving yourself. Change your perception of life. Upgrade your eyes from black and white to high-definition color. Release the cold emotions of pain, resentment, and fear, and open the widow of your mind, heart, and soul to the warm healing light of forgiveness.

Forgiving yourself will change your anxiety into contentment and your depression into hopefulness. It will resurrect the faith, hope, and love that has been dormant inside your spirit. Forgiving yourself will allow you to forgive others. Once the Light consumes your thoughts and emotions, it will influence your words and actions. This will enable you to think, feel, and see like Jesus—to forgive all those who betrayed you, persecuted you, inflicted pain upon you, and deserted you (Matt 5:9–10).

EXAMINATION OF CONSCIENCE

Because the tenth station describes Christ reaching his final earthly destination and being nailed to a cross, I thought this would be a perfect time for you to examine your conscience. Peter Kwasniewski has created a series of questions based on the writings of Saint Benedict.[5] In his commentaries, Saint Benedict wanted Christ's disciples (followers) to hold a mirror up to Christ and see themselves in that mirror. By contemplating each question, you will see yourself in this mirror. Take note in which areas you see a blurred reflection, a distorted reflection, or no reflection at all. I would suggest that you complete this exercise at the quarter point of the year (once every three months). This will allow you to examine the strength of your spiritual flame as well as recommit yourself to your conversion to Jesus Christ. Please keep in mind, your conversion is not a one-time event. It is a daily journey of words and action to achieve an intimate relationship with the Lord.

5. Kwasniewski, "New Examination of Conscience"; reproduced below with permission.

Like other exercises in previous chapters, take your time answering each question. I would suggest that you not answer every question in one sitting. Find a comfortable, private setting where you can become one with your spirit. Open your meditation session with a thanksgiving prayer to the LORD. Ask him to give you the clarity to answer each question truthfully. Also, ask him to provide you guidance in finding strength in your weakness (Isa 35:4).

Examination of Your Conscience
General
Have I neglected to love the Lord God with all my heart, all my soul, and all my strength, and my neighbor as myself? If so, in what specific ways?
In deed *or in thought,* have I killed, committed adultery, stolen, coveted, or borne false witness?
Have I failed to honor all people?
Did I do to another what I would not have had done to me?
Did I prefer anything, whether great or small, to the love of Christ?
Self-Denial
Have I been self-indulgent instead of denying myself in order to follow Christ?
Have I pampered my body or sought after delicate living, rather than chastising my body?
Have I neglected fasting or abstinence?
Have I overindulged in wine or other beverages, or verged on gluttony?
Have I been drowsy or slothful?
Did I immerse myself in worldly affairs rather than keeping aloof from them?
Did I fulfill the desires of the flesh rather than hating my own will?
Have I sinned against chastity, modesty, or purity?
Charity Toward Neighbor
Have I neglected, when it was possible, to relieve the poor, clothe the naked, visit the sick, bury the dead, help in affliction, or console the sorrowing?
Have I welcomed anger or harbored a desire of revenge?
Have I fostered deceit in my heart or made an insincere peace?
Have I failed to utter truth from heart and mouth?
Have I rendered evil for evil or done wrong to anyone?
Did I feel or exhibit impatience when wronged?
Have I hated my enemies or any person?

Did I neglect to pray for my enemies in the love of Christ?
Have I avoided making peace with any adversary?
Have I fled persecution for justice's sake?
Have I rendered cursing for cursing, rather than a blessing?
Have I been guilty of disparaging others?
Have I avoided wasteful words, vain words, and needless laughter?
Have I uttered evil and wicked words?
Have I been jealous or given way to envy?
Have I loved strife?
Did I give into vanity?
Have I been egotistical?
Did I fail to reverence my elders in Christ?
Did I fail to love those who are my brothers/sisters, juniors, or dependents?
Have I, in any other way, forsaken charity?
Seek First God's Kingdom
Did I neglect in my prayer the daily confessing of past sins?
Have I faltered in putting my hope in God?
Have I subtly or openly attributed the good that I see in myself to myself rather than to God?
Have I run away from acknowledging the evil I have done, or tried to blame it on someone else?
Have I delayed taking the steps necessary to amend my sins and failings?
Have I been remiss in smashing my evil thoughts on the rock of Christ the instant they came into my heart?
Have I been lax in applying myself to frequent prayer?
Did I fail to keep death daily before my eyes, with fear of the day of judgment and dread of hell?
Have I not been desiring everlasting life with all spiritual longing?
Have I failed to keep guard over the actions of my life by bearing in mind that God sees me everywhere?
Have I not sought the counsel of my spiritual Father when I should have done so?
Have I hidden evil thoughts from him?
Have I shown poor obedience to the commands of those who are placed in authority over me?
Did I seek a reputation for holiness rather than holiness itself?
Have I been lax in fulfilling the commandments of God each day?

Have I ever abandoned God's mercy?

Come near to God and he will come near to you.
—Jas 4:8

Chapter 7
Mission

Let us not become weary in doing good, for at the proper time we will reap a harvest if we do not give up.

—Gal 6:9

THE CARPENTER'S HOUSE

An elderly carpenter was ready to retire. He told his employer-contractor of his plans to leave the house-building business to live a more leisurely life with his wife and enjoy his extended family. He would miss the paycheck each week, but he wanted to retire. . . . The contractor was sorry to see his good worker go and asked if he could build just one more house as a personal favor. The carpenter said yes, but over time it was easy to see that his heart was not in his work. He resorted to shoddy workmanship and used inferior materials. It was an unfortunate way to end a dedicated career.

When the carpenter finished his work, his employer came to inspect the house. Then he handed the front-door key to the carpenter and said, 'This is your house . . . my gift to you.' The carpenter was shocked! What a shame! If he had only known he was building his own house, he would have done it all so differently.[1]

1. Live Life Happy, "Short Stories About Life."

Mission

YOUR HOUSE

Chapter 7 will focus on your life's journey. It will help you reflect upon where you have been, where you are now, and where you plan to go. Hopefully, it will provide insight into your life's mission. To make this content a bit easier to digest, I will once again lean on construction metaphors to help you understand your past, current, and future location. If you recall in the summary of part 1, I spoke to you about how your life will always be a construction site. I stressed that you will be constantly building, rebuilding, and/or reorganizing depending on your life's experiences. We talked about the importance of assessing the "soil conditions" of your life. We concluded that this assessment would help you decide the placement of your life's "footings," as well as how deep and wide your life's footings need to be.

In part 2's summary, I spoke to you about the importance of a "cornerstone" in your life. In an architectural sense, I expressed to you how a cornerstone is the first stone set in the construction of a masonry foundation. I described it as the largest, most solid, and most carefully constructed of any other stone. I stressed to you that this stone determines the position of the entire structure. The content in chapters 3, 4, and 5 helped you recognize that Jesus Christ must be the cornerstone of your life so that he can position you to follow his will and do his work while you are on your life's journey.

This brings us to the introduction of chapter 7. Did the story of the elderly carpenter surprise you? As you were reading the story, I bet you predicted that his last build would be his most magnificent accomplishment! What were your thoughts when you learned that his heart was not in his work? What emotions stirred within when you learned about his shoddy workmanship and use of inferior materials? Why do you think his employer gifted the house to him? Did you find any meaning behind the carpenter's reaction after he was given the keys to the house?

You may be asking yourself, "What does this story have to do with me?" Well, you are the builder of your "house" (life). You build it every day.

Is your heart in your work?

How is your workmanship?

What kind of materials are you using?

Do you realize that you must live in the house that you are currently building?

Looking back into the days, weeks, months, and years of building, would you do anything differently?

Lessons lost are lessons learned. What I mean by that is life is a one-way street. You can only go one way—forward. If your house is not what you want it to be, all is not lost! Today is another construction day! How will you use it? What do you plan to work on? Are you willing to ask others for help? These are some of the questions that chapter 7 will ask you to explore. Get ready to put on your overalls, work boots, hard hat, and tool belt. Chapter 7 is going to help you build, rebuild, and/or reorganize your house!

Yesterday's the past, tomorrow's the future, but today is a gift. That's why it's called the present.

—*Bil Keane*[2]

YOU ARE THE ARCHITECT OF YOUR LIFE

There is only one you and you will only live one life. You are responsible for being what you were created to be. When you unroll the blueprints of your life what do you see?

What does the structure of your current "house" look like?

Is it animated or jaded?

What is the size of your "house"?

Is it bigger today than it was in the past?

What is the condition of your "house"?

Does it exhibit and utilize advanced features or is it old and dilapidated?

Does your "house" exude warmth from the "Light," or is it cold and dark?

2. Used in one of Keane's *Family Circus* comics, in *Parsons Sun*, Aug. 31, 1994.

Regardless of how your current "house" looks and feels, you have the power to improve it. You should never be satisfied with the minimum but always strive for the maximum. As the architect of your house, you need to keep in mind that your structure will never remain the same. It will always get bigger or smaller, more advanced or obsolete, warmer or colder. Your daily faith, hope, and love will determine whether your blueprints match your reality.

YOUR EMPLOYER IS GOD

Whatever has been given to you (physically, mentally, socially, emotionally, spiritually) is not owned by you. All that you had, have, and will have is owned by the LORD. Through his grace, love, and compassion, he has gifted to you all that you are and all that you own. In return, he expects you to serve his will.

TIME

In their hearts, humans plan their course,
but the Lord establishes their steps.
—Prov 16:9

We all have been given the same three things from the LORD but not in the same amount. The first thing that the LORD has given all of us is *time*. We all have time but not the same amount of time. We are not all going to die at the same age, month, and day. However, God has granted us an allocation of time. The question then for you is, how will you invest in the limited amount of time that you have? Will you assign a portion of each day to take care of your mind, body, and spirit by reading, writing, working, dieting, exercising, praying, and studying Scripture? Will you create and foster relationships? Will you value and respect everyone you meet? Will you remember and celebrate important milestones in other people's lives like birthdays, graduations, weddings, anniversaries, etc.? Will you forgive others by word and action for the way they treated you? Will you love your neighbor regardless of their color, creed, or condition? Will you prioritize your daily tasks and not stress over things that you cannot control? These are only some of the questions that need to be answered in your life's investment portfolio.

I just heard you ask yourself, "What is a life investment portfolio?" Well, it is like a financial investment portfolio, but it has nothing to do with your finances and/or retirement. Once you enter the career of your choice, it is highly recommended that you seek and hire a financial advisor to create an investment portfolio for you. This simply means that every month, you will take a portion of your pay and give it to your financial adviser so that they can invest it into stocks, bonds, etc. for you to receive a return (profit) when you enter retirement. Have you ever seen a commercial talk about 401(k)s or IRAs? If so, they are referring to financial investment portfolios.

Careers, financial advisors, investment portfolios, stocks, bonds, 401(k)s, and IRAs are all things that you will explore in the future. However, I'm speaking to you on the most important day of your life—which is today! I want to help you create your own life investment portfolio. A strong life investment portfolio will help you maximize the time that God has granted you on this earth. It will provide you a quality of life defined by productivity. It will also prepare you for the afterlife. Simply stated, your life investment portfolio consists of the moral, ethical, and spiritual assets that you accumulate throughout your life. The greatest adviser to seek and hire to help you expand your life investment portfolio is Jesus Christ. He will provide you with full disclosure and help you create the portfolio that you will need to enter his kingdom. He will take all that you say and do daily and compare it to his Father's standard. He will test you, challenge you, and inspire you to find and fulfill the assets that promote his kingdom and accomplish his will. The return on this investment is an everlasting life with the LORD in paradise (Luke 23:42–43).

Because time is the most valuable asset that you have, you should begin your life's investment portfolio by measuring it. Are you using God's gift of time accordingly, or are you letting it slip through your fingers? Are you harnessing the full power of your time to fulfill or foil God's will? Take this opportunity to reread and answer the questions that I asked you in the previous paragraph concerning time. Make note on how many times you answered yes or no for each question. The more that you answered yes, the closer you are to maximizing the gift of time (Mark 12:34).

As mentioned earlier, these questions are just the first of many that you will need to ask yourself throughout your life while measuring your productivity compared to time. I strongly encourage you to create a document entitled "My Life's Investment Portfolio." Copy and record your answers to the questions that were posed to you in this section. Make it a monthly goal to review and generate new questions to help you practice and perfect the moral, ethical, and spiritual assets that you will need to live a healthy, productive, fulfilling life.

I would like to conclude by asking a thought-provoking question that will hopefully change your perspective about the life that you are currently living:

How would you change if you counted your birthdays *down* instead of *up*?

The future's uncertain, and the end is always near.

—Jim Morrison[3]

ABILITIES

For we are God's handiwork, created in Christ Jesus to do good works, which God prepared in advance for us to do.
—Eph 2:10

The second thing that the LORD has given all of us are *abilities*. These are the Holy Spirit–inspired talents that God has provided every individual. He has provided everyone with some type of capability or capacity so that he can utilize it for the benefit of his kingdom. Have you discovered an ability that God has given you? If so, are you using it to glorify God? If you haven't discovered one of the many God-given talents that Jesus Christ has given you, why the delay (Acts 22:16)?

In the Gospels of Matthew (13:31–32), Mark (4:30–32), and Luke (13:18–19), Jesus speaks to you about the parable of the mustard seed. He begins this story by telling you that this seed is the smallest of all seeds. However, when sown into the ground, it springs up to become the largest of all plants and provides food and shelter to birds. Jesus uses this parable as an analogy so that you can realize how much potential is packed into your soul. Jesus has placed you on this earth (like the mustard seed) to grow. He wants to bring forth from your life glorious blessings into the world. The only thing that he asks from you is to allow him to do his

3. Morrison, "Roadhouse Blues."

work through you. Like the mustard seed, you must allow yourself to be planted in the fertile soil of the LORD by surrendering yourself to his divine will. You must allow yourself to be watered by daily prayer. Finally, you must allow the rays of the Son of God to shine upon you so that he can bring forth from you all that he desires. God has packed your soul with incredible talents. It is your responsibility to search and find these talents and put them into action for the benefit of his kingdom.

If you haven't yet discovered one of the many abilities that God has gifted to you, start the exploration process with the following steps. First, humbly pray to him to cure your "blindness," to help you see yourself and the world through the spirit instead of the flesh. Through this divine perspective, he will allow you to see yourself as he sees you, as well as to see the world as he sees it. This will set you on "the Way" to unleash the extraordinary potential and opportunity that awaits you. Secondly, open your mind, heart, and soul to everything that you experience each day. Focus on your thoughts, words, and actions. Listen to those who interact with you. Be aware of the needs of family, friends, and strangers that intersect your life. Create a mindset in which you truly believe that Jesus Christ has placed you into situations (good and bad) to share your talents with others. If you realign your thoughts, behaviors, and actions in these ways, your abilities will blossom and grow just like the mustard seed. Thirdly, since God has packed these abilities into your soul, you will have to devote time and energy to uncover them. The best tool to use to accomplish this task is self-reflection. Here are a few questions to ask yourself to start the mining process:

What do you enjoy doing?

What makes you feel accomplished and at ease?

What activities do you gravitate toward when you have free time?

What character traits are you complimented on?

What do people say they like or admire about you?

Congratulations, you have just made your soul an excavation site! Pay careful attention of what you are unearthing. You may discover that the LORD has granted you a talent as big as a mountain or as small as a mole hill. Remember, according to the mustard seed parable, size does not matter. What does matter is that you take ownership of a particular ability and use it to bring glory to God! You may still be asking yourself,

"How will I know when I find a God-given talent, or what does a God-given talent sound like or look like?" Refer to the questions that I asked you above. A God-given talent simply comes down to things that you enjoy doing because you are good at it! Let me try to give you a few examples of God-given abilities that can be used to glorify God.

Does one of your talents lie in *music*? Has God blessed you with the acuity to write, read, or play music? Did God bless you with an angelic voice? If so, put these talents to use by providing others with a slice of heaven through your performances. Share these talents in church by performing religious music or singing in the choir. Sharpen your musical talents in your school's orchestra, marching band, and/or choir. Have the courage to audition for your school's musical or create your own band or vocal group. Maximize your talents by creating original pieces and perform them for free for the less fortunate in your community.

Does one of your talents lie in the *arts*? Has God blessed your hands with the gift of drawing and/or painting? Has he given you the ability to build artwork out of clay, stone, wood? Maybe he has given you the talent to act, dance, or make people laugh. If so, it is time to share these abilities with others. Maybe you can draw a portrait of your favorite teacher and present it to him/her as a token of appreciation for all the time and effort they have spent with you. You could also paint a mural at the community center in your neighborhood to create a sense of unity. What if you created the manger scene out of wood, clay, and stone and presented it to your church so that they can display it during the Christmas season? I bet you could put on a puppet show during the summer to entertain children.

Has God gifted you a *compassionate heart*? Does he allow you to easily empathize with others? If so, strengthen your heart by volunteering your time to worthy causes. Maybe you can volunteer down at your local library and tutor others who are struggling in certain academic areas that you are strong in. You can always go to your local food bank and unload, pack, and/or serve food to the needy. Maybe you can make the earth greener and cleaner by "adopting" a road, highway, or park to bag and recycle the litter that is left by others.

These are just a few examples of abilities and talents that God gives to his "children." The number of gifts that he has given you are more numerous than the stars in the universe. Like stars, he wants you to shine upon others so that they have a navigational point to help them return to the "Good Shepherd"!

Success is not measured by what you do compared to what others do. It is measured by what you do with the ability God gave you.

—Zig Ziglar[4]

TREASURE

For where your treasure is, there your heart will be also.
—Luke 12:34

The third thing that the LORD has given all of us is *treasure*. When you hear the word *treasure*, I bet you picture an old, dirty wooden chest full of precious metals, gems, or other valuable objects that has been dug up by following specific coordinates on a secret map. The film industry has created blockbuster movies using this premise as its plot. How many times have you watched the *Pirates of the Caribbean* movies or *National Treasure*? These movies made Walt Disney Pictures over a billion dollars! Everyone loves to look for and find treasure! However, the LORD doesn't picture treasure like we do. The treasure that he provides comes in the form of resources. His picture of treasure aligns more with the definition that *Merriam-Webster*'s dictionary provides: "wealth of any kind or in any form."[5] Whether you know if or not, the LORD provides you with priceless treasures each day. Just like *time* and *abilities*, he wants you to use these resources to serve the purpose of the kingdom of heaven.

Christ's treasures are never buried underground (Matt 25:18). They are ever present and always available to you at a moment's notice. They come in many forms. They can be tangible or abstract, active or static, literal or symbolic, apparent or mysterious. The form of the treasure isn't important—its essence is. Any resource provided to you should be viewed as a treasure from God and used appropriately.

I know, you are probably asking yourself, "How in the world am I supposed to recognize a treasure sent to me from God when they come in all these different forms?" To answer your question, you must make a U-turn and revisit chapter 6. Most of the content in chapter 6 focused on the human eye. What you see and how you see it directly correlates with

4. Ziglar, "Success Measured."

5. *Merriam-Webster*, s.v. "treasure," https://www.merriam-webster.com/dictionary/treasure.

the type of relationship you have with the Lord. Perception is reality. You are either a believer or nonbeliever (Matt 12:30). You either see with your eyes or your heart (Eph 1:18).

Throughout this book, I have helped you see your current mental health situation from a different perspective. I have introduced you to your Lord and Savior, Jesus Christ. I encouraged you to make a conscious effort to build an intimate relationship with him. I ensured you that if his will becomes your will, your entire life (and afterlife) will change. Hopefully all these themes have helped improved your eyesight. By using your heart and soul to see, you will be able to recognize and use the treasures that Jesus Christ has gifted to you, which in turn will bring a new life, better health, and more prosperity and productivity.

In the last six chapters, I have expanded upon treasures that are available to you 24/7. Whether it was the lessons that faith, hope, and love provide or the power that you receive from prayer and Scripture reading or the holistic approaches to help heal the symptoms of anxiety and/or depression, the Lord constantly provides you with detailed instruction on how to find, open, and use his gifts for the greater good of his flock and his kingdom. I would like to take this space to describe additional resources that are available to you in his treasure chest.

Your Family

Did you choose your family? Did you choose your siblings or make the decision not to have any siblings? Did you have any decision-making power over the structure of your family? I am guessing that your answers to these questions are *no*. The reason the answers were no is because you and your family are part of God's plan. God is omnipotent, which means he is all-knowing, all-powerful, and able to do anything. He has specifically placed you into the family that you currently cohabitate with because they have been provided resources that will help you accomplish your earthly mission. This means that you and your family have a contract with each other and God. The terms of these contracts are clear and binding. All of you have been created by God and have been predestined to be with one another to aid and support each other's cause and fulfill the promises made by the Lord.

Sometimes you may think that your family members are barriers. However, they are just the opposite. God has placed them into your life to be bridges. He has provided them resources to help you cross over obstacles so that you can continue your journey. Regardless of their age or title, the treasures that are packed into your family's souls were intended to help you blossom and grow. Therefore, recognize the importance they have in your life. Value the time that you spend with them. Listen and learn from their experiences. Jesus Christ told his disciples, "The harvest is plentiful, but the workers are few. Ask the Lord of the harvest, therefore, to send out workers into his harvest field" (Matt 9:37–38). Your family members have been sent to you to make sure that you have all that you need to do God's will. Allow them to nourish you so that you can grow as tall and strong as the mustard plant.

Your Friends

Did you choose your friends? Did you make a conscious choice about the number of friends you have? Did you have any decision-making power over the type of people that you want to be associated with? I am guessing that your answers to these questions were *yes*. The reason your answers were yes is because God provides you free will. Even though he is omnipotent, he allows his children to make their own decisions. He grants you the opportunity to choose your own pathways in life. Unlike your family members, you are given the responsibility to choose who you want to invest your time with outside of your home. How have you done thus far in fulfilling this responsibility?

It has been popularly cited that a person meets approximately eighty thousand people over a lifetime. This number can be compared to the number of fans that fill up a college football stadium on any given Saturday in the fall. When meeting these eighty thousand people, you will have an opportunity to impact their life, and they will have an opportunity to impact yours. What an awesome thought! The eighty thousand people that you meet will all be part of God's plan for you. You will not meet these people by coincidence. Your life will be intersected by them because each of you possess specific resources that will help the other accomplish their earthly mission. If your will is aligned with God's will, he will provide you with the vision that is necessary to give and receive these resources. However, if you live by the flesh, then you will both pass each other like two ships in the night.

If you take a moment to think in these terms, you will begin to comprehend how much the Lord loves you. Because his love for you is infinite (Rom 38–39), he is willing to provide you multiple opportunities to give and receive treasures that will promote his kingdom and protect yours daily. But it all begins with you! He loves you too much to force you to do anything. Take advantage of what the Bible has to offer so that you can begin to walk "the street named Straight" (Acts 9:11) and follow his map to the treasures he has stored up for you!

Your Dreams

The treasures of your future are beating inside of you like a drum. It is a melody that you love to listen to because you have created it. Most people like to title this instrumental piece "The Dreams I Have for the Future." Your aspirations and dreams are conceived with a spiritual imagination. Your soul sends messages to your brain, instructing it to expand upon certain thoughts created in you by God. Dreaming in a figurative sense is essential to creating a better life for yourself and others. Envisioning where you will be and what you will be doing soon allows you to engage in the exercise of hope. You are preparing your mind, body, and soul for the work that must be done to ensure the future that you imagine comes to fruition.

In the Bible, dreams and visions were often used by God to communicate with people and to reveal his plan. God utilized this method to create a bridge between the realm of the divine and the realm of flesh. Ultimately, God the Father decided to send Jesus, his only begotten Son, into the world to promote the kingdom of heaven and rebuild the kingdoms here on earth. When you were conceived, God planted in you seeds to help him promote and rebuild both these kingdoms. Therefore, it is necessary that you allow your spiritual imagination to work independently from your other bodily systems. This will allow your projected future to be based on the principles of love, compassion, sacrifice, humility, faithfulness, and justice. These embedded principles will act like guardrails and protect your future dreams from veering off into the lanes of destruction and damnation.

Allow yourself to dream as high and far as your spiritual imagination will take you. Collect and record the thoughts that rise from your soul. Never decapitate a dream sequence, and always accept where the dream takes you. Don't try to connect the dots from one dream to another. Random dreams or reoccurring dreams with different endings encourage mobility. This mobility will provide hope for the future and set you on a path to turn your dreams into reality.

If, in your current mental state, you are lacking in dreams and aspirations, turn to the Savior and ask him to insert his light into your soul. This will reactivate your spiritual imagination and allow you to dream once again. A lack of dreams and aspirations can be a cause for concern. It can lead to the paralysis of your soul. If you lack the mobility to dream, then you are destined to be enslaved by your flesh and be forced to participate in the "culture of death."

As already mentioned in the introduction of this chapter, your life will always be under construction. Work will be required to progress to get to where you want to be. Who you are, what you are, where you are, and how you feel will always be fluid. You must find, possess, and use your faith, hope, and love to reignite and/or fuel your dreams and aspirations. You must be willing to fight for the right for your dreams to become reality.

For where your treasure is, there your heart will be also.
—Matt 6:21

THE LORD'S GIFTS COME WITH EXPECTATIONS

The first theme of this chapter focused on you being the architect of your life. If the elderly carpenter knew that his employer was going to give him the last house that he built for a retirement gift, I'm sure he would have planned and worked diligently to create a magnificent structure that would have protected him and his family for the remainder of his life. However, he chose a different strategy. This section was created to inform you that you only have one life to live and that you are responsible for building your life. The good news is you do not have to build it on your own. There are others in your life that will help you become the person that you were meant to be.

The person willing to help the most is your employer—Jesus Christ. He has gifted you a certain amount of time, ability, and treasure to maximize the structure of your life. As your employer, he will only give you gifts based on your capacity to handle them. In other words, God doesn't give you simply the things you ask for, he gives you what you ask for in the amount that you can handle. He will not give it to you because you merely want it. He will give it to you because he knows you have the capacity to handle it. He wants you to manage what he gives you properly.

God expects you to multiply the things he gives you. He wants you to take advantage of the time, talents, and treasures that you have already acquired. He wants you to acknowledge the spiritual connections between what you have, where it came from, and what you should do with it. God will not micromanage you. He will provide you with his gifts and allow you to invest them as you see fit. Subsequently, he allows you to become the architect of your "house" and ultimately grants you full responsibility for the product.

After you spend your last day on earth, you will go in front of the LORD for your final judgment. While you stand at the front gate of heaven, will you see anyone already inside because of your influence? Will there be any testimonies in heaven from others on how you helped them? Will you be able to show God the time that you served him and not simply the time you prayed for him to serve you? When God evaluates your life, will he uncover hard evidence of how you used the gifts he granted you to benefit his kingdom?

You don't know when Jesus is coming back or when he will be calling you home; therefore, you need to pick up the pace in constructing your "house." Maximize your time, abilities, and treasures so that you can strengthen your life's investment portfolio and earn a profit here on earth as well as in the kingdom of heaven.

Doing what we can with what we have is the most we should expect of ourselves or anyone else.

—Fred Rogers[6]

IS YOUR HEART IN YOUR WORK?

> Reaching into his bag and taking out a stone, he slung it and struck the Philistine on the forehead. The stone sank into his forehead, and he fell face down on the ground. (1 Sam 17:49)

6. King, *World According to Mister Rogers*, 14.

Have you ever tried your hand at the game of poker? If so, how did you do? If you haven't played, have you ever witnessed others playing this card game? I'm betting (pun intended) that all of you have come across this popular game somewhere in your past. Maybe you have played a few rounds with family/friends at a party or watched your favorite celebrity play in a televised tournament. One of the main reasons poker has become one of the most popular card games is because it parallels life. The skills needed to win in poker are the same skills needed to win in life. Tell any poker player that he or she was lucky to win a pot and you'll likely find yourself on the receiving end of a cold death stare. The fact that someone would have the nerve to suggest that a player's hard work and efforts were nothing more than luck merely displays their ignorance of the game. You see, poker is a game of strategy and skill, and while the rules may seem straightforward enough, learning how to play is no simple task. Yes, you may understand the rules, but it takes years of hard work and practice to master the various intricacies of the game. Reading a player's actions and reactions, learning how to switch strategies when the unexpected happens, and knowing when to quit versus play are skills that only the best players have mastered. These are some of the same skills that are needed when playing the game called *life*. One thing is for sure, whether we are talking about poker or life, luck has nothing to do with winning or losing.

Poker Imitates Life, Life Imitates Poker

Poker and life are one and the same. Let me prove it to you. First, if you want to participate in either activity, more than one person needs to play. Second, to win, you must be willing to gamble. Third, all participants play from the same deck. Fourth, the cards are shuffled and randomly distributed. Finally, the outcome of the game will be determined by the action of each player based on their knowledge of probability, psychology, and game theory. So, what does all this "casino" talk mean? It means that life is just like a game of poker: the only reason you are playing is to win the "jackpot"! What do you define as your life's jackpot, and what are you willing to do to win it?

If you want to be dealt into a game of poker, you will be asked to "ante up" before the game begins. This means that a forced bet is required by all players before any cards are dealt. The ante ensures two important characteristics of the game. First, it establishes a pot (the sum of money that the players wage during a single game). Second, it incentivizes each player to play to win. If a player folds (forfeits their hand), they have no chance of winning and therefore lose their investment in the game.

Each morning, life forces you to ante up. It encourages you to invest your time, talents, and treasures into the pot. Life will provide you with daily opportunities to lead a productive life. How is your game going thus far? Are you winning or folding? How much do you ante up each day? What is your strategy? Are you committed or content? Are you multiplying your chips (time, talent, treasure) or wasting them?

God is the dealer in the game of life. He provides everyone with the same deck of cards. These cards guarantee you twenty-four hours in a day and 365 days in a year. He shuffles these cards thoroughly each day and deals you a hand. Some days the cards are great, and other days they are poor (Matt 5:45). Either way, he expects you to ante up and use the cards you receive to the best of your ability. Because of his infinite love and compassion, he will always provide you with the cards that you need. You may not want or like the cards you have been dealt, but if you persevere and commit to play, you will grow in faith, hope, and love and eventually win the "jackpot" (Luke 6:38).

W. I. N. (What's Important Now)

In Mark 4, Jesus tells his disciples the following parable:

> Listen! A farmer went out to sow his seed. As he was scattering the seed, some fell along the path, and the birds came and ate it up. Some fell on rocky places, where it did not have much soil. It sprang up quickly, because the soil was shallow. But when the sun came up, the plants were scorched, and they withered because they had no root. Other seed fell among thorns, which grew up and choked the plants, so that they did not bear grain. Still other seed fell on good soil. It came up, grew and produced a crop, some multiplying thirty, some sixty, some a hundred times. (Mark 4:3–8)

What is so interesting about this portion of the Gospel is that Jesus explains this parable to his disciples (us). He goes on to say,

> The farmer sows the word. Some people are like seed along the path, where the word is sown. As soon as they hear it, Satan

> comes and takes away the word that was sown in them. Others, like seed sown on rocky places, hear the word and at once receive it with joy. But since they have no root, they last only a short time. When trouble or persecution comes because of the word, they quickly fall away. Still others, like seed sown among thorns, hear the word; but the worries of this life, the deceitfulness of wealth and the desires for other things come in and choke the word, making it unfruitful. Others, like seed sown on good soil, hear the word, accept it, and produce a crop—some thirty, some sixty, some a hundred times what was sown. (Mark 4:14–20)

How important is this parable? Jesus begins it with a one-word sentence, "Listen!" and ends it by bluntly explaining its meaning. This parable is another example of the power of a seed. Seeds are necessary to sustain life. Without seeds, reproduction would be impossible. Through this parable, the Lord teaches you that he provides you with ample seeds daily to help you grow physically, mentally, and spiritually. How you respond to these seeds will determine whether they will promote growth or stagnation. Where are the seeds in your life? Are they located on the path, in rocky places, among thorns, or in good soil? Do you allow Satan to steal these seeds from you? Do you permit your flesh to blind you so that you never acknowledge them? Do you invite the culture of death into your life to poison them? Or do you allow the spirit to cultivate them so that they can multiply?

If you reflect a little deeper into this parable, you will uncover that God also wants you to be a farmer. For your seeds to produce, you must act. You must possess the courage to go forth every day and spread your time, talents, and treasures among others. Don't fret about where your seeds are landing. Focus on spreading your seeds wherever life takes you each day. Sharing your seeds requires a positive spiritual attitude and a maximum physical effort. You must be willing to toil and labor whether your seeds produce fruit or not. Tap into the deep hope and confidence that radiates from your soul and believe in the fact that your seeds will reach the soil that your Lord desires it to reach. Commit yourself to sowing; God will worry about the rest.

David and Goliath

The first Scripture quoted in this section came from 1 Sam 17. It described the outcome of the battle between David and Goliath. I would like to conclude this section by examining certain scenes from this battle and convert them into lessons to help you build your structure (life).

The introduction of chapter 17 sets the stage for a battle between the Philistines and the Israelites. As both armies took their positions on the battlefield, the great Philistine warrior, Goliath, marched to the middle of the battlefield so that all his opponents could see him. Goliath was nine foot nine inches tall! The total weight of his armor was 164 pounds! "Goliath stood and shouted to the ranks of Israel, 'Why do you come out and line up for battle? Am I not a Philistine, and are you not the servants of Saul? Choose a man and have him come down to me. If he can fight and kill me, we will become your subjects; but if I overcome him and kill him, you will become our subjects and serve us'" (1 Sam 17:8–9). In other words, he challenged the Jews to a one-on-one battle in which the winner would win the "jackpot." In this case, the jackpot was slavery. "For forty days the Philistine came forward every morning and evening and took his stand" (1 Sam 17:16). "Whenever the Israelites saw the man, they all fled from him in great fear" (1 Sam 17:24).

The Israelites were facing a giant, the biggest human being they have ever seen before. You are also facing a giant in the form of anxiety and/or depression, something that you have never experienced before. The Israelites were intimidated by the size of their problem. Their problem (Goliath) was so big and so well armored that it kept them insecure, afraid, and terrorized for forty days. Has your anxiety and/or depression made you insecure, afraid, and terrorized over the past forty days? Are you allowing your anxiety and/or depression to act like Goliath? Is it threatening your present and future with slavery?

In 1 Sam 17:12, we are introduced to David, the youngest of Jesse's eight sons. Jesse tells his teenage son to take food to his three older brothers, who were entrenched on the battlefield. When David delivered the food to his brothers, "Goliath, the Philistine champion from Gath, stepped out from his lines and shouted his usual defiance" (1 Sam 17:24). This was the first time that David saw Goliath and heard his challenge. Upon seeing and hearing this, David changed the situation the Jews found themselves in. What David had that the rest of the Israelites didn't have was a different perspective on the problem. It was the same problem, but David wasn't looking at it in the same way everyone else was. How do you see your anxiety and/or depression? Have you always looked at it the same way? Is it possible for you to see it from a different perspective? If all you see is what you see, you don't see all there is to be seen!

The issues that the Israelites dealt with were spiritual in nature. The issues that you are currently dealing with are also spiritual in nature. This is a complicated fact to understand because the Israelites saw their problem and you feel yours. Both look and feel like they are nine foot nine inches tall! However, the "father of lies" (Satan) specializes in keeping you blind from spiritual reality. He tries to keep you insecure, afraid, and terrorized by controlling your physical reality—the circumstances that you currently find yourself in. But David teaches you that when God becomes part of your equation, Goliath (your problem) will shrink. The Lord will change your circumstance when you change your perspective!

"David said to Saul [king of Israel], 'Let no one lose heart on account of this Philistine; your servant will go and fight him'" (1 Sam 17:32). To slay your giant, you must listen to your heart. Allow it to fill you with courage so that you will be armed with a belief that you can and will conquer your mental ailments. Allow it to strengthen your resolve so that you will commit to battle. Whatever the diagnosis, symptom, or stressor, approach it with David's perspective and allow your spirit to guide you to victory.

"Then he took his staff in his hand, chose five smooth stones from the stream, put them in the pouch of his shepherd's bag and, with his sling in his hand, approached the Philistine" (1 Sam 17:40). God provided David all that he needed to defeat Goliath. He sent him to the battlefield when the Israelites needed him the most (time). He battle-tested David prior to him facing the Philistine (talents; 1 Sam 17:34–37). He gave him the ammunition that he needed for his weapon (treasures). David's destiny was fulfilled by following the "spirit."

Stop reading for a moment and take inventory of what God has given you to defeat your "Goliath." Think about your time, talents, and treasures. How did you do? Were you able to provide yourself with examples? If so, the Spirit is already moving within you (John 14:16). If not, let me provide you with some examples. He created this day for you to begin the fight (time). He has packed your mind, body, and soul with the seeds of faith, hope, and love (talents). He has surrounded you with family and friends that will support you in any and every way (treasures).

Did you notice the last three words of verse 40? David "approached the Philistine." When you allow your spirit to guide you, it will move you forward. With God as your copilot, you will always be on offense. This perpetual forward motion will allow you to fight the good fight, to finish the race, and to keep the faith (2 Tim 4:7). Because David was willing to act, it made all the difference for himself, his family, and his nation. Are you willing to move quickly to the battle line, like David, and take on your "Goliath" (1 Sam 17:32)?

"So, David triumphed over the Philistine with a sling and a stone; without a sword in his hand, he struck down the Philistine and killed him. David ran and stood over him. He took hold of the Philistine's sword and drew it from the sheath. After he killed him, he cut off his head with the sword" (1 Sam 17:50–51). David's victory over Goliath is extraordinary. Not only did it take tremendous courage and perfect skill (hitting the Philistine between the eyes) to defeat the giant, but it took a complete faith in God. This Scripture passage proves that no matter how fortified an obstacle in your life may be, it can be defeated. With the right perspective, courage, skill, and faith, victory can be achieved!

Submit yourselves, then, to God. Resist the devil, and he will flee from you.
—Jas 4:7

Put on the full armor of God, so that you can take your stand against the devil's schemes. So that when the day of evil comes, you may be able to stand your ground.
—Eph 6:11, 13

If God is for us, who can be against us?
—Rom 8:31

Moral of the story is: I chose a half measure when I should have gone all the way. I'll never make that mistake again. No more half measures, Walter.

—Mike Ehrmantraut, Breaking Bad[7]

7. Bernstein, "Half Measures."

HOW IS YOUR WORKMANSHIP?

For every house is built by someone, but God is the builder of everything.
—Heb 3:4

How strong is your "house"? Have you built it on rock or sand? Can it withstand the rain and wind that life brings, or will it fall with a great crash? Do others describe you as wise builder or a foolish one (Matt 7:24–27)? These are the questions that Jesus asked his followers over two thousand years ago and continues to ask today. Your answers to these questions will allow Jesus to evaluate your daily workmanship. He is paying very close attention to see if you are following the building codes that were established by his Heavenly Father.

Your workmanship will determine the structural integrity of your "house." Structural integrity is an aspect of engineering which deals with the ability of a structure (your life) to hold together under a load (stress, anxiety, depression, etc.) without breaking or deforming excessively. Superior workmanship will ensure that your "house" will perform its designed function (to be productive) for as long as its intended life span.

How would you describe your workmanship? Is it comparable to Jesus Christ, the master carpenter, or more comparable to the elderly carpenter that was described in the introduction of this chapter? Do you approach your daily build in a systematic or haphazard way (Luke 14:28–30)? Are you working off a set of blueprints? If so, who created them: you or the Lord? Are the structures you are building temporary or everlasting? Do you choose to work on your house by yourself, or do you allow others to help you? If others help you, are they skilled or unskilled laborers? These are some of the questions that will help define the quality of your workmanship.

The Lord's Training Center

If your workmanship is substandard, today is the day to retrain and rebuild (Eccl 3:1). Is your current foundation built on sand? Jesus Christ will turn it into bedrock! Is your current structure flimsy and weak? Jesus Christ will make it strong as steel! Is your house dark and empty? Jesus Christ will fill it with light and love! Training sessions on how to build the house (life) you always dreamed of are now available to you. The only prerequisite needed to receive this training is to "repent and turn to him" (Acts 3:19). "For the Lord your God is gracious and compassionate. He will not turn his face from you if you return to him" (2 Chr 30:9).

The Lord's training center is open 24/7. It is always accepting applicants, and no one is ever denied. The only textbook needed for these training sessions is the Holy Bible. His "words" will provide you with the time, talents, and treasures that are necessary to build the house that he has envisioned for you. He will slowly but surely retrain you so that you can earn the title master builder. However, building this house is not an easy task. It is going to take planning, patience, purpose, passion, perseverance, performance, participation, persuasion, possessions, praise, prayer, preparation, prevention, production, promises, promotion, protection, pushing, pulling, and any other verb you can think of that starts with the letter *p*!

Apprentice

If you apply to the Lord's training center, he will enroll you into his apprenticeship program so that you can acquire all the knowledge and skill needed to build a mansion here on earth and in heaven (John 14:2–3). As a new enrollee, the Lord will position you as an *apprentice*. Depending upon the structure of your current "house," this portion of the training may last months or years. As an apprentice, you will learn the most basic and rudimentary skills on how to build your house by imitating Jesus Christ. Your entire experience will revolve around the concepts of *faith*, *hope*, and *love*. These foundational concepts will be taught through Scripture reading (Old and New Testament). The Lord will also use his primary teaching assistant (the Holy Spirit) to provide you with homework assignments that will allow you to experience and practice these concepts (John 14:26).

Also, you will have the advantage of seeing Jesus Christ at work. Whether it is learning lessons from his parables or witnessing miracles, you will receive personal instruction on the importance of compassion, service, love, forgiveness, commitment, gentleness, patience, self-control, and humility (Matt 7:12). In addition, you will have total access to him to engage in conversation and ask questions. Most importantly, you will have the opportunity to try out new skills beneath his watchful and correcting eye.

Journeyman

Once you acquire the knowledge and understanding that comes from being an apprentice, the LORD will elevate you into the second phase of training—a *journeyman*. This title symbolizes that you are no longer a novice and have earned the reputation of being a competent builder in the eyes of the LORD. As a journeyman, you are still under the supervision of the LORD, but he grants you the free will to begin building/rebuilding your house with the lessons that you learned under his tutelage. However, before the building begins, the LORD will demand that you inspect your house. You will be asked to analyze your foundation, engineering, and capacity. In other words, you will access the condition of your current life and discover what needs changed, reinforced, or added to increase your productivity.

Once this inspection is complete, action will be required. This is where the journey begins. All the theoretical concepts that you learned as an apprentice will now be turned into physical, emotional, and spiritual labor. All restorations and/or additions to your house must be built with your Heavenly Father in mind. You must accept full responsibility for your work (Gal 6:5) and understand that "everyone who has been given much, much will be demanded; and from the one who has been entrusted with much, much more will be asked" (Luke 12:48). The LORD has high expectations for his journeymen and is prepared to test them to prove they have what it takes to be a builder for the kingdom of God. The time that it takes to fulfill the requirements of being a journeyman depends upon the quality of your house. Your house must be built upon a hill for everyone to see. It must shine light before others so that they may see your good deeds and the glorification of the Heavenly Father (Matt 5:14–16). Until this occurs, you will be designated a journeyman at the LORD's training center.

Teacher

The third and final phase of training is to earn the title of *teacher*. It is the highest rank you can receive from the LORD. Those who complete this stage are forever known as saints. The entry to this level is not exclusive but inclusive. You can reach this stage by *always* performing God's will. The emphasis at this level centers around others. Through God's grace, you no longer focus on yourself because he has brought great satisfaction and fulfillment in your life. Your burning desire for God has transformed your whole outlook on life and has given you a clear and certain direction in all that you do. Every relationship you form and every decision you make is endorsed by the Lord. You realize that the house you have spent a lifetime building does not exist to serve you but to serve others (Mark 10:45).

Practicing teachers begin each day with a renewal ritual. Renewal is a daily process that helps combat sin. It inspires the teachers to live their life in a Christlike manner. Teachers are called to be set apart from the worldly culture around them, to live in the world but not be of the world (John 15:19). This is made possible by renewing their bodies, minds, and spirit. Physical renewal simply means they receive enough sleep each night (eight or more hours) so their imperfect bodies acquire enough rest to function at their best. Mental renewal is accomplished by reading and meditating on God's word. This allows them to capture the mind of Christ (1 Cor 2:11–16) so they can see the things of the world as he sees them. Spiritual renewal develops when they focus on God and rely on his strength to sustain them. God's strength comes in the form of asking, receiving, and giving forgiveness (1 John 1:9, Matt 18:21–35). It comes from fervent and constant prayer (Mark 1:35).

Once the daily morning renewal ritual is completed, they spend the rest of their day in service of the Lord. They are motivated and led by the Holy Spirit to spread the seeds that are taken from the kingdom of God. Either by word (evangelization) or by action (an unselfish deed), they do not let an opportunity pass them by until they shine the light of salvation onto that given situation. Conversations are illuminating! Interactions are life-changing! Inspiration is all-encompassing! These teachers become the scarred hands and feet of the Lord. They help heal the sick; house, clothe, and feed the poor; forgive those who are stained by sin; defend those who cannot defend themselves; visit the lonely and imprisoned; condemn the culture of death; challenge the wealthy and powerful to govern fairly; fight for justice for those who are oppressed; renounce materialism; promote love; strive for peace; and practice mercy. They are ordinary people that do extraordinary things for their Lord and Savior!

What Is the Condition of Your House?

Hopefully, this section allowed you to pause and think about your "house." I encourage you to inspect your house every six months. This will allow you to repair any holes or leaks that are not allowing you to live in the most effective and efficient manner. Secondly, it will refocus you on the new structures that you are currently installing. Finally, it will allow you to compare your existing structure with the house that you created in your heart, mind, and soul.

Remember, each day is a workday. Be prepared to sweat and get dirty. Always have a plan. Don't panic if things don't go as planned. Make sure your toolbox contains a Bible. Don't be afraid to ask for help, and always keep your front door open so you can help others find the Lord and Savior.

Commit to the Lord whatever you do,
and he will establish your plans.
—Prov 16:3

You, Eternal Trinity, are my Creator, and I am the work of Your hands, and I know through the new creation which You have given me in the blood of Your Son, that You are enamored of the beauty of Your workmanship.

—Catherine of Siena[8]

WHAT KIND OF MATERIALS ARE YOU USING?

You are the salt of the earth.
—Matt 5:13

You are the light of the world.
—Matt 5:14

What kind of materials are you using to build your "house"? Are they made from the finest quality or are they generic? Are they natural substances or synthetic materials? Are they tested or unreliable? Are they

8. Noffke, *Dialogue of the Seraphic Virgin*, 383.

timeless or temporary? The value of your house depends upon the time, talent, and treasures you use to build it. Without the proper materials, your house will never match the blueprints that God created for you.

Building your house is not a passive exercise. It takes time, patience, prayer, and energy to gather the specific materials needed to complete your unique house (Matt 7:7). Because the size and shape of your house is different from every other house, it is your responsibility to diligently choose the materials you will need to complete it. God has given you the free will to design and build the *exterior* of your house but has instructed you on how to construct the *interior*. In Matthew chapter 5, he explicitly tells you that the interior of your house must be erected by using "salt" and "Light" (Matt 5:13–14).

Salt

You are called to be the "salt of the earth." And just like salt, you are not made to simply be the star and center of attention. You are not made only for yourself. Instead, it is your Christian duty to enter the world and add to it, helping to transform it into a world of grace and mercy, full of the "flavor" of God's kingdom. This is done, especially, by the building up of relationships. It's done by striving to touch one person at a time to enhance their lives and help them to be closer to Christ. The love of God that you bring into the world, and into the lives of those whom you encounter, can be seen analogously as salt entering food and enhancing it.

Light

> A little boy was sitting in church with his mom one day. As he looked up at the beautiful stained-glass windows, he saw faces in the glass. "Mom, who are those people in the window?" he asked. "Those are the saints," she answered. The little boy thought for a while and then said, "Oh, I know who the saints are. They're the ones that let the light in."[9]

The Lord has predestined you to become a saint (teacher). He has given you time, talents, and treasures so you can share your eternal "light" with others. The bright light that others see is the good works

9. Pritchard, "Salt and Light Brigade."

that you do. This includes your character, your conduct, your actions, and your spoken testimony. When people see you, they will glorify God because they will recognize that it is by the grace of God that you are what you are. They will see that your light is his light and that your works are his works done in you and through you. That is how you will let the light of Jesus Christ come into them.

Essential Building Materials

You are unique. You are special. Your Father (God) has created you in his own image. His life-giving breath is inside of you (Gen 2:7). He loves you and wants the very best for you. He wants your "house" to be filled with "good news"! His goal for you is to be what you were meant to be. To accomplish his goals and your goals, you must add the following building materials to your house.

Love: True love is a choice, not a feeling. It deliberately expresses itself in action and always seeks the welfare of others. Love is dependent on your character, not emotion. Love chooses to set aside your own preferences and desires so you can put other people first (Phil 2:1–3).

Joy: It is a feeling of gladness based on your circumstances. Sadly, most of us define joy based on fleeting, physical circumstances. But the joy of the Lord is established in our spiritual, eternal circumstances. As you grow in your relationship with him, you will experience the fullness of joy he promised (John 15:4–11).

Peace: The world doesn't offer much peace; take a moment and think about what you see, hear, and feel daily. However, the peace of Christ is possible, no matter your circumstances (John 14:27). You can reject the chaos of the world and embrace God's peace by laying all your worries, fears, and concerns at the foot of his cross (Phil 4:4–9).

Patience: One of the many goals of the culture of death is to destroy the concept of patience. The fast-paced, "I want it now" society that you live in doesn't value this virtue. However, by accepting your circumstances and walking in faith, you will learn to use endurance and perseverance as fuel to finish the "race" (Rom 5:3–4).

Kindness and Goodness: Together these characteristics present the picture of a person who not only possesses moral goodness and integrity but also generously expresses it in the way they act toward others. Their moral compass always points toward the Lord, which allows them to love themselves and their neighbors (Matt 22:34–30).

Faithfulness: To be faithful is to be reliable or trustworthy. It is a continued and consistent submission and obedience to the Lord and the plan he has created for you. Regardless of the twist and turns that life presents, you will be steadfast in the knowledge the Jesus Christ died on his cross and rose from the dead so that you would have everlasting life in his kingdom (Luke 23:43).

Gentleness and Meekness: Closely linked to humility, gentleness is grace of the soul. It is not weakness, but instead it is strength under control. Gentleness, being the opposite of self-assertiveness and self-interest, is also a key ingredient in unity and peace within the body of Christ (Eph 4:2).

Self-Control: This gives you the power to say yes to the Spirit and no to the flesh; yes to salvation and no to damnation; yes to virtue and no to sin. It gives you the confidence to trust in the Lord (Prov 4:27)!

> *But the fruit of the Spirit is love, joy, peace, forbearance, kindness, goodness, faithfulness, gentleness, and self-control. Against such things there is no law.*
>
> *—Gal 5:22–23*

How Aesthetically Pleasing Is Your House (Life)?

When someone views your "house," what do they experience? Do they see a life that is fulfilling its function? Do they see balance, proportion, and order? Do they sense a combination of color, texture, and lines that radiate a positive ambience? Can they connect a harmonious flow between your interior and exterior? Can they feel a culture, environment, and lifestyle that promotes the kingdom of God? Do they notice the "Light" in your eyes, heart, and soul? Do they want what you have? Hopefully this section gave you some insight into these questions.

> *Give careful thought to your ways. Go up into the mountains and bring down timber and build my house, so that I may take pleasure in it and be honored says the Lord.*
>
> *—Hag 1:7–8*

Part 3 | The Way, the Truth, the Life

The Happiness of your Life depends on
the Quality of your Thoughts.
—Marcus Aurelius[10]

DO YOU REALIZE THAT YOU MUST LIVE IN THE HOUSE YOU ARE CURRENTLY BUILDING?

If a house is divided against itself, that house cannot stand.
—Mark 3:25

Have you ever taken a virtual tour of the Sistine Chapel in Rome? If you haven't, I suggest that you stop reading for a moment and take the tour. Well, did you take my advice? What were your thoughts and emotions when viewing this awe-inspiring ceiling? It took Michelangelo four years to paint 343 figures! Each year, over five million people head to Vatican City to visit this chapel to see what Michelangelo did with the time, talent, and treasures that God gave him.

One the most famous frescoes on the Sistine Chapel ceiling is entitled the *Creation of Adam*. This painting illustrates story in the book of Genesis of God breathing life into Adam, the first human being. The painting is laid out in a rectangle. On the left, Adam is reclining and lazily stretches out his limp left hand toward God. On the right, God is in motion amid a cluster of angels. He extends his right hand toward Adam to discharge the spark of life. Their fingers are depicted only millimeters apart.

Michelangelo's paintbrush masterfully compares divine dynamic energy (illustrated in the movement of the Creator, who appears to radiate action) and human apathy (represented by Adam's aura of slothfulness). God's index finger is fully stretched and tense with energy; Adam's fingers are so limp that they cannot even be fully extended. No image better sums up the physical and conceptual chasm between God and man.

10. Aurelius, *Emperor Marcus Antoninus* 3.9.

The Deadly Sin of Slothfulness

So how does this painting relate to you? Since Adam and Eve are the ancestors of all humans, you are related to them. This means that they have passed all their traits on to you. Unfortunately, one of the traits that you have received from Adam is the deadly sin of slothfulness. Slothfulness was one of many tools used by Satan to banish Adam and Eve from the garden of Eden (Gen 3:23), and he continues to use it on you today to block you from properly building your "house." The devil relishes every time you choose to be lazy. He cheers when you stay in your pajamas all day to binge-watch Netflix. He applauds when you stay in the house on a beautiful day to play video games. He dances when you isolate yourself in your bedroom for hours surfing social media. He sets off fireworks when you skip out of school, show up late for work, disobey your parents, break your promises, procrastinate, and forget to pray. The evil one's goal is to manipulate you so he can drain your time, talents, and treasures. The more time you spend with him, the less time you have to complete your house.

How much more time do you invest into your flesh rather than your spirit? Are you allowing the devil to manipulate you? Did he trick you into living in his den instead of building your house for the kingdom of heaven? The following questions will help you determine your current address. It will also help you measure the amount of slothfulness that currently preoccupies your life. This exercise focuses on six categories that the devil will infiltrate to slow or stop the building process from occurring. Circle the response that best answers each question.

What Is Your Current Address?	
Category #1—Making Soft Choices	
1. How do you go about making decisions?	
a. base it on the path of least resistance	b. base it on finding a positive outcome
2. What is more important to you in the decision-making process?	
a. maintaining comfort	b. solving the problem
3. What is the first thing that you do when your alarm clock goes off in the morning?	

a. hit the snooze button	b. get out of bed and prepare for the day
4. What do you with "extra" time that is built into your schedule (study hall / work break)?	
a. play a game on your phone / surf the web	b. complete unfinished tasks / start a new task
Category #2—Disregarding Time	
5. How would you describe yourself?	
a. unambitious	b. self-starter
6. What best describes your daily approach?	
a. there is always tomorrow	b. *carpe diem*—seize the day
7. What do you value more?	
a. money	b. time
8. What best describes your life's philosophy?	
a. live in the moment—there is no tomorrow	b. live for today but plan for tomorrow
Category #3—Leaving Tasks Unfinished	
9. How would you describe yourself?	
a. lethargic	b. energetic
10. What is your attitude about work?	
a. it's a mountain that I'm forced to climb	b. it's a doorway to opportunity
11. If given a task, what's the likelihood you will complete it?	
a. not likely	b. very likely
12. How important is it for you to complete a task successfully?	
a. not important	b. very important

Category #4—Living in a World of Wishful Thinking	
13. What do you value more?	
a. wants	b. needs
14. What do you want out of the next phase of your life?	
a. I don't know / I haven't thought about it	b. I know what I want / I have a plan to get it
15. What is the best way to describe your general outlook on life?	
a. pessimist	b. optimist
16. Which emotion do you experience more often?	
a. restlessness	b. contentment
Category #5—Being Unproductive at School/Work	
17. How would you describe the influence you have in your school/workplace?	
a. neutral / negative	b. positive
18. How would you describe your initiative and follow through at school/work?	
a. below average	b. excellent
19. How would others describe you at school/work?	
a. individual	b. team player
20. What is your typical response when you underperform at school/work?	
a. blame others	b. take responsibility
Category #6—Limiting Activities by Self-Induced Fears	
21. What is your typical response to failure?	
a. give up / blame yourself	b. learn from your mistakes / try again
22. When you find yourself in a stressful situation, what kind of outcomes do you predict?	

a. negative outcomes	b. positive outcomes
23. What is your approach when dealing with your fears?	
a. avoid them	b. confront them and control my response
24. Do you allow your fears to stop you from experiencing desires and opportunities?	
a. sometimes	b. never

Thank you for completing this exercise. It is now time to evaluate your score. Tally up the number of times you circled option *a* and compare it to the number of times you circled *b*. Which letter did you circle the most? If you circled *a* more than *b*, Satan has taken an interest in you. He is making sure that you are exercising your flesh so that it can dominate over your spirit. If you circled *b* more than *a* this means you have successfully defended against the deadly sin of slothfulness. Don't raise the championship belt just yet. You are going to have to defend your spirit tomorrow, next week, next month, next year (Luke 4:13). The devil is persistent and patient. He is willing to fight you as many rounds as it takes to knock out your spirit. Also, keep in mind that he has more than one punch (in this case, it was *slothfulness*) in his repertoire. He is willing to use any temptation to take your heavenly championship belt from you!

Next, focus of the difference between your *a* and *b* responses. How large or small is that number? If you circled *a* more than *b* and the difference is significant, then Satan has you on his roster. Accept this like you would a streetlight. The light is currently red, which means you need to stop what you are currently doing. A change is needed in your life. You need to experience a transformation (Rom 12:12) to receive a radical newness. You can live in the springtime of your life if you choose to open your eyes, ears, heart, and soul to the Lord. Jesus Christ will change that streetlight to green so that you can move away from the "darkness" and enter "light." In Matt 17:1–8, Peter, James, and John experienced the transfiguration of Jesus Christ as well as their own transformation. They received an important message on that day that changed their life (and afterlife) forever. I would like to share this message with you so that your life (and afterlife) can be changed: "A bright cloud covered them, and a voice from the cloud said, 'This is my Son, whom I love; with him I am well pleased. Listen to him!'" (Matt 17:5).

Finally, I would like you to tally up your responses for each category. What category did you score the best in—more *b*'s than *a*'s? What category did you score the worst in—more *a*'s than *b*'s? This is important data for you to calculate. If changes are needed in your life, you can focus daily on specific strategies that will change specific behaviors. Daily improvement in one category can have a positive ripple effect on the other categories. In time, you will be making better decisions, valuing time, completing tasks, accepting reality, becoming more productive, and experiencing everything that life has to offer. You will be evicted out of the Devil's Den and given a new address on Everlasting Lane!

Decisions Have Consequences

When Adam and Eve willfully chose to disobey God in the garden of Eden, they created the right for you to practice free will—to freely make your own decisions. The one thing that Adam and Eve quickly learned (and that you must learn) is that decisions have consequences (Gen 3:14–19). You are free to make your own decisions, but you are not free to control the consequences of your actions.

To receive free will, you must accept responsibility for your actions. Every decision you make changes the shape of your "house." What you build today, you will live in tomorrow. Your present and future are interwoven together. Today's eating habits, exercise, and health choices will affect how you feel tomorrow. What you buy and spend money on today will affect you in some way tomorrow. How you treat others today will have a direct impact on how fruitful your relationships will be tomorrow. What your mental, emotional, and spiritual outlook are today will determine your faith, hope, and love for yourself and the LORD tomorrow. Your actions cause reactions, and these reactions create consequences. These consequences (positive or negative) impact your future. The secret of life is to keep one eye on today and the other eye on tomorrow!

Be very careful, then, how you live—not as unwise but as wise,
making the most of every opportunity, because the days are evil.
—Eph 5:15–16

Watch and pray so that you will not fall into temptation.
The spirit is willing, but the flesh is weak.

—Matt 26:41

One day or day one, you decide.
—Attributed to Paulo Coelho

WOULD YOU DO ANYTHING DIFFERENTLY?

> "Truly I tell you," Jesus answered, "this very night, before the rooster crows, you will disown me three times." (Matt 26:34)

Have you ever heard the story about the fisherman who was down on his luck? He always caught seaweed, shells, and smelly socks, but no fish. One day, he caught something else that looked quite useless: an old bottle. As soon as the fisherman took out the stopper and cast it aside, a huge genie appeared. "You have released me from a thousand years of imprisonment!" he cried, "For this I will grant you three wishes."

If you were that fisherman, what would you ask for? Would you ask for money? Would you ask for power? Would you ask to be a famous athlete, singer, or movie star? The old carpenter at the beginning of this chapter would have used one of his wishes to go back in time and restart the last house he built. How do I know this? When his employer handed the front-door key to him and said, "This is your house . . . my gift to you," the carpenter exclaimed, "If I had only known that I was building this house for myself, I would have done it all so differently."

In this section, we will discuss regret. Regret is usually the most common emotion people mention in their daily life. Unfortunately, regret is a negative emotion because it carries with it a tremendous amount of guilt and psychological pain. It's a human condition that we all suffer from. We would all like to find a genie in a bottle so that we, like the carpenter, could go back in time and right our wrongs so that our current lives would be a carbon copy of our dreams. But (I hate to be a dream crusher) you are not going to find a genie in a bottle anytime soon. So, you are going to have to learn to love and respect who you are and where you are in your life. Practicing faith, hope, and love will lead you to be the man or woman you were meant to be.

What Is Regret and How Can You Control It?

When looking back into your past, do you play the "what if" game? Do you ask yourself, "What if I made a different decision?" or "What if I responded in a different way?" It is very difficult to evaluate an experience without self-judgment. Sometimes playing the "what if" game is helpful because it enables you to learn valuable lessons by analyzing your behavior and its consequences. However, if you play the "what if" game every time you reminisce, you increase the chances of flooding your body with regret. Regret is a negative cognitive or emotional state that involves blaming yourself for a bad outcome, feeling a sense of loss or sorrow at what might have been, or wishing you could undo a previous choice that you made. Regret can be a painful experience that can trigger chronic stress that damages the mind, body, and soul.

Regret, like all emotions, has a function for survival. It is your brain's way of telling you to take another look at your choices, a signal that your actions may be leading to negative consequences. If you get stuck blaming yourself and regretting past actions, find a way to forgive yourself and let it go. Consider the circumstances that may have made it more difficult to make good choices in that instance, or the fact that you had limited knowledge at the time. Perhaps you had to make a quick decision under time pressure or had multiple stresses going on.

You are the by-product of your choices and actions. Various researchers estimate that the average person makes about thirty-five thousand conscious decisions each day. Of those thirty-five thousand choices, some are bound to be wrong. You are human, which means you are going to make mistakes—plenty of them. Instead of allowing these past mistakes to haunt your present and future, use them as opportunities to learn important lessons about yourself—including your values, vulnerabilities, and triggers—as well as about other people. Use them to decide how to take better care of yourself in the future.

The Denial of Peter

One of the great stories of regret can be found in all four Gospels in the New Testament. It is when Peter denied Jesus. The story begins at the Last Supper when Jesus told his disciples, "This very night you will all fall away on account of me" (Matt 26:31). After hearing this, Peter stood up and replied, "Even if all fall away on account of you, I never will"

(Matt 26:33). Jesus answered, "Truly I tell you, this very night, before the rooster crows, you will disown me three times" (Matt 26:34). But Peter declared, "Even if I have to die with you, I will never disown you" (Matt 26:35).

When Jesus was arrested in the garden of Gethsemane, "all the disciples deserted him and fled" (Matt 26:55). While the soldiers marched Jesus to the house of the high priest, "Peter followed at a distance" (Luke 22:54). Peter finally arrived at the courtyard and sat down around a fire with the soldiers.

> A servant girl came to him. "You also were with Jesus of Galilee," she said.
>
> But he denied it before them all. "I don't know what you're talking about," he said.
>
> Then he went out to the gateway, where another servant girl saw him and said to the people there, "This fellow was with Jesus of Nazareth."
>
> He denied it again, with an oath: "I don't know the man!"
>
> About an hour later, those standing there went up to Peter and said, "Surely you are one of them; your accent gives you away."
>
> Then he began to call down curses, and he swore to them, "I don't know the man!" (Matt 26:69–74).

> Just as he was speaking, the rooster crowed. The Lord turned and looked straight at Peter. Then Peter remembered the word the Lord had spoken to him: "Before the rooster crows today, you will disown me three times." And he went outside and wept bitterly. (Luke 22:60–62)

Even though Peter knew that Jesus Christ was the Messiah, the Son of the living Father (Matt 16:13–20), he still fulfilled the LORD's prophecy by denying him three times. Why did Peter do it? The Scriptures never give us an answer, but maybe he was frightened, distraught, vulnerable, defeated. Maybe peer pressure made him do it. He certainly was with the wrong people (nonbelievers) in the wrong place at the wrong time, about to do the wrong thing. We know that Peter regretted his decisions and actions because the Gospels report that after the cock crowed, "he went outside and wept bitterly" (Matt 26:75, Mark 14:72, Luke 22:62).

Jesus Reinstates Peter

But this story is not over! After the empty tomb was discovered and Jesus appeared to Mary Magdalene and his disciples (including Thomas), Peter and the rest of the disciples go back home to their families and their profession—fishing. After a long night of catching no fish, Jesus was seen standing on the shore as dawn was breaking (Light of the World).

> But the disciples did not realize that it was Jesus.
>
> He called out to them, "Friends, haven't you any fish?"
>
> "No," they answered.
>
> He said, "Throw your net on the right side of the boat and you will find some." When they did, they were unable to haul the net in because of the large number of fish.
>
> Then the disciple whom Jesus loved said to Peter, "It is the Lord!" . . .
>
> When they landed, they saw a fire of burning coals there with fish on it, and some bread. . . .
>
> When they had finished eating, Jesus said to Simon Peter, "Simon son of John, do you love me more than these?"
>
> "Yes, Lord," he said, "you know that I love you."
>
> Jesus said, "Feed my lambs." Again, Jesus said, "Simon son of John, do you love me?"
>
> He answered, "Yes, Lord, you know that I love you."
>
> Jesus said, "Take care of my sheep." The third time he said to him, "Simon son of John, do you love me?"
>
> Peter was hurt because Jesus asked him the third time, "Do you love me?" He said, "Lord, you know all things; you know that I love you."
>
> Jesus said, "Feed my sheep." (John 21:4–7, 9, 15–17)

This time when Peter found himself sitting around a fire, things were much different. He was fearless, balanced, protected, and full of hope. He was surrounded by the right people (disciples) in the right place (with Jesus) at the right time (witnessing the resurrection), about to do the right thing (evangelize the Lord's name). The series of questions that Jesus asked Peter allowed him to redeem himself from the poor decisions and actions he made days earlier (denying Christ three times). Jesus asked Peter one simple question three times, "Do you love me?" Peter responded each time, "Yes, Lord, you know that I love you." After each question and response, Jesus gave Peter a command: "Feed my lambs";

"Take care of my sheep"; "Feed my sheep." In the end, Jesus taught Peter a very important lesson. That lesson is *love* conquers all!

Jesus Christ is asking you the same question that he asked Peter. The difference is that he not going to ask, "Do you love me?" three times. He is going to ask you this question every day of your life. How do you plan to respond? Do you want to feel the power of forgiveness? Say, "I do!" Do you want to experience true love? Say, "I do!" Do you want the spiritual fulfillment that comes with giving and serving? Say, "I do!"

Stop Searching for a Genie in a Bottle

I crushed your dreams earlier in this section by telling you that you will not find a "genie in a bottle" anytime soon. As a matter of fact, you should stop wasting your time and energy and end your search today. I bet you have been wondering this whole time what that fisherman did with his three wishes. Allow me to end the suspense. The fisherman's first wish was that the genie was to return into the bottle. With this command, the genie shrunk back into the bottle and the fisherman put the stopper in, trapping him once more. The fisherman returned to his fishing, and this time he succeeded in catching a fish for dinner!

The fisherman teaches all of us a life lesson. We do not need a genie to make our wishes come true. When you have the Lord and Savior Jesus Christ in your life, you are guaranteed to catch a fish! The fisherman did and so did the disciples when Jesus told them to "throw their net on the right side of the boat" (John 21:6). In Jesus, you have direction, hope, life, meaning, and purpose. In Jesus you have love and forgiveness. The one thing that you will never have with Jesus Christ is regret!

Repent, then, and turn to God, so that your sins may be wiped out, that times of refreshing may come from the Lord.
—Acts 3:19

It is better to look ahead and prepare than to look back and regret.

—Jackie Joyner-Kersee[11]

11. Joyner-Kersee, "Letter to My Younger Self."

HOLISTIC APPROACH #2: THERAPEUTIC SURRENDER

> Unless I see the nail marks in his hands and put my finger where the nails were, and put my hand into his side, I will not believe. (John 20:25)

Saint Thomas

Thomas was one of the twelve main disciples of Jesus Christ. He's not a major Bible character by any means; he's only mentioned eight times in the entire New Testament, and four of those times are just lists of the twelve apostles. However, Thomas was one of the people who was closest to Jesus. He spent three years living with him, witnessing his miracles, and hearing his teachings. He saw numerous demonstrations of Jesus' power—including his power to raise people from the dead—and he heard Jesus predict his resurrection. As a disciple, he displayed great courage and loyalty. When the other disciples tried to keep Jesus from going to Bethany to raise Lazarus from the dead because of the danger from those in the area who had just earlier tried to stone him (John 11:8), Thomas said to them, "Let us also go, that we may die with him" (John 11:16). Thomas also asked him one of the most famous questions: "Thomas said to him, 'Lord, we don't know where you are going, so how can we know the way?' Jesus answered, 'I am the way and the truth and the life. No one comes to the Father except through me'" (John 14:5–6).

Do you know Thomas? What if I give you his nickname, "Doubting Thomas"? Now do you know who he is? He was given this label because he simply did not believe that Jesus had risen from the dead. Scripture explains that Jesus appeared to some of the disciples, but Thomas was not with them the first time. "So, the other disciples told him, 'We have seen the Lord!' But he [Thomas] said to them, 'Unless I see the nail marks in his hands and put my finger where the nails were, and put my hand into his side, I will not believe it'" (John 20:25). Eight days later, Jesus appears before his disciples again:

> A week later his disciples were in the house again, and Thomas was with them. Though the doors were locked, Jesus came and stood among them and said, "Peace be with you!" Then he said

> to Thomas, "Put your finger here; see my hands. Reach out your hand and put it into my side. Stop doubting and believe."
>
> Thomas said to him, "My Lord and my God!"
>
> Then Jesus told him, "Because you have seen me, you have believed; blessed are those who have not seen and yet have believed." (John 20:26–29)

Understanding the life and times of Saint Thomas will help you unleash the power of *therapeutic surrender*. Surrender is defined as giving oneself over to something. This occurs at an unconscious level. Simply put, a conversation takes place.

Conversation + Surrender = Systematic Change.

To eliminate your mental and spiritual afflictions, you will need to understand the process of surrender.

Therapeutic Surrender

No surrender, no cure! One of the main goals in therapy is for you and your mental health professional to establish a therapeutic alliance. This means to create a psychological and emotional bond with one another during sessions. If you *believe* your therapist is emphatic, trustworthy, experienced, skilled, and engaged in the communication process, you have a great chance to experience surrender. If your therapeutic alliance is absent or weak, you are wasting each other's time, and you need to find a new therapist.

Once a bond is formed between you and your therapist, you both can focus on setting goals for your time in therapy. These goals can range from short-term to mid-term to long-term. You and your therapist will begin to identify broad motives, hopes, and dreams that you have. You will begin to choose a theme you want to focus on (anxiety and/or depression). You will narrow that theme onto a specific target ("I want to prevent panic attacks"). You will create SMART (specific, measurable, achievable, relevant, time-bound) goals to help change behaviors around that target ("I want to reduce the number of panic attacks from five per month to one to two per month by the end of the year"). Finally, you will create an action plan to track and achieve your goal.

The outcome of this experience will depend on your reaction to this plan. If you *submit* to this plan, you may reduce your panic attacks. If you *surrender* to this plan, you will no longer experience anxiety. As you can see, there is a major difference between submission and surrender. Submission is a conscious decision in which you voluntarily *give up* your power to someone or something. Surrendering is an unconscious decision in which you *retain* your power over someone or something.

If you *submit* to the plan described above, you may see it as something that you are forced to do—something that is not needed. You may allow your ego to hijack your thoughts and behaviors. You may give yourself permission to fight, reject, ignore, and push against the plan that you submitted to. You may purposely sabotage the therapeutic process to free yourself from this unwelcome bondage.

If you *surrender* to the plan described above, you will see it as something that you must do. You unconsciously recognize that you have a problem and that you need help. Your ego has run its course and no longer controls your thoughts and behaviors. You have forgiven yourself for past mistakes and are prepared for a new beginning. You have hope for the future but live in the present. You fully embrace the therapeutic plan because it provides you an opportunity to heal. You welcome the challenge of renewal and are motivated to experience everything that it has to offer. You are full of gratitude, grace, hope, and joy. A sense of relief and peace guides you through the therapeutic process and beyond.

A recent study found that in the United States, the dropout rate for therapy is between 40 percent to 60 percent. What's even more troubling is that one-third of those who drop out do so after the initial visit.[12] The findings in this study are not a surprise. Though there may be many explanations for this phenomenon, the ulterior reason is that most clients only *submit* to therapy. It's funny how everything we discuss goes back to flesh versus spirit. If you enter therapy under the control of your flesh, you may suffer the same fate as your ancestor Adam. Adam's sense of superiority, need for control, thirst for freedom, and pride exiled him from the garden of Eden. He went on to a life of toil, doubt, fear, guilt, shame, blame, enmity, loneliness, and frailty. The same can happen to you if you *submit* to therapy.

Deny your flesh and sanctify your spirit. Drown the yearnings of your ego and baptize the aspiration of your soul. Strike the serpent's head and bow down at the foot of the cross. Free your spirit and follow it to a

12. Roseborough, et al., "Attrition in Psychotherapy," 804; Simon et al., "First Psychotherapy Visit," 705.

conversion. Accept *surrender* and experience the joy of healing. No surrender, no cure!

Peace Be with You

I introduced you to Saint Thomas in the introduction of this section. I stated that knowing the story of Saint Thomas will help you unleash the power of therapeutic surrender. Let's review the life and times of Thomas and see how he dealt with *submission* and *surrender*. Thomas was born to play an important role in God's plan. Thomas was so important to God that his only begotten Son sought him out so that he could spend his last three years on earth with him. Wherever Jesus went, Thomas followed. Whatever Jesus preached, Thomas heard. Whoever Jesus healed, Thomas witnessed. Even though Thomas was blessed to receive a VIP pass to experience Jesus' ministry on earth, he only partially *submitted* to him. Like the rest of the disciples, Thomas was devoted to Jesus right up until the time he was arrested, tried, and crucified. After Jesus died on the cross, the disciples passed through a phase of doubt, unbelief, trouble, and confusion. Jesus ended their mourning by showing himself on the day that he rose from the dead. The dilemma for Thomas was that he wasn't present for this event. Thomas became a skeptic and rejected the testimony that Jesus had risen from the other disciples.

Because Thomas was living in his "flesh," he made his own individual test for believing in the resurrection: "Unless I see the nail marks in his hands and put my finger where the nails were, and put my hand into his side, I will not believe it" (John 20:25). This was an absolute condition and a nonnegotiable term for believing. His ego did not permit any other evidence to be admissible. Eight days later, Jesus accepted the challenge of Thomas and invited him to proceed with the demanded test. The unbelieving disciple not only saw Christ but was instructed to complete the test by touching the hands and of the side of Jesus. Instantly, Thomas went from *submitting* to *surrendering*. Without any other words, explanations, or apologies, he responded with an astonishing confession of faith: "Thomas answered him, 'My Lord and my God'" (John 20:28). A conversion took place, and Thomas's life was radically changed forever!

Enter Your Spirit

Do you believe? Can you overcome your doubts? Can you trust that therapy is a way to heal your mental afflictions? Therapeutic surrender (like spiritual surrender) is attained through faith, hope, and love. Prior to entering therapy, you must recognize that you are not functioning at your maximum capability. More importantly, you must internally accept this assessment. Coming to terms with your affliction will pause the battle from within. Acknowledging a mental health issue will bring peace to your mind, body, and soul. It will shed "light" on the reasons why you have been struggling with your emotions, thought patterns, and biological functions. It brings faith to your fight!

Surrendering to therapy also allows you to wear an armor of hope. You realize for the very first time that you are not the only person battling this enemy. There are millions of other adolescents and/or young adults who fight on the same battlefield as you. You are not alone in this fight. Family, friends, and mental health professionals are by your side helping you advance on the battlefield.

Finally, surrendering to therapy is the ultimate form of love. If you only learn one lesson from this book, I hope it is that *love conquers all*! Loving the Lord, loving yourself, loving your neighbor, and loving the therapeutic process will always cleanse any ailment that life tries to stick on you. True love can only be found in the "spirit" and only in the "spirit" will you declare victory over the enemy.

There's No Surrender without Full Surrender!

—Dina Rolle[13]

HOLISTIC APPROACH #3: THE POWER OF JOURNALING

It is true! The Lord has risen and has appeared to Simon. (Luke 24:34)

13. Rolle, *Adversities and Triumphs*, 50.

The Road to Emmaus

Are you familiar with the Scripture passage that describes a conversation that two men had with a stranger while they were walking to a town called Emmaus? The road to Emmaus Bible story is the first of three resurrection appearances found in Luke. The story begins when two men are traveling to Emmaus (which was seven miles from Jerusalem) just days after the crucifixion of Jesus. As they were walking, a third man drew near to them. Together they walked and discussed the life of Jesus of Nazareth and how he might still be alive since his tomb was found empty. When the men get to Emmaus and join in supper, the third man is recognized as Jesus as he breaks and blesses the bread. Jesus then vanishes, and the two men return to Jerusalem where they pronounce to the "Eleven" that Jesus has risen!

This Scripture passage is important because it has a deep connection with the third holistic approach—*journaling*. While walking with the "stranger," the two men give a very detailed and accurate description about what happened over the past three days in Jerusalem.

> "About Jesus of Nazareth," they replied. "He was a prophet, powerful in word and deed before God and all the people. The chief priests and our rulers handed him over to be sentenced to death, and they crucified him; but we had hoped that he was the one who was going to redeem Israel. And what is more, it is the third day since all this took place. In addition, some of our women amazed us. They went to the tomb early this morning but didn't find his body. They came and told us that they had seen a vision of angels, who said he was alive. Then some of our companions went to the tomb and found it just as the women had said, but they did not see Jesus." (Luke 24:19–24)

This description is very detailed and informative. It provides fact as well as opinion. You can feel emotions seesaw from sadness and frustration to hope and joy. The story is packed with everything a Hollywood script would want. The men were able to tell this story to the "stranger" in this fashion because it was fresh in their minds; it just happened over the past three days. Journaling is powerful in the same way because it captures your thoughts, emotions, struggles, fears, and accomplishments as they are occurring. If these men came across this "stranger" a year after all these events took place, I'm sure their story would lack the insight that only a fresh perspective can give.

After receiving all of this "breaking news" from these men, Jesus (the "stranger") begins to provide them personal tutoring in the meaning of Old Testament Scripture. "He said to them, 'How foolish you are, and how slow to believe all that the prophets have spoken! Did not the Messiah have to suffer these things and then enter his glory?' And beginning with Moses and all the Prophets, he explained to them what was said in all the Scriptures concerning himself" (Luke 24:25–27). Jesus' response can also be tied into the importance of journaling. Because Jesus is the Son of God, he provided these men with all the words and events that occurred in human history that predicted his triumphant glory. By journaling, you can trace back your own thoughts and events to understand how you arrived at your current stage in life.

When writing this passage, Luke used the word *open* three times. The repetition of this word directs you to the message of this passage as well as the importance of using journaling as a holistic treatment. The first mention of *open* occurred at the beginning of the story when the two men were leaving Jerusalem and heading to Emmaus. Luke tells us, "All along the journey, the eyes of the two disciples were not open to recognize Jesus" (Luke 24:16). The *open* reference in this verse tells you that these two men were closed (the opposite of *open*) when conversing with the risen Christ. The reason that they were blind to Jesus is because in their hearts, they believed that Jesus was dead even though they heard reports about the empty tomb earlier that day.

Have you closed yourself off from events that have occurred in the past? Are there flaws in your character that you refuse to recognize? Do you intentionally create blind spots so you don't have to deal with reality? Do you have cataracts on your soul because you refuse to forgive someone that has caused you pain? If so, journaling can "open" you by removing the filters you have created over time. Journaling will allow you to freely explore your inner dynamics. It will allow you to express your emotions without guilt or judgment. It will help shine a "light" on the dark spots of your mind, heart, and soul.

The second mention of *open* is when they urged the stranger to stay with them since it was late in the day. "When Jesus was at the table with them, he took bread, gave thanks, broke it, and began to give it to them. Then their eyes were opened, and they recognized him, and he disappeared from their sight" (Luke 24:30–31). The two men experienced a conversion when Jesus repeated the ritual that occurred at the Last

Supper. They recognized the Lamb of God when he served them his body and blood.

When was the last time you reflected upon your needs? What item did you secure to meet one of these needs? How long ago did that occur? In times of stress and struggle you must take care of yourself before you can help others. You must have the courage to find a direction out of the pain. Journaling will provide you with a compass that will move you in the right direction. Writing is a cathartic release. It provides psychological relief and a path to recovery. Journaling can help you discover who you were, are, and will be.

The last mention of the word *open* occurred when Jesus vanished from the sight of the two men. "They asked each other, 'Were not our hearts burning within us while he talked with us on the road and opened the Scriptures to us?' They got up and returned at once to Jerusalem. There they found the Eleven and those with them, assembled together and saying, 'It is true! The Lord has risen and has appeared to Simon'" (Luke 24:32–34). The two men were now truly "opened" to the risen Lord. They *surrendered* their hearts, mind, and soul to Jesus Christ. They were so excited about the good news that they immediately walked the seven miles back to Jerusalem to report what they witnessed to the rest of the disciples. When arriving back at Jerusalem, they "opened" the door where the disciples were staying and exclaimed, "The Lord has risen!"

Journaling is a holistic approach that can open your eyes, heart, and mind. It can help you deal with your experiences and feelings. It can help you cope with the world. It can help you uncover your inner identity and voice. It can help you make sense of the past and present. Most importantly, it can change the trajectory of your future. Are you ready to journal?

Journaling While in Therapy

Are you spending time in therapy, or are you investing time in therapy? Therapy is not something that you do for one hour per week. It is a daily process of introspection. Your thoughts and emotions don't act like the water faucet in your kitchen. You just can't turn them on and pour them out to your therapist during a session. They flow at unpredictable times. Maybe you experience them when you are at peace or when you are stressed. Maybe they gush when your senses are stimulated (something you hear, smell, taste, touch). Maybe your unconscious unleashes them while you are sleeping. For these and other reasons, it is good to have a record of them when they appear. Journaling is the best way to capture them.

Journaling is not diary writing. It is not a daily log of the events that occurred in your life. It is much more than that. It helps you to explore and understand yourself. It helps you release mental blockades so that you can fully experience your desires, priorities, and worries. Journaling is not as complicated as you think. The first thing you need to decide is what your journal will look like. You can keep a journal in many forms, from digital to analog and aural to visual. The important thing is that you choose a journal medium which inspires you to write. The second decision will be when to use your journal. You may use it when a thought and/or emotion reveals itself, or you may get into a daily habit to examine your conscious and record your reactions. You must not approach journal writing as homework but as extra credit!

When writing a journal entry, make sure that you date it and title it. This will allow you to take a snapshot of a time and place in your life. The title will also give you a quick description about the content in that entry. Before writing, take a moment to meditate and brainstorm the ideas that you want to describe. This will allow your entry to be concise but potent. Write quickly, naturally, and honestly. These entries are for you (and your therapist if you would like to share). The words and ideas that are presented in your journal should come from your inner core. Be real with your thoughts, feelings, and opinions. Be as candid as you can. Your entries should take between five to twenty minutes to write. If you are spending less than five minutes writing, you haven't given yourself enough time to explore your thoughts and/or emotions. If you go over twenty minutes, you may lose interest in journaling because of the demand on your time and energy. You don't have to write in paragraph form. You are not turning this in to your English teacher as a graded assignment. Be free to write in fragments, outlines, or checklists. The goal is to capture your thought and/or emotion and react to it. Make sure to reread your entry when you complete it so that it makes sense. This will allow you to go back to a certain place and time in your life and understand what you were thinking, feeling, and experiencing.

Another idea would be to reserve a section in your journal for your therapy sessions. After each session you can review and reflect upon the discussions and exercises that were covered. Writing a summary of your session can help you process any new information that you discovered. It can also provide additional questions that you may want to ask at your next appointment. This summary can also help you set the agenda for your next session. For example, maybe you want clarification on a strategy that was introduced or you want to discuss the pace and progress of the goals that were established. Journaling about your thoughts, sensations, questions, challenges, breakthroughs, attitude, and behavior during therapy sessions increases the chances of growth and healing between appointments. What are you waiting for? The creation of your journal is just a thought away!

It is like whispering to one's self and listening at the same time.

—Bram Stoker[14]

CHAPTER 7 SUMMARY

My people will live in peaceful dwelling places, in secure homes, in undisturbed places of rest.

—Isa 32:18

This chapter continued to provide you with the opportunity to discover "the Way," "the Truth," and "the Life." Its content focused on the "house" (life) that you are currently building for yourself. Each section helped you inspect your structure in different ways. The first step in this self-inspection process was to look at the paperwork that came with your "house." The deed of the house belongs to God. He has hired you to build a structure on his plot of land. He has made you the primary architect but is willing to help you throughout the construction process. He has given you three important building materials: time, talents, and treasures. He has gifted you these resources so that you can maximize your house. He has also provided you a set of blueprints that he wants you to follow. These blueprints represent the life that he has planned for you. Are you following these blueprints or have you created your own?

The second step in the self-inspection process was to gauge the stability of your house. There were a series of test questions that examined your structure's integrity. These questions focused on your work ethic,

14. Stoker, *Dracula*, 79.

workmanship, expectations, judgment, and atonement. Did you pass the test? Have all the LORD's building codes been met?

The final step in the self-reflection process focused on sustaining and bolstering your life. Two holistic approaches were presented to help you mentally and emotionally overcome the self-doubt and fear that comes with building. Because God is your landlord, he wants to ensure that his investment is profitable. Therefore, he will continue to provide for you if you earn a daily wage in his workforce and pay him the rent that you owe every Sunday in church.

> *By wisdom a house is built, and through understanding it is established; through knowledge its rooms are filled with rare and beautiful treasures.*
>
> —*Prov* 24:3–4

THE ROAD RESURRECTION

ELEVENTH STATION: JESUS PROMISES HIS KINGDOM TO THE GOOD THIEF

> Two rebels were crucified with him, one on his right and one on his left. (Matt 27:38)

We adore you, O Christ, and we bless you.

Because by your holy cross you have redeemed the world.

> One of the criminals who hung there hurled insults at him: "Aren't you the Messiah? Save yourself and us!"
>
> But the other criminal rebuked him. "Don't you fear God," he said, "since you are under the same sentence? We are punished justly, for we are getting what our deeds deserve. But this man has done nothing wrong."
>
> Then he said, "Jesus, remember me when you come into your kingdom."
>
> Jesus answered him, "Truly I tell you, today you will be with me in paradise." (Luke 23:39–43)

LORD, grant us perseverance that we may never stop seeking you.

ELEVENTH STATION: REFLECTIVE EXERCISES AND QUESTIONS

On Good Friday, three men were nailed to crosses on Calvary. Two of them were criminals and one was a king. Each of them faced agonizing pain and death. Their suffering was the same, but they reacted very differently to their experience. The Gospels do not tell us much about the criminals. We do not know how much they stole or how often. We do not know who they stole from or why. It does not matter what they did. What's important is what they became because of their encounter with Jesus. Isn't that true? All that matters one hundred years from now is what you did with the person of Jesus Christ!

The First Criminal

The first criminal's heart is so dark and thick that he was willing to mock Jesus hours before his own death. Scriptures tell us that this man was hostile and full of rage. He "hurled insults" at Jesus while hanging next to him. This nonbeliever asked Jesus sarcastically, "Are you not the Messiah? Save yourself and us!" He was focused only on his immediate pain and need. His mind was fixed on himself. He cursed Jesus for his suffering, as if he was not to blame for his own fate. He was blind to anything good, special, and divine about Jesus. He was blind to his own failings that had brought him to his cross and blind to the person next to him who could have still given him salvation. Living in his "flesh" sealed his fate.

People in great pain will say anything. Have you ever acted like the criminal above? Have you looked at Jesus and asked, "What have you done for me lately?" Have you ever demanded him to take you down from the cross that you currently hang from? Have you challenged the LORD to get you out of a situation? Do you treat Jesus like a spare tire instead of your steering wheel? Do you only call on him when you need help? If so, your destiny could be like that of the criminal. Being estranged from the LORD is a lonely experience. It will render you blind, mute, and deaf. You will experience the same response that Jesus gave this criminal—silence!

The Second Criminal

The second criminal reacted in a very different way than the first. There were four things that distinguished this man from the first criminal. First, his perspective was different. He wasn't riddled with self-pity. He was dying, and he knew he was not in a good place with God. Second, he took responsibility for his actions. He accepted his punishment. There was no doubt that he regretted the way he had lived, but there was no denial of his sin. He knew that he lived against God. Third, he recognized who was hanging next to him. He stated, "This man has done nothing wrong." Somehow, someway, he knew Jesus was innocent. He knew that Jesus did not deserve ridicule because he was a good man. Finally, his plea to Jesus was different than the other criminal. The first criminal's words were taunting. The second criminal's words were appealing: "Jesus, remember me when you come into your kingdom."

The Father would not allow his Son to die alone. He blessed him with a strange companion during his last hours. He gave him a believer! A believer with mighty faith. A believer who looked past the raw wood and nails and blood to the heavenly kingdom that Jesus would inherit. He was a believer who wanted *in*. Jesus, full of grace, told his prodigal son, "Yes, you'll be with me there—today in paradise. We'll go together, you and I." What faith! What a promise! What a privilege! What glory!

How do you see yourself? As a victim or a victor? As a worrier or a warrior? Do you let God shape you or do you allow the world to shape you? Do you trust yourself more than you trust the Lord? Do you know where you came from? Do you know why you exist on earth? Do you know where you are going after death? The second criminal asked himself these questions while he hung on the cross from nine in the morning until three in the afternoon. The answers to these questions guided him to salvation. He experienced a conversion and surrendered himself to Jesus. He left this earth knowing that Jesus is the way, the truth, and the life.

Choose like Your Life Depends on It

Often, the choices before you are not crystal clear. There are complex factors that you need to consider, pros and cons to calculate, various angles that need to be investigated. But occasionally, the contrast between options is stark and the choice unambiguously clear. This station presents two options for you to entertain. The first is to remain stuck in a self-centered world where all that matters is what you can get out of any given situation. The other is to admit that you are fallible and that you need the Lord's help to give you meaning, purpose, and direction. The two criminals in this station portray two clear choices: disbelief and contempt, or faith and confidence. It is up to you to choose what cross you want to bear.

If you declare with your mouth, "Jesus is Lord," and believe in your heart that God raised him from the dead, you will be saved.
—Rom 10:9

TWELFTH STATION: JESUS SPEAKS TO HIS MOTHER AND THE DISCIPLE

> [Jesus] replied to him, "Who is my mother, and who are my brothers?" Pointing to his disciples, he said, "Here are my mother and my brothers. For whoever does the will of my Father in heaven is my brother and sister and mother." (Matt 12:48–50)

We adore you, O Christ, and we bless you.

Because by your holy cross you have redeemed the world.

> Near the cross of Jesus stood his mother, his mother's sister, Mary the wife of Clopas, and Mary Magdalene. When Jesus saw his mother there, and the disciple whom he loved standing nearby, he said to her, "Woman, here is your son," and to the disciple, "Here is your mother." From that time on, this disciple took her into his home. (John 19:25–27)

Lord, grant us constancy that we may be willing to stand by those in need.

TWELFTH STATION: REFLECTIVE EXERCISES AND QUESTIONS

Jesus was now in the depth of his own sufferings, yet when he saw his mother and her companions, their grief greatly affected him, particularly the distress of his mother. Therefore, though he was almost at the point of death, he spoke a few words in which he expressed his most affectionate regard to her. He said, "Woman, behold your son," meaning John. His words were intended to assure her that the disciple whom he loved would become her son after he was gone. He also gave John a token of his high esteem. He said to him, "Behold, your mother." Thus, singling him out as the disciple that he trusted to fulfill the role and duty of a son.

With these words, Jesus demonstrates his divine love. His love is ever-flowing regardless of his condition or your condition. His love and mercy are available to all those who are suffering. His words compel you to love your parents unconditionally. To provide for them as they provided for you. To honor them with your words and actions. His words also obligate you to love your friends as well as your enemies: "But I tell you, love your enemies and pray for those who persecute you, that you may be children of your Father in heaven. If you love those who love you, what reward will you get? And if you greet only your own people, what are you doing more than others? Be perfect, therefore, as your heavenly Father is perfect" (Matt 5:44–48).

Jesus' love is perfect! It turns tears into laughter and sorrow into joy. It mends broken hearts, restores lost souls, and heals fractured relationships. At this station, he offers his love to you. He also makes you a promise: "Very truly I tell you, whoever believes in me will do the works I have been doing, and they will do even greater things than these, because I am going to the Father. And I will do whatever you ask in my name, so that the Father may be glorified in the Son. You may ask me for anything in my name, and I will do it" (John 14:12–14).

Exercise Your Love

For this reflective exercise, you will imitate the love that the Lord has modeled for you in the twelfth station. I would like you to handwrite two letters. That's right—no texting, no typing, but actual writing coming from your own hand! The recipient of these letters will be someone that you truly love and someone you have a strained relationship with. Both letters will express the extreme love that you have for both. Pick your favorite stationary and pen, and let your heart do the rest.

The three most powerful statements you can make to someone are "I love you," "I forgive you," and "I'm sorry." These sentiments are compelling because they come directly from your soul. They are based on the teachings of God. Throughout his earthly mission, Jesus taught you to use these principles to expand his heavenly kingdom. Make it a point not only to use these phrases but repeat them and support them with examples. Don't set a limit on the length or topics that you would like to express in your letters. "Open" your heart and allow it to flow. Organize your content so that your loved one can make connections and understand your emotions in a coherent way.

When you have completed each letter, put it in an envelope, attach a stamp, and take it to the post office so that it can be delivered. Even if your loved one lives in the same house as you, mail the letter. The content in these letters deserves a special delivery. When your loved one opens the envelope, a heavenly light will escape and shine upon them. Your thoughts and words will fill their mind, heart, and soul with the love and mercy that Jesus gave to you. Don't be surprised if a miracle takes place because of your letter. At the very least, your relationship will be strengthened or restored with each other and with the Lord!

Above all, let your love for one another be intense, because love covers a multitude of sins.
—1 Pet 4:8

Chapter 8
Resurrection

He is not here; he has risen, just as he said.
—Matt 28:6

VICTORY

Alleluia! The Lord is risen! The Lord is risen indeed! Alleluia! Do you have your noise maker? Did you blow up balloons? Are you ready to throw confetti in the air? Put on your best suit or dress. Gather your family, friends, and neighbors. It is time to celebrate. Our Lord and Savior Jesus Christ has conquered death! The rock has been rolled away! The tomb is empty! You have been saved! No longer do you need to wander aimlessly in the dark. Today is the day to be reborn in the bright light of Jesus Christ.

The greatest news that your ear has ever heard is the news that Jesus Christ has risen from the dead, as he had promised. He is the new Adam and Mary is the new Eve. Obedience has overcome disobedience. Love has conquered sin. Everlasting life now can be obtained because the Son of Man has finished the work that his Father gave him to do (John 17:4). Sin and death have become powerless over you because Jesus has shown you the way (Ps 32:8). This chapter will be one big celebration that we will share together. We will trace the Lord's victory over evil during his earthly mission. His victory is your victory. His joy is your joy. His peace is your peace. His salvation is your salvation.

But thanks be to God! He gives us the victory through our Lord Jesus Christ.

—*1 Cor 15:57*

IMMORTALITY

Our greatest fear is when the Lord will take back the breath of life that he blew into our nostrils (Gen 2:7). We bury this inevitable event deep into our subconscious because it is too painful to face. Death carries with it a certain dread. It has always been the enemy, the great mystery that makes us quake with fear. We do all that we can to avoid it and fight it, but ultimately, we must come to terms with it (Eccl 9:5).

The Bible contains much warning about death, speaking as frequently on this subject as it does about any other. When God formed the universe, he understood the power of sin and death and did his very best to protect us from these scourges. In the garden of Eden where death had never entered, Adam and Eve were instructed by God to refrain from eating from the tree of the knowledge of good and evil. He provided them with a clear consequence if they disobeyed him: "For when you eat from it you will certainly die" (Gen 2:17). We know that they did eat the forbidden fruit; and at that very moment, the judgment of God passed upon them and their bodies began the process of death and decay. This is the first of many examples that links sin with death (1 Cor 15:56). The Bible says that "through one man [Adam] sin entered the world, and death through sin, and thus death spread to all men, because all sinned" (Rom 5:12).

The Bible presents historical records from the past. From BC to AD, it describes encounters that men and women had with God. Names, stories, and outcomes with the Divine are reported. However, you cannot study the life of any Bible character without being reminded that they all died—except Enoch and Elijah. There is no escaping death. Try as hard as you can, the Grim Reaper will pay his visit to each of us. He is blind to all tears and deaf to all prayers and pleadings. He must come to us, for he is sent by appointment (Heb 9:27). It is the judgment of the Almighty. Man and woman must die (Job 14:10–12).

Is there any hope? Long ago Job asked the question of the ages: "If someone dies, will they live again?" (Job 14:14). The answer can be found at the empty tomb owned by Joseph of Arimathea. "After the Sabbath, at dawn on the first day of the week, Mary Magdalene and the other Mary went to look at the tomb. There was a violent earthquake, for an angel of the Lord came down from heaven and, going to the tomb, rolled back the stone and sat on it. His appearance was like lightning, and his clothes were white as snow. The angel said to the women, 'Do not be afraid, for I know that you are looking for Jesus, who was crucified. He is not here; he has risen, just as he said'" (Matt 28:1–6).

Jesus Christ has answered Job's question. The evidence is irrefutable. He died on Calvary (Luke 23:46). He was buried (Luke 23:50–55). He rose (Luke 24:1–8). He will come again (Acts 1:10–11)! The stone from his tomb has been rolled away (Luke 24:2). "The strips of the burial linen are laying by themselves" (Luke 24:12). The tomb is empty (Luke 24:2). The angel of the LORD has pronounced, "He is not here; he has risen!" (Luke 24:6). These are the facts, and they cannot be disputed. Jesus Christ lives!

Jesus Christ was the first to rise so that the rest of us can follow him. His resurrection is your resurrection. His promise of everlasting life is your promise of everlasting life. His victory over sin and death is your victory over sin and death. Just like his earthly mission prepared him for his heavenly throne, your earthly mission will prepare you to witness the resurrected body and spirit of the Savior of the world. Jesus wants you to come to his tomb and witness for yourself the miracle of his resurrection. He wants to prove to you that your tomb will be empty like his. Come to Jesus and experience immortality.

For those who find me find life and receive favor from the Lord.
—Prov 8:35

FIDELITY

Even though God is sovereign, he empowered humanity with free will. The power of choice and the right to decide has been given to you as a gift from God. When it comes to God, you have a binary choice: to believe or not to believe, to obey or disobey. These choices will not only define the kind of relationship that you have with the Heavenly Father but will also predict where your soul will spend eternity.

Obedience

Jesus is very concerned about you because he wants to redeem your soul. He wants to be reunited with you after your earthly mission has ended. For this to occur, your relationship with him must supersede all other relationships in your life (Matt 22:36–38). You must submit to and obey all that he commands (John 14:15). Before you can follow him, you must allow him to lead. Being attentive to his laws, ways, and words will place you on the path of redemption. You can't follow Jesus unless you know where to find him.

The first place to look for the LORD is from within. Jesus Christ has already deposited all the navigational tools you will need to find him. They are stored within your spirit. Where is your spirit? It is where the light shines. It's that bright, warm, peaceful place you visit during your darkest hours. It is the place where you feel most protected. Go to that place and humbly speak to the LORD and ask him for guidance. Jesus, being the "Great Provider," will joyfully send you to your soul (Ps 145:16). There is where you will find the keys to the kingdom of heaven.

The key chain inside your soul is large and holds many keys. These keys are unique because they will only open the doors that God has planned for you to open. Jesus has grouped these keys in a particular order so that you will have an opportunity to use them and become all that he wants you to be. The first set of keys will give you access to him. These opened doors will ignite an internal passion so you can learn about who God is, what he has done, and what he will do for you. Unlocking these doors will teach you about worship, obedience, love, forgiveness, and service. They will introduce you to the Living Word by leading you to the Holy Bible and a place to worship.

The second set of keys will strengthen your faith. These opened doors will allow you to accept everything that you learned about the LORD. Acknowledging the Father, Son, and Holy Spirit means that you truly believe without your eyes ever seeing or your ears ever hearing (1 Cor 2:9). Walking through these doors enables you to approach each day of your life knowing that the Son of Man sacrificed himself on a cross so that your sins may be forgiven and that you can share everlasting life with him.

The third set of keys will allow you to change lives. The first key on this set will unlock the door that will change your life. You will be baptized by the blood and water of Jesus Christ and become his child. Your sins will be washed away, and you will walk in the newness of life through Jesus Christ (Rom 6:4). You will proclaim his name and make known his deeds to everyone you encounter (Ps 105:1). You will persecute your flesh and live in the spirit (Col 3:5). Once you can talk the talk and walk the walk for the Savior of the world, you will be ready to use the rest of the keys in this set. These keys are reserved for the hearts, souls, and minds of all those you encounter in your house, school, work, church, social events, etc. These doors need to be opened, and God has assigned you to do this job. He wants you to take his laws, ways, and words and put them into action. It may be difficult to open some of these doors, but this is your duty as a Christian (Acts 13:47). You already have the keys to open these doors; you just need the courage to turn the locks. A smile, hug, or small gesture may be just enough to allow the "Light" to enter a family member, friend, or stranger.

The last key on the key chain opens the gates of heaven. If you use the keys of knowledge, acceptance, and service throughout your life, God will be waiting for you when you return to him. The funny thing is, you will not need this last key because the gates of heaven will already be open for you.

Jesus Christ had a relentless love for his Father and a selfless obedience to do his will. He used all the keys that his Father gave him and opened the kingdom of heaven to those who accepted him (John 6:38–40). He is the Son of God, and you are one of his sheep. He has given you everything that his Father gave him. Will you use your keys to open doors?

Disobedience

What has God given people? It is difficult for the mind to comprehend such a question. The depth and breadth of God's gifts are staggering. It would be impossible to tally up a list. The best that you can do is go to the Holy Bible for answers. One of the Scripture passages that succinctly answers this question states, "His divine power has granted to us all things that pertain to life and godliness" (2 Pet 1:3). In other words, God has given you everything you need to live. His gifts preserve and elevate your physical, spiritual, and eternal life. His love, mercy, and grace provide you with comforts, joy, pleasures, blessings, and support. His gifts are life-changing and world-changing. If this is all true, why do you turn your back on God?

You have been chosen to play *Who Wants to Be a Disciple of Jesus Christ?* This game is the Christian version of *Who Wants to Be a Millionaire*. If you answer every question correctly, you will receive an all-expenses-paid trip to "Paradise." Just like the televised game, you will be given three lifelines to increase your chance of winning: the Holy Bible, Prayer, and Worship. You can use these three as many times as you want to help you answer each question. Are you ready to play? Let's dim the lights and start the music!

Let's Play . . . Who Wants to Be a Disciple of Jesus Christ?	
Question 1 is worth $100	Do you believe in God, the Father Almighty, Creator of heaven and earth?
Question 2 is worth $200	Do you believe in Jesus Christ, his only Son, our LORD, who was born of the Virgin Mary, was crucified, died, and was buried, rose from the dead, and is now seated at the right hand of the Father?
Question 3 is worth $300	Do you believe in the Holy Spirit, the holy church, the communion of saints, the forgiveness of sins, the resurrection of the body, and life everlasting?
Question 4 is worth $500	Do you reject Satan?
Question 5 is worth $1,000	Do you reject all Satan's works?
Question 6 is worth $2,000	Do you reject all Satan's empty promises?
Question 7 is worth $4,000	Why do you get lost on "the Way"?
Question 8 is worth $8,000	Why do you ignore "the Truth"?
Question 9 is worth $16,000	Why do you reject "the Life"?
Question 10 is worth $32,000	Why is your faith so fragile?
Question 11 is worth $64,000	Why have you lost hope?
Question 12 is worth $125,000	Why is your love fading?
Question 13 is worth $250,000	Why do you suffer from the disease of "me instead of he"?

Question 14 is worth $500,000	Who is stopping you from obeying the LORD?
Question 15 is worth $1 million	What is stopping you from obeying the LORD?

Are your bags packed? Did you answer every question? Are you ready for your trip to Paradise? I'm guessing that you probably didn't qualify for that all-expenses-paid vacation. Being a disciple of Jesus Christ is much more difficult than being a millionaire. Let's break down these questions and see how you responded. The first three questions tested your belief. Each of these questions began with "Do you believe . . ." These questions separate the "believers" from the "nonbelievers." The correct answer to the first three questions was *yes*! What is your score so far? Three out of three? That's fantastic! Because you are a believer, you have purchased a ticket to Paradise.

Questions four through six tested your faith. Each of these questions began with "Do you reject . . ." These questions reinforce the deep act of faith that believers have in the Father, Son, and Spirit. By renouncing Satan, the LORD provides his believers authority and protection over Satan so that they can bring down his strongholds (2 Cor 10:4). The correct answer for these questions was *yes*! Now what is your score? Six out of six? That's awesome! Because you have faith, you have earned your boarding pass to Paradise.

Questions seven through thirteen tested your commitment. Each of these questions began with "Why . . ." These questions probed your lifestyle. They required more than a simple yes or no answer. They demanded deep contemplation and introspection. Did you use any of your lifelines? Were you able to answer all these questions? Being a disciple of Jesus Christ is about more than just making declarations. It's about action and reaction, giving and receiving, teaching and learning, falling and rising, following and leading. It's about becoming "fishers of men" (Matt 4:19). There is no shame or blame if you had to stop the game. Spend more time using your lifelines as a resource. They will lead you to the correct answers. Before we get to the top of the board, what is your score? Did you say thirteen out of thirteen? If that is the case, be on the lookout for Elijah and his chariot of fire and horses because he is coming to lift you up in a whirlwind and take you to heaven (2 Kgs 2:3–9).

You have reached the top of the board! Questions fourteen and fifteen had the highest monetary value because they asked the most important questions when it comes to discipleship. These two questions tested your obedience. In the letter that Saint Paul wrote to the Galatians, he writes, "You were running a good race. Who cut in on you to keep you from obeying the truth?" (Gal 5:7). Saint Paul wants to know who is stopping you from becoming a disciple? The first person you may want to visit is that person you see when you look into a mirror. That person may be the main reason why you haven't reached discipleship. Have a conversation with that person and ask them to explain their motives behind blocking you from reaching your full potential. Tell that person your hopes and dreams and how you need them to support you to fulfill your destiny. Make peace with that person so that they will provide you with assistance instead of resistance in becoming a disciple of Jesus Christ.

The final question that will catapult you to the gates of heaven was, "What is stopping you from obeying the LORD?" Consciously or subconsciously, you will refuse to answer this question because it will expose who you really are. Even though these answers will free you to experience and express the mission and miracles of Jesus Christ, you would rather hide in your fear and embarrassment. No one ever wants to be exposed. Your pride and ego will do all that it can to prevent you from surrendering. Your natural inkling is to justify independence over authority, law over love, transaction over intimacy, and controlled relationships over kingdom relationships. You don't need God because you believe you are your own God and you can do a better job than he can when it comes to your life! Paul instructed the Galatians, "You are not to do whatever you want" (Gal 5:17). He went on to tell them, "I warn you, as I did before, that those who live like this will not inherit the kingdom of God" (Gal 5:21).

Now you know why this was the million-dollar question. This question forces you to come to terms with things you do not want to say or hear. It forces you to admit that you are no different than Adam or Eve—a disobedient sinner. You yearn for the forbidden fruit that the culture of death offers and disregard the consequences of your actions. Temptation and sin will follow you like a dark shadow. Even when the "Light of the World" shines down upon you, this shadow will be present. Rebellion and disobedience will always act like a thorn in your side (2 Cor 12:7). They will always force you to make a binary choice: to believe or not to believe, to obey or disobey. Your choice will define the fidelity that you have with the Lord.

> *Do not conform to the pattern of this world but be transformed by the renewing of your mind. Then you will be able to test what God's will is—his good, pleasing, and perfect will.*
> —*Rom 12:2*

TO OBEY OR DISOBEY . . . THAT IS THE QUESTION

In both the Old and New Testament, you can read accounts of people who obeyed the Lord and disobeyed the Lord. They exercised their free will in deciding whether they wanted to follow or lead, listen or ignore, answer or question. Each of these people had to weigh the following categories before they made their final decision.

Silence

A decision doesn't need to be made until a request is offered. To hear the voice of the Lord, you must choose silence over chaos. How loud is the world? Scientists tell us that you are interrupted at least once every three minutes. It may seem impossible to tune out the voices of others (especially on social media) and prioritize the demands on your time. The white noise of your life can fill up your thoughts, behaviors, and actions. It can cause a spiritual inner ear infection in which you lose your sense of balance and become deaf to God's call.

During the time of the great prophet Elijah, the Israelites suffered from a spiritual inner ear infection. They abandoned the Lord's commands, tore down his altars, and sentenced his prophets to death. Because Elijah was the last of the Lord's prophets, he had to flee for his life. God guided him on a journey of forty days and forty nights until he reached Horeb, the mountain of God. He was directed to climb to the top of the mountain and go into a cave, where he rested.

> Then an angel said to Elijah, "Go out and stand on the mountain in the presence of the Lord, for the Lord is about to pass by."
>
> Then a great and powerful wind tore the mountains apart and shattered the rocks before the Lord, but the Lord was not in the wind. After the wind there was an earthquake, but the Lord was not in the earthquake. After the earthquake came a

> fire, but the LORD was not in the fire. And after the fire came a gentle whisper. When Elijah heard it, he pulled his cloak over his face and went out and stood at the mouth of the cave. Then a voice said to him, "What are you doing here, Elijah?" (1 Kgs 19:11–13)

Like Elijah, the LORD is sending you on a journey. The purpose of this journey is for you to come to God. By surrendering your will, he will guide you to his mountain. When you reach this destination, he will speak to you in a whisper. He will ask you the same question that he asked Elijah, "What are you doing with the life that I gave you?" Actively seeking moments of silence can help you answer this question (Luke 5:16). The voice of the LORD will quiet you, calm you, and heal you (Ps 46:10). You will be amazed at what you can hear in silence.

Attentiveness

How many times a day do you talk to someone who isn't paying attention to you? How many times a day do you have a conversation with someone and you don't hear a word they are saying? I'm sure it happens more times than you want to admit. It is very difficult to give your full attention to something or someone for an extended period. Your life is full of distractions. Your mind constantly needs attention. Your buds are in your ears, and your phone is in your hand to make sure that your mind stays satisfied. You have conditioned yourself to shorten your attention span and devalue the present moments that you live in. Your lack of focus has hindered your relationship with others and with God. Your self-conscious approach has forced you to become independent.

After Jesus Christ resurrected from his tomb, several people had contact with him but did not recognize him. The three main places where it is mentioned are in John 20:14, John 21:4, and Luke 24:15–16. In the first passage, John 20:14, Jesus appears to Mary Magdalene near the tomb, but she does not recognize him until he says her name. Why didn't Mary recognize him? Was it because of her blurry vision from weeping? Was it because it was predawn and still dark out? Was it because Jesus was so far away from her that she couldn't recognize his features (John 20:1, 15–16)?

In John 21:4 Jesus meets seven of the disciples while they are fishing and calls to them from the shore. Why didn't his disciples recognize him?

Was it because they were about one hundred yards from the shore when he called out to them (John 21:8)? Was it because it was twilight and they could not see Jesus? In the third passage, Luke 24:15–16, Cleopas and his friend walk and talk to Jesus for several miles but think that he is a visitor in Jerusalem. They do not recognize him until they invite him into their home and he breaks bread and gives it to them.

Three encounters with the resurrected Lord, and not one of his followers recognized him. How could this be? Dimness of light and other natural causes are clearly not the reason for their misidentification. The reason that they did not recognize the risen Lord is because they were not living in the moment while they were with him. Their minds were preoccupied on Jesus becoming the king of Israel. They focused more on their ranking as a disciple than they did on the Lord's ministry. They ignored the word of the Lord when he predicted to them many times over that "the Son of Man must suffer many things and be rejected by the elders, the chief priests and the teachers of the law, and he must be killed and on the third day be raised to life" (Luke 9:22). Their independence prevented them from not recognizing the living Savior.

The Lord wants you to change your self-conscious approach into a God-conscious approach. He wants your soul quenched before you indulge your mind. He wants you to surrender your independence. He wants your undivided attention so that you can experience him when he comes to you every day with his resurrected body. Do you see him? Do you recognize him? Shut off your mind and turn on your spirit so that you can identify your loving Father!

Service

Obedience is much harder than disobedience! Obedience demands sacrifice, commitment, and selflessness. Disobedience provides comfort, choice, and self-service. Obedience directs you in a straight line (Ps 86:11–17). Disobedience removes your rudder. Obedience requires you to love others. Disobedience teaches you to love yourself. Obedience increases your faith. Disobedience creates skepticism. Obedience maintains hope. Disobedience promotes fear. Who you are, what you are, and where you are depends upon your obedience or disobedience to the Lord's words and ways.

Will you serve the LORD, or will you serve yourself? This is the question that Jonah asked himself when he heard the voice of the LORD. Jonah received a calling from the LORD to preach repentance to the people of Nineveh. Jonah disliked this town and wanted God to punish its people. Instead of obeying and going straight to Nineveh, he went to the next town over to board a ship so that he could cross the sea. After he boarded the ship there was a great storm. During the storm, the sailors found Jonah in the bottom of the ship asleep. When they woke him, he confessed that he was running away from God. Jonah asked the men to throw him overboard because he thought that if he were dead, then God would stop punishing him. The sailors agreed to throw him into the sea. While in the water, Jonah was swallowed by a whale. He was in the whale's belly for three days and three nights. Jonah awoke in the belly of the mammal and cried out to God. He confessed his disobedience and told God that he would accomplish the task that the LORD had called him to. God then instructed the whale to vomit Jonah out onto dry ground. Jonah ran to the city of Nineveh. To his amazement, and disappointment, the people of Nineveh did repent and asked for the LORD's salvation. Even though Jonah preached to the people, he was not happy. He climbed to the top of a mountain to watch the LORD destroy the city. Because the people of Nineveh repented, God did not destroy them or their city

Jonah willfully disobeyed the LORD. He chose comfort over sacrifice because he didn't want to walk through the city of Nineveh. He was selfish instead of selfless because he disliked the people of Nineveh and wanted them to be punished by God. He found himself far from home and lost at sea because he was rudderless instead of purposeful. He put others in danger because he loved himself more than anyone else. He was full of fear instead of hope when he confessed his disobedience. Finally, he was skeptical instead of faithful in God's mercy when he watched and waited for the LORD to destroy the city. Being disobedient to the LORD's words and ways can change the trajectory of your life. You may find yourself lost, lonely, confused, incapacitated, and bitter just like Jonah. Ignoring a service call by the LORD can place you into the belly of hell!

Fortitude

In your life, many situations will arise in which it will become difficult to do the right thing, even when you know what it is. It is very challenging to do the right thing and suffer the consequences. Many times, doing the right thing causes you grief, sorrow, heartache, sadness, blame, regret, misery, resentment, shame, insecurity, embarrassment, worry, panic, frustration, cynicism, jealousy, weariness, pain, anxiety, fright, and fear. If doing the right thing (obeying the LORD's words and ways) brings some or all these negative emotions to you, why would you ever want to be obedient to the LORD? To help you in the decision-making process, the LORD has given you the seven gifts of the Holy Spirit (wisdom, understanding, counsel, fortitude, knowledge, piety, and fear of the LORD). These gifts exist to help you maintain balance when temptation tries to tip the scales.

To stay strong amid evil, the Holy Spirit has given you fortitude. Fortitude is often identified with courage but also embodies endurance. Fortitude gives you the willingness to stand up for what is right in the sight of God, even if it means accepting rejection, verbal abuse, or physical harm. It prepares your mind to make Christlike decisions while enduring evil.

The greatest example of fortitude is offered in the book of Job. Job was a wealthy man that lived in a land called Uz with his large family and extensive flocks. He was "blameless" and "upright," always careful to avoid doing evil (Job 1:1). One day, Satan appeared before God in heaven. God boasted to Satan about Job's goodness, but Satan argued that Job was only good because God had blessed him abundantly. Satan challenged God that if he were given permission to punish the man, Job would turn and curse God. God allowed Satan to torment Job to test this bold claim, but he forbade Satan from taking Job's life in the process.

In one day, Job received four messages, each bearing separate news that his livestock, servants, and ten children all died due to invaders or natural catastrophes. Job mourned this news but still blessed God in his prayers. Satan appeared in heaven again, and God granted him another chance to test Job. This time, Job was afflicted with horrible skin sores. His wife encouraged him to curse God and give up and die, but Job refused and accepted his circumstances while maintaining his faith in God. Even though Job did not understand why he was experiencing so much misfortune, he trusted God and did his very best to persevere during these tragic events. Because of Job's fortitude, God returned Job's health, provided him with twice as much property as before, blessed him with new children, and granted him an extremely long life.

Like Job, have God and Satan placed a wager on you? They are both willing to gamble on your soul. Each of them feels that they have influence over your instincts. The relationship that you have with each is fluid. Each day, you are either advancing to the Lord and retreating from the devil or advancing to the devil and retreating from the Lord. There is no such thing as being static in these relationships. The difference between God and Satan is that God loves you and trusts you. He is willing to grant Satan permission to test your loving relationship with him (1 Pet 4:12–13). God will allow the devil to place struggle, pain, heartbreak, and loss in your life (2 Tim 3:12). He doesn't view these things as punishments but as gifts (Jas 1:2–4). He wants you to be grateful for everything that occurs in your life (2 Cor 4:17). He wants you to accept all things with faith, hope, and love.

God is everywhere and God is everything. Once you accept this fact, you will be open to receive the gift of fortitude. It will lead, transform, and guide you out of doubt and temptation and into belief and prevention. It will supply inspiration, enthusiasm, contentment, calmness, serenity, peace, trust, bliss, delight, happiness, pleasure, joy, ease, satisfaction, fulfillment, confidence, optimism, passion, harmony, excitement, gratitude, kindness, affection, and love. With one heart, one mind, and one soul dedicated to the Lord, you are guaranteed to make the right decision every time, all the time (Acts 4:32)!

Discernment

In its simplest definition, discernment is nothing more than the ability to decide between truth and error, right and wrong. Discernment is the process of making careful distinctions in your thinking about truth. Pontus Pilate famously asked Jesus, "What is truth?" while trying to determine his fate (John 18:38). Truth is in the eye of the beholder. Everyone doesn't see the same thing in the same way. For example, God sees things based on the written word. His decisions are made by the commands and lessons that are recorded in the Holy Bible. His discernment is very clear and concise. He sees the truth in terms of black and white. Satan, on the other hand, contradicts the written word. He twists the word of God to justify his decisions. His discernment is dark and confusing. His vision of the truth is always in shades of gray. How do you determine what is right and wrong? Do you measure your decision by your spirit or your ego? Is your discernment diverse or particular? Do you see truth in black and white, gray, or high-definition color? How you view truth will determine if you obey or disobey the LORD's words and ways.

Let's travel back to the garden of Eden to further explore the concept of discernment. In Genesis chapter 2, God places Adam and Eve into Eden. He created this garden so that all their *needs* would be met. Inside of the garden were fruit trees, livestock, and four life-sustaining rivers (Gen 2:8–14). Now God knew that the serpent already lived in Eden before he placed Adam and Eve there. To protect them, he gave them his word: "And the LORD God commanded the man, 'You are free to eat from any tree in the garden; but you must not eat from the tree of the knowledge of good and evil, for when you eat from it you will certainly die'" (Gen 2:16–17).

The garden of Eden contained the first test for mankind concerning discernment. The test was quite simple: obey God's word and live forever, or disobey God's word and die. Sounds like an easy test to pass. Unfortunately, Adam and Eve failed the test! How did they choose the wrong answer? Let me introduce you to the serpent. It didn't take long for the serpent to find Eve in the garden. The serpent initiated the conversation by asking Eve a question. There is a reason why Gen 3:1 says, "Now the serpent was craftier than any of the wild animals the LORD God had made." By asking Eve a question, it required her to give a response. This means that Eve had to take Satan's thought and contemplate it. The serpent asked, "Did God really say, 'You must not eat from any tree in the garden'?" (Gen 3:1). This question took the black-and-white command of God and turned it gray. God said, "You are free to eat from any tree in the garden; but you must not eat from the tree of the knowledge of good and evil." The serpent skipped the first part of the command and emphasized the second part. He didn't want Eve to focus on the goodness of God but wanted her to react on the restrictions of God. He wanted her to consider alternative facts. He wanted her to ask herself, "Has God put limitations on me? Is he restricting me? Is he holding me back? Is he telling me what I can and cannot do?"

"The woman said to the serpent, 'We may eat fruit from the trees in the garden, but God did say, "You must not eat fruit from the tree that is in the middle of the garden, and you must not touch it, or you will die"'" (Gen 3:2–3). Eve's response shows you the power of the serpent. He accomplished his mission by only asking her one question. Did you notice her response was different from the command that God gave? She consciously or subconsciously eliminated the phrase "you are free to eat." She told the serpent, "We may eat . . ." This omission is a sign of independence. She lost sight of the goodness of God because she was influenced by the devil to only see what she couldn't have. The devil blinded Eve to all the privileges, rights, joys, and opportunities that Eden had to offer. Eve now saw truth in gray instead of black and white.

Once the color of the truth changed, the "father of lies" darkened the gray by telling Eve two additional lies: "'You will not certainly die,' the serpent said to the woman. 'For God knows that when you eat from it your eyes will be opened, and you will be like God, knowing good and evil'" (Gen 3:4–5). Eve's newfound independence authorized her to disobey God and willfully pick the forbidden fruit to satisfy her, and her husband's, *wants* (Gen 3:6).

God will never mandate obedience; he will always present it as a choice. The same test that God gave Adam and Eve in the garden of Eden he gives to you one thousand times a day. He trusts that you will choose the right answer every time. How you see truth depends on your relationship with the LORD. The more intimate your relationship becomes, the easier it will be to confront the "serpent" and obey the words and ways of God.

What Do You Prefer?

To obey or disobey, what will you do? Isn't this a shocking question to ask? However, it is something that you must answer many times each day. God the Father sent his Son into the world to be a Light for you. The world in the twenty-first century is full of darkness because people prefer it that way (John 3:19). Many choose their own sins over freedom from sin. Why is that? Today, more than ever, the truth is under attack. The "serpent" has tricked your generation to challenge the truth. He has taught you to exercise your free will and demand that everything be given to you without cost (obedience). He has empowered you to eat the forbidden fruit without guilt or regret. These attitudes and actions have darkened your world.

What are you drawn to? Are you in search of the "Light"? Are you attracted by those things that brighten your day? Are you drawn to the many ways that God is present and active in the world around you? If so, your obedience is heightening the intimacy that you have with the LORD.

Are you in search of your independence? Are you attracted to those things that fulfill your wants? Are you drawn to the illusion of money, power, and fame? Is so, your disobedience is pushing you out of the kingdom of God (Eden).

To obey or disobey is a binary choice. The consequences of your choice will lead to everlasting life or certain death. Before you make your decision, seek silence, be attentive, answer the call to service, accept the gift of fortitude, and sharpen your skill of discernment. These actions will guide your free will to make the appropriate choice.

Peter and the other apostles replied: "We must obey God rather than human beings!"
—Acts 5:29

The reward of eternal life requires effort.
—Thomas S. Monson[1]

THE TRIALS AND TRIBULATIONS OF JESUS CHRIST

Before the rock was rolled away on the first Easter morning, Jesus had to endure emotional, psychological, and physical pain over a seventy-two-hour period. It began just after midnight on Friday in the garden of Gethsemane when Judas led Jewish officials and a band of Roman soldiers to Jesus to issue him a warrant for his arrest. Judas approached Jesus and kissed him on his cheek so that he could be identified. With that kiss, Judas completed his betrayal and initiated Jesus' pain (Matt 26:47–51). The Jewish leaders and Roman soldiers shackled Jesus and led him into Jerusalem so that he could be put on trial. The first preliminary trial took place at a palace owned by Annas. Annas was the former high priest of the Jewish nation. Annas questioned Jesus about his disciples and his teachings. When Jesus responded to his questions, Annas disapproved of his answers and ordered one of the officers to strike Jesus with his hand. Jesus' pain continued as Annas sent Jesus "bound" to Caiaphas, who was the current high priest of the Jewish nation (John 18:19–23).

Caiaphas, along with some of the members of the Sanhedrin, attempted to find witnesses who would give false evidence to build a case

1. Monson, "Three Rs of Choice."

against Jesus. They found many but could not find matching testimony that would prove guilt. Frustrated and angry, Caiaphas asked Jesus, under oath, if he was the Christ, the Son of God. Jesus replied, "I am, and you will see the Son of man sitting at the right hand of power and coming with the clouds of heaven" (Mark 14:62). With this acknowledgment, Jesus was accused of blasphemy (acknowledging that he was the Son of God). He was then mocked and physically tortured for the rest of the night (Matt 26:57–67). The entire Sanhedrin reconvened at sunrise and again asked Jesus if he was the Christ. Jesus again professed that he was, so they bound Jesus and led him away to the Roman governor, Pontius Pilate (Luke 22:66–71).

When they delivered Jesus to Pontius Pilate, they added charges to his arrest sheet by telling Pilate that he incited people to riot, forbade his followers to pay Roman taxes, and claimed to be a king. Because Pilate deemed the last charge as a serious accusation, he interrogated Jesus. Pilate simply wanted to know if Jesus was a king. After having a conversation with Jesus, he took him out in front of the Jews and reached a verdict of *not guilty*. Not satisfied with the acquittal, the Sanhedrin accused Jesus of additional crimes. Hesitant to retry Jesus, Pilate sent him to King Herod since most of Jesus' treasonable teachings occurred in Galilee (Luke 23:1–6).

When Jesus arrived in front of Herod, the king was happy to see him because he hoped that Jesus would perform a miracle in front of him and his guests. Herod heard the testimony of the chief priests and scribes and asked Jesus many questions, but Jesus did not respond. Irritated by the refusal of Jesus to perform miracles or answer questions, he and his soldiers put a king's robe on Jesus and mocked him. Herod never intended to put Jesus on trial for treason because he knew that it was illegal and that Pilate had already acquitted him. Because of this, he sent him back to Pilate (Luke 23:8–12).

When Pilate found Jesus back in front of him, he made another attempt to release Jesus because of the lack of evidence in the case. Pilate reminded the chief priests, scribes, and the people of the custom of releasing a prisoner of their choice during Passover. He told the mob that if they chose Jesus, he would be scourged before his release as a compromise. The chief priests and elders persuaded the people to demand the release of a notable robber named Barabbas and to crucify Jesus. After three attempts to release Jesus, Pilate finally succumbed to their threats and outcries and sentenced Jesus to be crucified (Luke 23:13–25).

Biblical scholars tell us that Jesus participated in six trials in six hours.[2] The pretrial examination with Annas began at 2:00 a.m. on Friday morning, and Pilate's crucifixion sentence ended at 8:00 a.m. The first three trials were religious in nature, and all ended in guilty verdicts. The final three trials were civil in nature, and all ended in innocent verdicts. All six trials took an emotional, psychological, and physical toll on Jesus. Unfortunately, this was only a small sample size of the pain that he would have to endure on that day. From 8:00 a.m. to 12:00 p.m., Jesus was mocked, scourged, and forced to carry his cross to Calvary. At 12:00 p.m., he was nailed to his cross and hung on it until his death at 3:00 p.m. Joseph of Arimathea was given permission by Pilate to take the body of Jesus. With the help of Nicodemus, they prepared his body for burial by washing it, anointing it, and wrapping it. Late in the afternoon, his body was placed in a new tomb and sealed by a large stone.

THE TRIALS AND TRIBULATIONS OF (ENTER YOUR NAME)

When it comes to your earthly existence, you and Jesus are no different. The world treated him no differently than it treats you. What he experienced, you will experience. The moments of opportunity that were offered to him will be offered to you. How you react to these opportunities will define your existence. Jesus never wasted a moment to teach others about his Father's love and mercy. Whether he was experiencing positive or negative emotions, he always modeled his Father's ways. In your life, Jesus wants you to seize the positive moments and experience the joy, gratitude, pride, serenity, interest, amusement, hope, inspiration, awe, and love that life provides. Not only does he want you to accept these feelings, but he wants you to produce them in others. He wants you to grow in the light that the Holy Spirit provides.

Nature teaches us that vegetation can't sustain life without rain. The same can be said about your spiritual life. You cannot grow in your relationship with God without pain. Trials and tribulations will come in and out of your life to strengthen your bond with God. The suffering that occurs in your life acts like spiritual fertilizer that provides nutrients to your relationship with God so that it can strengthen and grow. Things like anger, annoyance, sadness, guilt, fear, anxiety, discouragement,

2. Lawrence, *Six Trials*.

despair, apathy, disappointment, and frustration become visible during challenging times. This is precisely when the LORD wants you to come to him so that he can help you remove these "weeds" and purify your relationship with him.

Suffering causes a tremendous amount of pain. You, like Jesus, will struggle socially, emotionally, psychologically, and physically when you are put on trial. You may feel betrayed when one of your family members or friends calls a mental health professional to seek help for you. You may feel embarrassed when your symptoms won't allow you to engage in normal daily activities. You may feel abandoned when your friends don't sympathize with your diagnosis and choose others over you. You may feel fear when your anxiety brings on panic attacks or your depression generates thoughts of self-harm. You may feel lost when you are constantly being evaluated by physicians, psychiatrists, psychologists, and therapists. You may feel trapped when you begin therapy and/or medication and it doesn't seem to help. You may feel fatigue from carrying your anxiety and/or depression everywhere you go. You may feel shame because others can't relate to your mental health issues. You may feel resentment because you never asked for the diagnosis that you were given. In other words, you will feel what Jesus felt during the seventy-two hours before his death on the cross!

Trails, tribulations, and suffering bring these and other unwelcome feelings into your life. They push you to places you never experienced internally or externally. They make you question everything. They bring you to your knees! This is exactly where the LORD wants you to be. He wants you on your knees in front of his crucifixion. At the base of his cross is where you will find peace. It is where you will find healing. It is where you will find miracles. It is where you will find love and forgiveness. It is where you will find the Blessed Virgin. It is where you will find the body and blood of Jesus Christ. It is where you will find hope. It is where you will find faith. It is where you will find safety and security.

When you enter your next trial, remember it was given to you so that you can grow emotionally, psychologically, and spiritually. The LORD wants you to embrace it and accept it. He wants to strengthen your faith, hope, and love through his grace. Even though suffering may temporarily put you into a dark tomb, know that Easter morning will come, and the earth will quake when the angel of the LORD comes down from heaven to roll back the stone from your tomb so that you can be reunited with the LORD (Matt 28:2–3).

TRIAL BY FIRE

In chapter 3 of the book of Daniel, a story is presented about three young men who were put on trial because of their obedience to God. They were sentenced to death because they refused to uphold man's word above God's word. Does this story sound familiar? The story takes place about six hundred years before Jesus Christ was born, when King Nebuchadnezzar of Babylon invaded Jerusalem. Because of the king's might and power, he was able to conquer Jerusalem and deport their finest citizens back to Babylon. Among those held captive were three young men named Shadrach, Meshach, and Abednego.

In Babylon, King Nebuchadnezzar had a huge golden image built as a symbol of his power and glory. The Bible states it was sixty cubits high and six cubits wide—that is, approximately ninety feet high and nine feet wide (Dan 3:1). He commanded that his people bow down and worship this image whenever they heard music. Those who disobeyed the order would be thrown into an immense, blazing furnace. Shadrach, Meshach, and Abednego, however, worshiped only the one true God and refused to bow down to the false idol. They were brought before Nebuchadnezzar to face their fate but remained courageous in the face of the king's demand to bow down before the golden statue. They said, "King Nebuchadnezzar, we do not need to defend ourselves before you in this matter. If we are thrown into the blazing furnace, the God we serve can deliver us from it, and he will deliver us from Your Majesty's hand. But even if he does not, we want you to know, Your Majesty, that we will not serve your gods or worship the image of gold you have set up" (Dan 3:16–18).

Furious, Nebuchadnezzar ordered the furnace to be heated seven times hotter than average. Shadrach, Meshach, and Abednego were bound and cast into the flames. The fiery blast was so hot it killed the soldiers who had escorted them. But as King Nebuchadnezzar peered into the furnace, he marveled at what he saw: "Look! I see four men walking around in the fire, unbound and unharmed, and the fourth looks like a son of the gods" (Dan 3:25). Then the king called the men to come out of the furnace. Shadrach, Meshach, and Abednego emerged unharmed, with not even a hair on their heads singed or the smell of smoke on their clothing. Nebuchadnezzar declared, "Praise be to the God of Shadrach, Meshach, and Abednego, who has sent his angel and rescued his servants! They trusted in him and defied the king's command and were willing to give up their lives rather than serve or worship any god except their own God" (Dan 3:28). Through God's miraculous deliverance of Shadrach, Meshach, and Abednego that day, Nebuchadnezzar declared that the remaining Israelites in captivity were now protected from harm and were guaranteed freedom of worship, and Shadrach, Meshach, and Abednego received a royal promotion.

Who was the fourth man Nebuchadnezzar saw in the flames? Some scholars say it was Jesus, and others say it was an angel. Regardless, a heavenly bodyguard was sent by God to protect Shadrach, Meshach, and Abednego during their intense time of need. Who is inside the blazing furnace with you as you deal with the symptoms of anxiety and/or depression? Is it your mother, father, brother, sister, cousin, grandparent, friend, or therapist? Look through your pain and suffering and you will see that you are not alone in the furnace. God has sent a heavenly bodyguard to protect you just like he did to protect Shadrach, Meshach, and Abednego. He wants you to recognize that person and allow them to help you exit this furnace with a stronger resolve so that you can receive a physical, psychological, and spiritual promotion.

The trial that you are currently going through isn't just a physical, emotional, and psychological experience. It is a spiritual experience. It is testing the state of your soul. If you commit yourself to his words and ways, Jesus will provide you with the truth that will set you free from any challenge (John 8:31–32). You will be able to confidently walk through any fiery furnace knowing that the Son of God walks side-by-side with you, giving you the grace and strength that you need to be victorious. Trials are part of the human experience. They will emerge at any given time to challenge your faith, hope, and love. They will reveal your inner strengths and weaknesses. They will test your loyalty to the LORD. During these difficult times, remind yourself that Jesus specifically came to earth to free you from the bonds of death. His victory over earthly trials guarantees your victory over earthly trials. His resurrection over death guarantees your resurrection over death. Everlasting life only comes through trials and tribulations.

My grace is sufficient for you, for my power is made perfect in weakness.
—2 Cor 12:9

Beautiful souls are shaped by ugly experiences.
—Attributed to Matshona Dhliwayo

THE HEALING POWER OF JESUS CHRIST

God anointed Jesus of Nazareth with the holy Spirit and power. He went about doing good and healing all those oppressed by the devil, for God was with him.
—Acts 10:38

The Gospel of Jesus

Throughout his earthly life, Jesus spent his waking hours teaching and preaching about the coming of God's kingdom. He did not speak his own words but the words that his Heavenly Father gave him (John 12:49–50). His gospel was focused on repentance and belief (Mark 1:14–15). To help his followers understand grace, faith, redemption, justification, sanctification, salvation, and glorification, Jesus used his divine powers to perform miracles. These miracles were essential to his ministry because they allowed him to put his words into action. Not only did these miracles supplement his teachings, but they ultimately proved he was indeed the Son of God. He used his divine powers to comfort, heal, and purify the "lost sheep" of the world. The LORD healed the blind and the lame, he restored children and friends to life, and he reconciled all those who were alienated by sin and despair. He did all these things so that you can believe in him. Put your faith, hope, and love into Jesus so he can transmit his divine healing powers onto you.

Miracles of Healing

I would like to share a few Scripture passages with you so you can witness the healing power of Jesus Christ. A power he is willing to share with you. In these passages, I want you to place yourself into the sandals of those that he healed. I want you to associate your affliction with their affliction. I want you to focus on the words and actions of Jesus before, during, and after the healing miracle. I want you to feel the love, compassion, and empathy that he expressed while healing others. I want you to study the reaction of the person who was healed and the people who witnessed it. I want you to make note of the physical, emotional, and spiritual change that occurred after each convalescent encountered Jesus.

I want you to do all these things because I want you to be prepared when Jesus Christ heals you! You are next in line. He is calling your name. He wants to relieve your pain and suffering so you can live a productive life and evangelize his power and glory. He is waiting for your submission and permission. Are you ready to declare your dependence upon the Lord? Are you willing to ask the Lord for help? If your answers are *yes*, be prepared to experience the healing power that Jesus Christ has in store for you.

Jesus always uses the opportune time and place to heal others. He chooses to perform miracles when others are experiencing trials and tribulations. When the agent of evil, Satan, spreads sin, suffering, illness, disease, disaster, and death into the world, the Son of God appears to destroy his work (1 John 3:8). The following events will confirm the Lord's physical, mental, emotional, and spiritual victory over Satan. His way, truth, and life restores the sick, allows the deaf to hear and the mute speak, cleanses lepers, frees the possessed, enables the lame to walk, and raises the dead. Complete victory is his and can be yours if you walk with him!

The Sick Are Restored

> Jesus left the synagogue and went to the home of Simon. Now Simon's mother-in-law was suffering from a high fever, and they asked Jesus to help her. So, he bent over her and rebuked the fever, and it left her. She got up at once and began to wait on them. (Luke 4:38–39)

> *Then he returned to Cana in Galilee, where he had made the water wine. Now there was a royal official whose son was ill in Capernaum. When he heard that Jesus had arrived in Galilee from Judea, he went to him and asked him to come down and heal his son, who was near death. Jesus said to him, "Unless you people see signs and wonders, you will not believe." The royal official said to him, "Sir, come down before my child dies." Jesus said to him, "You may go; your son will live." The man believed what Jesus said to him and left. While he was on his way back, his slaves met him and told him that his boy would live. He asked them when he began to recover. They told him, "The fever left him yesterday, about one in the afternoon." The father realized that just at that*

> *time Jesus had said to him, "Your son will live," and he and his whole household came to believe.* (John 4:46–53)

In these two passages, sickness, in the form of fevers, came to both households. The illness which affected Simon's mother-in-law was called a "high fever," and that which nearly proved fatal to the nobleman's son was also called a fever. These fevers were so severe that family members specifically sought out Jesus for help. This is the most important lesson that you can extract from these passages. When trials and tribulations come into your life, so does Jesus. With great afflictions come great blessings. Make it a daily practice of telling the Lord about your concerns. Make Jesus aware of your struggles, troubles, and anxieties. Do not keep any secrets from him since he keeps none from you. Tell him the causes and symptoms of your current "fever." Provide him insight into your physical, psychological, emotional, and spiritual complications. Allow his sympathetic heart to be afflicted by your afflictions. Through his words and actions, he will provide you with the right prescription for your recovery!

In the first passage, Peter asked the Great Physician to make a house call so that he could heal his mother-in-law. Even though Jesus spent most of his day in the synagogue praying and debating the true meaning of the kingdom of God, he graciously accepted the invitation. This gesture illustrates that Jesus will always make time for those who are in need. When he arrived, he went directly to her. In Matt 8:14 you are told that "she was lying in bed." When she opened her eyes and looked up, she saw the Lord Jesus Christ standing over her. The Lord touched her hand, and the fever left (Matt 8:15). Jesus then raised her up and she immediately began to serve.

Today is the day to open your mind, heart, soul, and eyes to Jesus. If you do, you will see him standing over you. With his tender love and infinite compassion, he will look down upon you and protect you. He will take your troubles, fears, anxiety, and depression and replace them with comfort and confidence. He will take your hand and "rebuke the fever." All the pain, suffering, and mental anguish will disappear. The shackles of your affliction will be pulled loose (Acts 16:26). Jesus will raise you up and renew your strength. With this new-found freedom, he will expect you to immediately start serving him and ministering to those who are around you.

In the second passage, Jesus returns to a place (Cana) where he performed a miracle in the past. This introductory sentence is important because it conveys that Jesus will return to you each time you call upon him. Jesus is not your one-time Savior; he is your all-the-time Savior. Victory over a trial yesterday doesn't mean a new trial won't happen today. Just because God healed you in the past doesn't mean you won't need him to heal you in the present. New trials often come in the same areas where victory was previously experienced. For example, learning what triggers your panic attacks doesn't mean you will no longer experience a panic attack. Recognizing you are entering a psychological or emotional decline doesn't mean you won't feel the symptoms of depression. One miracle doesn't stop the need for a new miracle. The reason that Jesus came back to Cana is because another miracle was needed.

A nobleman traveled from Capernaum to Cana (about a day's journey) to seek out Jesus. Because of his power and status, he could have sent his subordinates to relay a message to Jesus, but he chose to take this long arduous trip alone. He did not wrap himself in pride, nor did he care about what others thought of him. Neither time nor distance nor egoism would hinder him from receiving the knowledge, mercy, and power of the Lord. Is there anything keeping you from coming to Jesus?

This man was facing a severe disaster in life, and he came to the only person who could help—Jesus. His son was severely ill and was on the verge of death. Unfortunately, it usually takes "a desperate need" for many to come to the Lord. The day eventually comes when every person needs help. The severe disasters of life (accidents, illnesses, disease, suffering, and death) are beyond any person's control. No one is exempt from experiencing these things—not even a rich, powerful nobleman. How will you react to such events when they come to you? What will you do? Will you allow them to break you, or will you triumph over them in complete victory?

When the nobleman finally had a chance to interact with the Lord, he begged him to travel back to Capernaum so that he could provide a life-saving miracle. God new he was a man of faith because he was separated from his son for many hours but believed that he would not die because Jesus would heal him from his affliction. The fact that he persevered and kept his eyes on the hope of Jesus showed the faith in his heart. However, Jesus wanted this man's faith to advance to a higher level. He wanted to teach the nobleman that his word alone was enough to heal his son's suffering. Do you need to witness to believe, or do you believe to witness?

Jesus tested the nobleman by telling him that his son would live. This miraculous statement placed the nobleman into a predicament. If he refused to return to Capernaum without taking Jesus with him, he would show that he did not believe Jesus' word. If he followed Jesus' order, he would be returning to the dying boy with no outward assurance that his son would recover (he didn't see a sign or wonder). He was forced to make the difficult choice between insisting on evidence or exercising faith without any tangible proof to encourage him. He chose to believe in the Word of God and was rewarded for it. Do you need to see signs and wonders, or do you believe in the Word of God?

Throughout your life you will experience "fevers." These fevers will disrupt your physical, psychological, and emotional health. Their severity and duration will vary, but each episode will require a remedy to return you to optimal health. Regardless of the type, cause, or symptom of your affliction, Jesus Christ has a treatment plan for you. If you search for him and call upon his name, he will make a house call. Through his power, glory, and grace, he will cure your illness. Not only will your fever subside, but he will provide you with lessons that are needed to enter his kingdom.

The Deaf Hear and the Mute Speak

> *Again he left the district of Tyre and went by way of Sidon to the Sea of Galilee, into the district of the Decapolis. And people brought to him a deaf man who had a speech impediment and begged him to lay his hand on him. He took him off by himself away from the crowd. He put his finger into the man's ears and, spitting, touched his tongue; then he looked up to heaven and groaned, and said to him, "Ephphatha!" (that is, "Be opened!") And [immediately] the man's ears were opened, his speech impediment was removed, and he spoke plainly. He ordered them not to tell anyone. But the more he ordered them not to, the more they proclaimed it. They were exceedingly astonished and they said, "He has done all things well. He makes the deaf hear and the mute speak."* (Mark 7:31–37)

Mark introduces this passage by providing us with a detailed look at Jesus' passport. He is very specific in the direction and places that Jesus visited before arriving in Decapolis. The travel habits of Jesus symbolize that God's work is never done. He is willing to travel anywhere and everywhere to accomplish his Father's will. Today, more than ever, billions of lost sheep are scattered throughout the world looking for the Good Shepherd. Jesus is willing to do whatever it takes to find, protect, and nurture his flock (Luke 15:1–7). Jesus is waiting for you to join him on his journey. Have you ever walked with Jesus? When was the last time you walked the "extra mile" to help someone who was in need? When was the last time you proclaimed the good news to someone who needed it? When was the last time you fed the hungry, satisfied the thirsty, comforted the lonely, clothed the needy, cared for the sick, and forgave those that hurt you (Matt 25;31–46)? "The harvest is plentiful, but the workers are few" (Matt 9:37). Check your passport and see how many locations you have traveled with Jesus. If you can count these experiences on one hand, today is the day to ask the Lord of the harvest to send you out into his harvest field (Matt 9:38).

When Jesus entered a region, a multitude of people gathered around him. Why did Jesus attract so much attention? Throughout his three-year ministry, Jesus built a reputation of being a holy man that preached a new message of repentance, generosity, forgiveness, love, and justice. Additionally, reports circulated throughout Israel that he was a miracle worker. For these reasons, people wanted to see, hear, and touch the Lord. It was no different in Decapolis. Their citizens gathered around Jesus to witness his message and divine power. When was the last time you were in the presence of the Lord? When was the last time you heard him speak his word? When was the last time you witnessed a miracle?

While teaching and preaching in Decapolis, Jesus was introduced to a man who could not hear and could barely speak. Jesus' emotions were moved, not only for this afflicted man but also for the citizens of Decapolis. Jesus knew their hearts were pure because they exercised a loving act of kindness toward this man. Jesus realized that they did all they could to help him but were limited when it came to communicating with him. They could not restore the man's hearing, nor could they free his speech, but they knew Jesus could! Because of their faith, Jesus was willing and able to help. Have you ever given your best, but it wasn't enough? Have you reached your limitations over an unsolved issue? If so, you must turn to Jesus and ask him to do what you cannot do. Like the citizens of Decapolis, present Jesus your problem and have faith in him that he will solve it for you!

The first thing that Jesus did when he met this man was take him away from the crowd. Why did he do this? The Scripture passage does not give a reason, but if you put yourself in this man's sandals, you may come up with an answer. This need for privacy was the first step in the healing process. When Jesus looked upon this man, he saw more than just physical defects; he saw internal conflicts. During this time, if a person was deaf and mute it was a lifetime sentence of solitude. Not only did it mean that communication was impossible, but it also meant that they were going to be disconnected from social engagement, education, effective employment, and friendship. In essence, Jesus sensed a lonely, frustrated man. Jesus needed to heal him internally before he could heal him externally. Jesus took this man to a quiet, private place to show him that he loved him and that he could fulfill his internal needs. Do people notice your physical affliction? Do these physical afflictions create internal strife? Do you feel like you spend your days in solitary confinement? Does your affliction disconnect you from social engagement? Does it disrupt your education? Has it stopped you from finding employment? Has it made relationships difficult to sustain? If so, you know exactly how the deaf and mute man felt. Allow Jesus to take you away from the noisy and pressing throng of life. Follow him to a quiet place so that you can become more attentive and receptive to him. Give him permission to love you and heal you from within.

The methods that Jesus used for healing this deaf-mute man were unique. He was not doing some kind of ritual to bring about healing. Jesus does not need to perform any rituals to summon his power. A simple thought or word from the Lord can heal any alignment. Instead, Jesus chose this procedure because he wanted to enter this man's world of silence and speak to him in a language that he could understand. Jesus chose to use a primitive form of sign language to explain to the man how and when the healing would take place. For Jesus, the most important part of the healing process is for the patient to be an active participant. Jesus placed his fingers in the man's ears and removed them. He was telling the man, "I am going to remove the blockage in your hearing." He spat and touched the man's tongue. He was telling him, "I am going to remove the blockage in your mouth." He looked up toward heaven to tell the man, "It is God alone who is able to do this for you."

Jesus spoke the first words that this man ever heard: "Be opened!" With this command, the man's mind, body, and soul were aligned and opened. For the first time in his life, he was free from the ailments that controlled him. The Scripture passage details the first words that this man heard but not the first words that he spoke. I often wondered what he said to Jesus. If you were this man, how would you have responded to God? It's safe to say that for the rest of his life, he proclaimed that his affliction was a blessing instead of a curse because it allowed him to see, hear, and speak to the Son of God.

Are you spiritually deaf? Are you spiritually mute? Do you need Jesus to put his fingers in your ears? Do you need him to touch your tongue? The following quiz will help you determine your spiritual tone.

1. Do you listen to the Word of God through daily Scripture reading?
2. Do you comprehend and accept his words and ways?
3. Do you profess your obedience to him through your words and actions?
4. Do you speak to the LORD through daily prayer?
5. Are you sharing the word of God in your house, at school, or in your workplace?
6. Do you love others and treat them with respect as Jesus did?

If you were able to answer yes to every question, you are on a journey with Jesus. You are continuing his mission and are providing comfort, protection, and mercy to his flock. If you answered no to some of these questions, you need to find Jesus and request some private time with him so he can help you identify your internal conflicts and spiritual defects. If you answered no to all these questions, you are in desperate need of a miracle. Jesus is waiting to heal you. No one is excluded from an encounter with him. If you accept his offer of salvation, you will be set free from sin, sorrow, inner emptiness, and loneliness. Jesus has traveled a long distance to see you. He is with you at this very moment. Humbly go to him and ask him for a miracle. Today is the day you can see, hear, and speak to the Son of God. Today is the day that your affliction becomes a blessing!

The Lepers Become Clean

> *As he continued his journey to Jerusalem, he traveled through Samaria and Galilee. As he was entering a village, ten lepers met him. They stood at a distance from him and raised their*

> *voice, saying, "Jesus, Master! Have pity on us!" And when he saw them, he said, "Go show yourselves to the priests." As they were going they were cleansed. And one of them, realizing he had been healed, returned, glorifying God in a loud voice; and he fell at the feet of Jesus and thanked him. He was a Samaritan. Jesus said in reply, "Ten were cleansed, were they not? Where are the other nine? Has none but this foreigner returned to give thanks to God?" Then he said to him, "Stand up and go; your faith has saved you."* (Luke 17:11–19)

Before Jesus was born to his mother Mary, he already knew how his earthly existence would unfold. He knew how many days, hours, minutes, and seconds he had on this earth. Everything that he would experience was already predestined by his Father. The places he traveled, the people he met, the miracles he performed were all part of his Father's plan. He selflessly relinquished his will and placed his faith in his Father so he could carry the sins of the world on his back and hold them on the cross! Each step that Jesus took and each word that he spoke prepared him for the events that would occur in Jerusalem.

In the first sentence of this Scripture passage, Luke tells you that Jesus was making his way to Jerusalem. This means that Jesus knew that his earthly existence was rapidly coming to an end. Even though Jesus could vividly sense what was waiting for him in Jerusalem, he faithfully followed his Father's plan. The essence of Jesus' life was to be productive every waking second while he was on the earth. His Father programmed him to promote the kingdom of God through his words and actions. Jesus never wasted an opportunity to preach, teach, and model the lessons needed to be one with his Father. Take a moment a think about your life. Unlike Jesus, you do not know the day, hour, minute, or second when your earthly life will cease to exist. You don't have the divine power to vividly see and hear what will happen to you in the future. However, the Father has a plan for you just like he did for his Son. Have you selflessly relinquished your will over to him? Do you have faith in him and the plan that he has for you? Are you following his plan by being productive during your waking hours? Are you preaching, teaching, and modeling the precepts of the kingdom of heaven? Are you harnessing the gifts that the Father has given you to advance yourself and others closer to your heavenly destiny? Luke tells you in the first sentence of this passage that Jesus traveled to the border of Samaria and Galilee to continue his Father's work and complete the mission that he was given. Where will you travel today, and what will you do to complete the mission that the Father has given to you?

Jesus was still on the outskirts of the village when ten men who were suffering from leprosy met him. Biblical leprosy included a variety of skin diseases. Some of these diseases were highly contagious and were not curable. During the time of Jesus, priests were responsible for diagnosing leprosy. If a priest determined that someone had leprosy, it was regarded as a death sentence. Those that suffered from these skin diseases were required to be isolated from all healthy people. In addition, this diagnosis carried with it a sign of God's judgment, meaning people believed that a person who suffered from this disease brought it upon themselves by the sins that they committed. Therefore, society had less compassion for those who suffered from leprosy. For these reasons, these ten men met Jesus before he entered the village he was traveling to.

When these men saw Jesus, they stood at a distance from him as they did with anyone they met. It seems that they knew who Jesus was because they called him by his name, "Jesus, Master." In unison, they made a simple request to Jesus, "Have pity on us!" Luke emphasizes that Jesus "saw them," which symbolizes that even though the rest of society decided to make these lepers invisible (label them as outcasts) Jesus accepted them and recognized their pain and suffering. Jesus does not heal the lepers immediately but instead commands them to show themselves to the priests for inspection as if they had been healed. As mentioned in the last healing summary, for Jesus, the most important part of the healing process is for the patient to be an active participant. Because of this, the healing of these ten men would only take place if they exercised their faith and obeyed the Word of God. Because they believed and willingly followed the instructions of Jesus, their bodies were "cleansed." They were "reborn" into a new life that provided them faith, hope, and love.

Were you surprised that only one out of the ten returned to Jesus? If they were all healed, why did only one return? Jesus wanted to know where the other nine went. It's easy to read this passage and criticize the other nine, but I'm sure if you reflect long enough on past events, you will recognize yourself as one of those nine! Have you ever prayed long and hard for something that you needed or wanted? Were your prayers answered? When the Lord delivered on his promise, how did you respond to him? Did you praise him in a loud voice? Did you throw yourself at his feet and thank him, or did you go on with your life thinking and feeling that you deserved the miracle that Jesus graciously granted you? How often do you stop each day and thank God for your blessings? How often do you forget to thank God?

The man that came back to Jesus was given the ultimate gift. Because of his faith, obedience, gratitude, praise, humility, and love, Jesus saved this man's soul. He commanded him to "rise and go" so he could be a witness for the kingdom of heaven. Not only did Jesus give this man new skin, but he also gave him a new mind, heart, and soul! The next time you make a request to Jesus and he fulfills it, make it a priority to return to him with praise and thanksgiving. If you do this, not only will you be healed, but you will be saved!

Have your mental afflictions made you into a leper? Do you feel as though you are an outcast? Have you allowed your anxiety and/or depression to isolate you from your family and friends? Do you blame yourself for your diagnosis? Do you believe that you will never experience mental wellness? If so, be on the lookout for the LORD. He is coming to your town, your house, your room. Have the courage to call out his name and ask him to have pity on you. He will accept you as you are and recognize your pain and suffering. Your healing will take place with words and actions—his words (Scripture), your actions (faith and obedience). When your stress, strain, and pain disappear, don't forget to return to the LORD with praise and thanksgiving for his grace. Jesus will do whatever it takes for you to become his productive disciple!

The Lame Walk

> *He entered a boat, made the crossing, and came into his own town. And there people brought to him a paralytic lying on a stretcher. When Jesus saw their faith, he said to the paralytic, "Courage, child, your sins are forgiven." At that, some of the scribes said to themselves, "This man is blaspheming." Jesus knew what they were thinking, and said, "Why do you harbor evil thoughts? Which is easier, to say, 'Your sins are forgiven,' or to say, 'Rise and walk'? But that you may know that the Son of Man has authority on earth to forgive sins"—he then said to the paralytic, "Rise, pick up your stretcher, and go home." He rose and went home. When the crowds saw this they were struck with awe and glorified God who had given such authority to human beings.* (Matt 9:1–8)

Have you ever seen the movie *The Wizard of Oz*? I bet you have—several times! Do you remember the final scene? Glinda (the Good Witch of the

North) tells Dorothy that the ruby slippers she is wearing have the power to return her to Kansas. After sharing a tearful farewell with Scarecrow, Tin Man, and Lion, Dorothy follows Glinda's instructions by closing her eyes, tapping her heels together three times, and repeating, "There's no place like home." Dorothy wakes up in her bedroom surrounded by her family and friends, including Toto. Everyone dismisses her adventure as a dream, but Dorothy insists it was real and says she will never run away from home again before declaring, "There's no place like home!"[3]

Jesus spent much of his earthly existence at home in Nazareth. Luke indicates that Jesus ventured beyond this village at least once when he was twelve years old to travel with his parents, family, and friends to the holy city of Jerusalem (Luke 2:42–52). The next recorded event about his life occurred eighteen years later. According to Matthew, Mark, and Luke, Jesus left Nazareth in search of John the Baptist so that he could be baptized (Matt 3:13–17). This event officially marked the beginning of his ministry (Luke 3:23). He then was led by the Spirit into the wilderness for forty days and nights where he was tested and tempted by Satan (Luke 4:1–13). After this purification, Jesus returned to Nazareth on the Sabbath and entered the synagogue to declare to his family, friends, and neighbors that he is the Son of God (Luke 4:16–20). Upon hearing this news, the people that he knew and loved tried to stop his message and end his life by throwing him off a cliff (Luke 4:22–30)! I often wonder, after this episode, did Jesus share the same feeling about Nazareth as Dorothy did about Kansas?

You can force the Son of Man out of Nazareth, but you can't take Nazareth out of the Son of Man. Throughout his three-year ministry, his followers and foes associated him with his hometown (John 1:46). Even at the end of his earthly life, Pilate prepared a sign that was placed on the top of his cross that read, "Jesus of Nazareth, the King of the Jews" (John 19:19). Regardless of the hurtful words and actions from his kin, Jesus continued to love and forgive them. Jesus returned home several times but was never fully welcomed. He was consistently met with friction and rejection (Mark 6:1–6). Have you ever been in a social situation where you were not welcomed? How did you react? Did you ever place yourself back in that situation?

Why did Jesus continue to go back to a place where he would expose himself to emotional pain and physical danger? The answer can be found

3. Fleming, *Wizard of Oz*.

in Jesus' heart. Jesus doesn't judge you on a single action or reaction. He won't allow your sins to be final and fatal. He will return to you until your discord turns to harmony, confusion turns to certainty, disbelief turns to faith, fear turns to hope, pain turns to comfort, and hate turns to love. "If today you hear his voice, harden not your heart" (Heb 3:15).

In this healing Scripture, Jesus once again returns to Nazareth. Not everyone in his hometown were nonbelievers, at least one crippled man and his friends had hope in him. Jesus was moved by the actions from the friends of the crippled man. These men were so sure that Jesus could heal their crippled friend, they literally carried him and placed him at the feet of the Lord. This is an important lesson that cannot be overlooked. Without their faith and effort, their friend would have never been healed! Jesus recognized what was in the hearts and minds of these men and was willing to reward them for it.

It's hard to determine the faith of the crippled man. His physical alignment caused suffering his entire life. It's only natural that this suffering jaded his emotional and psychological outlook as well. When Jesus looked at the crippled man, he saw a lost soul who was stagnant from physical, emotional, and spiritual paralysis. Therefore, Jesus addressed this man with a kind, hope-inspiring phrase, "Take heart, son; your sins are forgiven." This command initiated the healing process because it filled him with the faith, hope, and love he would need to walk the road toward discipleship. Do you relate with the crippled man in the story? Has your pain jaded your emotional and psychological perspective? Has it caused you to question your faith in God? If so, "take heart"! When you find yourself idle and lost, don't be afraid to reach out to your family and friends. Their faith and effort will carry you to the nail-scarred feet of Jesus. Jesus will reward their intercession by providing you with the grace, wisdom, and faith you will need to become an active disciple of the Lord.

It shouldn't surprise you the response Jesus received from the scribes after declaring to the crippled man that his sins were forgiven. Jesus already experienced their ridicule, scorn, and rejection of his claim for being the Messiah. However, he was providing them another opportunity to accept the "truth." Your thoughts and opinions of God are open to him and are of interest to him. He wants you to truly believe that he is the Father, Son, and Holy Spirit. So much so that he is willing to humble himself and prove it to you time after time. Because the scribes could not see Jesus forgive the crippled man's sins, he needed another way to show the nonbelievers that he is the Almighty. To prove to them that he had the power of God to both heal and forgive sins, he commanded the crippled man to get up and walk! This miracle of healing made it undeniably clear that Jesus was God incarnate.

Do you believe Jesus Christ is the Alpha and the Omega, the beginning and the end of everything? Do you believe he is the only teacher from whom you must learn? Do you believe he is the only Lord on whom you should depend, the only Head to whom you should be united, and the only model that you should imitate? Do you believe he is the only Physician that can heal you, the only Shepherd that can feed you, the only Way that can lead you? Do you believe that he is the only Truth? Do you believe that he alone can satisfy all your needs and desires? If you answered no to any of these questions, ask him to prove it to you and he will!

The Possessed Are Freed

Then they sailed to the territory of the Gerasenes, which is opposite Galilee. When he came ashore a man from the town who was possessed by demons met him. For a long time he had not worn clothes; he did not live in a house, but lived among the tombs. When he saw Jesus, he cried out and fell down before him; in a loud voice he shouted, "What have you to do with me, Jesus, son of the Most High God? I beg you, do not torment me!" For he had ordered the unclean spirit to come out of the man. (It had taken hold of him many times, and he used to be bound with chains and shackles as a restraint, but he would break his bonds and be driven by the demon into deserted places.) Then Jesus asked him, "What is your name?"He replied, "Legion," because many demons had entered him. And they pleaded with him not to order them to depart to the abyss. A herd of many swine was feeding there on the hillside, and they pleaded with him to allow them to enter those swine; and he let them. The demons came out of the man and entered the swine, and the herd rushed down the steep bank into the lake and was drowned.

When the swineherds saw what had happened, they ran away and reported the incident in the town and throughout the countryside. People came out to see what had happened and, when they approached Jesus, they discovered the man from whom the demons had come out sitting at his feet. He was clothed and in his right mind, and they were seized with fear. Those who witnessed it

> *told them how the possessed man had been saved. The entire population of the region of the Gerasenes asked Jesus to leave them because they were seized with great fear. So he got into a boat and returned. The man from whom the demons had come out begged to remain with him, but he sent him away, saying, "Return home and recount what God has done for you." The man went off and proclaimed throughout the whole town what Jesus had done for him.* (Luke 8:26–39)

In this healing Gospel, Jesus traveled across the Sea of Galilee to a foreign land. It would be the first and only time in Luke's Gospel that Jesus would enter a gentile (non-Jewish) territory. This region's culture, values, beliefs, attitudes, and behaviors were vastly different from what Jesus and his disciples were accustomed to. Why did Jesus invest his time and energy and travel to a place where he and the inhabitants had nothing in common? Who or what was there that needed his immediate attention? The answer to any question about Jesus that starts with the words *who, what, where, when, why,* and *how* have the same answer. He does all things because his love for others is infinite, and he wants to stop sin and suffering from impeding his Father's work. Has your anxiety and/or depression made you feel like a foreigner in your own body? Have your symptoms changed your values, beliefs, attitudes, and behaviors? If so, cast your eyes to the horizon. Jesus is coming to you with his might and mercy so that he can bless you with mental wellness.

The forces of good and evil are colliding around you at this very moment. These forces are in a tug-of-war to see which one of them can influence you the most. Both forces are exerting tremendous energy so that they can enter your mind, heart, and soul. Both want to control your thoughts, words, and actions. Do you ever feel this battle taking place? Do you sense prevention and/or temptation in your daily life? Think back over the last three days about your thoughts, words, and actions. Which force influenced you the most?

This Gospel provides insight into the strength and weakness of each force. As soon as Jesus stepped out of the boat, the answer becomes very clear as to why he chose to travel to this gentile region. Evil was causing sin and suffering and wasn't allowing a certain man to complete his Father's work. Jesus went across the Sea of Galilee to save a life. Did you notice how this demon-possessed man immediately fell at the feet of Jesus? Did you also notice how these unclean spirits tried to negotiate with the Lord? When Jesus comes, evil goes! Satan and his fallen angels have no power to do what they want to do without Christ's permission. When it comes to good versus evil, good is the undisputed champion. A battle between the two never takes place because evil always submits before the fight begins. It only becomes a twelve-round heavyweight championship fight when you get involved. Even though good wears the championship belt around its waist, evil is the number one ranked contender willing to use you to knock out the champion. Temptation is very powerful because it exclusively focuses on your wants. It appeals to your flesh. When you grant evil entry into your mind, heart, and soul, the fight begins from within. Evil provides you pleasure for a moment but torture for a lifetime. It leaves you naked, homeless, and crestfallen. It imprisons you and sentences you to solitary confinement. There are only two ways that it relinquishes its control over you: Jesus commands the impure spirits to leave you or they completely suck the life out of you until you expire.

This Gospel provides another example of the infinite love and mercy the LORD has for his children. Jesus Christ is the answer to your problems. He can command a legion of demons out of you and into the abyss. He can give you back what you once had. He can realign your psychological, emotional, and spiritual state and place you on the street named Straight (Acts 9:11). He is willing and able to heal you so that you can "return home and tell how much God has done for you" (Luke 8:39). This all can be given to you if you: accept Jesus Christ, obey his word, and do his work (Matt 7:7)!

The Dead Are Resurrected

When Jesus had crossed again in the boat to the other side, a large crowd gathered around him, and he stayed close to the sea. One of the synagogue officials, named Jairus, came forward. Seeing him he fell at his feet and pleaded earnestly with him, saying, "My daughter is at the point of death. Please, come lay your hands on her that she may get well and live." He went off with him, and a large crowd followed him and pressed upon him. While he was still speaking, people from the synagogue official's house arrived and said, "Your daughter has died; why trouble the teacher any longer?" Disregarding the message that was reported, Jesus said to the synagogue official, "Do not be afraid; just have faith." He did not allow anyone to accompany him inside except Peter, James, and John, the brother of James. When they arrived at the house

> *of the synagogue official, he caught sight of a commotion, people weeping and wailing loudly. So he went in and said to them, "Why this commotion and weeping? The child is not dead but asleep." And they ridiculed him. Then he put them all out. He took along the child's father and mother and those who were with him and entered the room where the child was. He took the child by the hand and said to her, "Talitha koum," which means, "Little girl, I say to you, arise!" The girl, a child of twelve, arose immediately and walked around. At that they were utterly astounded. He gave strict orders that no one should know this and said that she should be given something to eat.* (Mark 5:21–24, 35–43)

What a scene! I have saved the best for last. Jesus is returning home from across the Sea of Galilee where he healed the demon-possessed man from Gerasenes (the healing miracle we just discussed). Waiting at the shoreline was a man named Jairus who was a prominent member of the community. His title was that of synagogue leader. This is an important detail of the story because the last time Jesus visited his hometown synagogue, the people became so angry at his declaration of being the Son of God that they tried to kill him. Now, the leader who represented the resistance toward Jesus was in desperate need of his help. How long are you willing to wait for Jesus? How much time and energy are you willing to invest to see him, touch him, and speak to him?

When Jesus stepped off the boat, Jairus fell at his feet. Jesus must have felt the sensation of déjà vu. Jairus and the man who was possessed by demons had the same reaction when they saw Jesus. They both humbled themselves in the presence of the LORD. An important question to ask while reading this Scripture passage is, why the sudden change in Jairus? The last time Jairus saw Jesus, he was leading an angry mob to the top of a cliff to push him off. Now, he is bowing down in reverence to him. After hearing Jairus's request, it is not so difficult to understand why he had a change of heart. A parent of a dying child will do nearly anything to save their child.

On that day, Jairus decided to experience his "coming to Jesus" moment. It has been said that all of us will experience a "coming to Jesus" moment (or multiple) in our life. A "coming to Jesus" moment consciously occurs when your fundamental priorities and/or beliefs are challenged, reassessed, or reaffirmed. It is a moment of epiphany, enlightenment, or intuition regarding the "truth," which leads you to choose to accept Jesus Christ as your Savior and to follow the Christian faith. This moment usually occurs during adverse times when the only one you can turn to for help is the LORD. In the case of Jairus, his daughter's illness stripped him of his status, ego, and pride and humbled him to wait for the only person who can save his daughter and his soul! Have you experienced a "coming to Jesus" moment in your life? If so, what situation or circumstance caused you to turn to the LORD for help? Did you seek Jesus out? Did you patiently wait for his arrival? When he came to you, did you humble yourself in his presence? Did you earnestly request his help?

Jairus invited Jesus to his home. This act of faith moved the heart of Jesus. Jairus never expressed any doubt but instead expressed confidence that Jesus would restore his daughter's health if he only laid his hands on her. To reward Jairus's faith, Jesus accepted his invitation. Have you ever invited Jesus into your home (your heart)? Have you grown in your faith, hope, and love in the LORD? Do you trust that the LORD will meet your every need?

When Jesus and Jairus arrived at his home, mourners approached them and told them that the young girl died. There is a lot of information contained in this book, but if you can only remember one quote and use it the rest of your life, I hope it will be what Jesus told Jairus after he heard the devastating news that his daughter died: "Don't be afraid; just believe"! This simple command not only raised Jairus's daughter from the dead, but it will also raise you from whatever afflictions, heartaches, pain, loss, failures, etc. that life brings to you.

It was only a matter of time until Jesus would face ridicule from his kin. It came when he declared that this young girl was not dead but only sleeping. Jesus knew that the miracle he was about to create would be a lesson in the resurrection. His hometown folk laughed at him when he told them that she was suffering from a temporary condition—sleep. The people of Jerusalem and the surrounding area were not yet familiar with the concept of resurrection. However, Jesus wanted to give them a prequel of what was to come on the first Easter Sunday. By raising Jairus's daughter from the dead, he was showing his kin and the rest of humanity that he is the resurrection and the life. Anyone who believes in him will live, even though they die; and whoever lives by believing in him will never die (John 11:25).

The final point that I would like to make about this Scripture passage is once you have your "coming to Jesus" moment, be prepared to be ridiculed. When you commit yourself to the LORD and always put him first, the culture of death will treat you like an outcast (Luke 8:37). When you model your thoughts, words, and actions after Jesus Christ, you will be accused of being out of touch with reality (Mark 3:21). When you witness to others about how the Lord has changed your life, you will be perceived as a radical (Acts 28:24). When you evangelize the word of God, you will be labeled an agitator (Heb 4:12). "Don't be afraid; just believe"! The work that your Heavenly Father asks you to do is important in expanding his kingdom. He has entrusted you to continue his work here on earth. He has given you all that you will need to accomplish the tasks that he has assigned to you. He will never give you an assignment that you will not be able to complete, nor will he ever put you into a situation you will not be able to handle. Nothing comes to you that doesn't pass through his fingers first. Accept the challenge of being a disciple of Jesus Christ. He has made the path for you. Have the courage to follow it!

The Anxious and/or Depressed Are Relieved

This section has been reserved for you to describe how Jesus has healed or will heal you from the symptoms of anxiety and/or depression. Create a gospel story in which you are the main character. Describe for me a scenario when your surroundings trigger your panic attacks and/or depressive thoughts. Provide detail on how you meet Jesus. Do you seek him out? Does he seek you out? Does a family member or friend bring you to him or him to you? Describe the interaction you have with Jesus. What do you say and/or do? How does he respond? What does he say and/or do? How do you respond? Illustrate the way Jesus goes about healing you. Does he command your affliction to leave you? Does he use the power of touch to free you? Does he send you to a person or place to cleanse you? Finally, what is the outcome of the miracle that takes place? What does he instruct you to do? How has your life changed without the physical, psychological, and emotional burden of anxiety and/or depression?

Allow the Holy Spirit to inspire you as you complete this activity. Don't be surprised if the shackles of your anxiety and/or depression begin to loosen as you participate in this exercise. The more time and energy that you invest in this process, the more strongly you will feel the healing power of Jesus Christ within you. God works in mysterious ways. Maybe at the end of this exercise you will experience his power and glory!

> *Is anyone among you sick? He should summon the elders of the church, and they should pray over him and anoint him with oil*

in the name of the Lord, and the prayer of faith will save the sick person, and the Lord will raise him up. If he has committed any sins, he will be forgiven.
—Jas 5:14–15

The wound is the place where the Light enters you.
—Rumi[4]

HOLISTIC APPROACH #4: SPONTANEOUS PRAYER

And we have this confidence in him, that if we ask anything according to his will, he hears us. (1 John 5:14)

Pray Throughout the Day

Prayer is the vehicle that allows you to communicate with God. It is the medium that leads you into a conversation with the Almighty. The more you converse with the Lord, the stronger your relationship becomes. Therefore, instead of speaking to him once a day, speak to him throughout the day.

Each day consists of twenty-four hours. Hopefully, at least eight of those hours you are sleeping. If that is the case, what are you doing with the sixteen hours that remain? I'm sure you can provide a long list of commitments you have that fill up those hours. However, you and I both know that these commitments do not absorb every waking minute. As a matter of fact, you have more idle time each day than you realize. "Idle time" refers to periods when you are not engaged in essential work. Examples of essential work include school, job, chores, individual/ family management, etc. Even when you are at school, work, and/or home, there is always down time between activities. This is the perfect time to speak to the Lord. In these moments, he doesn't expect you to open your Bible or recite long ritual prayers. He wants you to speak to him in short phrases that come from your inner core. This gesture will help prioritize your life by setting a daily agenda that places him first on the list of

4. Barks, *Illuminated Rumi*, 128.

people that you need to interact with throughout each day. These spontaneous conversations will help optimize your focus, patience, and energy to accomplish the tasks that your Heavenly Father has placed before you. Investing your idle time communicating with the LORD is better than wandering into the devil's workshop (Prov 16:27–29).

To help you begin this spontaneous daily conversation with the LORD, I have provided you with some small but powerful phrases you can use during idle time as well as stressful times throughout each day. These phrases come in the form of *praise*, *petitions*, and *guidance*, depending upon the circumstances you are experiencing. Remember, these phrases are meant to be short informal prayers that bubble up from your soul.

Spontaneous Daily Conversations with the Lord	
Praise	
Jesus, I trust in you!	Jesus, I give my life totally to you.
This is the day the LORD has made; let me rejoice and be glad in it.	Jesus, may all my actions, words, and thoughts glorify you.
LORD, you are the only way.	Father, may all who see me think of you.
LORD, let me glorify you through my work.	Jesus, I choose to love you and reject selfishness.
May I live no longer for myself but for Jesus.	Jesus, my LORD, my God, my all.
Jesus, I devote my life to you.	Give thanks to the LORD, for he is good.
Father, thank you for days like today: days of hope, love, and joy.	Jesus, you are my only hope and the only hope I need.
LORD, I do believe!	Jesus, I welcome you as LORD of my life.
Jesus, I welcome you in my heart.	Father, everything I have is yours.
Father, I love you with all my heart, all my soul, all my mind, and all my strength.	Jesus, thank you for making my life worth living.
Petitions	
LORD, save me.	Jesus, give me your mind and your standards.
Father, send me the Holy Spirit to teach me your ways.	Father, send the Spirit of truth to make me a person of truth.
Father, fill me with love for Jesus.	Father, make me a messenger of hope.

Father, teach me how to witness with power for the risen Jesus.	Father, increase my faith so that I become a new person.
Father, make me a missionary of mercy.	Jesus, make me one of your disciples.
LORD, make me an instrument of your peace.	Lord Jesus, have mercy on me.
Jesus, teach me the meaning of humility.	LORD, give me a humble and docile heart.
Jesus, cleanse me of my sins and make me holy.	Father, make me a peacemaker.
Father, make me perfect in love.	LORD, fill me with joy.
Jesus, come visit me.	Father, mold me into the image of Jesus.
Jesus, don't let me go to sleep tonight without forgiving everyone who has ever hurt and rejected me.	Jesus, help me to reform my life and believe in the gospel.
Father, may I do it your way, all the way and all the time.	Father, may I love those considered unlovable.
Jesus, remember me.	Father, may I realize that you don't owe me anything and I owe you everything.
LORD, increase my faith!	Jesus, help my unbelief.
Jesus, fill my emptiness.	Jesus, keep me near the cross.
Father, give me enough love to repent.	Jesus, make my heart like yours.
Father, free me from sin.	Father, guard me against complaining.
Guidance	
Jesus, may your will be done.	Jesus, never leave me in times of trial.
Jesus, allow me to serve instead of being served.	Jesus, give me the strength to love my enemies.
Father, may I live a life of obedience.	Jesus, save me from myself.
Father, may your love drive out my fear.	Father, may I want what you want.
Jesus, forgive me for I have sinned.	Jesus, allow me to always hope.
Father, may I increasingly read, study, pray, share, live, proclaim, obey, and teach your word.	Father, grant me the courage to obey your will.
Father, may I make every effort to build unity.	Jesus, may I never get tired of you.

Risen Jesus, may I repent of living for selfish pleasure.	Father, never let me forget you, even for a moment.
Father, may I never be used by Satan.	LORD, guide me to all truth.
LORD, never allow me to give in to fear.	Jesus, may I receive joy and be a joy for you.
May my love for the people in my life reflect your love for them.	Father, may I decrease so that Jesus may increase.
Jesus, I throw myself on your mercy. Cleanse me of sin.	Father, may I be free from the sins of racism, impurity, and laziness.
Jesus, may I do it your way.	Father, let me be faithful to your teachings.
Jesus, my will is to do your will	LORD, may I walk by faith in you, not by sight.
May I spend my life spreading the good news of your merciful love.	Jesus, may I see obedience and disobedience as you do.
Father, fulfill every detail of your plan for my life.	Father, may I build your kingdom wherever you put me.
Jesus, let me live each day by your standards.	Father, may I desire mercy like Jesus does.
Jesus, ruin any plans of mine that are not yours.	Jesus, may I never erase you from any part of my life.
Father, forgive me as I forgive my betrayers.	Father, help me fix my eyes on Jesus.
Father, may grace come constantly to me and through me.	Father, I surrender myself to you and worship you.
Father, may I not only receive a blessing but be a blessing.	Father, open my eyes to the reasons behind all my behaviors toward those who dislike me.
Father, may I not move to the right or to the left but be set in your ways.	Father, may I never give in to discouragement.
Jesus, do anything to me you want, even things I don't understand.	Keep me faithful to your teaching and never let me be parted from you.
I have decided to follow Jesus instead of him following me.	Father, may I see problems as opportunities to claim your victory.

By reading the above prayers, you have just started your spontaneous conversation with the LORD. The goal now is to continue the conversation throughout the rest of today, tomorrow, and the remainder of your life until you experience your resurrection. At first, you may want to make a copy of this list and use it as a reference when you are in between times of essential work. The more you converse with the Lord, the less you will need this reference sheet. Your heart and soul will know what to say and when to say it. By exercising this holistic approach, you will quickly realize that the one ear that will always listen and the one voice that will always respond is that of the resurrected Lord!

If you ask anything of me in my name, I will do it.
—John 14:14

God's purposes and plans will not fail.
Before you spend all your prayer time telling Him about yours, ask about His.

—Louie Giglio[5]

HOLISTIC APPROACH #5: CHOOSE YOUR WORDS CAREFULLY

> She said to herself, "If I only touch his cloak, I will be healed." (Matt 9:21)

Speaking Without Saying a Word

I have a challenge for you. Starting tomorrow morning, I want you to take a twenty-four-hour vow of silence. The rules for the challenge are simple: you are to follow your normal daily routine with one exception, you are not allowed to open your mouth and speak. You are allowed to communicate with others, but you cannot use your vocal cords as a means of communication. No one can hear your voice for a twenty-four-hour period. Are you up for this challenge? Do you think you can be productive for one full day without using your voice? Do you want to put your money where your mouth is (pun intended)? Let's place a friendly wager on this matter. If you are successful in completing this challenge, I promise to post your name on my "Wall of Fame" on my website. If

5. Louie Giglio (@louiegiglio), "God's purposes and plans," X, Feb. 20, 2013, https://x.com/louiegiglio/status/304265363879784448.

you fail to complete this challenge, you must promote my book on your social media platforms to help others who are struggling with anxiety and/or depression. Do we have a deal? Good luck, because you are going to need it!

Stop reading until you complete the challenge!

Well . . . how did you do? Did you win the bet? If so, please email me the details of how you were able to accomplish this minor miracle of not talking for twenty-four-hours. I will make sure that you receive all the accolades that you deserve by putting your name up on my prestigious "Wall of Fame." By the way, tell all your family, friends, coworkers, teachers, etc. I'll accept all their gratitude since they didn't have to hear you complain for one day (cue smiley face). For those of you that lost the bet, what happened? When, where, and why did the breakdown occur? What was so important that you needed to use your voice? I'm sorry to hear that you did not cross the finish line. You can always try again tomorrow, but for now, get on your social media platforms and promote this book! With your help, we can bring some *Faith, Hope, and Love* into someone's life today.

This was a very difficult challenge. I commend all of you that accepted it. Humans are social in nature. We all, consciously and/or subconsciously, search to make connections with others. The easiest way to make these connections is through verbalization. When this challenge removed this mode of communication, I'm sure you felt a sense of uneasiness because the main bridge that you normally use to communicate with others was shut down for twenty-four hours. You needed to find another form of communication (that was probably much more time consuming) to regain the connections that you so strongly desire.

If this exercise worked the way I wanted it to, then you spent less time than normal communicating with others during this twenty-four-hour period. If this is true, then you had ample time to speak with the two most important people in your life—God and yourself! Did you take this opportunity to speak to both? If so, how did the conversations go? Did you give yourself time to listen to each of them? Did you learn anything? It is important that you communicate with each of them every day. I promise, every conversation you have with them will be productive. The exchange of words and ideas with each of them will present a moment of growth and understanding that will allow you to become all that you were meant to be.

Time slips away very quickly. The famous fictional movie character Rocky Balboa once said, "Time takes everybody out; time's undefeated."[6] Because time is finite, you have a limited amount of people you will come in contact with in your life. What you say to them and how you say it will make a difference in their life as well as yours. Therefore, you need to choose your words very carefully before you use them. Your words, whether silent or audible, are just as important as your actions. What you say and/or pray are the building blocks of your personality and reputation. Invest wisely in your limited time and make sure you are communicating with others in a way that leaves each of you a better person and the world a better place.

Sticks and Stones

I'm sure you are familiar with the child's expression "Sticks and stones may break my bones, but words will never hurt me." As far back as I can remember, when I used this expression, I was always hurting inside. For me, this was an ego defense mechanism that allowed me to send a message to someone that their words didn't do psychological or emotional damage to me, but they *did*! Therefore, I learned early on those sticks and stones did hurt, and so do words. Sticks and stones create temporary pain and may cause cuts and/or bruising or a need for a cast, but over time a person will witness their physical healing. However, words can pierce deep into a person's psyche and never completely heal because those wounds remain open as long as that person recalls the original event in which these words were used against them. Unfortunately, the damage caused by words cannot be healed by using medical supplies that you can find in a first-aid kit. These wounds can only be healed by using the antibodies found in your psychological, emotional, and spiritual systems.

Do you recall the last time someone weaponized words to hurt you? Who was it? What was it about? What words did they turn into "bullets"? How much damage did these bullets cause? Do you still carry these bullets around with you? If so, why?

Do you recall the last time *you* weaponized words to hurt someone else? Who was it? What was it about? What words did you turn into "bullets"? How much damage did your bullets cause? Do you regret using these bullets against that person? If so, why?

6. Stallone, *Rocky Balboa*, 0:45:22.

Do you recall the last time you weaponized words to hurt *yourself*? Why was there a need to tell yourself those things? What did you tell yourself? How much damage did your words cause? Do you regret telling yourself those words? If so, why?

Words have tremendous power. They can heal or hurt, help or hinder, encourage or discourage, compliment or criticize. They can act like seeds or weeds. They have the power to move heaven or hell. Whether words are silent or audible, they can change a person's mind, body, and soul. What a tremendous force that each of us possesses. Choose your words wisely and decipher what you hear so that you can guard against despair.

Jesus Heals a Sick Woman

I would like to conclude the "Resurrection" chapter with one more miracle story for you to reflect upon. This miracle was created and completed strictly through words. It provides witness to the power of silent and audible words.

> *A woman suffering hemorrhages for twelve years came up behind him and touched the tassel on his cloak. She said to herself, "If only I can touch his cloak, I shall be cured." Jesus turned around and saw her, and said, "Courage, daughter! Your faith has saved you." And from that hour the woman was cured.*(Matt 9:20–22)

This nameless person (which could be you) had been suffering from a medical condition for twelve years. Even though she suffered, she always found time each day to speak to the Lord through silent petitions. Because of her loyalty, the Lord blessed her with faith, hope, and persistence. He gave her the strength to never give up or give in to this affliction. After twelve long years, Jesus led her to a place and time where he could free her from this medical burden. Because of the large crowd surrounding Jesus, it was impossible for her to get close to him. Through a silent prayer, "If I only touch his cloak, I will be healed," Jesus heard her and responded. Jesus sought her out and told her, "Take heart, daughter, your faith has healed you." With his audible message, the woman was healed immediately! This woman received a blessing because of the power of her words (silent petitions) and actions (faith).

Do you have the same strength within you? I know that you are also currently facing a medical challenge as well. I know dealing with the symptoms of anxiety and/or depression is very difficult for you, and you can't seem to overcome the stress, strain, and pain you are experiencing. I know that sometimes you just want to give up and give in to this pain and frustration and accept that this is who you are and how the rest of your life will be. *But take heart, son or daughter of God!* Choose to be like the nameless person in this Scripture and continue to have hope and faith that God will heal you and free you of your burdens. I know that faith and patience are hard to come by in the twenty-first century because we all want our challenges and sufferings to be over today. However, Jesus is leading you to a time and place where he will free you from your anxiety and/or depression. He wants to have a conversation with you daily so that he can provide you with the faith, hope, and persistence that you will need to triumph over your obstacles. Finally, find the virtue of patience to seek out Jesus, however long it takes, to receive your healing.

All you need to say is a simple "Yes" or "No."
Otherwise you will be condemned.
—Jas 5:12

Every positive thought is a silent prayer which will change your life.
—Bryant McGill[7]

CHAPTER 8 SUMMARY

Blessed be the God and Father of our Lord Jesus Christ, who in his great mercy gave us a new birth to a living hope through the resurrection of Jesus Christ from the dead.
—1 Pet 1:3

This chapter opened with a personal invitation for you to join in the victory celebration. Devoted Christians around the world want you to join them in proclaiming the events that took place on the first Easter Sunday. The crucifixion of Jesus Christ wasn't the end of his story but only the beginning. He has conquered your biggest fear—death! He saved his best miracle for last. Jesus Christ was the first to rise so that you can follow him. His resurrection is your resurrection. His promise of everlasting life

7. McGill, *Simple Reminders*.

is your promise of everlasting life. His victory over sin and death is your victory over sin and death.

To share in Christ's victory, this chapter expanded upon several things that will help you vacate your tomb and be reunited with Jesus. The one thing that all these topics had in common was the theory of self-determination. In other words, the LORD has granted you exclusive power to decide where you want to spend eternity. This means, your capacity of commitment will determine your ultimate destination. For example, are you a believer or nonbeliever in Jesus Christ? Do you submit to and obey all that he commands, or do you create your own life parameters? Have you taken time out of your daily schedule to study and reflect upon the trials and tribulations of Jesus Christ, or are you only infatuated with your own suffering? Have you asked Jesus to walk with you as you travel the road of human experience, or are you making this trip a solo adventure? Do you seek the LORD for physical, psychological, emotional, and spiritual healing, or do you prescribe to self-healing? Do you use your silent and audible words to productively speak to Jesus and yourself, or do you selfishly use them as weapons to gain an advantage in this world? The answers to each of these questions begin and end with you. How you answer them will determine your future. Will the Light of the World penetrate your tomb and lead you to his Heavenly Father, or will you deteriorate in empty darkness?

Let us end this chapter where it started: the first Easter Sunday. On the evening of the first Easter Sunday, Jesus entered a locked room where his disciples were gathered. When they saw him, "they were startled and frightened, thinking they saw a ghost. He said to them, 'Why are you troubled, and why do doubts rise in your minds? Look at my hands and my feet. It is I myself! Touch me and see; a ghost does not have flesh and bones, as you see I have.' When he had said this, he showed them his hands and feet" (Luke 24:37–40).

The resurrected Christ still had the marks of death (crucifixion) on his hands, feet, and side. The wounds of the cross were not forgotten but transformed and made sacred. No longer were they a source of death but a place of life. What a great comfort that is for you. Your pain, suffering, and frustration may be the precise place where amazing transformation can occur. The resurrection of Jesus Christ can be found in wounds. His hands, feet, and side no longer caused pain but created hope. The same can be said for you. The wounds that you carry from the symptoms of anxiety and/or depression may cause pain and strain today but will be a source of faith, hope, and love tomorrow. Your wounds will lead you toward your resurrection. Your wounds will lead you to amazing blessings. Your wounds will lead you to the risen Christ!

Alleluia! The Lord is risen! The Lord is risen indeed! Alleluia!

Where, O death, is your victory?
Where, O death, is your sting?
—1 Cor 15:55

RESURRECTION

THIRTEENTH STATION: JESUS DIES ON THE CROSS

> And about three o'clock Jesus cried out in a loud voice, "Eli, Eli, lema sabachthani?" which means, "My God, my God, why have you forsaken me?" (Matt 27:46)

We adore you, O Christ, and we bless you.

Because by your holy cross you have redeemed the world.

> It was now about noon and darkness came over the whole land until three in the afternoon because of an eclipse of the sun. Then the veil of the temple was torn down the middle. Jesus cried out in a loud voice, "Father, into your hands I commend my spirit"; and when he had said this he breathed his last. (Luke 23:44–46)

LORD, grant us trust in you that when our time on earth is ended our spirits may come to you without delay.

THIRTEENTH STATION: REFLECTIVE EXERCISES AND QUESTIONS

The final statement that Jesus made while hanging on the cross was, "'It is finished.' With that, he bowed his head and gave up his spirit" (John

19:30). It's significant that he said, "It is finished," as his last words. What does this mean? What is finished? This spiritual statement from Jesus is one that affirms that his mission to redeem the whole world has been accomplished. "It" refers to his perfect sacrifice of love offered to you. His death is the perfect sacrifice which takes away the sins of all. What a gift! And what a sacrifice Jesus endured for you!

At the end of each day, before you fall asleep, what is your last statement? What simple statement do you make that encapsulates the day that you just lived? How do you arrive at it? What is the meaning behind it? Who is it intended for? You are dishonoring God's gift of life if you commonly lay your head on your pillow and simply fall asleep at the end of each day. It is important that you value the twenty-four-hour period you just experienced. The way to value life is to reflect upon all the events and opportunities that occurred on any given day. Creating a final statement for each day brings closure and clarity on what you were able to accomplish or not accomplish in your earthly kingdom as well as in God's heavenly kingdom.

The following set of questions will guide you in creating your last statement for each day. Consider all these questions before turning to the next page of your life. Keep in mind, your final statement will vary from day to day because it will be based upon your thoughts, attitudes, words, actions, reactions, accomplishments, disappoints, etc. It may be therapeutic to keep a log of these final statements so you can find themes and patterns that define your physical, psychological, emotional, and spiritual direction.

Ten Questions to Consider Before Creating Your Twenty-Four-Hour Statement
Did I consider today to have been productive or wasteful?
Did I take advantage of the opportunities that were given to me to improve my life?
Did I take advantage of the opportunities that were given to me to improve the lives of others?
What did I say or do today that improved my life and/or the lives of others?
What did I say or do today that hindered my life and/or the lives of others?
What was my greatest accomplishment today?
What was my greatest disappointment today?
Did I tell someone today that I loved them?
Did I serve others before I served myself?

Did my words and actions promote the kingdom of God?

I hope these ten questions help you begin to evaluate and appreciate each twenty-four-hour window of your life. Measuring yourself in these daily increments will help you gain a better understanding of yourself, others, and God. Creating a final daily statement will honor God in a very special way because it will allow you to maximize your time, talents, and treasures by being all that he wants you to be while carrying out his mission!

You must have accurate and honest weights and measures, so that you may live long in the land the Lord your God is giving you.
—Deut 25:15

RESURRECTION

FOURTEENTH STATION: JESUS IS PLACED IN THE TOMB

> Now in the place where he had been crucified there was a garden, and in the garden a new tomb, in which no one had yet been buried. So they laid Jesus there because of the Jewish preparation day; for the tomb was close by. (John 19:41–42)

We adore you, O Christ, and we bless you.

Because by your holy cross you have redeemed the world.

> When it was evening, there came a rich man from Arimathea named Joseph, who was himself a disciple of Jesus. He went to Pilate and asked for the body of Jesus; then Pilate ordered it to be handed over. Taking the body, Joseph wrapped it in clean linen and laid it in his new tomb that he had hewn in the rock. Then he rolled a huge stone across the entrance to the tomb and departed. (Matt 27:57–60)

Lord, grant us your compassion that we may always provide for those in need.

FOURTEENTH STATION: REFLECTIVE EXERCISES AND QUESTIONS

Jesus' mission in life was to take away the sins of the world. His entire existence was based on this premise. His earthly journey would lead him to that fateful Friday in Jerusalem where he would carry our sins to the top of Mount Calvary and sacrifice himself to free us from the shackles of sin and death. His unconditional love and commitment to us was confirmed when he allowed others to nail his hands and feet to a cross that we created. After he had faithfully fulfilled his Father's will, he bowed his head and gave up his spirit. At this exact time, Joseph of Arimathea arrived at the top of Calvary with paperwork, signed by Pontius Pilate, giving him the authority to bury the body of Jesus. Joseph, a secret disciple of Jesus, took the body of Jesus to a garden adjacent to where he was crucified. There he prepared a proper burial for Jesus and placed him into the new tomb, which was cut out of the rock.

How does this station impact your current situation? Like Joseph of Arimathea, you have a mission to complete in your life. Do you know the specific mission Jesus has given you? Do you have a sense of your God-given gifts? Have you worked to strengthen these gifts, or have you chosen to ignore them? If you are lost and need help in finding your mission and/or unique talents, go to the top of Mount Calvary and find Jesus. He is waiting for you to show you "the Way." His ultimate sacrifice will have such a profound impact on you that you will abandon the current road you are on and willfully become his public disciple. Jesus will lead you to the people and places that need your God-given talents. Like Joseph of Arimathea, he will position you in the right place and time and give you his authority to accomplish your mission. The result of your work will be identical to that of Joseph of Arimathea—a miracle will occur!

Please review the following Venn diagram. The answers that you provide will help you find and fulfill your life's purpose. It will also provide you the opportunity to find your God-given talents and utilize them in a way to serve the kingdom of God.

Do You Hear the Call of Jesus?

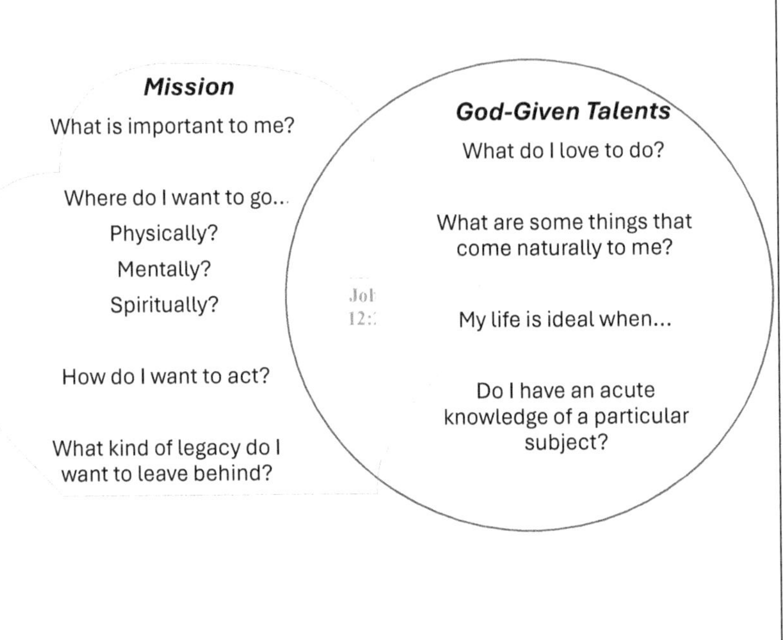

Each of you should use whatever gift you have received to serve others, as faithful stewards of God's grace in its various forms.
—1 Pet 4:10

Chapter 9
Ascension

I came from the Father and have come into the world. Now I am leaving the world and going back to the Father."
—John 16:28

Congratulations, you have reached the last chapter! How do you feel? It is my hope that these last eight chapters have led you on a journey of self-discovery. Words, sentences, and paragraphs were constructed to recalculate your direction. Reflection exercises were created to analyze your current thoughts, words, and actions. Assessments were provided to measure internal growth. Stories were told to help uncover hidden characteristics and values. Finally, Scripture passages were delivered to help you pursue a purpose-driven life. I am praying that each of you took at least one step forward on the road to mental, emotional, and spiritual wellness. However, if your mind, heart, and soul are still stuck in neutral, this last chapter has been written for you!

The content in the first eight chapters were based on past events. These chapters traced stories that already had an ending. Whether the main character in these stories was you or others, the events already happened. Chapter 9 is not about the past or the present, it's about the future. Chapter 9 is about where you are going! It's about your physical, mental, emotional, and spiritual appearance after you receive the gift of healing. It's about a new way of thinking, feeling, acting, and experiencing life. It's about the awareness of your full potential as a descendent of Jesus Christ!

Chapter 9 is titled "Ascension" because you have been given a promise by the Lord that he intends to keep. Jesus wants you to look toward the horizon to see what he has planned for you. Tomorrow's "light" will melt your past and present negative experiences away. The warm glow of the "Son" will lead you to your hopes and dreams. All these things are available to you. It is in your reach but not in your hand. You are going to have to work today to receive it tomorrow! The good news is that tomorrow is just one day away. If you can take one step forward each day, you will meet your future self and live the life that God has planned for you.

I came so that you may have life and have it more abundantly.
—John 10:10

The plan of God is in motion in your life. He has sent people into your life to help you fulfill his plan. God is always with you and wants the very best from you. He wants to relieve your suffering and bring you joy and glad tidings. God will never forget or neglect the plan that he has for you. God wants you to act with curiosity and wonder about his plan instead of disbelief and hesitance. God wants you to tap into his grace so that you can recognize and receive his blessings. He has invited you to reflect on his plan. Through prayer and meditation, you will hear the LORD speak to you about your future. He will share with you something new and wonderful. It is my hope that you will respond to his call in a spirit of hope and faith.

Do you see the blessings that God has given you?

Are you looking for the ways in which God continues to break forth into your life?

Are you looking for the ways in which grace is being presented to you and is present before you?

Are you looking for the ways in which God has invited you to grow deeper in your love for him and others as you share the gifts of your life?

Are you actively seeking for the ways in which God is at work in your life and in the world?

I would like to conclude this introduction with a lesson that is provided to us by nature. Did you know that an eagle can foresee when a storm is approaching long before it breaks? It is popularly believed that instead of hiding, the eagle will fly to some high point and wait for the winds to come. When the storm hits, it sets its wings so that the wind can pick it up and lift it above the storm. While the storm rages below, the eagle soars above it. The eagle does not escape or hide from the storm but instead uses the storm to lift it higher. It rises on the stormy winds which others dread. When the storms of life hit you, you can rise above them and soar like an eagle. Don't be afraid of the storms in your life; use them to lift you. Ascend!

The Lord your God is with you,
the Mighty Warrior who saves.
He will take great delight in you;
in his love he will no longer rebuke you,
but will rejoice over you with singing.
—Zeph 3:17

THE ASCENSION OF JESUS

> While they were looking intently at the sky as he was going, suddenly two men dressed in white garments stood beside them. They said, "Men of Galilee, why are you standing there looking at the sky? This Jesus who has been taken up from you into heaven will return in the same way as you have seen him going into heaven." (Acts 1:10–11)

The events that occurred on the first Easter Sunday marked the first day of Christ's everlasting reign as the Savior of the world. His story was not concluding but commencing! Jesus would spend the next forty days appearing, teaching, preaching, and proclaiming his Father's heavenly kingdom to his disciples (Acts 1:3). During this rite of redemption, Jesus informed his followers that they would receive power from the Holy Spirit to embolden them to be his witnesses and travel the world proclaiming the "good news" (Acts 1:8). On the fortieth day after his resurrection, Jesus took his disciples to the Mount of Olives in Bethany (Acts 1:12). There he instructed his disciples to wait in Jerusalem until the Holy Spirit came down upon them. While he was providing his final blessing, he rose from the ground gradually and visibly. He was received onto a cloud and taken from their sight. As his disciples were gazing intently into the sky, two men in white clothing stood beside them and said, "Men of Galilee, why do you stand here looking into the sky? This same Jesus, who has been taken from you into heaven, will come back in the same way you have seen him go into heaven" (Acts 1:11). The disciples returned to Jerusalem with great joy and continually stayed at the temple praising God (Luke 24:52–53).

What is the meaning and importance of the ascension of Jesus Christ? More importantly, how does it relate to you in your current circumstance?

JESUS CHRIST IS THE KING OF THE UNIVERSE

On the first Easter Sunday, Jesus became the undisputed King of the universe and Satan could do nothing about it. He conquered the last two strongholds that Satan held over all mankind—sin and death. Through his resurrection and ascension, your debt has been forgiven (Heb 10:11–14). You have been freed from the chains of the evil one. No longer do you need to weigh yourself down with the shame and guilt that temptation and sin bring. You have been released from your prison cell to pursue happiness and fulfillment. Jesus Christ has defeated death and has ascended into heaven. He is seated at the right hand of his Father. He will come again in glory to judge the living and the dead, and his kingdom will have no end. His resurrection and ascension have provided you with transformation and mobilization. You now have the confidence to move forward in your life with hope and joy because the king of the universe has proven his love for you. He has completed his work and is waiting for you to complete yours. He has sent down the Holy Spirit to help you find and fulfill your mission in this life so that you can be with him in the afterlife.

Forty Days

After the first Easter Sunday, Jesus spent forty days on the earth before ascending to his Father. Forty days—does this number sound familiar to you? In chapter 6 we discussed the Scripture passage provided in Luke 4:1–14 when Jesus was tested in the wilderness by Satan for forty days. It seems Jesus needed this time of preparation before he moved into momentous moments in his life. The forty days in the desert prepared him for his ministry and mission. The forty days after the resurrection prepared him for his life-everlasting reign in his Father's heavenly kingdom.

These forty-day increments remind me of the bulletin board that hung in my classroom as a middle school and high school social studies teacher. On the first day of each grading period (which lasted forty days),

I would spend several minutes reviewing the five *P*s with my students. The five *P*s were listed vertically to complete the following sentence: *Prior Planning Prevents Poor Performance!* Prior planning is like the moving walkways you find at airports. It gets you to your destination more effectively and efficiently. Whether you are the Savior of the world or a student who wants to earn an A in American history, prior planning will give you the best opportunity to maximize your potential.

Before the Lord's ascension, he used his forty days to continue the work of his Father. He turned cynics into disciples, students into teachers, and agnostics into missionaries. He forever put in motion the ministry of the Christian faith. How do you plan to use your time of preparation before your ascension takes place? What are your goals for the next forty days? How will your thoughts, words, and actions bring relief to your current mental health crisis? What are some rituals you are willing to participate in to help you rise above the pain and suffering you are currently experiencing?

I have created the following table to help you organize your prior planning for the next forty days. Please take some time and effort to complete each sentence. Make sure you are committed to the words that you put down into this book. Putting ink to paper will not be enough. It is essential that you hold yourself accountable for carrying out these directives for the next forty days. The LORD's work is never finished, and neither is yours. The next forty days will help cleanse your mind, body, and soul as you journey toward mental wellness.

My Forty-Day Guide to Ascension: What I Plan to Do During My Time of Preparation
My one goal for the next forty days will be . . .
The one thought that I will mediate on for the next forty days will be . . .
The one word that I will chose to say to myself, or others, for the next forty days will be . . .
The one action I will choose to do for myself, or others, for the next forty days will be . . .
The one ritual I plan to participate in for the next forty days will be . . .

The Mount of Mental Wellness

Everything Jesus did in his life was filled with significance. The places he traveled and the people he interacted with always displayed great symbolic value. For example, Jesus seemed most comfortable on a mountaintop as he fulfilled his Father's will. Many pivotal Scripture events occurred on a mountain. Whether Jesus was teaching, preaching, healing, feeding, or praying, it usually occurred on a mountain. This shouldn't be too much of a surprise because mountains dotted the landscape of the surrounding area of Jerusalem. Therefore, it was not uncommon for people to live and work in higher elevations. However, Jesus chose to visit these areas for more spiritual reasons. Mountains seemed to symbolized constancy, eternity, firmness, and stillness. They served as a cosmic axis linking heaven and earth. They evoked a special sense of awe and power. For these reasons, Jesus reserved his most important work in this setting.

The Mount of Olives was a very special place for Jesus. He visited this mountain more than any other mountain in Jerusalem. When he traveled in the vicinity of Jerusalem, he often stayed and prayed on the Mount of Olives (Luke 21:37, 22:39). When he visited his friends Lazarus, Mary, and Martha (Luke 10:38–42, John 11:1–45), he stayed in Bethany which is on the eastern slope of the Mount of Olives. Scripture accounts report that Jesus spent the last week of his earthly life on the Mount of Olives. From Palm Sunday through Resurrection Sunday, the Mount of Olives was the backdrop of the new covenant between God and his chosen people.

The Mount of Olives was such a special place for Jesus that on the fortieth day after his resurrection, he took his disciples to this Mount to witness his ascension. For Jesus, the Mount of Olives was a place for prayer, healing, revelation, and commissioning. Jesus is calling you to the Mount of Olives. He is waiting for you at its peak. He wants you to use your time, energy, and courage to journey toward him. He no longer wants you to stay stagnant in your current psychological, emotional, or social state. He wants you to begin the ascent toward mental wellness. He wants you to experience a state of full consciousness so you can find the true meaning of your life.

Making this climb will not be easy. You will need the proper climbing gear to reach the peak of mental wellness and bask in the glow of the Lord's glorious presence. I have provided you with some of the gear you will need to ensure a successful climb.

Climbing Essentials That Will Ensure Your Ascent	
Item	*Rationale*
Backpack	to carry faith, hope, and love
Walking Stick	to lean on the LORD when you need him
Climbing Boots	to provide traction and stability on unfamiliar terrain
Canteen	to carry holy water so as to provide daily blessings
Safety Ropes	to keep you physically, mentally, and spiritually attached to God
Headlamp	to use in climbing when the shadows of life fall upon you
Waterproof Jacket and Pants	to help you repel the storms of life
Bible	to use as a navigation device
Daily Prayer	to use as a beacon to alert God about your progress

The only way to get to the top of the Mount of Olives and the Mount of Mental Wellness is to start climbing today! It's not about how much terrain you scale on any given day, but it is about the willingness to put on your climbing gear and move onward and upward!

You Are on the Clock

Have you ever watched the NFL draft? It's an annual event that takes place in April. For professional football fans (like Steeler Nation), it's a three-day holiday in which they get to watch their favorite team (the Pittsburgh Steelers) draft college football players in the hopes of winning the next Super Bowl Championship (six Lombardi Trophies more than any other NFL team!). Once the draft starts, there is always a team "on the clock." This means that a specific team (depending on the draft order) has a specific amount of time to select a player. If a team does not decide within its allotted time, that team still can submit its selection at any time after its time is up, but the next team can pick before it, thus possibly "stealing" a player the team with the earlier pick may have been considering.

Why am I telling you all of this? When Jesus was taken onto a cloud and ascended into heaven, he was officially "on the clock"! Jesus chose you as his number one draft pick.

He has a starting role for you on his team (the "Angels"). He believes you are the missing piece that will help him win the battle over evil. You have everything he needs to win another championship. If you accept his invitation, he will train you to maximize your time, talents, and treasures. He will help you build up your physical, psychological, emotional, social, and spiritual muscles so you can defeat sin and temptation. He will put you through drills and increase your skills so when your play is called, victory will be delivered. All these guarantees are inside the contract he has prepared for you. He is waiting for you to sign it so that you can "officially" become a member of his team.

On the other hand, Jesus' number one rival (Satan) hopes you don't agree to the terms of the contract. Satan hopes you hire him as your agent so that a contract dispute occurs. This will allow him an opportunity to "steal" you for his own team (the "Devils"). The contract to join the "Devils" is easy to understand. The owner will offer you anything you want if you give him your soul after the game (your life) is over. Keep in mind, the owner doesn't always abide by the contract. He has been known to lie, cheat, and steal. Most of the time his empty promises will cost you everything in this life and the afterlife. I forgot to mention, expect to experience loss every time you play for Satan because the "Devils" have never beaten the "Angels," and they never will!

You have a decision to make. What team do you want to play for? What contract are you willing to sign? Jesus unconditionally loves you and wants you to join his team. He sacrificed his life on a cross to give you this opportunity to experience victory over sin and death. Satan despises you! The only reason he has an interest in you is because God is calling you. He will say and do anything to separate you from your Heavenly Father. The consequences of your decision are extreme. You will either experience ascension or descension. You are "on the clock"!

You Are the Hands and Feet of the Lord

As his disciples watched Jesus ascend into heaven, two men in white clothing stood beside them and said, "Men of Galilee, why do you stand here looking into the sky?" My translation of this question is, "Followers of Jesus, why are your eyes distracted and your feet still?" Jesus has called you by name and has commissioned you to continue his mission. Today is the day to cast your eyes toward the horizon and move forward in completing the work God has entrusted in you.

Jesus' mind, heart, soul, and body are now in heaven. Sometime in the future, you will be reunited with him. You will see him as his disciples saw him on the Mount of Olives before he ascended. Between now and then, Jesus wants you to take his place while you inhabit the earth. He wants you to be his hands and feet. He wants you to continue his ministry through prayer and action. But before you can use the Lord's nail-scarred hands and feet, you must accept him into your heart and life. You must be willing to follow him. Jesus said "follow me" thirteen times in the Gospels. He used these two simple words to call Peter, Andrew, James, and John as his disciples (Matt 4:18–20, 21–22; 9:9). Each time Jesus offered this invitation, these men immediately abandoned their old lifestyle and accepted a radical new calling. They humbly submitted their entire self to him. This is the cost of being a disciple of Jesus Christ! His plan for your life is something that you have never considered. It is full of healings, blessings, and miracles. Yet, the only way you will experience these things is if you say yes to his invitation and take your place behind him.

I have created three simple statements that you can add to your daily prayer life to confirm to God that you are committed to being his disciple.

Three Daily Statements That Confirm Your Commitment to God
I want to follow the LORD.
I wish to have my life be informed by what God teaches.
I want to receive God's love, grace, and strength.

These daily declarations will grant your insight into the LORD's mind, heart, soul, and body. They will allow you to use Jesus' holy hands and feet to accomplish your life's mission. These daily declarations will bring peace of mind and productivity to your social, emotional, and spiritual life.

Jesus is calling you to share in his work. This work will take on different forms according to your vocation and mission. The question that you need to ask yourself is, "Am I responding to the call from Jesus in the way he is directing me?" This is an important question. The mission Jesus has given you is not entrusted to anyone else. You must come to realize that the Father has sent you to continue his work. You have a mission that he wants you to accomplish. Whatever you are currently doing in your life, God wants more from you. His plan for you requires that you step out in faith, be courageous, move out of your comfort zone, or face some fear. The comforting news about your situation is that God does not just send you, he also remains with you. He has not left you alone to fulfill the mission he has entrusted to you. He has promised his continued help in a very central way.

I have created a list of questions that you can ask yourself to help you hear the LORD's calling and uncover the plan that he has for you. The answer to these questions will lead you to the buried time, talents, and treasures that God has planted within you. The answers to these questions will probably change over time as God's plan develops and grows throughout your life.

Five Questions That Will Uncover God's Calling and Plan for You
1. LORD, where are you calling me to carry on your work in my life right now?
2. LORD, how can I teach others about the gospel?
3. LORD, how can I proclaim the kingdom of God through my actions?
4. LORD, where do I see some element of evil that I can or should be standing up to?
5. LORD, where can I do corporal works of mercy, especially for the sick and suffering?

The work of the LORD will come to you in your own unique package. You have different skills, abilities, talents, and resources than any other Christian. This is a big world, and the LORD needs your cooperation, communication, and collaboration so that his ministry can be passed onto your generation and the next. What you say and what you do has an impact on what Jesus said and did. There are a lot of needs in the world. There are a lot of places, whether in your own heart or the hearts of others, where you can offer an encouraging word or a kind action in the name of Jesus. This will require that you open your eyes and look for the opportunity to fulfill your life's mission. You must be vigilant in finding ways that you can be the hands and feet of Jesus so that you can display words and actions that bring hope and life. The only way that all of this can occur is if you roll up your sleeves and set your eyes and feet to the horizon!

Joyous, Faithful, and Patient

At this very moment, you are on the ultimate journey—it's called *your life*. From the moment you were conceived, your journey began. What an amazing ride you have already experienced, and the best is yet to come! Each breath you take is a gift from God. When you open your eyes each morning, you have a new opportunity to move forward in your life. Whether you realize it or not, you are going somewhere. Have you ever taken the time to ask yourself, "Where am I going? Where is my journey taking me? What is my life about? What am I searching for?" The fallen world can become so chaotic that it distracts you from asking these life-fulfilling questions. It can numb you into accepting your current circumstance and paralyze your present and future contemplation of the meaning of life. However, God can provide you the wisdom and grace to live each day to your fullest and accept what occurs within it and use those experiences and lessons to bear the fruit of the Spirit (Gal 5:22–23).

> I am the true vine, and my Father is the vine grower. He takes away every branch in me that does not bear fruit, and every one that does he prunes so that it bears more fruit. You are already pruned because of the word that I spoke to you. Remain in me, as I remain in you. Just as a branch cannot bear fruit on its own unless it remains on the vine, so neither can you unless you remain in me. I am the vine, you are the branches. Whoever remains in me and I in him will bear much fruit, because without me you can do nothing. Anyone who does not remain in me will be thrown out like a branch and wither; people will gather them and throw them into a fire and they will be burned. If you remain in me and my words remain in you, ask for whatever you want and it will be done for you. By this is my Father glorified, that you bear much fruit and become my disciples. (John 15:1–8)

Do you have a "green thumb"? Do you help a family member or friend create and sustain a garden in your/their backyard? If the answer is no, do you know someone who has a garden? Gardening is a very therapeutic activity because it requires faith and patience. It is a labor of love. Although it takes some knowledge to create a successful garden, the most important ingredients for maintaining a garden are time, commitment, and sacrifice. The joy of gardening is in the cultivation process. To take a small seed and nourish it until it blossoms into a mature plant is very gratifying. A gardener's true joy occurs when they reap what they sowed.

Harvest time, usually during the late summer and early fall, brings a bounty of fruits and vegetables to the gardener in which he/she inevitably shares with their family and friends over a meal and social activities. All the hours, days, and months of digging, planting, fertilizing, watering, and protecting their plants produce memories that last a lifetime.

In chapter 15, John paints an image about God's garden on earth. Each plant in God's garden represents every living soul. The vine of each plant symbolizes Jesus. The branch (or blossom) of the plant represents each living person (you). Finally, God the Father is the gardener and assumes responsibility of nurturing growth by trimming and pruning so that each branch (person) bears fruit.

The branch (you) needs to be attached to the vine (Jesus) to draw strength, nourishment, and life. In other words, apart from Jesus, you will wither and die. The relationship that you cultivate with the LORD is paramount. It is essential to find and fulfill the meaning of your life. The closer you are to Jesus, the stronger you are in your growth and in your life. The interesting thing about God's garden is that to grow and thrive, you are going to have to endure the painful process of pruning. God has a shape for you, a direction for you, and a path he wants you to follow. Sometimes your "flesh" manipulates you to grow in the opposite shape and direction than God the Father had originally planned for you. During these times in your life, God will need to help you conquer your flesh by pruning your selfish ways so that you can face his "Son" and grow through the Holy Spirit.

John ends this portion of his Scripture by reminding you to do your Heavenly Father's will by bearing much fruit and becoming his Son's disciple (John 15:8). John wants you to focus on your spiritual fruit. In chapter 7 ("Mission"), we discussed the essential building materials that you will need in your life to accomplish your goals alongside the goals that God has for you. These essential building materials were the fruits of the Spirit: love, joy, peace, forbearance, kindness, goodness, faithfulness, gentleness, and self-control. You are called by God to draw strength from Jesus so that you can live the joy of Jesus to those around you. His love, his joy, and his peace should be evident in the connections that you have among your family, friends, and community. God wants you to use his "Son" to cultivate your relationships to help his garden's expansion and production. Your family, friends, and neighbors may be struggling in their growth. They may be living with loneliness, depression, doubt, fear, and worry. God has positioned you at the right place and time to take the fruits of the Spirit and live it with the people that need it the most. Your family, friends, and neighbors are looking for hope, life, love, and faith. They are looking to be connected to the vine (Jesus).

Take a moment to reflect on the people that encompass your circle of love and friendship. Speak the names of those that are in desperate need to be connected to the vine. Brainstorm some creative ways you can reach out to them today to allow the love of Jesus to flow from his heart to your heart and into their hearts.

Today is the day to be fruitful for the LORD. The master gardener has spent his time and energy nurturing your growth. Now, he wants to harvest a piece of your spiritual fruit so that he can bring his light and love to those closest to you. He wants to tend to their needs so that they can find life in his garden. However, he cannot accomplish this mission alone. He needs your joy, faith, and patience to plant another seed in his garden.

Four Daily Statements That Will Help You Bear Fruit in Your Life
1. LORD, I want to be close to you.
2. LORD, I want to draw strength from you.
3. LORD, I love you.
4. LORD, I am asking you to give me whatever I need today to grow as a disciple and apostle.

Love is a fruit in season at all times, and within the reach of every hand.

—Mother Teresa[1]

CONFLUENCE

Being a "Yinzer" (a native of Pittsburgh), I can remember way back to first grade when I learned my first three-syllable word in English class. It was part of a vocabulary list titled "Words Connected to Pittsburgh." The word was *confluence*. For the exam, I needed to spell and define this word. Have you ever heard of this word? If so, do you know its definition?

1. Mother Teresa, *Love*, 5.

Every Yinzer knows this word and its geographic meaning! The meaning of this noun is the junction of two rivers, especially rivers of approximately equal width. When the city of "Pixburgh" (Yinzer talk) is shown in a photograph or on TV, it usually is a picture of "dahntahn" (as Yinzers say for *downtown*) at the Point. This is the iconic symbol of this great city! Point State Park's fountain sits directly at the confluence. This unique geographic feature is where the Allegheny River and Monongahela River form the Ohio River (see the map below).

Why am I teaching you this geography lesson? Is it to test your mental acuity? No! Is it to persuade you to come visit the most livable city in America? Maybe! The main reason I am introducing you to the word *confluence* is to help you become one with God! You are called to be so much more than just a physical brother or sister in Christ Jesus. You are called to the most intimate and transforming familial union imaginable. How can you experience oneness with God? The first thing you must do is locate "the Way" to your Lord and Savior.

Immediately Bartimaeus received his sight and followed Jesus on the way.
—Mark 10:52

Where is "the Way"? How far do you have to travel to get there? What modes of transportation will you need to arrive at your destination? These are all great questions that only your heart, mind, and soul can answer. Only you know your current position when it comes to the relationship that you have with God. There is a map somewhere within you that shows "You are here" and "God is there." It is up to you whether you are willing to invest the time and energy it takes to calculate the direction, distance, and time to become one with him.

Let's refer to the map that I provided above. This is a great visual for what your map from within may look like. I like this map because it depicts water systems. Usually in art, literature, and philosophy, water symbolizes life—in this case, your life! Water can be associated with birth, fertility, and refreshment. Its qualities are fluidity and cohesiveness. Flowing water usually represents change. It is one of the four elements essential to life (earth, air, fire, and water)!

In a Christian context, water has many correlations. Christ was baptized with water (Matt 3:13–17), transmuted water into wine (John 2:9), walked on water (Matt 14:25), discharged water when he was pierced by a spear after his death on the cross (John 19:34), and provides rivers of living water for those who believe in him (John 7:37–39). Thus, the confluence that occurs in "dahntahn Pixburgh" is a perfect symbol to follow to become one with God and his kingdom.

For argument's sake, and because I live near the north shore of "Pixburgh," let's designate the Allegheny River to represent Jesus. The Allegheny River is roughly 325 miles long and runs through New York and Pennsylvania. It's the main tributary of the Ohio River. The river flows alongside "Pixburgh" sports stadiums—Heinz Field and PNC Park—where, on occasion, home-run balls splash into their new home. Unfortunately, many of them are hit by whatever visiting team is playing the Pirates. Yes, that's right, I am a Pirates fan. Who says there is no such thing as purgatory on earth?

Let's get back on track before my blood pressure begins to rise! Directly on the opposite side of "dahntahn" flows the Monongahela. Let's designate this river system to represent you. Formed in West Virginia, the Monongahela, or the "Mon" (as Yinzers call it), flows south to north past Morgantown through Washington County and into "Pixburgh." The river is 130 miles long and flows below the Fort Pitt Bridge and the Liberty Bridge (the "City of Bridges" boasts 446 bridges, more than any other city in the world, including Venice, Italy). The Mon is a major barge route. You'll often find barges carrying natural resources along the river.

At the Point (confluence), the Allegheny and Monongahela form the Ohio River. Let's designate this river system as God the Father. It's the largest tributary of the Mississippi River. The river is 981 miles long and flows northwest out of Pittsburgh and goes through or borders six states.

As a result, the Ohio River is the source of drinking water for more than three million people.

So, let's review. The Allegheny River represents Jesus. It is roughly 325 miles long and is the main tributary of the Ohio River. The Monongahela River represents you. It is 130 miles long and joins the Allegheny River at the Point to form the Ohio River. The Ohio River is created by the Allegheny and the Mon and flows 981 miles and provides life to three million Americans. Is this starting to make sense to you? Jesus came to the earth through his Father (the main tributary of the Ohio River). The Mon (you) flows in the same direction as the Allegheny (Jesus). The Mon will help you carry your natural resources (time, talents, and treasures) to meet Jesus at Point State Park. The Ohio River (God the Father) would not exist without the Allegheny (Jesus) and the Mon (you). If you choose to travel "the Way" and unify with Jesus, God the Father can expand his kingdom and provide everlasting water (John 4:14) to over three million Americans. Who knew that a map of "dahntahn Pixburgh" could help you achieve your personal ascension!

Pittsburgh entered the core of my heart when I was a boy and cannot be torn out.

—Andrew Carnegie[2]

BAPTISMAL WATERS

> *Then Jesus came from Galilee to John at the Jordan to be baptized by him. After Jesus was baptized, he came up from the water and behold, the heavens were opened [for him], and he saw the Spirit of God descending like a dove coming upon him. And a voice came from the heavens, saying, "This is my beloved Son, with whom I am well pleased."* (Matt 3:13, 16–17)

When Jesus sought out his cousin John the Baptist, he was aware that his life was going to change dramatically. Since his birth, Jesus prepared his mind, body, and soul for this meeting. It was Jesus' destiny to enter the Jordan River and willfully participate in his baptismal ceremony so he could become one with his Father and the Holy Spirit. This event marked

2. Carnegie Medal of Philanthropy, "Legacy That Defines a City."

the inauguration of his public ministry. He would exit the water and begin to follow "the way." Through preaching, miracles, healings, and proclamations of mercy and forgiveness, he would become the symbol of repentance and conversion. Through the holy Triune, a new way of life is possible!

When will your life dramatically change?

Whom do you seek for miracles, healings, and proclamations of mercy and forgiveness?

When will you repent?

When will you convert?

When will you ascend?

Like Jesus, you need to enter baptismal waters (the Mon) to become one with God the Father and the Holy Spirit. The fastest way to the "confluence" is through the body and blood of Jesus Christ. By accepting Jesus Christ as your Lord and Savior you will begin your journey on "the way." Have you entered the Mon yet? Where are you on the Mon (your life) compared to the confluence? Wherever you are on the Mon, Jesus is at the exact point on the Allegheny. If you are still on the shoreline, he is on the shoreline. If you are scared and unsure and have decided just to wade out to where your feet can still touch, Jesus' nail-scarred feet are also still touching the bottom of the Allegheny. If you are in the middle of the Mon, Jesus is in the middle of the Allegheny. If you stop swimming, Jesus stops swimming. If you tread water, Jesus will tread water. Whatever you choose to do, Jesus will be right beside you, encouraging you to continue on "the way." Jesus won't arrive at the confluence without you (John 17:12). He will stay as patient as you need him to be so that he can be your lifeboat when you get tired, frustrated, or lost. He knows and his Father knows that without you there can be no Ohio River.

The waters of the Mon are calm and warm. This river is not something to look at or think about; it is meant for you to enter. These waters will bring you "new" life, growth, vitality, refreshment, hope, and security. Each day, God presents you an entry point into these waters. He has too much love and respect for you to force you into these waters. He wants you to walk in on your own volition. He doesn't want you to dive in but to walk in. He wants these life-changing waters to gradually cover your ankles, knees, and waist. This will allow a slow but steady relationship to form between you and his Son. As you grow more confident in his word, you will be willing to take another step on "the way." The more steps you take, the deeper your relationship becomes with Jesus. Eventually, your feet will no longer touch the bottom, and you will "float in your faith." You will depend less upon yourself and more on the Word of God. You will be submerged with his grace and obtain a "new" perspective on life. Jesus' healing hands and his holy currents will support you as you swim to the confluence (Ezek 47:1–12).

BECOMING ONE WITH THE FATHER, SON, AND HOLY SPIRIT

What will happen when you make your way down the Mon and reach the fountain at Point State Park? You will come to the realization that you have reached the first lock (a device used for raising or lowering boats between stretches of water on different levels on a river) on "the way." There, you will meet Jesus who has already paid for your toll to use this lock when he willingly hung on his cross to forgive your sins (John 15:13). He will embrace you and thank his Father for your safe arrival. This encounter will change your life for eternity. Jesus will allow you to experience his love, grace, peace, forgiveness, and hope. He will heal any of your physical, psychological, and/or emotional pain and purify your soul in preparation for your continued journey into the Ohio River to become one with the Father, Son, and Holy Spirit (Matt 10:40).

To help you to fully comprehend the impact of meeting and accepting Jesus Christ as your Lord and Savior, I have provided three brief summaries of others who have met Jesus in the New Testament.

The Magi Visit the Messiah

> *When Jesus was born in Bethlehem of Judea, in the days of King Herod, behold, magi from the east arrived in Jerusalem, saying, "Where is the newborn king of the Jews? We saw his star at its rising and have come to do him homage." When King Herod heard this, he was greatly troubled, and all Jerusalem with him. Assembling all the chief priests and the scribes of the people, he inquired of them where the Messiah was to be born. They said to him, "In Bethlehem of Judea, for thus it has been written through the prophet: Then Herod called the magi secretly and ascertained from them the time of the star's appearance. He sent them to*

Bethlehem and said, "Go and search diligently for the child. When you have found him, bring me word, that I too may go and do him homage." After their audience with the king they set out. And behold, the star that they had seen at its rising preceded them, until it came and stopped over the place where the child was. They were overjoyed at seeing the star, and on entering the house they saw the child with Mary his mother. They prostrated themselves and did him homage. Then they opened their treasures and offered him gifts of gold, frankincense, and myrrh. And having been warned in a dream not to return to Herod, they departed for their country by another way. (Matt 2:1–5, 7–12)

The Magi followed a star to help them along "the way." This star served as a messenger from God to guide them. In a sense, the star was an angel. It gave the Magi light, direction, and joy. The light from this angelic star provided them with the faith and courage they needed to take the long and arduous journey. It also gave them direction to find the manger that contained the Holy Family. Finally, it filled them with joy when they encountered the child and experienced his divinity.

Have you experienced an angelic star this year?

Has someone or something acted as God's messenger to direct you closer to the LORD?

When the Magi came upon Mary and the child, they bowed down and worshiped him. Then they opened their treasures and presented him with gifts of gold, frankincense, and myrrh. Today, the LORD is calling you to prostrate yourself before him and do him homage. Like the wise men, you should express your reverence by giving him your time, talents, and treasures. Maybe you want to give Jesus gold (donating your time and resources toward a Christian charity). You might want to give Jesus frankincense (committing yourself to daily prayer and fasting). Finally, you might want to give Jesus myrrh (accepting the spirit and rejecting your flesh in word and deed). Following and finding Jesus is only half the battle. Committing your life to his ways and means will lead you to discipleship and apostleship.

When was the last time you thanked God for the blessings he has bestowed upon you?

How will you use the gold, frankincense, and myrrh that God has graciously given you?

Why was King Herod, and the rest of Jerusalem, unable to see the star that guided the Magi? Could it be that the angelic messenger was for only the Magi to see? In your own life, God is constantly calling you to seek him out and worship him. He is using some of the most ordinary parts of your life to send forth that calling. How is he calling you? In what way is he sending you a star to follow? Many times, when God speaks you ignore his voice. You must learn from these Magi and diligently respond when he calls. You must not hesitate and must seek to daily be attentive to the ways that God invites you to deeper trust, surrender, and worship. The LORD is showing his love to you personally and calling you into a deeper relationship in a way unique for you. God is revealing his Son to you. Ask the LORD for faith to see, believe, and follow the angelic star he gives to you so you can experience the tender love of his Son.

Are you listening?

Are you responding?

Are you ready and willing to abandon all else in life to serve his holy will?

One final thought before we move on. For me, the last sentence of this Scripture passage may be the most important part of this event. "And having been warned in a dream not to go back to Herod, they returned to their country by another route" (Matt 2:12). In other words, no one comes to Jesus Christ and goes back the same way he/she came. Once you find and accept Jesus Christ as your Lord and Savior, your life will never be the same. Your mind, body, and spirit will experience a spiritual realm that you never knew existed. Your thoughts, words, and actions will align to advance the kingdom of God. You will become an angelic star for others to follow!

Anna the Prophet

> There was also a prophetess, Anna, the daughter of Phanuel, of the tribe of Asher. She was advanced in years, having lived seven years with her husband after her marriage, and then as a widow until she was eighty-four. She never left the temple, but worshiped night and day with fasting and prayer. And coming forward at that very time, she gave thanks to God and spoke about the child to all who were awaiting the redemption of Jerusalem. (Luke 2:36–40)

Because Joseph and Mary were devout Jews and followed the Mosaic law, they were required to wait a certain amount time after the birth of Jesus before they could present him to God (Lev 12). At the appropriate time, the Holy Family traveled to Jerusalem to fulfill this religious obligation. While in the temple, Joseph, Mary, and Jesus were introduced to Anna. The summary of Anna's life was described in a few words—her name, her father's name, her tribe, and her long life as a widow. Luke makes it a point to tell us that Anna was old! He gives us some hints to help us calculate her age. Some biblical scholars argue that she may have been 106 years old. Regardless of her age, God blessed her with much grace.

Anna was a remarkable woman. As a widow she knew pain and loss but had not become bitter. Although Luke doesn't provide any specifics, we get the sense that she experienced her share of challenges in her life. Can you relate to Anna? I'm sure your bouts with anxiety and depression have forced you to deal with disappointments. Have these experiences made you cynical and hopeless? If so, reflect more deeply into Anna's perspective on life. What stands out more than all her pain and loss is her faith. She is full of hope! She is a model of waiting, recognizing, fasting, prayer, and praise. In essence, she is presented to you as a model of discipleship. She has moved beyond her past and looks toward a new future. There is no looking back with regret with what life has brought her. She has grown strong and is filled with wisdom.

When you place God first in your life, you will also grow in strength and wisdom. Think of the joy that washed over Anna the moment she recognized God (baby Jesus) in human form. All her pain, frustration, and loss guided her to the temple to meet her Savior. She experienced the real presence of Christ: body, blood, soul, and divinity. You can experience the same as Anna if you allow God's grace to enter your heart, if you allow his love to enter your soul, if you allow his body to strengthen your body. Anna never lost hope, and neither should you!

What do you hope for? The hope which God places in your heart needs to be released into the world. It will be used as fertilizer to grow his kingdom as well as your happiness on earth. Hope grows with prayer and age. Anna was preeminently a woman of great hope and an expectation that God would fulfill all his promises. Filled with the Holy Spirit, she was found daily in the house of the Lord, attending to the Lord in prayer and speaking prophetically to others about the Lord's promises. If you follow this model, you will also experience the real presence of Christ in your life. By putting God first in your life and placing your trust in his promises, you will enter the Ohio River (become one with the Holy Trinity).

Below is a quiz that will provide you with some insight on whether you are putting God first in your life. Please circle *agree* or *disagree* for each statement.

Am I Putting God First in My Life?		
1. I have time to create a successful career.	*Agree*	*Disagree*
2. I don't have time to make myself a victorious Christian.	*Agree*	*Disagree*
3. I have time to experience everything the world has to offer.	*Agree*	*Disagree*
4. I don't have time to make sure that God is proud of me.	*Agree*	*Disagree*
5. I have time to read what's on my iPhone.	*Agree*	*Disagree*
6. I don't have time to read the Bible.	*Agree*	*Disagree*
7. I have time to talk to my friends.	*Agree*	*Disagree*
8. I don't have time to pray.	*Agree*	*Disagree*
9. I have time to serve myself.	*Agree*	*Disagree*
10. I don't have time to serve the kingdom of God.	*Agree*	*Disagree*

Take a moment to review your answers. How did you answer the even-numbered questions? This will give you a good idea about where you place God in your daily priorities. The answers to the odd-numbered questions are important to your mental and emotional well-being, but the answers to the even questions measure your spiritual well-being. In the Sermon on the Mount, Jesus told his disciples (you), "Seek first God's kingdom and his righteousness, and everything else will be given to you as well" (Matt 6:33).

Simon Peter

> Andrew, the brother of Simon Peter, was one of the two who heard John and followed Jesus. He first found his own brother Simon and told him, "We have found the Messiah" (which is translated Anointed). Then he brought him to Jesus. Jesus looked at him and said, "You are Simon the son of John; you will be called Cephas" (which is translated Peter). (John 1:40–42)

The calling of Saint Peter is recorded in all four Gospels (John 1, Mark 1, Matt 4, and Luke 5). In three of the four passages, Andrew and his brother Simon are hard at work as fishermen when Jesus approaches and offers them to become "fishers of men." The only Gospel that describes Andrew and Simon approaching Jesus is in John 1:40–42. There are many ways by which souls are brought to Jesus. Sometimes, people seek him earnestly and find him. Other times, by the intervention of another, a person is introduced to him. Most of the time, Jesus himself takes the initiative and finds those that do not seek him. In the Scripture passage above, Andrew's intercession brought Simon to Jesus. Have you been introduced to Jesus? If so, who coordinated the introduction? Did you approach him? Did he approach you, or did someone introduce you to him?

Andrew was a follower of John the Baptist and learned about Jesus through John's testimony. John taught that the kingdom of God was at hand and their "Messiah" was walking the earth. When Jesus approached John, John exclaimed, "Look, the Lamb of God who takes away the sin of the world" (John 1:29). Upon hearing these words, Andrew left John and began to follow Jesus. After spending a full day with Jesus, Andrew knew that he found the Messiah. Though he had not yet witnessed a miracle or a miraculous healing, his faith and the powerful words of Christ convinced himself of this. Nobody said to Andrew, "Go and look for your brother," and yet as soon as he had realized Jesus was the Messiah, he hurried away to find his brother to share his conviction with him. One lesson that you can learn from Andrew's encounter with Jesus is when a person finds Jesus Christ, there is a natural and instinctive impulse to tell someone else about him! Have you shared your conviction of Jesus Christ with your mother, father, brother, sister, relative, friend, neighbor? Have you told them that you have found the Messiah and you want them to meet him? This is the way to discipleship. This is the way to ascension!

Did you notice that when Andrew came to his brother with the "good news" that "we [instead of *I*] have found the Messiah," Simon did not argue with him? Simon could have told his brother to stop wasting his time and leave him alone so that he could finish his fishing duties. However, Simon listened, believed, and followed. Many people interact with you daily and offer you the "good news" through their words and deeds. When you receive this message, do you respond like Simon or someone who is too self-insulated to be bothered by others? When Jesus sees Simon, he looks at him intently and tells him who he is and where he came from (his family lineage). Jesus was making a point to Simon. He was simply telling him that he knew Simon long before this initial meeting. Jesus reveals to Simon that he possesses supernatural and thorough knowledge of all things. Do you believe this? Do you feel that Christ is looking at you? Do you believe that he knows you? Do you believe that he constantly searches your thoughts and feelings? Do you rejoice in this? Do you carry this with you as consolation and as strength in moments of weakness and times of temptation? Do you feel blessed in your relationship with the LORD?

The final thing that the Lord does for Simon in their first meeting is change his name. He will now be known as Peter. This name change signifies that Peter is now born again and belongs to God. By accepting this new name, Peter has abandoned the old and has accepted the new. He commits himself to a new life of serving the LORD. He is willing to sacrifice everything to follow the way, the truth, and the life (Jesus Christ). As you continue to read the New Testament, you will see that the transition from Simon to Peter will be a long process. On "the way," Peter will experience what all Christians experience: trials and tribulations. However, in the end, he will become the rock on which Jesus builds his church (Matt 16:16–19).

Are you willing to accept a name change from Jesus? Are you willing to be born again? Are you willing to abandon the old and accept the new? Are you willing to sacrifice everything to follow Jesus? This is what it will take for your life to ascend. The time has come to be all you want to be! God's timing is perfect—far better than yours. He has prepared everything for you before he has made this call to you. Harness your faith, hope, and love and get to the confluence ASAP so that you can become one with the Father, Son, and Holy Spirit.

TRANSITION AND CHANGE

One thing in life is for certain: you will experience transition. You will routinely deal with awkward, difficult times when you find yourself in unchartered waters (the Mon). In different stages and places in your life, you will be forced to swim in climates and currents you never experienced. It is profoundly important that you exit these waters differently from how you entered. You need timely transitions in your life because they will reform, reshape, and restore you. Transitions are always complicated, challenging, and ever-changing. However, they also are captivating and compelling. Welcome to the ascension!

Remember at the beginning of the chapter when we discussed when Jesus took his disciples to the top of the Mount of Olives after his resurrection? Talk about transitions. Think about the lives of the twelve disciples. They were living a normal, productive life before being called by Jesus. They then abandoned their old life and became active in Jesus' three-year ministry. All their time and energy led to the horror and tragedy of Jesus' crucifixion and death. Finally, they accepted and rejoiced over the resurrection and shared the risen Lord with one another. Then one day, Jesus tells them that he will be leaving to be with his Father in heaven. They experienced a lifetime of transitions within a three-year period. Unbeknownst to them, after the ascension, they would experience many more transitions as they proudly carried the title of *Christians*.

If you want to understand what it is like to deal with transitions and changes in life, then focusing on the twelve disciples is a great place to learn. There are three lessons the disciples learned about transition. The first was that the letter *t* in transition stood for *trust*. When they found themselves in a life-changing circumstance, they put their trust in God. They trusted that the Lord would give them what they needed. They never felt that the Lord would abandon them. They trusted that the Lord would walk with them every step on "the Way." They kept their eyes fixed of Jesus!

The second lesson the disciples learned about transition was that they needed to be comfortable while being uncomfortable. Transition brings about physical, social, emotional, and psychological changes. The key for the disciples was that they recognized and accepted those physiological changes because they knew growth would follow. If the disciples only did what was safe and comfortable after the ascension, the gospel of Jesus Christ would have never spread, and a new religion would have never been born. Being comfortable in uncomfortable situations allowed the disciples to face challenges, difficulties, and uncertainties with an undeniable faith and confidence that ultimately changed heaven and earth!

The third and final lesson the disciples learned about transition was they needed to respond to God's grace as it came to them. The disciples didn't have a clue about God's plans for them, but they let the Holy Spirit lead them. They didn't know how their necessities would be met (food, shelter, protection), but they let the Holy Spirit lead them. They had no experience in teaching, preaching, writing, proclaiming, and healing, but they let the Holy Spirit lead them. When the disciples opened their hearts to God's grace, God's grace worked through them. When the disciples were open to God's prompting, he led them to a new and improved circumstance in their life.

What is the difference between the original twelve disciples and you? Absolutely nothing. They went through multiple transitions in their life and so will you. The three lessons they applied to their circumstances you can apply to yours. If you put trust in God, learn to be comfortable in uncomfortable situations, and respond to God's grace, you too can experience a new and improved circumstance in your life and, more importantly, change heaven and earth for the better!

Change is hard at first, messy in the middle, and gorgeous at the end.
—*Robin Sharma*[3]

HOLISTIC APPROACH #6: DIET, EXERCISE, AND SLEEP

The pillars of mental wellness are diet, exercise, and sleep. They will allow you to gain and maintain a proper balance between your mind, body, and spirit. They will help accelerate the healing process and allow you to perform at your optimum level. Unlike your therapist (whom you will see once a week), these important members of your therapeutic team provide guidance and growth daily. The more you interact with them, the better you will feel. Recovery begins with a commitment toward a balanced diet, regular exercise, and adequate rest.

Diet

In 1826, a French lawyer (Jean Anthelme Brillat-Savarin) wrote, "Tell me what you eat, and I will tell you what you are."[4] Almost two hundred years later, the world of science and medicine have proven this statement. What you put into your body has a direct effect on your psychological,

3. Robin Sharma (@RobinSharma), "Change is hard at first," X, Apr. 8, 2014, https://x.com/RobinSharma/status/453472361421877248?lang=en.

4. Brillat-Savarin, *Physiology of Taste*, 3.

emotional, social, and physical state of being. What you eat, when you eat, and how much you eat plays a key role in mental wellness. Numerous studies have shown that those who practice poor eating habits have a higher risk of suffering from anxiety and depression than others who maintain a healthy diet. Professionals in the mental health field refer to this as nutritional psychiatry. A well-balanced diet produces internal and external energy. As your energy increases, so will your productivity. Higher productively will result in desired outcomes. Desired outcomes fuel a sense of pride and accomplishment. Pride and accomplishment protect against mental and emotional fatigue. The absence of mental and emotional fatigue promotes mental wellness.

I know that there are a million diet fads that come and go (usually before swimsuit season). However, nutritional psychiatry doesn't promote weight loss but stress loss. One important by-product of a well-balanced diet will be weight loss, but this will not be the main reason you choose to realign your eating habits. The priority of nutritional psychiatry is to reconnect your mind, body, and spirit. The type, time, and amount of food intake will be the first of three links (exercise and sleep being the other two) that will strengthen your human core.

It is my personal recommendation that you begin to follow the Mediterranean diet. I hate to describe it as a diet because it is more of a lifestyle than a diet plan. The Mediterranean diet is based on the traditional foods that people used to eat in countries like Italy and Greece back in 1960s. Researchers noted that these people were exceptionally healthy compared to Americans and had a low risk of many lifestyle diseases (including anxiety and depression). There is no one right way to follow the Mediterranean diet. The diet consists of general guidelines, not rules written in stone. The plan can be adjusted to your individual needs and preferences. You certainly can find books, articles, blogs, etc. that provide more information about this diet. However, I would like to list some basic dos and don'ts when it comes to participating in this plan. First and foremost, you should only eat three meals a day (breakfast, lunch, and dinner). If you happen to become hungry between meals, there are plenty of healthy snack options: nuts, fruits, vegetables, and Greek yogurt. Second, the recommended beverage to drink with your meals/snacks is water. You can drink as much water as you would like throughout the day. Most dietary experts promote at least eight full glasses of water per day. Third, your diet should consist of eating vegetables, fruits, nuts, seeds, legumes, potatoes, whole grains, breads, herbs, spices, fish, seafood, and extra virgin olive oil. You can moderately eat poultry, eggs, cheese, and yogurt. This plan recommends that you rarely eat red meat. The things that appear on the *don't ingest* list include sugar-sweetened beverages, added sugars, processed meat, refined grains, refined oils, and other highly processed foods.

Though there is not one defined Mediterranean diet, this way of eating is generally rich in healthy plant foods and relatively low in animal foods, with a focus on fish and seafood. It will certainly take courage, commitment, and a conscious effort to shop and prepare these types of foods. However, at the end of the day, the Mediterranean diet is incredibly healthy and satisfying. You won't be disappointed in the outcome, and your mind, body, and soul will thank you by repaying you with a long and prosperous life!

Exercise

It's no big secret that exercise is good for your body. Any type of exercise can improve your physical health and your physique, trim your waistline, and even add years to your life. However, did you know it can also boost your mood, improve your sleep, and help you deal with depression, anxiety, stress, and more? Research indicates that modest amounts of exercise can make a real difference. No matter your age or fitness level, you can learn to use exercise as a powerful tool to improve your psychological, emotional, social, and physical well-being.

For many, the thought of exercise can be intimidating. You may have manufactured preconceived notions that have prevented you from participating in weekly physical activity in the past. Maybe you are one of those people that tell yourself one or more of the following reasons/excuses for not exercising: (1) I'm too tired to exercise, (2) I can't afford the gym, (3) I don't have time, (4) I need to be motivated to exercise, (5) I don't like to exercise alone, (6) I get bored easily / exercise is no fun, (7) I'm too fat/uncoordinated/embarrassed to exercise, (8) I can't stick with a program, (9) I don't like to work out around the opposite sex, or (10) I don't like to sweat. If you used one or more of these excuses in the past, you are not alone! According to the Centers for Disease Control and Prevention, only about 24 percent of the US population exercise thirty minutes per day.[5]

5. Centers for Disease Control and Prevention, "Exercise or Physical Activity."

A weekly exercise routine is not complicated, nor is it time consuming. You don't need to devote hours out of your busy day to train at the gym, run a marathon, or exert blood, sweat, and tears to reap all the physical and mental health benefits of exercise. Just thirty minutes of moderate exercise five times a week is enough. And even that can be broken down into two fifteen-minute or even three ten-minute exercise sessions, if that's easier. There are endless activities that can get your heart rate up in a slow and safe manner. Some of these activities include walking, hiking, jogging, biking, stretching (yoga), swimming, dancing, skateboarding, weight lifting, gardening, etc. Remember, choose an activity that you enjoy. Exercising should be fun, not a chore. Another strategy than may help you commit to your exercise routine is to team up with a workout buddy. Sometimes it is hard to get motivated to exercise on your own. Having an exercise buddy can help. Exercising with a friend can make your workout time fly by and give you an extra incentive to push a little harder. Also, it is more difficult to make an excuse not to exercise when someone else is holding you accountable. The key is to commit to some moderate physical activity—however little—on most days. As exercising becomes a habit, you can slowly add extra minutes or try different types of activities.

The main reason that I would like you to commit to a weekly exercise routine is that physical activity will provide you with an enormous sense of well-being. It will make you feel more energetic throughout the day, sleep better at night, have a sharper memory, and feel more relaxed and positive about yourself and your life. Also, it's a powerful medicine that helps treat symptoms caused by anxiety and depression. Studies have shown that exercise can treat mild to moderate anxiety and depression as effectively as anti-anxiety and antidepressant medication—but without the side effects.[6]

Exercise is a powerful anxiety and depression fighter for several reasons. Most importantly, it promotes all kinds of changes in the brain, including neural growth, reduced inflammation, and new activity patterns that promote feelings of calm and well-being. It also releases endorphins, powerful chemicals in your brain that energize your spirits and make you feel good. Finally, exercise can also serve as a distraction, allowing you to find some quiet time to break out of the cycle of anxious and negative thoughts that feed anxiety and depression. Today is the day to feel better,

6. Craft and Perna, "Benefits of Exercise."

look better, and get more out of life. One medical and scientific way to do this is to exercise on a weekly basis!

Sleep

Have you ever "woken up on the wrong side of the bed"? I mean, as soon as your feet left the bed and hit the floor, you were in a bad mood. You started the day feeling stressed, fatigued, and mentally "down." Why did you feel this way the minute your eyes opened? There may be many answers to this question, but the most common reason is that you probably deprived yourself from the sleep that your mind, body, and soul needed to recover from the day before. Sleep and mental health are closely connected. Sleep deprivation affects your psychological state and mental health. Sleep problems are particularly common in patients with anxiety, depression, bipolar disorder, and attention deficit hyperactivity disorder (ADHD). While research is ongoing to better understand the connections between mental health and sleep, the evidence to date points to a bidirectional relationship. Mental health disorders tend to make it harder to sleep well. At the same time, poor sleep, can be a contributing factor to the initiation and worsening of mental health problems. Because of this fact, there is strong reason to believe that improving sleep can have a beneficial impact on mental health and can be a component of treating many psychiatric disorders.

I won't bore you with the medical research pertaining to your brain activity while you sleep; however, it is important that you know that sufficient sleep facilitates your brain's processing of emotional information. While you sleep, your brain works to evaluate and remember thoughts and memories. Research has shown that a lack of sleep is especially harmful to the consolidation of positive emotional content.[7] This means that poor sleeping habits can influence your mood and emotional reactivity and impact your mental health disorders and their severity. Therefore, sleep quantity is important for mental wellness. Too little sleep (less than eight hours) and too much sleep (more than twelve hours) can increase the symptoms associated with anxiety and depression. However, some studies suggest that sleep quality is more important than sleep quantity. This brings us back to the two other links (diet and exercise) that were discussed above. Increased awareness about the importance of good

7. Hogan et al., "Effect of Sleep Deprivation," 188.

quality sleep, along with a healthy diet and regular physical activity, can act to promote good mental health among adolescents and young adults. These three links can reconnect your mind, body, and spirit and redirect your life's value and satisfaction toward optimal levels.

To help you recapture sleep quality and quantity, I have provided some steps that can be taken to help you cultivate healthier sleep habits.

1. Set a bedtime and maintain a steady sleep schedule.
2. Find ways to wind down, such as with relaxation techniques, as part of a standard routine before bedtime.
3. Avoid alcohol, tobacco, and caffeine in the evening.
4. Dim lights and put away electronic devices for an hour or more before bed.
5. Maximize comfort and support from your mattress, pillows, and bedding.
6. Block out excess light and sound that could disrupt sleep.

Finding the best routines and bedroom arrangement may take some trial and error to determine what's best for you, but that process can pay dividends in helping you fall asleep quickly and stay asleep through the night. This will give your mind, body, and spirit enough time to recharge from today and prepare for tomorrow!

The Thirty-Three-Day Challenge

According to a 2009 study, it takes 18 to 254 days for a person to form a new habit. The study concluded that, on average, it takes 66 days for a new behavior to become automatic.[8] Because of this research, I decided to propose a challenge to you. I triple dog dare you (a reference from the movie *A Christmas Story*) to complete this challenge! No, I'm not going to ask you to stick your tongue on a cold flagpole, but I am going to ask you to change your diet, exercise, and sleep routine for the next thirty-three days. I chose thirty-three days for two reasons. First, Jesus Christ was thirty-three years old when he fulfilled his Father's will by sacrificing himself for the sins of humanity. The second reason is if you complete the

8. Lally et al., "How Are Habits Formed."

full thirty-three days, you are halfway to making these new habits turn into a lifestyle.

On the one hand this dare is challenging, but on the other hand it is simple. Over the next thirty-three days, I want you to change the way you eat, the way you move, and the way you sleep. I would like you to take the concepts from the Mediterranean diet and put them into practice. Specifically, I would like you to only eat three meals per day and completely remove sugar-sweetened beverages, added sugars, processed meat, refined grains, refined oils, and other highly processed foods from your diet. I would like you to exercise for thirty minutes a day three days a week for the first eleven days, four days a week during days twelve through twenty-two, and five days a week during days twenty-three through thirty-three. Finally, I would like you to track the number of hours that you sleep at night. Your goal is to get between eight and ten hours of uninterrupted sleep each night for thirty-three straight days. To complete this challenge, you may want to recruit your family members to join in on all this fun. You and your family can become a team and hoist the Healthy Choice Trophy at the end of thirty-three days! Like the challenge that I posed in the fifth holistic approach (twenty-four-hour vow of silence), our bet will remain the same. If you complete the full thirty-three days, I will make sure that you receive all the accolades that you deserve by putting your name up on my prestigious "Wall of Fame." However, if you fail at any point before the thirty-three days are complete, you will have to go on your social media platforms and promote this book! With your help, we can bring some faith, hope, and love into someone's life today.

I would suggest that you create or purchase a daily planner so that you can track your daily performance. This physical or digital planner will help supply motivation, dedication, and accountability toward completing this challenge. It will lead you to a more healthy, happy, hopeful, and hallowed life.

Take care of your body. It's the only place you have to live.

—Attributed to Jim Rohn

HOLISTIC APPROACH #7: RECEIVE A BLESSING / RETURN A BLESSING

A blessing a day will keep anxiety and depression away! I created this expression by tweaking a famous saying that was first coined way back in 1913. Can you guess what that expression is? The famous saying is, "An apple a day keeps the doctor away." This is a great proverb to live by because apples are loaded with important nutrients, including fiber, vitamins, minerals, and antioxidants. So, eating an apple every day can lower the risk of numerous chronic conditions and promote good health. The same can be said for gratitude. The more gratitude you express, the happier you will be. The happier you become, the less of a chance there is that anxiety and depression will invade your mind, body, and soul.

We as humans are cursed (refer to the garden of Eden). Our flesh demands that we evaluate the glass of life to always be half empty. We are constantly yearning for more. What defines more? More can be money, fame, power, prestige, popularity, assets, etc. This perspective on life always leaves us unsatisfied. The next item we possess is never enough. When we are constantly unsatisfied, we begin to break down physically, psychologically, emotionally, socially, and spiritually. We become hollow inside. We lose all our faith, hope, and love and replace it with envy and jealousy. These selfish emotions turn our eyes green and change the meaning of our life. Our only mission becomes to covet whatever everyone else has. We are willing to gamble our time, talents, and treasures to satisfy our wants. As time slips away, we are reduced to thoughts of *what ifs* and *should haves* and the pain of *what is.*

The way to avoid physical and psychosocial pain is to reverse the curse! Train your brain to focus on the fullness of life instead of the emptiness of wishful thinking. This mental approach will open a portal into your mind, heart, and soul that will fill you with gratitude, grace, and grit. Gratitude, grace, and grit will not only flip your life's perspective, but they will also help you to fill up your life glass to the brim with happiness, satisfaction, and peace of mind. There will be no room for feelings of emptiness because your life will become full of positive experiences.

An extra dose of gratitude each day can provide you with greater happiness, an increase in positive emotions, an ability to live in the moment, a consistent psychological approach, and an openness to build strong relationships. Accepting grace daily can allow you (with the help from God) to forgive yourself for past transgressions and to forgive others who trespassed against you. Finally, daily grit can provide you with the passion and perseverance to keep your life's glass always full. It will supply you with courage, endurance, resilience, optimism, confidence, creativity, and a pursuit toward excellence. Grit will keep you moving forward. Even when you stumble and fall, grit will make sure that you fall forward.

How do you obtain and sustain gratitude, grace, and grit? It's as simple as changing your perspective about your life. Instead of viewing your life from the ground, where obstacles can distract you and obstruct your vision, view your life from God's view. Look at your life from ten thousand feet above instead of three feet in front of you. By viewing your life from above, you can see where you came from, where you are now, and where you are headed. This view can be very therapeutic in nature because it will allow you to measure your past, present, and future growth. Viewing your life from God's point of view will allow you to experience all the blessings that he has provided you. It will grant you the opportunity to see your life through your spirit instead of your flesh. It will prove how unique and special you truly are in the plans that he has for you.

With God as your copilot, you control your altitude, gratitude, and attitude. Like all pilots, it is important to constantly check the instrumentation of your "plane" (life). You need to make sure that all instruments are reading normal as you move on your journey. It's important to be proactive in this approach by taking preflight, peri-flight and postflight checks. The more efficient and effective your plane runs, the faster you can reach your desired destination. The two most important instruments in your plane are your input and output readings. These two readings are critical in making sure your altitude, gratitude, and attitude are always at their maximum height.

The input reading tells you the external things you are allowing into your plane. There are only two types of air that can enter your plane: dirty or clean. What type of air are you letting in? Every waking second of your life, you control the stimuli that enter your mind, body, and spirit. You create and control your body's filtration system. Therefore, I must ask you again, what does your input gage read? Is your plane full of dirty air, clean air, or a mixture of both? Your copilot (God) demands that you only allow clean air into your plane's cabin (your mind, body, and spirit). For this to occur, you must add additional scrubbers to your plane's filters to stop the unwanted poisoned air. Some of these additional scrubbers include humility, sincerity, selflessness, purposefulness, steadfastness, and faithfulness. These extra layers will help stop and/or redirect the unwanted stimuli that come your way each day. Constant fresh, clean air will keep your plane safe and healthy as you move along your life's flight pattern.

Your output gage indicates the kind of things you are releasing from your plane. Have you ever peered in the sky on a bright day and seen crisscrossing white lines left behind by aircraft? These trails are officially called contrails, short for condensation trails. In short, contrails are formed when the water vapor in the exhaust from the plane's engines condenses into water droplets that then freeze into ice particles, composing a line-shaped cloud. I promise, you will not be tested on this at the end of the book! The reason I am providing you with these aeronautical facts is to help make an analogy.

What is your output gage reading? What is coming out of your plane daily? What do people see, hear, and think when they interact with you? What are the contents of your contrails? Are they full of hope or cynicism? Do they promote relief or burden? Are they created from benevolence or malevolence? What kind of impact do you have on those you communicate with? Are your contrails still visible to them hours after your communication, or do they disappear seconds after your conversation ends?

Whether you know it or not, your thoughts, words, and behaviors leave an indelible mark on those you interact with. Being good is not enough. Being good must be coupled with doing good for your output gage to reach its maximum level. You must be cognitively and spiritually driven to make the world a better place each day. Opportunities abound for those who think, say, and do the right things at the right time. Small, medium, and large gestures grow the kingdom of God equally. A smile, hug, word of encouragement, listening, visiting, and delivering random acts of kindness are just a few things that can make our world and your life better.

So how can you elevate your altitude, recognize the power of gratitude, improve your attitude, and find grace and grit? Incorporating the following daily ritual into your life will allow you to see yourself and others with your heart instead of your eyes. It will change the way you think, speak, and act! It will flip your perspective of being half empty to totally full! Do you believe this (John 11:1–44)? The only way to find out is to dedicate yourself to this daily exercise.

This exercise is simple but powerful. It is concise but timely. Most importantly, it will become a tracking device that will measure your movement toward mental wellness. What I would like for you to do is purchase a daily calendar or use the calendar app on your cell phone. At the beginning of each day, reflect on the prior day and simply write one blessing you received from God. At the end of the day (before your nightly prayers) write down one blessing you returned to God (a blessing you bestowed upon another). That's it! One blessing entry before you start your day, and one blessing entry before you end your day. You don't have to write proper sentences or answer in paragraph form. It may only take you a few words to complete an entry. Just make sure your description is complete enough to recall what blessing you received and what blessing you returned. Reflecting upon these entries will help track your growth. I would like you to try this for thirty-three days.

This straightforward yet thought-provoking exercise will begin to have a profound effect upon you. The lens through which you see the world will begin to change. Your actions and reactions from your inner and outer worlds will become less intense. Your levels of anxiety and depression will decrease as you become filled with faith, hope, and love. The trajectory of your life will change. No longer will your doubts and fears determine your altitude and direction. You will naturally climb above the recent storms in your life and clearly see the potential and value your life has in relation to God, yourself, and others! Two entries per day for thirty-three days. Sixty-six entries that will transfigure you into the person you were meant to be (Mark 9:2–10).

Receive a Blessing / Return a Blessing		
Day	Blessing Received	Blessing Returned
1		
2		
3		

God's grace and goodness creates miracles. God intervenes, sustains, and strengthens when you need him the most. This exercise will allow you to pause, at least twice a day, to give a proclamation of praise to him. Your entries will be a reminder that God is constantly at work in your heart, life, and relationships. Today is a good day to find God at work in your life. With gratitude and thankfulness, you will find his blessings. This exercise will teach you to accept the good things from God and from others without shame or guilt. More importantly, this daily ritual will compel you to reciprocate those blessings that you received. Receiving and returning God's blessings will jettison your life closer to mental wellness.

It is more blessed to give than to receive.
—Acts 20:35

CHAPTER 9 SUMMARY

Only a person who has passed through the gate of humility can ascend to the heights of the spirit.
—Rudolf Steiner[9]

Chapter 9's content helped you peer into tomorrow. The stories told, the questions posed, and the activities assigned were all created to project your future self. When Jesus rose from the dead, the universe and everything within it changed. His resurrected body is a symbol of your future body. Each day is a new beginning, and with faith, hope, and love you will transcend into a new creation—a resurrected psychosocial state. All of this is possible through ascension.

Beginning on Easter Sunday, Jesus took forty days to prepare himself to embrace his Father in the kingdom of heaven. During this time, he appeared, taught, preached, and proclaimed his Father's heavenly kingdom to his disciples. His words and deeds turned cynics into disciples, students into teachers, and agnostics into missionaries. He forever put in motion the ministry of the Christian faith. The introduction of this chapter asked the following key questions concerning your ascension: How do you plan to use your time of preparation before your ascension takes place? What are your goals for the next forty days? How will your thoughts, words, and actions bring relief to your current mental health crisis? What are some rituals you are willing to participate in to help you rise above the pain and suffering you are currently experiencing? Remember the five *P*s (Prior Planning Prevents Poor Performance) when generating answers to these questions. This mnemonic device will provide you the best opportunity to maximize your future potential.

9. Steiner, *How to Know Higher Worlds*, 17.

To ascend, Jesus will ask you to make the climb to the top of the Mount of Olives (mental wellness). It will take a substantial amount of time, energy, and courage to journey toward this peak. Making this climb will not be easy. Therefore, make sure you bring your backpack, walking stick, climbing boots, canteen, safety ropes, headlamp, waterproof jacket/pants, and your Bible. The only way to make it to the top is to put one foot in front of the other and continue to move forward until you reach the summit. You are on the clock! Today is perfect climbing weather to begin your journey toward ascension. Jesus has drafted you on his team (the "Angels") and has put you into a starting position. He has created special plays only you can perform. He has given you unique skills to execute his game plan. You are crucial for him to win back the lost sheep of his flock!

On your journey toward ascension, you will become one with the Father, Son, and Holy Spirit. While traveling on baptismal waters, you will never be alone. If you float with faith, you will be guided toward healing waters that will provide peace and relief. Many people before you (the Magi, Anna the Prophet, and Simon Peter) took similar journeys. Though they may have not taken the same route as you, they reached the same destination—accepting and embracing Jesus Christ as their Lord and Savior. Once they transcended from the "old" and ascended into the "new," their life was never the same. The same can and will be said for you. Your future is always a day away. Sometimes it will be complicated, challenging, and ever-changing. However, since your future is always ahead of you (and not behind you), it is always captivating and compelling.

Ascension is a natural progression in life. It will teach you benevolence, charity, dignity, forbearance, hope, humility, kindness, modesty, perseverance, piety, repentance, righteous, sacredness, sincerity, steadfastness, truthfulness, unity, and wisdom. It will change your diet, sleep pattern, fitness acuity, thought process, speech, and behavior. It will transfigure you into a spiritual being!

Then a cloud came, casting a shadow over them; then from the cloud came a voice, "This is my beloved Son. Listen to him."
—Mark 9:7

RESURRECTION

FIFTEENTH STATION: JESUS RISES FROM THE DEAD

> When Simon Peter arrived after him, he went into the tomb and saw the burial cloths there, and the cloth that had covered his head, not with the burial cloths but rolled up in a separate place.
> 8 Then the other disciple also went in, the one who had arrived at the tomb first, and he saw and believed. (John 20:6–8)

We adore you, O Christ, and we bless you.

Because by your holy cross you have redeemed the world.

> Then the angel said to the women in reply, "Do not be afraid! I know that you are seeking Jesus the crucified. He is not here, for he has been raised just as he said. Come and see the place where he lay." (Matt 28:5–6)

This is the day, LORD God, that you have made! Raising Christ from the dead and raising us with Christ, you have fashioned for yourself a new people. As we hear the word that brings salvation, make our hearts burn within us. Through the presence of every friend and stranger, reveal to us the face of the One who had first to suffer but who has entered now into glory, Jesus Christ, our Passover and our peace, living and reigning with you, forever and ever. Amen.

FIFTEENTH STATION: REFLECTIVE EXERCISES AND QUESTIONS

Do you sometimes feel like your anxiety and/or depression has placed you into a tomb? Do these mental health symptoms make you lifeless? Are they preventing you from experiencing the life that God wants you to live? Is so, have no fear (Ps 27:3). Keep your faith, hope, and love alive and know that there is a garden (life) right outside your current condition. Like Jesus, you will only be in this tomb for a very short time. The darkness inside this tomb will be taken over by light (John 1:5). The frigid feeling of isolation will turn into warm rays of acceptance (Num 6:24–26)! The feeling of emptiness will transform into fulfillment when you feast on the LORD's love and grace. This will all occur for you because it occurred for Jesus. The Father would not allow darkness, isolation, and emptiness to end his Son's story, and neither will he allow your current condition to be your final resting place. Today is the day to shatter the boulder that blocks your entry into the garden. The Father has given you his power and glory to move the obstacles that are currently in front of you so that you can freely move closer to your hopes and dreams.

PROVEN STRATEGIES TO BEAT ANY ESCAPE ROOM

Have you and your family or friends ever participated in an escape room? An escape room is an immersive, sixty-minute, real-life adventure game. If you haven't experienced this adventure, I would highly recommend that you do. Because it is good family fun and a great place to go on a date, most cities offer this opportunity. Most escape rooms have a theme attached to them. Themes range from exciting and action-packed missions to silly and lighthearted experiences. After you choose a theme, you and your family/friends will meet your game guide. The game guide takes you to your room, explains the rules, and answers any questions before you begin your adventure. Once you're ready to start the game, your team will watch a mission video. This video explains the world your team is now in, what you're trying to accomplish, and why you only have sixty minutes to do so! To escape, you will need to search the room. You will have to look for patterns or connections and communicate with your teammates. Together, you can find solutions. You'll solve puzzles, uncover clues, and crack codes to progress through the game.

So why am I taking up space on this page to explain what an escape room is and how it works? Because the strategies you need to exit an escape room are the same strategies you need to resurrect from your mental health tomb! These interchangeable strategies will make you the "life of the party" and "bring a party back to your life."

Strategy #1: Pick the Right Team

Escape Room: The most important ingredient in making your escape room experience fun is the people that you play with. You don't need to surround yourself with "geniuses" to win. Everyone on your team (including yourself) will bring a unique perspective to the game and will help throughout the game. Remember, the by-product of this game is to have fun!

Mental Health Tomb: The most important factor in exiting your current mental health condition is to surround yourself with people that you love, trust, and respect. Those in your mental wellness entourage may not have ever experienced your reoccurring symptoms, but their faith, hope, and love will help you continue the journey of recovery. Remember, the by-product of your mental wellness team is peace and healing.

Strategy #2: Be Positive

Escape Room: Escape rooms are meant to be challenging. If they were easy, then it would not be exciting. If you stay positive and see challenges as opportunities rather than obstacles, you will be so much more likely to escape successfully.

Mental Health Tomb: The symptoms of anxiety and/or depression can drain the human mind, heart, and soul. They can inflict psychological, emotional, and physical pain. They can become so manipulating that they can control your thoughts, words, and actions. However, your mind can overcome matter. Your attitude and effort can catapult you toward relief and rebirth. Positivity is the antidote for negativity. Approaching each day with a "half glass full" mentality hydrates your daily productivity. Without positivity, you will suffer socio-emotional dehydration.

Strategy #3: Understand the Rules of the Game

Escape Room: There may be certain items that you shouldn't touch in the room. Disrupting these can result in messing up a puzzle and causing lost time due to frustration and unwanted results. A game master may have to enter the room to fix the problem. All of this leads to lost time and momentum.

Mental Health Tomb: The pathway to exit your mental health crisis begins with your mental health crisis. This hearkens back to the beginning of the book (Part 1, "The Afflictions"). The more energy you invest in understanding your symptoms, the closer you come to exiting your crisis. Educating yourself on anxiety and/or depression opens a map for you and your team to determine your location, direction, and destination toward mental wellness. Expending negative emotions on specific aspects of your affliction leads to lost time and momentum toward recovery. Identifying the rules of the game that you unknowingly entered allows you and your team to properly strategize a winning game plan that will eradicate your opponent and earn your freedom back.

Strategy #4: Keep an Eye on the Clock

Escape Room: An hour goes by very fast. How fast? Think about earlier today when you entered your favorite social media site to scroll for a few minutes. I bet those few minutes turned into thirty, sixty, or ninety minutes depending on the videos you were watching, games you were playing, or content you were reading or commenting on. In the escape room, time is the most important commodity you have. When you run out of it, the challenge is over! Therefore, you need to have a plan before the challenge begins. Someone on your team needs to be designated as the clock manager. This person's added responsibility is to alert the team throughout the challenge to how much time has been exhausted and how much time is still available. This information is crucial because it allows the team to adjust their time and energy as needed.

Mental Health Tomb: How long do you plan to stay in your mental health tomb? Unlike an escape room, there is no time limit. No one is going to open the door from the outside after a certain amount of time elapses. In the end, you (with the help from your team) will determine how long you will allow your afflictions to entomb you. The way out is from within! Your mind, body, and soul must uncover clues to unlock the anxiety/depression door that is holding you captive. You have the key to escape the current tomb you are in. Education, motivation, dedication, reflection, and risk-taking are the clues that will lead you to the key. Faith, hope, and love in yourself, the Lord, and your team will turn the key and open the lock so that you can reexperience the wonderful world of mental wellness. Time will pass if you let it. The responsibility of clock manager has been given to you. You will ultimately determine how long you will stay in your current physical, psychological, emotional, and social condition. How long do you plan to stay in your mental health tomb?

Strategy #5: Keep a Consistent, Determined Approach

Escape Room: Escape rooms can be mentally challenging. They exist to increase a person's frustration and blood pressure. The clues that are embedded into an adventure demand careful thought and deliberate action. Attention to detail is usually the key for solving a problem. Unfortunately, once your team solves a problem, another clue appears to explore another problem. This stressful pattern usually causes emotional overload. The number one emotion that a great escape room creates is doubt. Over time, one or more team members will allow this powerful emotion to affect their body language, attitude, and actions. Once this occurs, doubt usually spreads like a virus until the entire group raises the surrender flag and gives up. Don't be like the rest, because you are the best! Ignore the doubt and other emotions that the escape room conjures. Remain focused on the task at hand. If you put your mind to it, you can do it. Read the clues and methodically solve the problem. Two brains are better than one. Therefore, use the team approach to maintain and sustain momentum. This will allow your team to strategically move through this challenging psychological maze and fulfill your mission.

Mental Health Tomb: The path that you travel with anxiety and/or depression is sometimes clear and sometimes overgrown. Through education, communication, and therapy, you will traverse clear paths that were created by those before you that battled the symptoms that you currently exhibit. These clear paths are tried and true and will move you in the right direction. However, it's only a matter of time until these clear paths disappear and turn into vegetation in the middle of the mental health woods. If this happens to you, don't panic! This is the natural progression of exiting your mental health tomb. As a matter of fact, when you find yourself off the beaten path, you are close to escaping into mental wellness. The reason you can't always travel on a clear path is because you are a unique individual dealing with unique decisions on your exit strategy. Many marathon runners will tell you the last mile (out of the 26.2-mile race) is always the toughest. Just like a marathon runner, the real work begins near the end when you need to clear your own path. Finding the proper direction and moving forward on new terrain is time consuming, energy consuming, and effort consuming. It will take a consistent, determined approach to find and enter internal and external peace.

Strategy #6: See Something, Say Something

Escape Room: Communication is vital for beating an escape room. Puzzles often link with various items around the room. So, you might come across an item with a particular symbol on it, and that might correspond to something on the opposite side of the room. If your teammate stumbled across that very item but neither of you said anything, well, you're probably both going to miss the significance of that piece. Talking to each other about the things you discover in the room will help you notice the crucial aspects and help you win! Work together; you're all on the same team.

Mental Health Tomb: You're are not alone in your mental health tomb. You are surrounded by loved ones and experts that are willing and able to help you defeat the current cross that you bear. Research tells us that most adolescents (and adults) choose not to fully utilize their team to relieve their pain. They are either too embarrassed or too prideful to admit they need help. These unnecessary emotions and attitudes lead to self-isolation. There are very few "Davids" (patients) in the mental health arena that can defeat "Goliath" (anxiety and/or depression) on the battlefield alone. You will need the maximum number of resources available to reclaim your physical and psychosocial life! They key weapon to slay your mental health enemy is communication. Expressing yourself (either verbally or in written form) will help those around you gauge your physical and/or psychosocial makeup. Also, it will help you personally measure your growth back to mental wellness. I strongly encourage you to express your every thought and emotion to your team and yourself through your recovery. "Oversharing" is a required battlefield tactic that will help you either hold your ground or advance against your current symptoms.

Strategy #7: Use Your Clues

Escape Room: Part of the rules for an escape room includes an opportunity for a team to receive clues if they happen to get bogged down on one part of the mission. It is a high probability that a team will get stuck somehow, someway, somewhere throughout their sixty-minute mission. These escape rooms are tricky, and most of the time a team can't solve a riddle or notice the key item required to progress. Receiving a clue usually gets them unstuck! In a typical escape room, there are usually twelve puzzles to solve to complete the mission. Therefore, an accepted strategy is to ask for a clue if a team is stuck on a step for longer than five minutes. Teams that enter an escape room with humility usually exit victorious. However, teams that enter with a macho, braggadocious attitude usually become deflated and defeated after sixty minutes.

Mental Health Tomb: Your body often gives clues to your mind and soul. Your mind often gives clues to your body and soul. Your soul often gives clues to your body and mind. Are you aware of these clues? Do you hear them? Do you feel them? Do you comprehend their meaning? The answer to these questions will help increase the understanding of your symptoms and allow you to recognize triggers that ignite certain thoughts and reactions (whether biologically or psychologically). During your recovery, *you will* experience stagnation and/or relapse. When this occurs, it's best that you ask for a clue. Give yourself ample time to listen to your body, mind, and soul. Allow these three entities to define their wants and needs. This pertinent information may change your exit strategy. It may provide you additional ways of healing that you never considered previously. It may allow you to scale an obstacle that you previously thought was unattainable. It may fuel your will to do whatever it takes to regain control of your life and live it to your fullest potential. Requesting clues is not a sign of weakness; it is a sign of strength. It is a humble approach to solving a sophisticated problem. Most importantly, it is a required step in the mental wellness process!

Strategy #8: Have Fun

Escape Room: This last strategy is the key ingredient for success in an escape room! Escape rooms were invented for entertainment purposes. They were created to generate fun. In the end, it's just a game. Don't let the pressure of the clock or the difficulty of the puzzles ruin your experience. Enjoy the lasting memories that you will create with your family and/or friends. Whether you win or lose, don't worry; be happy!

Mental Health Tomb: There is joy in struggle. That's right, read it again! There is joy in struggle. Scripture tells us we rejoice in our sufferings, knowing that suffering produces endurance, endurance produces character, character produces hope, and hope does not put us to shame, all because God's love has been poured into our hearts through the Holy Spirit who has been given to us (Rom 5:1–5). You are who you are because someone loves you, and that someone is God! You are not alone, nor do you stand alone. God has created you and all those who are in your life. Those who have created you (God) and shaped you (family and friends) will be above you to bless you, below you to support you, before you to guide you, behind you to protect you, beside you to comfort you, and inside you to give you strength. Therefore, never forget that you have the capacity to preserve joy. The culture of death will relentlessly push you on a joyless quest for insatiable pleasure. Titillation and stimulation fast-track you to isolation. The true joys in life are beneath superficial pleasures. However, the only way to experience this true joy is through struggle. True joy will force you to be bold. It will force you to take risks. It will force you to fall and fail. It will force you to experience loss and pain. It will force you to carry some type of cross throughout your life. Despite that, do not be afraid, because God has promised you ascension (chapter 9)—ascension from your physical, psychological, and emotional afflictions. Most importantly, he has promised you a guarantee of reunification with the LORD when he causes your soul to ascend!

Part 3 Summary

The eleven[a] disciples went to Galilee, to the mountain to which Jesus had ordered them. When they saw him, they worshiped, but they doubted. Then Jesus approached and said to them, "All power in heaven and on earth has been given to me. Go, therefore, and make disciples of all nations, baptizing them in the name of the Father, and of the Son, and of the holy Spirit, teaching them to observe all that I have commanded you. And behold, I am with you always, until the end of the age."

—*Matt 28:16–20*

PART 3 OF THIS book was titled "The Way, the Truth, the Life." This portion of the book took all the theory that was discussed in part 1 and 2 and put it into action. Part 3 challenged you to improve your physical and psychosocial life. It posed a fundamental question, "Do you want to get well?" (John 5:6), and a fundamental solution, "Get up! Pick up your mat and walk" (John 5:8).

Part 3 created a strategic action plan that provided you organized tools to begin the recovery and healing process. Chapter 6 ("Conversion") helped you realize an existence that is on the horizon. It described the possibility of a "new" world and a "new" life full of opportunity and growth. It shared Scripture passages about others who endured similar afflictions as you currently do. Whether it is me, you, Saint Paul, or Bartimaeus, we all are searching for less pain, blame, shame, and strain in our lives. To encounter relief, we need to claim a connection with Jesus Christ. We need to accept "conversion" as the first step in the recovery process!

The moment you were conceived, God had a plan for you. While you were growing in your mother's womb, he was granting you time, talents, and treasures to accomplish this plan. Your "mission" (chapter 7) began the day you were born! Each day of your journey is vital because there is something you need to accomplish and/or experience to complete your mission. The uplifting component of this mission is that God does not expect you to do it alone. He will provide the guidance of his Son and your family, friends, hopes, and dreams to push you to the finish line. He expects you to utilize everything and everyone that enters your world to teach and guide you to fulfill your destiny. You will be tested (playing the daily hand that you are dealt) and challenged (David and Goliath) so that you can earn the skill and will to attain self-fulfillment.

You will soon break free from the anxiety and/or depression that you are suffering with. How do I know this to be true? Chapter 8 ("Resurrection") told me so! You and Jesus Christ have a lot in common. You both experienced what it is like to be human. The world treated him no differently than it treats you! What he experienced, you will experience. The opportunities that his Father offered him will also be offered to you. The only question is whether you will listen to the Father and take advantage of these opportunities. Throughout the New Testament, Jesus has proven to you that grace, faith, redemption, justification, sanctification, salvation, and glorification is possible only through him. His divine powers allow him to provide restoration for those who believe in him. The sick are restored, the deaf hear, the mute speak, the lepers become clean, the lame walk, the possessed are free, and the dead are resurrected! If Jesus cured all these maladies, he certainly would cure you from your current medical condition. For Jesus said, "Don't be afraid, you will be healed" (Luke 8:50).

Your future is bright! It is bright because you have ascended (chapter 9) into the "Light." Think of the day when your excessive worrying ends; when your physical concerns (headaches, sweating, nausea, tiredness, etc.) disappear; when your mood, interests, and self-esteem are activated and are operating at their peak performance. This day is near, or here, for you. This is the day the LORD has made for you; rejoice and be glad (Ps 118:24). The LORD has taken away from you all sickness (Deut 7:15). He has brought you up from the realm of the dead; he spared you from going down to the pit (Ps 30:3). He has enabled you to share in the inheritance that belongs to his people, who live in the light (Col 1:12). You have been recreated, reborn, and reclaimed by God. The Holy Spirit has been poured onto you and has revitalized you. You have seen and heard the Father. He has commanded you to follow a new way, a new truth, and a new life. On this journey, he wants you to testify about his greatness by always having faith, hope, and love in him.

Epilogue

Anguish Turns to Joy

Amen, amen, I say to you, you will weep and mourn, while the world rejoices; you will grieve, but your grief will become joy. When a woman is in labor, she is in anguish because her hour has arrived; but when she has given birth to a child, she no longer remembers the pain because of her joy that a child has been born into the world. So you also are now in anguish. But I will see you again, and your hearts will rejoice, and no one will take your joy away from you. On that day you will not question me about anything. Amen, amen, I say to you, whatever you ask the Father in my name he will give you.
—John 16:20–23

THERE IS MUCH IN life that can cause anguish. As the old saying goes, "Life is not a bowl of cherries." You live in a fallen world polluted by chaos, confusion, deception, abuse, scandal, and conflict. You are bound to confront one or more of these pollutants throughout your time on earth. When you encounter these toxins, be prepared to be infected with fear, anger, and despair. Even though this forecast seems severe and hazardous, God wants you to remain in peace and to trust him always.

In chapter 8 ("Resurrection"), we focused on the trials and tribulations of Jesus. He was arrested, falsely accused, sentenced to death, and crucified. Through it all, he remained in peace, knowing that his suffering would become the very source of new life! In your current situation, it seems your mind, body, and spirit betray you daily. Whether these challenges are self-imposed or unjustly imposed, they are providing you an opportunity to trust. The life (and everlasting life) lesson you are presently learning is that God can use all things for good for those who love and serve him. Entrust all things to God—every suffering, every persecution, every tragedy, and every struggle. If God the Father could bring about the greatest good ever known through the brutal murder of his own divine Son, then he can certainly do the same with all that you offer to him in trust. Trust always and in all circumstances, and your all-powerful LORD will bring good from everything.

Also, in chapter 8 we discussed whether we should obey or disobey God. We used the beloved Old Testament prophet Jonah as an example. Do you remember Jonah? He was the one who was swallowed by a whale! Now do you remember him? During our discussion, we learned that God called Jonah to fulfill a particular mission, but Jonah ignored God and ran in the opposite direction. Jonah did all he could to avoid God's calling. But God was relentless. In the end, God won, and Jonah fulfilled his mission. Jonah's calling changed lives and saved lives!

God is divine; therefore, his plans are divine. Jonah endured unnecessary trauma because of his self-centeredness (selfishness). If Jonah listened to God from the very beginning, he would have experienced gain without the pain. However, God's divine plan allowed Jonah to go through conflict. Why would God do this? Most likely it was for your sake, in that Jonah becomes a great example for you. It seems clear that one of the main lessons from Jonah's life is that God is relentless in his love for you and is relentless in calling you to embrace his will. God does not give up on you. He does not simply throw you away. Instead, he takes your brokenness, your lack of resolve, your failings and weaknesses and uses them for his glory and his perfect plan. If you feel like you have failed in following the will of God, don't give up and don't lose hope. God has not given up on his plan for you and has not lost hope. In the end, you may discover that those parts of your life that seem to be the greatest burden and/or obstacle will be solved and leveled by God's grace, and become the very source that propels you into your glory and God's glory.

Way back at the beginning of this book (the prologue), I discussed who I wrote this book for, how to read this book, and the companion book (Bible) that you would need to fully experience the essence of the words on each page. I also concluded that the heart of this book was the final section of each chapter, titled the "Road to Resurrection." These spiritual exercises allowed reflection upon each Station of the Cross that commemorated Jesus Christ's last days on earth as the Son of Man. I based this fifteen-step Catholic devotion from a celebration led by Saint Pope John Paul II on Good Friday in 1991.[1] I chose this alternate version rather than the traditional interpretation because it was a way for you and I to reflect more deeply on the scriptural accounts of Christ's passion.

However, I would like to conclude this publication with four important stations that were not covered by Saint Pope John Paul II, but that were part of the original procession for the Stations of the Cross. The following four stations are found in the traditional Catholic stations that were passed on in early tradition but not found in the biblical Gospels.[2] These reflections appear as the third, seventh, ninth, and eleventh stations in the traditional version. It is my belief that the following meditations will inspire you to carry your own crosses in life (anxiety and/or depression) until your anguish turns to joy!

RESURRECTION

THIRD STATION: JESUS FALLS FOR THE FIRST TIME

> Carrying the cross himself he went out to what is called the Place of the Skull, in Hebrew, Golgotha.). (John 19:17)

We adore you, O Christ, and we bless you.

Because by your holy cross you have redeemed the world.

> They were on the way, going up to Jerusalem, and Jesus went ahead of them. They were amazed, and those who followed were afraid. Taking the Twelve aside again, he began to tell them what was going to happen to him. "Behold, we are going up to Jerusalem, and the Son of Man will be handed over to the chief priests and the scribes, and they will condemn him to death and hand him over to the Gentiles who will mock him, spit upon him, scourge him, and put him to death, but after three days he will rise." (Mark 10:32–34)

1. Catholic News Agency, "Stations of the Cross."
2. Liguori, *Way of the Cross.*

Lord, in times of distress, allow us to drink from the cup from which you drank and fill us with the flames of your baptism so we will have the strength to get up when we fall.

THIRD STATION: REFLECTIVE EXERCISES AND QUESTIONS

What caused Jesus to stumble and fall? Was it sleep deprivation? Was it the lack of food and water in his body? Was it a headache from the crown of thorns that was driven into his head? Was it his blurry vision from Roman soldiers and onlookers spitting in his face? Was it the loss of blood from the open wounds on his body from the scourging he received before he walked the road to Calvary? Was it the feeling of embarrassment and humiliation? Was it abandonment issues created by his disciples? Was it from his heavy heart as he witnessed his mother watching her son being tortured? Was it the panic he felt trying to accomplish the will of his Heavenly Father? Or was it simply the weight of the cross (sins of mankind) that brought him to his knees? Take some time to ponder the first question in this paragraph. It will help you uncover what Jesus was thinking and feeling when he reached his earthly destination—Jerusalem.

What causes you to stumble and fall? Is it your pride? Your lack of faith and hope? The erosion of your sense of purpose? The disappearance of ambition? The absence of persistence? The fear of failure? The disease of procrastination? Or the interpretation of your past, present, and future? In the end, it really doesn't matter when you fall or why you fall. The most important question is, are you willing to get up? Jesus fell early on his journey to the crucifixion. However, when his knees scraped against the cobblestone road, he used his mind, body, heart, and spirit to push himself back to his feet. He willed himself to stand erect to prove to you that you can do the same. When anxiety and/or depression trips you up, will you use all that the Lord has given you to get back up?

Take some time to reflect on your current mental health journey. Consider the number of seconds, minutes, days, weeks, months, and possible years you have been dealing with anxiety and/or depression. Recall the physical, emotional, psychological, and social struggles caused by this affliction. Replay in your mind the events and circumstances that were impacted due to the symptoms of your mental health diagnosis. Have any of these past experiences made you stumble and fall? I'm sure they have! Now, I want you to think about the people, places, and things that propelled you forward. What, when, how, and why were you able to pick yourself up, dust yourself off, and move forward in your life?

The answers that you generate in this exercise will allow you to track your mental wellness gains. Pain, stress, strain, and failure are all opportunities for progress. When these feelings and/or experiences bubble up in your life, it is a chance for you to move closer toward your hopes and dreams. Any professional boxer will tell you that when they get knocked down, they are conditioned to get up before the referee reaches the count of ten. Every boxer has been knocked down at least once in their career. As a matter of fact, the greatest boxers of all time have often said they became champion for one simple reason: they got up every time they were knocked down!

The same can be said for you. Life can be compared to a daily boxing match. Some days you win on the score card, and some days you lose. Some days you get a knockout (you get what you want), and some days you get knocked out (you deal with the unexpected). Either way, your goal is to fight the next day. Win, lose, or draw, you need to be ready when the alarm clock rings. If you win the day, stay humble. If you get knocked down, get up so the fight continues. If you follow these keys to victory, you will become a champion and get to wear a smile on your face each day!

To help you get into a fighter's mindset, I created a daily scorecard for you. This will help you track your mental wellness. At the end of each day, I would like you to score your performance over your opponent (life). Be honest in your assessment. Your opponent is tough. Don't expect to win every round, but train yourself to win most rounds. Remember, one round (day) does not constitute a lifetime. If you find yourself behind on the scorecard, don't be embarrassed to ask for help from your corner. Your team (God, family, friends, therapist) are there to guide you toward victory. Let's get ready to rumble! Good luck. The bell just rung for your next round!

Please score yourself each day from one to ten.

A score of one means life knocked you down (you were severely impacted by the expected or unexpected).

A score of ten means you seized the day (you maximized the opportunities you were given).

Scores from two to nine are subjective but based on your overall physical, psychological, and spiritual health.

Your Daily Scorecard		
Round	*Score (1–10)*	*Rationale for Score*
1		
2		
3		
4		
5		
6		
7		

Let me tell you something you already know. The world ain't all sunshine and rainbows. It's a very mean and nasty place and I don't care how tough you are it will beat you to your knees and keep you there permanently if you let it. You, me, or nobody is gonna hit as hard as life. But it ain't about how hard ya hit. It's about how hard you can get hit and keep moving forward. How much you can take and keep moving forward. That's how winning is done! Now if you know what you're worth then go out and get what you're worth. But ya gotta be willing to take the hits and not point fingers saying you ain't where you want to be because of him, her, or anybody! Cowards do that and that ain't you! You're better than that!

—*Rocky Balboa*[3]

3. Stallone, *Rocky Balboa*, 1:17:00–1:21:39.

SEVENTH STATION: JESUS FALLS A SECOND TIME

> The message of the cross is foolishness to those who are perishing, but to us who are being saved it is the power of God. (1 Cor 1:18)

We adore you, O Christ, and we bless you.

Because by your holy cross you have redeemed the world.

> Then Pilate took Jesus and had him scourged. And the soldiers wove a crown out of thorns and placed it on his head, and clothed him in a purple cloak, and they came to him and said, "Hail, King of the Jews!" And they struck him repeatedly. (John 19:1–3)

LORD, grant us the strength, courage, and perseverance to withstand the storms of life as we continue to row toward your kingdom.

SEVENTH STATION: REFLECTIVE EXERCISES AND QUESTIONS

Scripture tells us before Jesus was given his cross to carry, the Jewish and Roman laws were followed. He was issued a warrant, judged, and sentenced. This process placed him in front of Judas, the Roman soldiers, the high priest, the Sanhedrin, King Herod, Pontius Pilate, and the people of Jerusalem. After the chief priests and citizens demanded that Pilate arrest and sentence Jesus to death (even though Pilate found no guilt in him), Pilate had Jesus scourged. Historians tell us that Jesus' hands were likely bound to a whipping post while he was beaten by a *flagrum*, a short whip made of three or more leather straps that connect to the handle. This weapon was invented to rip human flesh from the bone. The Roman soldiers would have begun the scourging on Jesus' upper torso and then gone down his back. They would continue flogging his legs and finish with his arms. Isaiah 52:14 suggests that the Romans beat Jesus so brutally that people were appalled to look at him. His form did not look like that of a human. During this flogging, Jesus would suffer a tremendous amount of blood loss. This would send his body into shock. His breathing would labor while his blood pressure dropped. This would cause him to shake and tremble. He would also be dehydrated, causing his tongue to swell. All these symptoms occur when a body suffers from extreme trauma and exhaustion.

After the scourging ended, the governor's soldiers took Jesus into the Praetorium and gathered the whole company of soldiers around him. They stripped him and put a scarlet robe on him and then twisted together a crown of thorns and set it on his head. They put a staff in his right hand. Then they knelt in front of him and mocked him. "Hail, king of the Jews!" they said. They spit on him and took the staff and struck him on the head repeatedly. After they had mocked him, they took off the robe and put his own clothes on him. Then they led him away to crucify him (Matt 27:27–31).

Jesus was a victim of physical and psychological warfare. He was exposed to violence that no human could withstand. Therefore, when he fell the second time, he collapsed and fell on his face. Jesus' mind, body, and spirit were empty. He did not have the strength to get up on his own. Jesus needed help! He was yanked up by the Roman soldiers. Seeing the condition Jesus was in, they knew he would not make it to the top of the mountain on his own, so they forced Simon from Cyrene to carry his cross for him so he could be crucified on it.

Please stop reading this section for a moment and revisit the eighth station's reflective exercises and questions.

I hope this station reminded you that many times in your life, you will be physically, psychologically, emotionally, and spiritually exhausted. You will figuratively collapse and fall on your face. You will need someone to help you get up! Do you have "Simons" in your life, or have you evicted everyone who has come to help improve your current mental health status? If you do have "Simons" (those that love and support you), then you must allow them to use their time, talents, and treasures to get you back on your feet. It's amazing what you will receive if only you ask!

Another action that will get you back on your feet is to *be* a "Simon" for someone else. The Lord has given you time, talents, and treasures to help relieve others from their pain and suffering. You only need the heart of Jesus to see who needs help. You have the strength, courage, and wisdom to lift the burdens off these people's hearts, minds, and souls. You were placed in this time and space to extend your God-given gifts to them so they can rise and continue their journey to the kingdom of heaven. When you become a "Simon," you will become a blessing to those you encounter. When you become a "Simon," you will dedicate your time to do what God wants you to do. When you become a "Simon," you will discover and develop spiritual gifts. When you become a "Simon," you will experience the Lord's joy and peace. When you become a "Simon," you will become more like Jesus by being more humble, grateful, and forgiving. Finally, when you become a "Simon," you will experience personal breakthroughs and miracles that only God can award for being a good and faithful servant. Simply put, by serving God and serving others, you will serve yourself!

To help you further expand on becoming a "Simon," I created six questions to ponder. The answers to these questions will help you speak up and stand up for someone in need.

1. What can I do with the limited time the Lord has given me on earth?
2. What are the God-given talents I have been gifted?
3. What treasures have I graciously been given that can be multiplied?
4. How can I serve God?
5. How can I serve others?
6. How can I serve myself?

> *And the king will say to them in reply, 'Amen, I say to you, whatever you did for one of these least brothers of mine, you did for me.'*
> *—Matt 25:40*

NINTH STATION: JESUS FALLS A THIRD TIME

> He himself bore our sins in his body upon the cross, so that, free from sin, we might live for righteousness. By his wounds you have been healed. (1 Pet 2:24)

We adore you, O Christ, and we bless you.

Because by your holy cross you have redeemed the world.

> Those passing by reviled him, shaking their heads and saying, "You who would destroy the temple and rebuild it in three days, save yourself, if you are the Son of God, come down from the cross!" (Matt 27:39–40)

Lord, bless us with optimism, gratitude, self-respect, self-compassion, and personal resilience each time that we fall. Provide us the strength we need to rise and walk toward your kingdom.

NINTH STATION: REFLECTIVE EXERCISES AND QUESTIONS

As Jesus neared Mount Calvary, he fell for the third and final time. The weight of the sins of the world crushed him into the earth. The eyes of Jerusalem were on him to see if he would get up a third time. Throngs of people witnessed Christ's passion. One-third felt he was guilty and wanted him to suffer and die. Another third of them were followers of Jesus and wanted to comfort him as he fulfilled his Father's will. The final third were indifferent and were following Christ because they were attracted to the spectacle of a Roman crucifixion. Two thousand years later, the song remains the same. There are approximately eight billion people living in the world today. One-third are non-Christian. Another third claim to be Christian, and the final third are unaffiliated with a religion. Therefore, today's world population reflects the makeup of those who traveled the road to Calvary with Jesus.

In what category do you place yourself in? Do you blame God for your medical diagnosis? Has the weight of your symptoms manipulated your spiritual beliefs? Has your suffering evaporated your faith, hope, and love in the Lord? Have you turned your back on him because of your pain, plight, or pride?

Did you answer yes to the previous four questions? If so, I have one more important question for you: Has your mental health improved by taking sole ownership over it? I assume you answered no because you are reading this book! Today is the day to invite the living Savior into your life. Ask him to heal your mind, heart, and soul. Follow him on the road to Calvary, and leave your anxiety and/or depression at the foot of his cross. Use your mind and spirit to travel to his tomb and witness his triumph over pain, suffering, and death. Look toward the heavens and believe he has a room prepared for you in his kingdom. Finally, pray each day for forgiveness and reconciliation. If you do these things, I guarantee you will receive his grace and mercy and will be healed from your physical, emotional, and spiritual afflictions.

Are you a disciple of Jesus who prays each day to understand his words and ways? Do you consider yourself his humble servant who is willing to follow in his footsteps toward death, resurrection, and ascension? Have you fallen in the past only to rise again to fulfill his glory in you? Are you willing to accept the crosses that you must carry throughout your life, knowing that God is with you and for you every step of the way? Are your eyes, heart, and mind fixed on Jesus each day? Is your faith, hope, and love in Jesus as strong as the bond between the Father, Son, and Holy Spirit? If you answered yes to these six questions, then Jesus will say to you, "You are not far from the kingdom of God" (Mark 12:34). Your faith in him, your hope through him, and your love for him will save you! Because you are his brother or sister, the Lord will not and can not be outdone in generosity. If you pray in faith, hope, and love, you can be confident that God will give you the strength and wisdom needed to be healed from your afflictions so that you can return to the vocation that you have been called to do.

Do you consider yourself spiritual but not religious? Do you feel weekly attendance at church is optional but not mandatory? Do you feel prayer is unnecessary? Do you think for yourself rather than depend on a set of doctrines? If you answered yes to these questions, then you should listen to "Saint" Jelly Roll's song "Need A Favor" because his prophetic lyrics are about you. The message of the song is all about questioning how it is that we feel we can claim Jesus as our Savior when we only really approach him when we need something from him.[4]

There is an old military saying that suggests "there are no atheists in a foxhole." This means that most people will turn to a higher power during times of extreme fear, pain, and/or stress. If you recall in chapter 8 ("Resurrection") under the section "The Dead Are Resurrected," I told the story of a synagogue leader in Nazareth (Jesus' hometown) named Jairus. The first time Jesus returned home to see his mother, the people of Nazareth (led by Jairus) tried to kill him because he proclaimed that

4. Jelly Roll, "Need a Favor."

he was the Son of Man. However, when Jesus returned home for the second time, Jairus fell at Jesus' feet and pleaded with him earnestly to save his little daughter because she was dying. Jesus followed him home and resurrected his daughter. Jairus was placed in a metaphorical foxhole and found his faith. We all will find ourselves in metaphorical foxholes throughout our lives. We all will come to Jesus. Better it be sooner than later! You see the LORD makes his sun rise on the bad and good and causes rain to fall on the just and unjust (Matt 5:45). Therefore, it is never too late to return to the Father (Luke 15:11–24). Whatever category you placed yourself in while Jesus traveled the road to Calvary, today is the day to "stop doubting and believe" (John 20:27)!

RESURRECTION

ELEVENTH STATION: JESUS IS NAILED TO THE CROSS

> And they placed over his head the written charge against him: This is Jesus, the King of the Jews. (Matt 27:37)

We adore you, O Christ, and we bless you.

Because by your holy cross you have redeemed the world.

> Then they crucified him and divided his garments by casting lots for them to see what each should take. (Mark 15:24)

LORD, as I endure the many sufferings of life, may I always have faith in the saving power of your cross and resurrection. May I always call upon you to calm my pain and hear you speak to me the many truths I need to hear.

ELEVENTH STATION: REFLECTIVE EXERCISES AND QUESTIONS

If you recall in chapter 8 ("Resurrection") under the section "The Trials and Tribulations of Jesus Christ," I traced the events of Jesus' arrest and crucifixion. Biblical scholars tell us that after Jesus was arrested, he participated in six trials in six hours. All six trials took an emotional, psychological, and physical toll on Jesus. Unfortunately, this was only a small sample size of the pain that he would have to endure on that day. From 8:00 a.m. to 12:00 p.m., Jesus was mocked, scourged, and forced to carry his cross to Calvary. I want to emphasize that Jesus returned to his feet after he fell for the third time (an important event not noted in the ninth station's reflective exercises and questions).

As it neared noontime on this Good Friday, Jesus finally reached the top of Mount Calvary. Waiting for him at his crucifixion site were six-inch spikes for his hands and sixteen-inch spikes for his feet. Scriptures record at high noon the crucifixion procedures began. Jesus did not say a word, nor did he make a sound. He did not lash out with anger, nor did he claim himself to be a victim.

I once heard of a study that concluded that the average person complains three times every fifteen minutes. That must be an old study because I can admit that I complain a lot more than that! Not only do I complain but I also judge, and I seem to justify my attitude, words, and actions each time that I do these things. However, after reading the last paragraph I concluded if anyone ever had the right to complain, it would be Jesus. The things that he experienced from his unjust arrest until his death are hard to comprehend. The physical, psychological, and spiritual torture that he went through is unimaginable. Yet during the Easter Triduum, Jesus bore your griefs and sorrows, broke the power of sin, and won a victory over death which he now wants to share with you!

Whenever the good LORD gives you a challenge, whenever he gives you a sliver of his cross to carry, he will give you the strength and grace to overcome whatever situation you find yourself in. If he never gives you challenges (his cross), you will never fully grow. Complacency leads to contentment. Contentment leads to passivity. Passivity leads to object mediocrity. God's creations are not mediocre but magnificent. Therefore, accept your current circumstance and be willing to change it with the help of the Father, Son, Holy Spirit, family members, friends, loved ones, and your mental wellness team. You are too important to God to be defeated by the challenges that life places in front of you. For this reason, accept who you are, where you are, and what/where you need to be. Measure the distance and effort it will take to scale your current obstacle, and let your faith, hope, and love fuel you over the finish line!

Twenty-Two Ways to Measure Your Mindset While Battling Mental Health Challenges		
Please circle *agree* or *disagree* after reading each statement.		
1. How I feel determines how I function.	*Agree*	*Disagree*
2. My current feelings have no bearing on my functionality.	*Agree*	*Disagree*
3. My commitment levels are directly correlated to my emotional levels.	*Agree*	*Disagree*
4. My commitment levels are disconnected to my emotional levels.	*Agree*	*Disagree*
5. My resiliency decreases as my stress levels increase.	*Agree*	*Disagree*
6. My resiliency is not impacted by stress or strain.	*Agree*	*Disagree*
7. Because of my current condition, I very rarely experience gratitude.	*Agree*	*Disagree*
8. No internal or external stressor can deplete the gratitude that I possess.	*Agree*	*Disagree*
9. I am currently focused on my condition and not my recovery.	*Agree*	*Disagree*
10. I am currently focused on my recovery and not my condition.	*Agree*	*Disagree*
11. I have no way of knowing if I feel the same, better or worse.	*Agree*	*Disagree*
12. I create process, performance, and outcome goals to assess growth.	*Agree*	*Disagree*
13. My current mental health condition is personal and confidential.	*Agree*	*Disagree*

14. I am open and honest with others about how my current mental health condition impacts my physical, psychosocial, and spiritual state.	*Agree*	*Disagree*
15. I choose not to use the resources available to me for recovery.	*Agree*	*Disagree*
16. I have adopted a "mental wellness team approach" to help me reclaim my independence from my current afflictions.	*Agree*	*Disagree*
17. My current mental health condition has kidnapped my future hopes and dreams.	*Agree*	*Disagree*
18. My mental wellness recovery plan encourages me to focus on my life a day, week, month, year, and decade from today.	*Agree*	*Disagree*
19. My current mental health condition weakens my confidence.	*Agree*	*Disagree*
20. My current mental health condition strengthens my confidence.	*Agree*	*Disagree*
21. My current mental health condition weakens my faith, hope, and love in the Lord.	*Agree*	*Disagree*
22. My current mental health condition strengthens my faith, hope, and love in the Lord.	*Agree*	*Disagree*

Take a moment to review your answers. How did you answer the odd questions? If you agreed more than disagreed with these statements, then you may want to reset your mental approach to your current life challenge. Approaching each day with a positive mindset involves focusing on the good in a situation and expecting good things to happen. This will allow you to become more hopeful, courageous, kind, resilient, and accepting.

How did you answer the even questions? If you agreed more than disagreed with these statements, then your mindset is in alignment with your assignment: to scale any obstacle set before you and move forward with the work that God has entrusted to you!

What will ultimately make the difference is your mindset. How will you approach (interpret and respond to) situations that occur in your life? Will you allow the circumstance to control you, or will you control the circumstance? There is no other object in the universe that can compare to your mind. It can deliver you through the good, the bad, and the ugly, or it can derail you into extinction. The conversations that your inner voice has with your mind is apocalyptic in nature. If the voice within feeds your brain with positive anecdotes, then positive things will occur internally and externally. If you inject your brain with negative sensations, then a battle will ensue for your body, mind, heart, soul, and life.

Jesus knew his mission before he was born to Mary (John 10:17–18). He willingly chose an unjust crucifixion to conquer evil, sin, and death. His life's mindset was that of humility, thoughtfulness, obedience, and patience. He was delivered upon this earth to love and serve (Mark 10:45). He offered forgiveness and grace to all (Eph 1:7). This mindset was the reason he was able to endure over twelve hours of psychological and physical torture. This mindset allowed him to get up three times after he stumbled and fell. This mindset allowed him to resurrect on Easter Sunday and offer you hope, salvation, and eternal life!

During this calendar year, designate each month to one of the following mindsets of Jesus: humility, thoughtfulness, obedience, patience, love, service, forgiveness, or grace. Research the meaning of each mindset and put it into daily practice for a month. Once the month is completed, move to the next mindset. If these attitudes and behaviors worked for Jesus, I'm sure they will work for you!

"I'LL SEE YOU AFTER!"

Did you ever see the movie *Braveheart*? If you haven't, I strongly encourage you to do so. It ranks very high as one of my all-time favorite movies! This historical epic film (released in 1995) was loosely based on the story of the thirteenth-century Scottish leader William Wallace. The storyline traces the life of Wallace as he is spurred into revolt against the English when the love of his life is slaughtered. Leading his army into battles that become a war, his advancement into England threatens King Edward I's throne. Wallace then is captured and executed, but not before becoming a symbol for a free Scotland.

At the climax of the movie, William Wallace plans to meet with the heir to the Scottish throne (Robert the Bruce) to unite the clans and commit troops to the war against England. However, Robert's father conspires with other nobles to capture and hand over Wallace to the English. Wallace is captured, tortured, and beheaded in England for the crime of high treason. Yet, Wallace's legend leads Robert the Bruce onto the battlefield against England in 1314 to claim independence from them!

Prior to the meeting with Robert the Bruce, Wallace (knowing his fate) says goodbye to his loyal friends who fought beside him on the battlefield. One of his soldiers was an Irishman named Stephen. When Wallace approaches Stephen, Stephen says to him, "I'll see you after."[5] Since we have come to the end of this book, I would like to tell you the same.

I'll see you after you conquer your current mental health affliction!

I'll see you after you become a new creation in Jesus Christ!

I'll see you after you accomplish all your hopes and dreams!

I'll see you in the afterlife!

Nevertheless, if you need me prior to accomplishing these destinations, please contact me so that I may be your copilot on these journeys.

It's been fun, but we are done! I pray that you face your future with courage, acceptance, hope, and faith. May you increasingly read, study, pray, share, live, proclaim, obey, and teach the word of God. I pray for you, and I ask that you pray for me. This will be our bond that will always connect us with our Lord and Savior.

I will leave you with this final Scripture passage. May you reflect upon it daily and allow it to guide you throughout your life. Good luck! God bless! I love you!

> I do not think of myself as having reached the finish line. I give no thought to what lies behind but push on to what is ahead. My entire attention is on the finish line—life on high in Jesus Christ. (Phil 3:13–14)

5. Gibson, *Braveheart*, 2:07:00.

Let's Continue the Conversation

Join the Movement of Faith, Hope, and Love

Thank you for reading *Faith, Hope, and Love: The Space Between Therapy Sessions.*

However, this book is only the beginning!

If you are a teen or young adult seeking encouragement, a parent searching for guidance, a teacher or therapist supporting others, or someone passionate about mental wellness – you are part of this mission.

To continue the conversation, share your story, or connect about speaking events at schools, universities, parent groups, community organizations, or online platforms, reach me at

Email: heavnerdavidj@gmail.com

Website: throughservicewegrow.com

Instagram: @throughservicewegrow

TikTok: @throughservicewegrow

YouTube: https://www.youtube.com/@throughservicewegrow

Facebook: facebook.com/throughservicewegrow

LinkedIn: David Heavner

Together, let's build a world where young people feel seen, supported, and empowered.

Bibliography

Albom, Mitch. *Tuesdays with Morrie: An Old Man, a Young Man, and Life's Greatest Lesson*. 1st ed. New York: Doubleday, 2007.

Alighieri, Dante. *The Inferno of Dante: A New Verse Translation*. Translated by Robert Pinsky. New York: Farrar, Straus & Giroux, 1994.

Allmond, Joy. "He Is Risen!" *Decision*, Mar. 31, 2009. https://decisionmagazine.com/he-is-risen/.

American Academy of Child and Adolescent Psychiatry. "Violent Behavior in Children and Adolescents." AACAP 55 (2017). https://www.aacap.org/AACAP/Families_and_Youth/Facts_for_Families/FFF-Guide/Understanding-Violent-Behavior-In-Children-and-Adolescents-055.aspx.

American Academy of Family Physicians. "Persistent Depressive Disorder (PDD)." FamilyDoctor.org, last updated Aug. 2023. https://familydoctor.org/condition/persistent-depressive-disorder/.

American Psychiatric Association. *Diagnostic and Statistical Manual of Mental Disorders*. 5th ed. Washington, DC: American Psychiatric Association, 2022.

———. "Level 2: Repetitive Thoughts and Behaviors—Adult (adapted from the Florida Obsessive-Compulsive Inventory Severity Scale). "DSM-5® Online Assessment Measures, 2023, PDF. https://www.psychiatry.org/getmedia/a451f9f0-40b7-4262-8ef2-e7be2ea004f2/APA-DSM5TR-Level2RepetitiveThoughtsAndBehaviorsAdult.pdf.

———. "Severity Measure for Panic Disorder—Adult." DSM-5® Online Assessment Measures, 2023, PDF. https://www.psychiatry.org/getmedia/6ab8ea4f-e810-4c0c-b41c-16838293506d/APA-DSM5TR-SeverityMeasureForPanicDisorderAdult.pdf.

———. "Severity Measure for Social Anxiety Disorder (Social Phobia)—Adult." DSM-5® Online Assessment Measures, 2023, PDF. https://www.psychiatry.org/File%20Library/Psychiatrists/Practice/DSM/APA_DSM5_Severity-Measure-For-Social-Anxiety-Disorder-Adult.pdf.

———. "Severity Measure for Specific Phobia—Adult." DSM-5® Online Assessment Measures, 2023, PDF. https://www.psychiatry.org/File%20Library/Psychiatrists/Practice/DSM/APA_DSM5_Severity-Measure-For-Specific-Phobia-Adult.pdf.

———. "Severity of Posttraumatic Stress Symptoms—Adult." DSM-5® Online Assessment Measures, 2023, PDF. https://www.psychiatry.org/File%20Library/Psychiatrists/Practice/DSM/APA_DSM5_Severity-of-Posttraumatic-Stress-Symptoms-Adult.pdf.

American Psychological Association. "Anxiety." *APA Dictionary of Psychology*, last updated Apr. 19, 2018. https://dictionary.apa.org/anxiety.

Bibliography

Anderson, Danny. "5 Reasons to Grow Your Faith." Danny Anderson (website), 2017. https://www.dannyanderson.net/5-reasons-grow-faith.

Anderson, Monica, and Jingjing Jiang. "Teens, Social Media and Technology 2018." Pew Research Center, May 31, 2018. https://www.pewresearch.org/internet/2018/05/31/teens-social-media-technology-2018/.

———. "Teens' Social Media Habits and Experiences." Pew Research Center, Nov. 28, 2018. https://www.pewinternet.org/wp-content/uploads/sites/9/2018/11/PI_2018.11.28_teens-social-media_FINAL2.pdf.

Anxiety and Depression Association of America. "Anxiety Disorders: Facts and Statistics." ADAA. https://adaa.org/understanding-anxiety/facts-statistics.

———. "Clinical Practice Review for Social Anxiety Disorder." ADAA, last updated July 14, 2025. https://adaa.org/resources-professionals/clinical-practice-review-social-anxiety.

———. *Depression*. Silver Spring, MD: ADAA, 2025. https://adaa.org/sites/default/files/ADAA%20Depression%20Brochure%20Final.pdf.

———. "Obsessive Compulsive Disorder." 2025. https://adaa.org/sites/default/files/OCD_brochure_rev.2014.pdf.

———. *Panic Disorder*. Silver Spring, MD: ADAA, 2025. https://adaa.org/sites/default/files/panic-brochure.pdf.

———. *Posttraumatic Stress Disorder*. Silver Spring, MD: ADAA, 2025. https://adaa.org/sites/default/files/ADAA_PTSD.pdf.

———. "Screening for Panic Disorder." Last updated Oct. 19, 2021. https://adaa.org/screening-panic-disorder.

———. "Screening for Specific Phobias." https://adaa.org/living-with-anxiety/ask-and-learn/screenings/screening-specific-phobias.

———. *Social Anxiety Disorder*. Silver Spring, MD: ADAA, 2025. https://adaa.org/sites/default/files/ADAA%20Social%20Anxiety%20Disorder%20Brochure%20 2021_0.pdf.

———. *Specific Phobias*. Silver Spring, MD: ADAA, 2025. https://adaa.org/sites/default/files/July%2015%20Phobias_adaa.pdf.

———. "Symptoms: Generalized Anxiety Disorder." 2025. https://adaa.org/understanding-anxiety/generalized-anxiety-disorder-gad/symptoms.

———. "What Is Depression?" Last updated Nov. 6, 2024. https://adaa.org/about-adaa/press-room/multimedia/what-depression.

Arylo, Christine. "Do You Love Yourself?" Path of Self Love, May 12, 2022. https://pathofselflove.org/assessments/self-love-quiz/.

Aurelius, Marcus. *The Emperor Marcus Antoninus: His Conversation with Himself.* Translated by Jeremy Collier. London, 1702.

Barks, Coleman ed. *The Illuminated Rumi*. New York: Broadway, 1997.

Batterson, Mark. "The Sound of Silence." Proverbs 31 Ministries, Oct. 23, 2017. https://proverbs31.org/read/devotions/full-post/2017/10/23/the-sound-of-silence.

Bernstein, Adam, dir. "Half Measures." Season 3, episode 12 of *Breaking Bad*. Aired June 6, 2010 on AMC.

Better Health Channel. "Relationships and Communication." Feb. 24, 2022. https://www.betterhealth.vic.gov.au/health/healthyliving/relationships-and-communication.

Bloudoff-Indelicato, Mollie. "The 14 Questions You Should Ask a Therapist Before Your First Appointment." *Washingtonian*, Mar. 3, 2016. https://www.washingtonian.

com/2016/03/03/the-14-questions-you-must-ask-a-therapist-before-your-first-appointment/.

Bommersbach, Tanner J., et al. "Why Are Women More Likely to Attempt Suicide than Men? Analysis of Lifetime Suicide Attempts Among US Adults in a Nationally Representative Sample." *Journal of Affective Disorders* 311 (2022) 157–64. https://doi.org/10.1016/j.jad.2022.05.096.

Bond, Robert. "Violence Spreads like a Disease Among Adolescents, Study Finds." Ohio State News, Dec. 20, 2016. https://news.osu.edu/violence-spreads-like-a-disease-among-adolescents-study-finds.

Booth Cundy, Jamie. "Mental Illness and the Family." *Psychology Today*, Nov. 27, 2012. https://www.psychologytoday.com/us/blog/the-beauty-in-the-beast/201211/mental-illness-and-the-family.

Breakout Games. "10 Strategies for Winning in Escape Rooms." Breakout, Sept. 9, 2024. https://breakoutgames.com/escape-rooms/strategy.

Brillat-Savarin, Jean Anthelme. *The Physiology of Taste: Or, Meditations on Transcendental Gastronomy*. Translated by M. F. K. Fisher. New York: Liveright, 2004.

Bucknell, Paul. "The Preparation of Our Heart." Foundations for Freedom, 2008. https://foundationsforfreedom.net/References/NT/Gospels/Luke/Luke09/Luke09_57-62_Discipleship.html.

Bump, Philip. "2018 Has Been Deadlier for Schoolchildren than Deployed Service Members." *Washington Post*, May 18, 2018. https://www.washingtonpost.com/news/politics/wp/2018/05/18/2018-has-been-deadlier-for-schoolchildren-than-service-members/.

Butterworth, Eric. "Love: The One Creative Force." In *Chicken Soup for the Soul: 101 Stories to Open the Heart and Rekindle the Spirit*, by Jack Canfield and Mark Victor Hansen, 3–4. Deerfield Beach, FL: Health Communications, 1993.

Cantor, Paul A. *Pop Culture and the Dark Side of the American Dream: Con Men, Gangsters, Drug Lords, and Zombies*. Lexington: University Press of Kentucky, 2019.

Carnegie Medal of Philanthropy. "A Legacy That Defines a City: Pittsburgh." https://www.medalofphilanthropy.org/a-legacy-that-defines-a-city-pittsburgh/.

Catholic News Agency. "Stations of the Cross with John Paul II—1991." https://www.catholicnewsagency.com/resource/56333/stations-of-the-cross-with-john-paul-ii-1991.

Center for Behavioral Health Statistics and Quality. *Key Substance Use and Mental Health Indicators in the United States: Results from the 2015 National Survey on Drug Use and Health*. HHS Publication No. SMA 16-4984, NSDUH Series H-51. Rockville, MD: Substance Abuse and Mental Health Services Administration, 2016. https://www.samhsa.gov/data/sites/default/files/NSDUH-FFR1-2015/NSDUH-FFR1-2015/NSDUH-FFR1-2015.htm.

Centers for Disease Control and Prevention. "About Underage Drinking." Jan. 14, 2025. https://www.cdc.gov/alcohol/underage-drinking/?CDC_AAref_Val=https://www.cdc.gov/alcohol/fact-sheets/underage-drinking.htm.

———. "Exercise or Physical Activity." Last updated Dec. 10, 2024. https://www.cdc.gov/nchs/fastats/exercise.htm.

———. "Fast Facts: Vision Loss." Vision and Eye Health, last updated May 15, 2024. https://www.cdc.gov/vision-health/data-research/vision-loss-facts/index.html.

———. "Healthy Schools." Last updated June 26, 2024. https://www.cdc.gov/healthy-schools/about/index.html?CDC_AAref_Val=https://www.cdc.gov/healthyschools/about/index.html?CDC_AAref_Val=https://www.cdc.gov/healthyschools/obesity/facts.htm.

Charisma. "8 Ways Jesus Suffered for You." *Charisma*, Apr. 16, 2014. https://mycharisma.com/spiritled-living/eight-ways-jesus-suffered-for-you/.

Cherney, Kristeen. "Effects of Anxiety on the Body." Healthline, last updated Nov. 13, 2023. https://www.healthline.com/health/anxiety/effects-on-body.

Cherry, Kendra. "Maslow's Hierarchy of Needs." Verywell Mind, last updated Apr. 2, 2024. https://www.verywellmind.com/what-is-maslows-hierarchy-of-needs-4136760.

Christianity.com Staff. "What Miracles Did Jesus Perform?" Christianity.com, last updated Mar. 13, 2025. https://www.christianity.com/wiki/jesus-christ/what-miracles-did-jesus-perform.html.

Cleveland Clinic. "Adjustment Disorders." Last updated Dec. 29, 2022. https://my.clevelandclinic.org/health/diseases/21760-adjustment-disorder.

Cole, Steven J. "Lesson 100: Who's the Greatest?" Bible.org, Dec. 20, 2018. https://bible.org/seriespage/lesson-100-who-s-greatest-luke-2224-30.

Cox, John Woodrow, and Steven Rich. "Scarred by School Shootings." *Washington Post*, last updated Mar. 25, 2018. https://www.washingtonpost.com/graphics/2018/local/us-school-shootings-history/.

Craft, Lynette L., and Frank M. Perna. "The Benefits of Exercise for the Clinically Depressed." *Primary Care Companion Journal of Clinical Psychiatry* 6 (2004) 104–11. doi: 10.4088/pcc.v06n0301.

Curran-Hackett, Mary. "The WD Interview: Janet Fitch - Into the Light." *Writer's Digest*, Mar. 11, 2008. https://www.writersdigest.com/writing-articles/the-wd-interview-janet-fitch-into-the-light.

Deffinbaugh, Bob. "Jesus Before Pilate: Part 1." Bible.org, Aug. 20, 2004. https://bible.org/seriespage/42-jesus-pilate-part-i-john-1828-38.

Degges-White, Suzanne. "The 13 Essential Traits of Good Friends." *Psychology Today*, Mar. 23, 2015. https://www.psychologytoday.com/us/blog/lifetime-connections/201503/the-13-essential-traits-good-friends.

Denizet-Lewis, B. "Why Are More American Teenagers than Ever Suffering from Severe Anxiety?" *New York Times*, Oct. 11, 2017. https://www.nytimes.com/2017/10/11/magazine/why-are-more-american-teenagers-than-ever-suffering-from-severe-anxiety.html.

Dixon, Stacey Joe. "Most Popular Social Networks of Teenagers in the United States from Fall 2012 to Fall 2023." Statista, May 22, 2024. https://www.statista.com/statistics/250172/social-network-usage-of-us-teens-and-young-adults/.

———. "Reach of Social Media Used by U.S. Teens and Young Adults 2020." Statista, May 20, 2022. https://www.statista.com/statistics/199242/social-media-and-networking-sites-used-by-us-teenagers/.

Dvorak, P. "Millions of Kids Fear Being Killed at School. It's Time for Adults to Say: Enough." *Washington Post*, Dec. 27, 2018. https://www.washingtonpost.com/local/millions-of-kids-fear-being-killed-at-school-its-time-for-adults-to-say-enough/2018/12/27/faa0cf62-0a06-11e9-88e3-989a3e456820_story.html.

Dynamic Catholic. "What Are the Stations of the Cross?" Feb. 20, 2024. https://www.dynamiccatholic.com/lent/stations-of-the-cross.html.

Ebner-Eschenbach, Marie von. *Aphorisms*. Translated and introduced by David Scrase and Wolfgang Mieder. Riverside, CA: Ariadne, 1994.

Emerson, Ralph Waldo. *Essays: First Series*. Boston: James Munroe and Company, 1841.

Evans, William. *The Great Doctrines of the Bible*. Chicago: Bible Institute Colportage Association, 1912.

Fairchild, Mary. "Bible Story of a Brave Trio: Shadrach, Meshach, and Abednego." Learn Religions, last updated Sept. 23, 2024. https://www.learnreligions.com/shadrach-meshach-and-abednego-bible-story-700080.

Fleming, Victor, dir. *The Wizard of Oz*. Culver City, CA: Metro-Goldwyn-Mayer, 1939.

Frances, Allen J. "The Magical Healing Power of Caring and Hope in Psychotherapy." *Psychology Today*, July 6, 2015. https://www.psychologytoday.com/us/blog/saving-normal/201507/the-magical-healing-power-caring-hope-in-psychotherapy.

Fulghum Bruce, Debra. "Teen Depression." WebMD, June 24, 2024. https://www.webmd.com/depression/teen-depression.

Gabbey, Amber Erickson. "Causes of Depression." Healthline, Jan. 2, 2020. https://www.healthline.com/health/depression/causes.

Gander, Kashmira. "Gen Z Is the Most Stressed Out Group in America, Poll Finds." *Newsweek*, Oct. 20, 2020. https://www.newsweek.com/gen-z-most-stressed-out-group-america-poll-finds-1540549.

Gibson, Mel, dir. *Braveheart*. Los Angeles, CA: Paramount, 1995.

Goodman, Wayne K., et al. "Obsessive-Compulsive Disorder (OCD) Screening Tool." Anxiety and Depression Association of America. https://growingrootsllc.squarespace.com/s/OCD-ScreeningTool.pdf.

———. "The Yale-Brown Obsessive Compulsive Scale: I. Development, Use, and Reliability." *Archives of General Psychiatry* 46.11 (1989) 1006–11. doi: 10.1001/archpsyc.1989.01810110048007.

GoodTherapy. "Bibliotherapy: Benefits, Techniques, and How It Works." Last updated May 9, 2016. https://www.goodtherapy.org/learn-about-therapy/types/bibliotherapy.

Gordon, Jon, and Damon West. *The Coffee Bean: A Simple Lesson to Create Positive Change*. Hoboken, NJ: Wiley & Sons, 2019.

Got Questions. "What Are the Stations of the Cross and What Can We Learn from Them?" Got Questions Ministries, Jan. 4, 2022. https://www.gotquestions.org/stations-of-the-cross.html.

Gstalter, Morgan. "More People Have Died in Schools than Military Service Members in 2018." *Hill*, May 18, 2018. https://thehill.com/homenews/news/388375-more-people-have-died-in-schools-than-service-members-in-2018-report/.

Gunaratna, Shanika. "Millennials Reach a U.S. Population Milestone." CBS News, Apr. 25, 2016. https://www.cbsnews.com/news/millennials-surpass-baby-boomers-us-census-data-largest-living-generation/.

Hacking, Brian. "Hooked on Your Phone? This May Be Why." CBS News, Jan. 10, 2018. https://www.cbsnews.com/news/hooked-on-your-phone-this-may-be-why/.

Hales, Craig M., et al. "Prevalence of Obesity Among Adults and Youth: United States, 2015–2016." NCHS Data Brief 288 (2017). https://www.cdc.gov/nchs/products/databriefs/db288.htm.

Happy Money. "What Is Financial Stress?" Aug. 23, 2022. https://happymoney.com/articles/what-is-financial-stress.

Harvard Health Publishing. "10 Questions to Ask When Choosing a Therapist." Mar. 5, 2024. https://www.health.harvard.edu/mind-and-mood/10-questions-to-ask-when-choosing-a-therapist.

Herring, Ryan. "Envisioning a Better Future: The Importance of Dreaming." HuffPost, last updated Sept. 1, 2016. https://www.huffpost.com/entry/post_b_8071972.

History Lists. "9 Circles of Hell (Dante's Inferno)." Apr. 17 2023. https://historylists.org/art/9-circles-of-hell-dantes-inferno.html.

Hogan, Alexandra M., et al. "The Effect of Sleep Deprivation on Emotional Memory Consolidation in Participants Reporting Depressive Symptoms." *Journal of Psychiatric Research* 103 (2018) 187–95.

Howard, Kathy. "What Are the Fruits of the Spirit?" Crosswalk, last updated Dec. 16, 2024. https://www.crosswalk.com/faith/spiritual-life/what-are-the-fruit-of-the-spirit.html.

HuffPost. "Body Shame." https://www.huffpost.com/topic/body-shame.

Impelman, Craig. "John Wooden's 7-Point Creed: 'Be Thankful.'" Wooden Effect, Feb. 22, 2017. https://www.thewoodeneffect.com/john-woodens-7-point-creed-thankful/.

Jackson, Abby, and Tanza Loudenback. "The 10 Most Critical Problems in the World, According to Millennials." Business Insider, Feb. 27, 2018. https://www.businessinsider.com/world-economic-forum-world-biggest-problems-concerning-millennials-2016-8.

Jackson, Wayne. "The Conversion of Saul of Tarsus." Christian Courier, Feb. 22, 2022. https://christiancourier.com/articles/the-conversion-of-saul-of-tarsus.

Jaffe, Dennis. "The Essential Importance of Trust: How to Build It or Restore It." *Forbes*, last updated Dec. 10, 2021. https://www.forbes.com/sites/dennisjaffe/2018/12/05/the-essential-importance-of-trust-how-to-build-it-or-restore-it/.

Jelly Roll. "Need a Favor." Track 11 on *Whitsitt Chapel*. BBR, 2022.

John Paul II. *Evangelium Vitae*. Mar. 25, 1995. https://www.vatican.va/content/john-paul-ii/en/encyclicals/documents/hf_jp-ii_enc_25031995_evangelium-vitae.html.

Johnston, Lloyd D., et al. *Monitoring the Future National Survey Results on Drug Use, 1975–2015: 2015 Overview, Key Findings on Adolescent Drug Use*. Ann Arbor: Institute for Social Research, University of Michigan, 2016. https://monitoringthefuture.org/wp-content/uploads/2022/08/mtf-overview2015.pdf.

Joyner-Kersee, Jackie. "Letter to My Younger Self." Players' Tribune, July 17, 2015. https://www.theplayerstribune.com/articles/jackie-joyner-kersee-letter-to-my-younger-self.

Kalvapalle, Rahul. "Twice as Many Americans Have Died in School Shootings than at War in 2018, Data Shows." Global News, May 19, 2018. https://globalnews.ca/news/4219210/us-school-shootings-combat-deaths-comparison/.

Kann, Laura, et al. "Youth Risk Behavior Surveillance—United States, 2015." *MMWR Surveillance Summary* 65.6 (2016) 1–175. https://www.cdc.gov/mmwr/volumes/65/ss/pdfs/ss6506.pdf.

King, Maxwell, ed. *The World According to Mister Rogers*. White Plains, NY: Peter Pauper, 2006.

Kirkham, Elyssa. "No. 1 Source of Money Stress for Millennials Is Debt." LendingTree, Mar. 13, 2018. https://www.lendingtree.com/student/debt-most-common-for-millennials-money-stress-survey/.

Kreeft, Peter. *Jesus-Shock*. South Bend, IN: St. Augustine's, 2008.

Kroenke, Kurt, et al. "The PHQ-9: Validity of a Brief Depression Severity Measure." *Journal of General Internal Medicine* 16 (2001) 606–13.

Kuehner, Christine. "Why Is Depression More Common Among Women than Among Men?" *Lancet Psychiatry* 4 (2017) 146–58. https://doi.org/10.1016/S2215-0366(16)30263-2.

Kwasniewski, Peter. "Looking for a New Examination of Conscience? Try the Rule of St. Benedict." Life Site News, July 11, 2018. https://www.lifesitenews.com/blogs/looking-for-a-new-examination-of-conscience-try-the-rule-of-st.-benedict/.

Lally, Phillippa, et al. "How Are Habits Formed: Modelling Habit Formation in the Real World." *European Journal of Social Psychology* 40 (2010) 998–1009. https://doi.org/10.1002/ejsp.674.

Lawrence, John W. *The Six Trials of Jesus*. Eugene, OR: Kregel, 1996.

Leeuw, Jacobus Johannes. *The Conquest of Illusion*. New York: Knopf, 1928.

LeJeune, Marcel. "Catholic Evangelization 101—What Conversion Looks Like." Catholic Missionary Disciples, Mar. 12, 2021. https://catholicmissionarydisciples.com/news/conversion.

Liguori, Alphonsus. *The Way of the Cross: Traditional and Modern Meditations*. Holland, MI: Our Lady of the Lake Parish, 2024.

Linberg, Sara. "How Does Bibliotherapy Work?" Verywell Mind, Nov. 20, 2024. https://www.verywellmind.com/what-is-bibliotherapy-4687157.

Live Life Happy. "7 Beautiful, Uplifting, and Inspiring Short Stories About Life." May 11, 2024. https://livelifehappy.com/live-life-happy-stories.

Marcus, A. M. *The Elephant and the Rope: Children's Picture Book on Perseverance*. Scott's Valley, CA: self-published, CreateSpace, 2015.

Martin, Jim. "A Modern Parable About Change." From a Pastor's Heart, Nov. 30, 2010. https://pastorjimmartin.blogspot.com/2010/11/modern-parable-about-change.html.

Maslow, Abraham H. "A Theory of Human Motivation." *Psychological Review* 50 (1943) 370–96.

Mayo Clinic Staff. "Teen Depression." Mayo Clinic, last updated Aug. 12, 2022. https://www.mayoclinic.org/diseases-conditions/teen-depression/symptoms-causes/syc-20350985.

Mazzei, Nada. "Lent: A Season of Change." Catholic Stand, Feb. 24, 2018. https://catholicstand.com/lent-season-conversion/.

McEachern, Patricia. *A Holy Life: The Writings of St. Bernadette of Lourdes*. San Francisco: Ignatius, 2005.

McGill, Bryant. *Simple Reminders: Inspiration for Living Your Best Life*. Self-published, 2015. https://bryanthmcgills.blogspot.com/2018/06/simple-reminders-book-2015-2018.html.

McGrath, Ellen. "Teen Depression—Girls." *Psychology Today*, June 1, 2002. https://www.psychologytoday.com/us/articles/200206/teen-depression-girls.

Mental Health America. "Questions to Ask a Provider." Aug. 3, 2023. https://mhanational.org/resources/questions-to-ask-a-provider/.

———. "The State of Mental Health in America 2017." Jan. 1, 2017. https://mhanational.org/research/the-state-of-mental-health-in-america-2017/.

Millman, Dan. *Way of the Peaceful Warrior: A Basically True Story*. Tiburon, CA: Kramer, 1980.

Monson, Thomas S. "The Three Rs of Choice." *Ensign*, Nov. 2010, 67–70. https://www.churchofjesuschrist.org/study/ensign/2010/11/priesthood-session/the-three-rs-of-choice?lang=eng.

Morrison, Jim, vocalist. "Roadhouse Blues." Track 1 on The Doors, *Morrison Hotel*, Elektra, 1970.

Mother Teresa. *Love: A Fruit Always in Season*. Edited by Dorothy S. Hunt. San Francisco: Ignatius, 1987.

National Institute of Mental Health. "Seasonal Affective Disorder." Last updated Nov. 2023. https://www.nimh.nih.gov/health/publications/seasonal-affective-disorder.

National Institute on Drug Abuse. "Drug Overdose Deaths: Facts and Figures." Last updated Aug. 21, 2024. https://nida.nih.gov/research-topics/trends-statistics/overdose-death-rates.

———. "Opioid Overdose Crisis." Last updated Aug. 2024. https://www.drugabuse.gov/drug-topics/opioids/opioid-overdose-crisis.

Newman, Michelle G., et al. "Preliminary Reliability and Validity of the Generalized Anxiety Disorder Questionnaire-IV: A Revised Self-Report Diagnostic Measure of Generalized Anxiety Disorder." *Behavior Therapy* 33 (2002) 215–33.

Newman, Tim. "Is the Placebo Effect Real?" Medical News Today, Sept. 7, 2017. https://www.medicalnewstoday.com/articles/306437.

Newton, Isaac. *Sir Isaac Newton's Mathematical Principles of Natural Philosophy and His System of the World*. Translated by Andrew Motte. Revised by Florian Cajori. Berkeley: University of California Press, 1947.

Newton, John. "Amazing Grace." 1779. Hymnary.org. https://hymnary.org/text/amazing_grace_how_sweet_the_sound.

Nielsen. "Millennials Prefer Cities to Suburbs, Subways to Driveways." Mar. 4, 2014. https://www.panoramic.com/wp-content/uploads/2014/05/Millenials-Prefer-Cities-to-Suburbs-Subways-to-Driveways.pdf.

Nixon, Richard. "Remarks About an Intensified Program for Drug Abuse Prevention and Control." American Presidency Project. https://www.presidency.ucsb.edu/documents/remarks-about-intensified-program-for-drug-abuse-prevention-and-control.

Noble, Darla. "How to Find Your God-Given Talents." Faith Island, May 8, 2017. https://faithisland.org/faith/how-to-identify-your-god-given-talents/.

Noffke, Suzanne, trans. *The Dialogue of the Seraphic Virgin: Catherine of Siena*. New York: Paulist, 1980.

Partnership for a Drug-Free America. "This Is Your Brain on Drugs." Public service announcement, 1987. YouTube video, 00:30. https://www.youtube.com/watch?v=GOnENVylxPI.

Peck, M. Scott. *The Road Less Traveled: A New Psychology of Love, Traditional Values, and Spiritual Growth*. New York: Simon & Schuster, 1978.

Pew Research Center. "The American Family Today." Dec. 17, 2015. https://www.pewresearch.org/social-trends/2015/12/17/1-the-american-family-today/?utm.

Picoult, Jodi. *Sing You Home*. New York: Atria, 2011.

Price-Mitchell, Marilyn. "Disadvantages of Social Networking: Surprising Insights from Teens." Roots of Action, Sept. 6, 2019. https://www.rootsofaction.com/disadvantages-of-social-networking/.

Pritchard, Ray. "The Salt and Light Brigade: Matthew 5:13–16." Keep Believing Ministries, Mar. 17, 1996. https://www.keepbelieving.com/sermon/1996-03-17-the-salt-and-light-brigade/.

Ratner, Paul. "Teens Have One Key Agenda When Using Social Media." Big Think, Feb. 26, 2018. https://bigthink.com/mind-brain/teens-mostly-use-social-media-for-one-specific-purpose/.

ReachOut Content Team. "Teenagers and Social Media." Reach Out, Dec. 1, 2024. https://parents.au.reachout.com/staying-safe-online/social-media/teenagers-and-social-media.

Reagan, Nancy. *My Turn: The Memoirs of Nancy Reagan*. New York: Random House, 1989.

Richmond, Christine. "What Happens During a Panic Attack?" WebMD, Feb. 26, 2024. https://www.webmd.com/anxiety-panic/panic-attack-happening.

Robinson, Lawrence, and Melinda Smith. "Social Media and Mental Health: Are You Addicted to Social Media?" HelpGuide.org, last updated Aug. 20, 2025. https://www.helpguide.org/mental-health/wellbeing/social-media-and-mental-health.

Rolle, Dina. *Adversities and Triumphs in the Midst of It All*. Self-published, Xulon, 2011.

Roseborough, David John, et al. "Attrition in Psychotherapy: A Survival Analysis." *Research on Social Work Practice* 26 (2016) 803–15. https://doi.org/10.1177/1049731515569073.

Saint Catherine Catholic Church. *Scriptural Stations of the Cross*. ECatholic, Mar. 2, 2020. https://files.ecatholic.com/24609/documents/2021/3/Scriptural-Stations-2020.pdf.

Schuller, Robert. *Tough Times Never Last, but Tough People Do!* New York: Bantam, 1983.

Silva, Sandra. "What Is Psychotherapy and How Does It Help?" PsychCentral, July 25, 2022. https://psychcentral.com/lib/psychotherapy#what-is-psychotherapy.

Simon, Gregory E., et al. "Is Dropout After a First Psychotherapy Visit Always a Bad Outcome?" *Psychiatric Services* 63 (2012) 705–7.

Sit, Ryan. "More Children Have Been Killed by Guns Since Sandy Hook than U.S. Soldiers in Combat Since 9/11." *Newsweek*, Mar. 16, 2018. https://www.newsweek.com/gun-violence-children-killed-sandy-hook-military-soldiers-war-terror-911-848602.

Snyder, Charles R. "Hope Theory: Rainbows in the Mind." *Psychological Inquiry* 13 (2002) 249–75.

Snyder, Charles R., et al. "Hope and Health." In *Handbook of Social and Clinical Psychology: The Health Perspective*, edited by C. R. Snyder and D. R. Forsyth, 285–305. Oxford: Pergamon, 1991.

Snyder, Charles. R., et al., "The Will and the Ways: Development and Validation of an Individual-Differences Measure of Hope." *Journal of Personality and Social Psychology* 60 (1991) 570–85. https://doi.org/10.1037/0022-3514.60.4.570.

Spitzer, Robert L., et al. "Patient Health Questionnaire-9 (PHQ-9)." 2025. https://www.apa.org/depression-guideline/patient-health-questionnaire.pdf.

Stallone, Sylvester, dir. *Rocky Balboa*. Culver City, CA: Metro-Goldwyn-Mayer, 2006.

Standberry, Lee. "Top 10 Issues Facing Our Youth Today." Top Tenz (blog), Jan. 29, 2019. https://www.toptenz.net/top-10-issues-facing-our-youth-today.php.

Stanford Medicine. "Teens: Relationship Development." Mar. 15, 2022. https://www.stanfordchildrens.org/en/topic/default?id=relationship-development-90-P01642.

Steiner, Rudolph. *How to Know Higher Worlds.* Translated by Christopher Bamford. Hudson, NY: Anthroposophic, 1994.

Steingard, Ron J. "Mood Disorders and Teenage Girls." Child Mind Institute, Nov. 18, 2024. https://childmind.org/article/mood-disorders-and-teenage-girls/.

Stoker, Bram. *Dracula.* 1897. Repr., New York: Modern Library, 2014. https://www.google.com/books/edition/Dracula/39lCAQAAMAAJ?hl=en&gbpv=0.

Suni, Eric. "Mental Health and Sleep." Sleep Foundation, Mar. 26, 2024. https://www.sleepfoundation.org/mental-health.

SWNS. "Millennials Spend Nearly 20 Percent of Their Year Stressed Out." *New York Post*, Sept. 27, 2017. https://nypost.com/2017/09/27/millennials-spend-nearly-20-percent-of-their-year-stressed-out/.

Thomas, Geoff. "The Man Who Carried Jesus' Cross." Geoff Thomas Sermon Archive, Sept. 25, 2005. https://geoffthomas.org/index.php/gtsermons/1521-the-man-who-carried-jesus-cross/.

United Nations Office on Drugs and Crime. *Global Study on Homicide 2023*. New York: United Nations, 2023. https://www.unodc.org/documents/data-and-analysis/gsh/2023/Global_study_on_homicide_2023_web.pdf.

United States Conference of Catholic Bishops. "Scriptural Stations of the Cross." Dec. 1, 2022. https://www.usccb.org/prayers/scriptural-stations-cross.

US Census Bureau. "Families and Living Arrangements." Nov. 16, 2017. https://www.census.gov/newsroom/press-kits/2017/families.html

US Preventive Services Task Force. "Anxiety in Children and Adolescents: Screening." Last updated Oct. 11, 2022. https://www.uspreventiveservicestaskforce.org/uspstf/recommendation/screening-anxiety-children-adolescents.

———. "Depression and Suicide Risk in Children and Adolescents: Screening." Last updated Oct. 11, 2022. https://www.uspreventiveservicestaskforce.org/uspstf/recommendation/screening-depression-suicide-risk-children-adolescents.

———. "Eating Disorders in Adolescents and Adults: Screening." Last updated Mar. 15, 2022. https://www.uspreventiveservicestaskforce.org/uspstf/recommendation/screening-eating-disorders-adolescents-adults.

———. "Illicit Drug Use in Children, Adolescents, and Young Adults: Primary Care-Based Interventions." May 26, 2020. https://www.uspreventiveservicestaskforce.org/uspstf/recommendation/drug-use-illicit-primary-care-interventions-for-children-and-adolescents.

———. "Unhealthy Alcohol Use in Adolescents and Adults: Screening and Behavioral Counseling Interventions." Last updated July 29, 2025. https://www.uspreventiveservicestaskforce.org/uspstf/draft-update-summary/unhealthy-alcohol-use-adolescents-adults-behavioral-counseling-interventions.

———. "Unhealthy Drug Use: Screening." June 9, 2020. https://www.uspreventiveservicestaskforce.org/uspstf/recommendation/drug-use-illicit-screening.

Vargas, Erica. "Body-Shaming: What Is It and Why Do We Do It?" Walden Eating Disorders, June 22, 2023. https://www.waldeneatingdisorders.com/body-shaming-what-is-it-why-do-we-do-it/.

Velarde, Robert. "Learning from the Prayer Life of Jesus." *Focus on the Family*, May 23, 2024. https://www.focusonthefamily.com/faith/learning-from-the-prayer-life-of-jesus/.

Wager, Tor D. "Do We Need to Study the Brain to Understand the Mind?" Association for Psychological Science, Sept. 1, 2006. https://www.psychologicalscience.org/observer/do-we-need-to-study-the-brain-to-understand-the-mind.

Webber, Robin S. "Follow Me . . . Bearing Our Cross like Christ." United Church of God, May 18, 2013. https://www.ucg.org/good-news/good-news-magazine-march-april-2013/follow-me-bearing-our-cross-christ.

The Week Staff. "Is Social Media Bad for Your Mental Health?" *Week*, Sept. 28, 2021. https://theweek.com/checked-out/90557/is-social-media-bad-for-your-mental-health.

Williams, Anthony Douglas. *Inside the Divine Pattern*. N.p.: Gemini 11, 2008.

Willingham, A. J., and Saeed Ahmed. "Mass Shootings in America Are a Serious Problem." CNN, June 13, 2016. https://www.cnn.com/2016/06/13/health/mass-shootings-in-america-in-charts-and-graphs-trnd.

World Health Organization. "Depressive Disorder (Depression)." Last updated Aug. 29, 2025. https://www.who.int/news-room/fact-sheets/detail/depression.

Yonkers, Kimberly Ann, and Robert F. Casper. "Clinical Manifestations and Diagnosis of Premenstrual Syndrome and Premenstrual Dysphoric Disorder." UpToDate, last updated Apr. 30, 2024. https://www.uptodate.com/contents/clinical-manifestations-and-diagnosis-of-premenstrual-syndrome-and-premenstrual-dysphoric-disorder.

Zavada, Jack. "How to Love like Jesus by Abiding in Him." Learn Religions, Feb. 12, 2019. https://www.learnreligions.com/how-to-love-like-jesus-701512.

Ziglar, Zig. "Success Measured." Ziglar (website). https://www.ziglar.com/quotes/success-measured/.

www.ingramcontent.com/pod-product-compliance
Lightning Source LLC
LaVergne TN
LVHW020521100826
845148LV00010B/1302